Market Reforms in
Socialist Societies

Market Reforms in Socialist Societies

Comparing China and Hungary

edited by
Peter Van Ness

with contributions by

George Barany
Valerie Bunce
James Caporaso
Jiasheng Chen
Joel Edelstein
Guocang Huan
János Kornai

William Loehr
Paul Marer
Satish Raichur
György Ránki
Su Shaozhi
Stephen C. Thomas
Peter Van Ness

Lynne Rienner Publishers • Boulder & London

Published in the United States of America in 1989 by
Lynne Rienner Publishers, Inc.
1800 30th Street, Boulder, Colorado 80301

and in the United Kingdom by
Lynne Rienner Publishers, Inc.
3 Henrietta Street, Covent Garden, London WC2E 8LU

Library of Congress Cataloging-in-Publication Data
Market reforms in socialist societies.
  Bibliography: p.
  Includes index.
    1. China—Economic   policy—1976- . 2. Capitalism—
China. 3. Hungary—Economic policy—1968-
4. Capitalism—Hungary. I. Van Ness, Peter. II. Barany,
George, 1922–
HC427.92.M39 1989   338.951   88-34563
ISBN 1-55587-096-1 (alk. paper)

British Cataloguing in Publication Data
A Cataloguing in Publication record for this book
is available from the British Library.

Printed and bound in the United States of America

The paper used in this publication meets the requirements of
the American National Standard for Permanence of Paper for
Printed Library Materials Z39.48–1984.

In memory of
György Ránki and Satish Raichur—
colleagues, scholars, and
friends

Contents

Acknowledgments

This book is the result of efforts by many people and organizations. It is my pleasure to acknowledge their intellectual, material, and moral support.

The project began as an international seminar on market reforms in socialist societies sponsored by the Institute for the Study of Development at the Graduate School of International Studies, University of Denver. Participants in the seminar, held in April 1985, included Jonathan Adelman, Bogdan Denitch, William Joseph, James Mittelman, Ann Seidman, Vicki Spencer, and Zhou Xingbao—in addition to contributors to this volume. Financial support for the seminar and for the publication of this volume was provided by the Frederick Wulsin and Janet Coon Memorial Trust and the Exxon Education Foundation.

Preparing a volume for publication that includes contributions by fourteen authors is no easy task. George Barany provided assistance in many ways, especially in editing the chapters on Hungary; Steve Barr orchestrated the project for Lynne Rienner Publishers; Ida May Norton copyedited the manuscript; and Asma Barlas typed the original manuscript. Many thanks to all.

Finally, several colleagues were especially helpful in providing criticism and advice about sources: Ian Bell, John Burns, James Caporaso, Anne Gunn, David Kelly, Robert F. Miller, Don Parker, Harry Rigby, Christopher Thorne, and members of the International Relations Seminar at the Australian National University.

Peter Van Ness

1

Introduction

Peter Van Ness

This book is a comparative study of the process of dismantling the Soviet-type command economy in China and Hungary, and the problems of implementing a market mechanism in its place. The two countries are in a critical transformation phase, no longer command economies but not yet market systems. The future they want to avoid is the present situation in Yugoslavia. Still in transition after forty years of market reforms, Yugoslavia is suffering its worst economic crisis in the postwar period (inflation averaging 217% annually in late 1988, high unemployment, and an estimated $21 billion foreign debt) and unprecedented political protests prompted at least in part by the economic crisis.

The studies in this book focus on this critical phase of transition, from which no socialist country has yet emerged. The problems of the command economy are clear and sufficiently serious to have prompted ruling communist parties to attempt market reforms, but the future is by no means certain even if market economies can be successfully introduced. What communist-party states lack is a political process capable of fully implementing market reforms. Hungary has been reforming on and off for twenty years, and China for ten—but Yugoslavia after forty years of reform still does not have an operational market system in place.

My objective in this introduction is to set an agenda for the book—that is, to raise some of the central questions about market reforms in socialist societies and to suggest a conceptual perspective for addressing them in our case studies of China and Hungary. Why have communist governments introduced market reforms in their socialist societies, and what specifically are they trying to achieve? What problems do they expect the market to help them solve, and how? How successful have they been? What are the implications of adopting this approach to socialist development for the Marxist objective of reaching communism?

These are paradoxical times. During late October and early November 1987, as the world capitalist stock markets suffered their worst crash in history,[1] the

1

leaders of the two most important socialist countries, China and the Soviet Union, reaffirmed their commitment to use market reforms to revitalize their socialist command economies.[2] In fact, virtually every ruling communist party in Asia and Eastern Europe either has considered adopting market mechanism reforms for its socialist command economy or has already begun to implement them. Yugoslavia was first, then Hungary, China, and now the Soviet Union. But why should communists in power choose to reform their economies by utilizing the basic structural feature of the capitalist system, the market? Doesn't this mean, as a result, that they are inevitably "going capitalist"?

If there was ever a subject that required a political economy approach for analysis, this is it. Politics and economics are inextricably intertwined in this phenomenon of market reforms in socialist societies. The question, however, remains which political economy? What conceptual approach or paradigm would be most analytically useful? How significant are these reforms? Some accounts describe China and Hungary as headed for capitalism, but other analysts point to what they see as the "totalitarian" character of communist-party states and note that so far none of these regimes has ever been successfully reformed.

One feature that communist-party states generally have in common is a Soviet-style command economy—a planned economic system that operates on the basis of output quotas set by the state rather than a market responsive to supply and demand. This is a part of their Stalinist heritage.[3] The majority of the world's ruling communist parties came to power (either by making their own revolution as China did, or with the help of the Soviet Red Army as in the case of Hungary) during the period of Stalin's rule in the Soviet Union. Stalin insisted that "socialist construction" for communists in power meant, among other things, adopting the Soviet system as a model and building a command economy.[4]

Despite staggering human costs, the Soviet-style command economy was initially successful in the Soviet Union and in China as a method for building an industrial infrastructure in what were basically nonindustrialized societies.[5] Command economies at later stages of development, however, seem inevitably to suffer from problems of declining rates of growth in productivity (especially in comparison with the more dynamic industrialized countries of the West and East Asia) that apparently cannot be resolved within the central design features of the system.[6] Mikhail Gorbachev in his analysis of these problems in the Soviet Union concludes:

> We first discovered a slowing economic growth. In the last fifteen years the national income growth rates had declined by more than a half and by the beginning of the eighties had fallen to a level close to economic stagnation. A country [the USSR] that was once quickly closing on the world's advanced nations began to lose one position after another. Moreover, the gap in the efficiency of production, quality of products, scientific and technological development, the production of advanced

technology and the use of advanced techniques began to widen, and not to our advantage.[7]

The purpose of employing the market as an instrument of reform in a command economy is to force competition and thereby to enhance efficiency. Because of the inefficiencies of centralized state planning and the priority placed on achieving rigid output quotas that characterize the command economy, such systems do not produce what is needed and desired by consumers, and they stifle both workers' enthusiasm and managerial initiative. Thus, one intended function of market mechanism reforms in a socialist command economy is to establish a direct link between the quality and quantity of what workers and enterprises produce and the material benefits they receive in return, thereby increasing productivity.

Clearly, however, market reforms in socialist societies are controversial. In the debate over the reforms in the different communist-party states, one can identify three distinct positions with respect to their assessment of the classical Stalinist-model socialist society (i.e., a social system combining a command economy and a so-called dictatorship of the proletariat). They are the conservatives, the reformers, and the radicals. Each position entails linking politics and economics in a distinctive way.[8]

The conservative position is the orthodox view. Conservatives, often older party leaders who are veterans of the struggle for power and who typically might have responsibilities in the military or public security organs, defend the party's monopoly of political power and the economic control maintained by the planning bureaucracy as hallmarks of what it means to be a socialist society. They cite ideological chapter and verse from Lenin (and sometimes even from Stalin and Mao) to defend their position, and point to the achievements of ruling communist parties since the Soviet Communists first won power in 1917. Although they might agree to a minor role for the market in a socialist society, the conservatives generally see systemic market reforms as a "capitalist" heresy, one that contains the danger of undermining party control and reversing progress already achieved on the road to communism.[9]

Reformers, by contrast, point to the inefficiencies that have become apparent in the command economy and argue that the best way to restore vitality and initiative to socialist societies in an increasingly competitive global environment is to introduce systemic market reforms. Moreover, they postulate that the prerequisite to socialist construction is a more substantial economic foundation (more developed "forces of production") and argue that unless sustained and substantial economic growth is achieved, communism must continually be postponed.[10] The reformers attempt to justify their initiatives in terms of Marxist ideology, even when their reform policies are designed to operate in terms of a logic borrowed from Western neoclassical economics.

Finally, many (but not all) of the radicals reject Marxism as a philosophical orthodoxy for determining the future of socialist societies. The most prominent radicals are former or even current party members. Most would probably agree with the outspoken radical, Chinese astrophysicist Fang Lizhi, who said in an interview, "Marxism is a thing of the past. It . . . belongs to a precise epoch of civilization which is over. It is like a worn dress that must be put aside."[11] The radical critique focuses on political change: the democratization of what Marxists call "dictatorship of the proletariat" and what the West tends to understand as "totalitarianism."[12] Radicals argue that the market reforms can never be successful without a basic political transformation. Their principal target is the party's monopoly of political power.[13]

To summarize the basic differences among the three positions, *the conservatives* want to keep the Soviet-type system fundamentally intact (a little market reform perhaps, but nothing that would change the fundamentals of the system); *the reformers* want to change the operation of the economy in order to make it more efficient, while preserving the party's monopoly of political power and continuing to proclaim loyalty to Marxism; and *the radicals* want to throw out the entire Soviet-type social system, politics as well as economics, and begin with a democratization of the dictatorship of the proletariat.[14]

Not every one of the participants in the reform debates fits precisely into one of these categories, but these generally are the main positions represented. To cite examples from China in 1987 just before the 13th Party Congress, veteran Politburo Standing Committee member Chen Yun and National People's Congress Standing Committee chairman Peng Zhen represented the conservative position; Deng Xiaoping and his protégé, Premier Zhao Ziyang, were prototypical reformers; and the jailed dissident Wei Jingsheng and astrophysicist Fang Lizhi were two of the most prominent Chinese radicals.[15] The 13th Party Congress was a resounding victory for the reform position, especially when four key conservatives (Chen Yun, Peng Zhen, and ideologues Hu Qiaomu and Deng Liqun) were retired from their top party jobs.

The studies collected in this volume primarily reflect the reform position. Some authors are reform leaders; others are academic proponents of reform. However, alternative positions are also represented. For example, Su Shaozhi, who presents in Chapter 9 a commentary on the Hungarian reforms as seen from a Chinese perspective, was sacked in 1987 as director of the Institute of Marxism–Leninism–Mao Zedong Thought because of his allegedly radical, "bourgeois liberal" views.

This book attempts to evaluate the present status of market reforms in socialist command economies by focusing on a comparison of China and Hungary. It is a collection of assessments by Chinese and Hungarian scholars of their own and each other's problems and achievements, plus commentaries by U.S. specialists. The project was begun as a conference held at the University of Denver in 1985. Subsequently, all of the papers were revised for publication, and several additional chapters were commissioned to complete the analysis.

Comparing China and Hungary

China and Hungary are at present pioneering these fundamental structural changes in the command economy, and the Soviet Union under Mikhail Gorbachev has now begun to follow suit. All other communist-party states see that their futures are also at stake in this ambitious experiment. Moreover, other than Yugoslavia, China and Hungary are the two socialist countries in which market mechanism reforms have been most fully implemented. Although Yugoslavia was the first communist-party state to undertake market reforms, in the three years between the party's revolutionary victory at the the end of World War II and Tito's break with Stalin in 1948, Yugoslavia never fully established a command economy on the Soviet model. Yugoslavia's experience, therefore, is not really comparable with the other communist-party states in this respect.

Yet, one might well ask what benefit there can be from an effort to compare China and Hungary, two countries that are different in so many ways: in their history and cultural tradition, geographical location, population and resource endowment, degree of industrialization, general standard of living, communist road to power, and degree of autonomy and extent of global influence. China is a large (the world's largest in population, third largest in land area), resource-rich, energy-exporting, low-income country. In contrast, Hungary is a small (only one-hundredth China's population), resource-poor, energy-importing, upper-middle-income country.[16]

In short, China and Hungary are different in virtually every way but one. They have a similar social system comprised of a Leninist communist-party state and a Soviet-type command economy, and as a result, despite their many differences, China and Hungary face many of the same kinds of economic and political problems.

When communist parties came to power in the two countries in the late 1940s (albeit under very different circumstances), they set up Soviet-type centrally planned economies as part of a close economic and political relationship with Stalin's Soviet Union. The problems that the market-mechanism reforms are designed to treat derive from that legacy, and in this sense, the problems that Hungary and China have experienced are representative of a common set of serious difficulties faced by the entire communist world. Similarly, their solutions, the market reforms, may provide answers that are widely applicable outside the two countries.

The rest of the communist world is observing the progress of those reforms most attentively, with an eye to emulating part or all of what Hungary and China have attempted in their own socialist systems. No matter what the outcome, their success or failure will have a significant theoretical and practical influence on the future of socialism. Market reforms are the most important structural changes in the Soviet-type social system that have been attempted since Stalin's death in 1953.

The phenomenon we are investigating is often referred to as "market socialism," and for lack of a better alternative, we will also use this shorthand term.[17] But isn't *market socialism* a contradiction in terms? Socialism by some Marxian definitions should be a society without commodity production and, instead, with allocation by plan—a long-term objective of socialism being to do away completely with the market. On the other hand, the market is the central feature of a capitalist economy—the "invisible hand" that almost magically is supposed to link supply and demand. So how then can *market* and *socialism* be combined?

Upon empirical investigation, one finds that all modern economies are some combination of both plan and market. Moreover, there are several different kinds of markets (e.g., markets for consumer goods, capital equipment and technology, labor, and equities), and one or more kinds operate in all contemporary societies. Thus, a kind of market socialism is a fact of life in all contemporary socialist societies (just as, one might say, a kind of planned capitalism is a fact of life in all contemporary capitalist societies). In this sense, "market socialism" is not a contradiction in terms.

For the purpose of this study, we define market socialism as a development strategy undertaken by a ruling communist party that employs a market mechanism to effect systemic change in an existing command economy. This definition is not as restrictive as some. For example, János Kornai has written: "The idea of market socialism is associated with the expectation that the 'marketization' of the socialist economy creates equilibrium of supply and demand. It is a crucial litmus test of reform to see whether such equilibrium has been established."[18] In other words, for Kornai, the implementation of market reforms in a socialist economy must have reached the point at which an equilibrium of supply and demand has been created before that system could properly be labeled "market socialist." The definition used in this volume, however, is not so demanding. By "market socialism" we simply mean a strategy for development in a command economy that is designed to bring about basic change in that economic system by employing market-mechanism reforms. This definition focuses on the demonstrated policy intentions of a ruling communist party, not (like Kornai's) on how successful those policies have been in transforming the command economy.

It should be noted that each economic system operates on the basis of a particular logic, usually either a market logic or a plan logic with the other aspect of the system playing a secondary role. The United States, for example, has essentially a market economy, but one that is shaped by various kinds of planned governmental interventions to constrain market forces (e.g., to minimize the adverse effects of recession and inflation). China and Hungary are the opposite: They have basically planned economies with an increasing role permitted to market forces under the control of the plan. For example, the current slogan in China is "the state regulates the market, and the market guides enterprises."[19]

But does this mean that when a ruling communist party attempts to use the market to reform its command economy that the country is inevitably "going capitalist"? The answer to this question obviously depends on what one means by "capitalism"—what definition and criteria are applied. If, for example, "taking the capitalist road" is defined as Mao Zedong specified it during the Cultural Revolution (1966–1976) in China, then, *yes*, China and Hungary are indeed going capitalist. For Mao, party policies that, for example, permit foreign investment and private enterprise, emphasize individualized material incentives, decollectivize agriculture, and generally enhance the role of the market definitely constitute "taking the capitalist road" rather than building socialism.[20]

If, instead, the existing social systems of the United States, Japan, and Western Europe define "capitalism" for the purpose of answering this question and one puts the question from the perspective of Western neoclassical economics, then the answer is *no*. To achieve a market economy in the Western sense would require political reforms that would change the nature of the "dictatorship of the proletariat" and undermine the party's monopoly of political power—something that no ruling communist party so far has been prepared to do.

Thus, so-called political reforms are at the heart of the matter. Certain fundamental changes in the communist-party state system might indeed facilitate the development of capitalism. But the Deng Xiaoping leadership in China, for example, has insisted on maintaining what it calls the *four fundamental principles*: "upholding the socialist road, the peoples's democratic dictatorship [i.e., the dictatorship of the proletariat], the leadership of the Communist Party, and Marxism-Leninism and Mao Zedong Thought."[21]

Conceptual Approach

This collection of essays is an analysis of similarities—what China and Hungary have in common. It is an examination of the Stalinist command economy and market-mechanism strategies for reform in the two countries.

No existing paradigm or intellectual perspective seems satisfactory to grasp the fullness of what is happening in countries like China and Hungary today. Analysts typically employ either the conceptual perspective of Marxist political economy or Western neoclassical economics. Both are represented in this volume. Each has obvious analytical utility, but both paradigms also have their blind spots.[22] Unfortunately, they cannot be combined successfully because the two paradigms are based on different assumptions, designed to answer different questions, and constructed out of incompatible theories.

There is a deep crisis in Marxist theory at present, both with respect to employing the Marxist paradigm to comprehend what is happening in capitalist societies and especially with regard to understanding how socialist societies might best be reformed. The ideological justifications for market socialism put forward by party leaders and propagandists are by and large rationalizations for pragmatic change rather than serious theoretical arguments, because, generally speaking, a reintroduction of a market mechanism into a socialist economy cannot be justified in Marxist theory short of admitting a complete bankruptcy of party leadership in the earlier stages of development, or accepting that the ultimate objective of communism is utopian.

The Chinese Communist Party has opted for an argument that China is still in the "primary stage of socialism" that will last into the middle of the next century (an important change from being well on the way to achieving communism, as Mao had claimed during the Great Leap Forward in 1958)[23] and that the principal task at present is to build up sufficient "forces of production" ultimately to sustain the material requirements of communism.[24] The obvious contradiction between using capitalist means to achieve supposedly communist objectives is not addressed. As economists in China and Hungary have focused increasingly on analyzing the operation of markets in their socialist societies, they have, perhaps inevitably, shifted their frame of reference from Marxian political economy to neoclassical economics.

Market reforms in socialist societies will presumably at some point produce a new paradigm—that is, a whole new way of understanding contemporary socialism (and probably capitalism as well). Unfortunately, we are not there yet, so this unavoidably must be a progress report.[25] In my judgment, five studies in the general literature best help to set the agenda. Each illuminates a key dimension of the phenomenon.

The five are books by Ota Sik, Milovan Djilas, Charles Lindblom, and Alec Nove, plus the debate between Christopher Chase-Dunn and Albert Szymanski in *Socialist States in the World-System*. To my mind, their work represents some of the most promising paths of intellectual inquiry for analyzing market reforms in socialist societies. Taken together, they provide a framework for integrating the fourteen chapters that comprise this volume.

The best-argued theoretical case by a Marxist economist for precisely why and how a market mechanism should be incorporated into a socialist planned economy is a 1967 book, *Plan and Market Under Socialism*, by the Czech economist Ota Sik. Although labeled a "naive reformer" twenty years later for failing to foresee the great practical difficulties of combining market and plan,[26] Ota Sik in this early book nonetheless spelled out in clear and concrete terms the nature of the economic problem for command economies and the logic of the market mechanism solution.[27]

A party planner and economic theorist of the "Prague Spring" reforms in Czechoslovakia in 1968 (before they were snuffed out by the Warsaw Pact military intervention), Sik focuses his criticism on the shortcomings of the command economy, which is characterized by (1) public ownership of the "means of production," generally meaning state ownership of industry and collective ownership of land and agricultural equipment, and (2) centrally planned, bureaucratic coordination of the economy. The planning bureaucracy exerts institutionalized, vertical control over the state-owned sector of the economy through a multilevel hierarchy that sets output targets and input quotas, allocates labor and investment, and appoints managers of state-owned firms. The bureaucracy controls the collective economy by establishing quotas for compulsory sales to the state (of grain and cotton, for example) and by setting the prices of key commodities.[28] Among other purposes, the command economy was designed to do away with the evils identified by Marx as inherent in a capitalist, market economy (e.g., class domination through ownership of the means of production, capitalist exploitation of hired labor, and worker alienation) and to establish a process for achieving communism.

The economic problems produced by the command economy are a declining rate of growth in productivity; a stifling of managerial initiative and worker enthusiasm at the production unit level; an economic sector imbalance (typically in favor of heavy industry and at the expense of light industry); and a failure to meet consumer demand. Even when assisted by sophisticated computers, party planners have not been able to anticipate demand as well as a market, and the command economy has characteristically not produced goods of a quantity and quality desired by consumers. (See Chapter 2 by György Ránki.)

Ota Sik's 1967 book laid out a theoretical design for employing a market mechanism to reform the classicial command economy. Permitting a greater role for the market would force production units to compete and would reward the more efficient with direct, material incentives. A decentralization of power from the bureaucracy to enterprise managers would carry with it the requirement that firms now would be responsible for their own profits and losses. Managers and workers who did more and better work would reap the rewards of higher salaries and bonuses.

In addition, a modest private sector would be permitted to develop, and collective enterprises would be encouraged—both potentially in competition with state-owned firms (although they were usually in different industries). As the economy was increasingly shaped by the market forces of supply and demand rather than rigid quotas set by the central plan, imaginative entrepreneurs would be rewarded with higher profits, and consumers would enjoy a wider selection of consumer goods. The overall economy would benefit from increases in productivity.

Market socialism for communist-party states has also meant opening their economies to the West, seeking foreign capital and technology by inviting foreign investment and participating in international financial institutions like the International Monetary Fund and the World Bank. In addition, China, for example, has established a major foreign tourist industry in order to earn hard currency income, and Beijing has sent thousands of Chinese scholars and students abroad for advanced training. For Ota Sik, one of the benefits of expanding an export trade with the West is that successful competition in the global market should increase the standards of product quality for domestic production as well.

In practice, market reforms have not been as easy to implement as Ota Sik suggested they might be in his theoretical discussion. Party conservatives especially balk when initial reforms begin to produce inflation, contribute to unemployment problems, and result in budget and foreign trade deficits. The key problem, however, seems to be political: Will the bureaucracy be willing to give up enough power to allow the market to function—in Kornai's terms, so that "the 'marketization' of the socialist economy creates equilibrium of supply and demand."[29] Thus far, the communist parties of China and Hungary have not been willing to go that far.

Whereas the reformers want to use the market to remedy the inefficiencies of the command economy but keep party political power intact, the radicals go much further. They would like to use market reforms to erode and ultimately to destroy the party's monopoly of political power. As one Yugoslav scholar put it, the central objective of reform is political, not economic. At issue is the Communist-party state. (See Chapter 5 by George Barany.)

An early Marxist critique by the Yugoslav dissident Milovan Djilas is still, in my opinion, one of the most penetrating commentaries on the communist-party state. Djilas's *The New Class*, first published in English in 1957, argues that the communist bureaucracy in contemporary socialist societies has become a new ruling class. Citing Marx's argument that the dominant class in any society is the group that owns the principal means of production, Djilas turns Marxian analysis against communists in power, asserting that because of its control over the publicly owned means of production, the communist bureaucracy in socialist countries has become the ruling social class. He writes: "Property is legally considered social and national property. But, in actuality, a single group manages it in its own interest."[30]

Djilas observes that successful communist revolutions did not occur in the most developed capitalist countries as Marx had expected, but rather in countries (like Russia, China, and Yugoslavia) where for a variety of reasons capitalism had failed to take hold. The historical task of communists in power became to carry out a forced industrialization of underdeveloped societies. The Soviet-type social system that Stalin created in the Soviet Union, ruled by a communist party ("the backbone of the entire political, economic, and ideological activity" of the society), became the prototype, the model: "Lenin's dictatorship was strict, but Stalin's dictatorship became totalitarian."[31]

If Djilas is indeed correct that the foundation of communist party power resides in its control over a publicly owned economy, then market reforms calling for changes in ownership and the freeing of economic activity from bureaucratic control have important implications for the party's monopoly of political power. Analysts have long observed that "totalitarian" systems are very resistant to change, and never has party power in a Soviet-type social system been successfully challenged. Perhaps in the market, radicals have found an answer.

From a different analytical perspective, Charles Lindblom seems to confirm this supposition. Lindblom opens his book *Politics and Markets* with the comment:

> Aside from the difference between despotic and libertarian governments, the greatest distinction between one government and another is in the degree to which market replaces government. Both Adam Smith and Karl Marx knew this. Hence, certain questions about the governmental-market relation are at the core of both political science and economics, no less for planned systems than for market systems.[32]

Investigating the role of politics and markets in socialist and capitalist societies, Lindblom focuses on methods of social control. He identifies three types: exchange, authority, and persuasion. Noting that every modern society employs some combination of plan and market and arguing that theoretically there is a wide variety of market and nonmarket systems of exchange, Lindblom shows that only in market-oriented systems does one find democracy: "Not all market-oriented systems are democratic, but every democratic system is also a market-oriented system." Later, Lindblom directly addresses the political implications of market reforms in socialist societies.[33] One implication of Lindblom's analysis is that market reforms may be the best hope for reforming the communist-party state.

Yet, the history of market reforms in Hungary and China so far is a telling commentary on how successful the bureaucratic establishment at various levels (center, region, and even the firm) can be in resisting full market implementation.[34] Nonetheless, if the party leaders want to achieve the economic benefits promised by the market, it is in their interest to fully implement the reforms. Moreover, once the required structural changes have been made, they are not easy to reverse: New vested interests develop, and the public quickly acquires new expectations (especially when the market increases their consumption possibilities).

One thing that is needed is a new way of thinking about these problems. Neoclassical economics can help party leaders understand and benefit from the market, but it provides no help with respect to understanding the politics of a Soviet-type system. Marxian political economy is not much better.[35]

Alec Nove in his *Economics of Feasible Socialism* concludes that "there is no Marxist political economy of socialism."[36] Nove, one of the West's most thoughtful analysts of the Soviet economy, argues after a careful analysis of Marxist theory that the assumptions underlying the Marxian view of socialism as a vehicle for achieving communism are utopian. For example, there is the assumption of abundance rather than a serious assessment of how to deal with problems of scarcity. Also, under socialism, supposedly the division of labor is to be overcome. But, Nove asks, how is the control and coordination that is so vital to modern society to be achieved? "Modern production is complex, integrated. Unless it is integrated, it will disintegrate."[37] Nove also questions the usefulness of the Marxian law of value for making practical decisions regarding how much and of what quality to produce in a socialist society.

Echoing some of Lindblom's analysis, Nove argues moreover that "an incentive scheme seems to be the only conceivable substitute for compulsion." For both Nove and Lindblom, the necessary but not sufficient condition for democratizing the Soviet-type political system is a market economy. Nove writes: "Marketless socialism can only mean *centralised* planning, in which a large and necessarily hierarchical and bureaucratic organisation issues instructions, allocates and co-ordinates. Such a form of organizing production can only have as its counterpart the hierarchical and bureaucratic organisation of politics."[38]

Marx, who spent his life investigating capitalism in the nineteenth century, is of little help today in understanding contemporary socialist societies, according to Nove. Regarding the legacy of Marx, Nove concludes:

> I think that it can be demonstrated that Marxist economics is either irrelevant, or misleading, in respect to the problems that must be faced by any socialist economy which could exist. This is because the very possibility of these problems was assumed out of existence. Attempts to adapt the labour theory of value are doomed to failure, both because Marx did not intend that it be applied to socialism and because of its high level of abstraction.[39]

If Nove is correct, orthodox Marxist theorists will never make sense in their interpretations of contemporary socialist society. At most, their arguments will be only rationalizations for party policies determined on the basis of pragmatic considerations. Yet, it is most unlikely that ruling communist parties will reject Marxist theory because of the extent to which their power is legitimated by Marxist dogma.

One solution for Marxists is to construct alternative designs for socialism by drawing on different theoretical roots in the Marxist tradition.[40] (See Joel Edelstein's conclusion in Chapter 14.) Among the more influential neo-Marxist interpretations of international relations is Immanuel Wallerstein's concept of "world-system."

Wallerstein, focusing on the influence of economic relationships on state behavior and the importance of a country's role in the global market economy, argues that a single division of labor is the central defining characteristic of the global social system. In the contemporary capitalist world-system, countries are identified in terms of their role in this division of labor as dominating "core," ambiguous "semi-periphery," or exploited "periphery."

In a book called *Socialist States in the World-System*, the editor, Christopher Chase-Dunn, debates one of his coauthors, Albert Szymanski, with regard to whether the Soviet Union and the East European countries associated with the Council for Mutual Economic Assistance (CMEA) are in fact an integral part of the world capitalist economy or should instead be seen as a separate world-system. In other words, they debate the question: In today's world, is there only one Wallersteinian world-system (the capitalist world economy) or two (capitalist and socialist)? Szymanski, in my opinion, makes the more convincing case, arguing that there are two.

Wallerstein's world-system paradigm is unsatisfactory by itself as an explanation of international relations because of its economic reductionism, as economics and the global division of labor alone cannot explain much of the conflict and cooperation in world politics. But the world-system concept and especially the debate between Chase-Dunn and Szymanski about the role of socialist countries in the capitalist world economy do raise critically important questions for all states about the costs and benefits of their choosing to integrate their economies with the capitalist world market. For example, for Chase-Dunn, even socialist countries become "functional parts" of the capitalist world-system, and achieving true socialist construction in one country becomes, if not theoretically impossible, most unlikely.[41] (See Valerie Bunce's analysis in Chapter 10.)

On the other hand, if Szymanski is correct, socialist states have three choices with respect to their international economic policies: to become a part of the Soviet-led East bloc world economy; to integrate their economy with the world capitalist market; or to go it alone—to opt for autarchy and self-reliance. The People's Republic of China (PRC) has tried all three.[42] During the 1950s, China built its industrial infrastructure on the basis of economic cooperation with the Soviet Union and Eastern Europe, although it was never a member of CMEA. After the break with Moscow in 1960, Mao insisted on a strategy of self-reliance for China until his death in 1976. And since the beginning of market reforms in China in 1978, the PRC has progressively integrated its economy more and more into the world capitalist market.

No matter what one's judgment regarding the Wallerstein paradigm, there is no question that important implications follow from a country's choice of international economic policy. This choice is especially significant for socialist countries when considering whether or not to integrate their economies into the capitalist world market. (The four chapters by Valerie Bunce, Loehr and Van Ness, Huan Guocang, and James Caporaso in Part 3 of this volume assess the different options).

The socialist countries attempting market reforms have generally accepted Western notions of "interdependence" and "international division of labor" and are attempting to design their own market-socialist growth strategies in order to benefit from greater participation in the world market economy. They are assuming that those countries that do not compete in the world market will be left behind.

The Soviet Union, as an example of the problems facing socialist countries before the implementation of market reforms, is currently responsible for some

20 percent of world industrial output but less than 3 percent of world trade. Moreover, only 25 percent (some estimates claim only 7 percent) of Soviet-manufactured goods are of world quality. Value-added products are a very small component in Soviet exports to the West, most of the trade being in oil and grain, and in the end, the Soviet Union benefits little from foreign trade.[43]

Increasingly, East Asia is setting the global standard for economic performance, for both capitalist and socialist countries. Japan and the East Asian newly industrialized countries (NICs) (Hong Kong, Singapore, South Korea, and Taiwan) and their export-led growth strategy have challenged the world to perform more efficiently. Socialist countries are competing economically with each other as well as with the capitalist world. Yet it is by no means clear how much any of the socialist countries can benefit from the East Asian NIC experience.

As the comparative data show (see the Appendix), China has by far the largest percentage of its foreign trade (over 90 percent) with nonsocialist countries, but for the PRC to achieve benefits similar to those enjoyed by South Korea and Taiwan from their export-led growth strategies, Chinese reformers will have to undertake very substantial additional reforms.[44] A 1987 Pacific Forum seminar, for example, pointed to the particular importance in the NIC developmental model of having highly competitive domestic markets, control of monetary growth, and proper exchange rate policies.[45]

But why is the international dimension of market reforms so important? What are the immediate benefits that socialist countries are attempting to gain from opening to the West?

There is a growing consensus that science and technology are the driving force of economic growth and modernization. Richard Cyert, president of Carnegie Mellon University, has argued that "new knowledge is now the only source of true economic power"; and Jean-Jacques Servan-Schreiber extends the argument to national security, claiming that "true security is higher knowledge."[46] Even if one finds these views extreme, there is no denying the importance of science and technology for increasing productivity.

New knowledge can be acquired through trade, foreign investment, and scientific cooperation. Probably the best way to achieve technology transfer is through the training of students. For example, in 1988, China had some 40,000 students studying abroad, about 27,000 of those in the United States, for just this purpose.[47]

Patterns of Reform

As Chen Jiasheng and other authors in this volume argue, there is no precedent, no blueprint for the market reforms that Hungary and China have been carrying out. Moreover, there is relatively little theory and certainly no accepted model of what market socialism, once achieved, would look like—especially regarding the political aspects and the role of the party.

The impetus to reform, as we have seen, is economic (the need to reverse the declining productivity and poor technological competitiveness of the command economy) but the measure of success of market reforms is more the ability of the state to achieve economic and political restructuring of the system than to improve short run economic performance. Increases in economic output, and especially increased supplies of consumer goods, are important as incentives to sustain public support for further reforms and as tangible evidence that reform will bring material benefits, but the central objective of the market reforms is to change the basic character of the social system.[48]

The real measures of success are: economically, the extent to which the economy has begun to operate on the basis of supply and demand (as Kornai has suggested); and, politically, the degree of restraint that has been achieved in controlling the party's monopoly of political power in areas critical to economic reform.[49]

Political opposition to market reforms in socialist societies is substantial. It comes from conservative party leaders who do not want to give up their special power and privilege; workers in state-owned firms who fear losing their entitlements to lifetime employment with fixed material benefits;[50] committed Marxists who see the reform effort as ideological heresy ("taking the capitalist road"); and consumers unfamiliar with inflation, unemployment, and debt or victims of growing income inequalities.

A successful politics of reform involves the ability to produce immediate benefits for a substantial part of the population so as to make tangible a rationale for their support for further structural change. This was achieved in China, for example, by giving first priority to agricultural reform, thereby providing new incentives for the 80 percent of China's population that lived in the rural areas to produce more, and then using the increase in agricultural output to meet consumer demand throughout the country. Grain production increased by one-third from 1978 to 1984, sharply increasing the food supply throughout the country.[51] Market reforms, as Ed Hewitt has argued, promise higher living standards in return for accepting greater economic insecurity, but if workers see only threats to job security and lower incomes because of inflation with no rewards in sight, they cannot be expected to support the reforms.[52] The analyses by Djilas and Lindblom, as we have seen, demonstrate some of the opportunities presented by market reforms for challenging the party's monopoly of power, but a democratization of the "dictatorship of the proletariat" does not necessarily follow from an economically successful market reform strategy. In the case of China, Vivienne Shue warns, for example, that the market is destroying what she calls "the honeycomb pattern of the polity under Mao" in the Chinese countryside, so that now, in her judgment peasants are more vulnerable to state power than at any time in Chinese history.[53]

Under a "dictatorship of the proletariat," the party's monopoly of power is manifest in at least four key areas: 1) deciding who rules (by means of the *nomenklatura* system for selecting leaders in government and society);[54] 2) shaping the cultural foundation of the society and the basis of individual morality and political legitimacy (through an insistence on Marxist-Leninist ideological orthodoxy); 3) maintaining the established social order (by exerting control over mass communications, the police, and the military); and 4) controlling the individual citizen (in China, for example, by means of the personal dossier kept on citizens [*dang'an*], residence permits [*hukou*], and the work unit [*danwei*] system). (See Stephen Thomas' chapter on human rights in China.)

Not all of these dimensions of party power must be modified in order to achieve an economy that operates on the basis of supply and demand. The key political requirements of market socialism are that the party give up running the economy; end its arbitrary exercise of political power; permit the selection of leaders mainly on the basis of merit instead of party loyalty; and loosen controls on the individual citizen to allow the operation of a labor market and to encourage individual entrepreneurial initiative.

With regard to running the economy, this would mean, among other things, separating the functions of party and government; cutting party secretaries out of the direct management of state-owned firms and giving enterprise directors exclusive responsibility for running their factories;[55] letting inefficient companies go bankrupt; and permitting managers to fire unwanted employees—all of which raise controversial ideological issues from the point of view of Marxist orthodoxy. In both Hungary and China, all of these changes have been proposed, but none of them have been accomplished in a comprehensive way to date.

By mid-1988, reform efforts in both China and Hungary were at a critical juncture. At the top of the restructuring agenda was price reform—which, if implemented, would almost inevitably lead to higher rates of inflation, but without which, full market operation could not be achieved. Price increases, to the extent that they cut into rising standards of living, obviously undermine public support for reform.[56]

As Marer writes in Chapter 3, the reforms have not yet been able to solve the problems they are intended to resolve. In the meantime, there is the danger of chaos: *political chaos* resulting from struggles within the party about how far to take the reforms as the party's monopoly of power comes under serious threat, and conflicts between the party and those who reject its legitimacy and denounce its record of arbitrary and self-serving rule; *economic chaos* due to inflation, unemployment, corruption reaching into the highest level of ruling party families, widening income inequalities, and growing national debt (and dislocations resulting from a situation in which the economy is no longer a command economy but not yet one that operates principally on the basis of supply and demand); and *cultural chaos* if Marxism as the defining ideology of the social order becomes so bankrupt that party rule virtually loses its legitimacy and there is nothing to replace it.[57]

Ruling parties in Hungary and China by 1988 no longer enjoyed the predictability and control of the command economy, nor had they achieved the promised competitiveness and efficiency of the market system. Enjoying the full benefits of neither alternative, communist leaders meanwhile were confronted with the serious difficulties of transition. Especially after the initial euphoria produced by lifting the repressive lid a bit has passed, these problems of transition have proven immensely difficult to resolve in the typical "dictatorship of the proletariat" communist polity.

No ruling communist party has yet succeeded in dismantling its command economy to the point of achieving "market socialism" in János Kornai's sense. Moreover, just a little market reform has not proven enough to force competition and thus to achieve significantly greater economic efficiency. Hence, Janos Kornai is probably right when he calls for a market socialism that is designed to establish an economy based on an equilibrium of supply and demand.

To sustain citizen support for the reform process, economic policies during the transition must produce improvements in general standards of living; however, when things go bad (e.g., inflation skyrockets, unemployment becomes serious, and the national debt and trade deficits build up), reform leaders cut back their initiatives, and the conservative opposition within the party counterattacks. Thus, the reformers are besieged all around: by skeptical citizens, demanding as the price of their loyalty to the reform leadership, sustained improvements in their standard of living; by party conservatives ideologically opposed to the direction of the reforms and especially anxious about reform initiatives that undermine the party's traditional monopoly of political power; and by radical dissidents convinced that the reforms have not gone half far enough, and quick to capitalize on the stalemate that has resulted. This may explain why market reform efforts in both countries have proceeded in a wave-like manner (i.e., a recurring pattern of reform initiatives followed by retrenchment),[58] and why those socialist countries that are most advanced in implementing market reforms seem to have gotten stuck short of full implementation of the market—in a dangerous situation in which citizen protests against declining living standards can become politically volatile.

The crux of the political dilemma in communist-party states is that the very monopoly of political power that the party enjoys prevents the evolution of the political mechanisms required to successfully implement such fundamental economic reforms. There is much talk about political reform, but what is most needed is a political process capable of dealing with the critical problems of restructuring, one which provides a mechanism for establishing accountability and resolving policy debates. One Yugoslav scholar, generalizing from the forty-year reform experience in his own country, suggests an independent judiciary and effective rule of law, an autonomous trade union movement (like Solidarity in Poland), or an independent communications media as examples of the kind of check on party power that could help provide this vital function.[59] A multi-party system might also work but is even more controversial.

Without such a political mechanism, it seems virtually impossible to expose corruption, to hold government and party officials accountable for illegal activities, to check abuses of power, to replace incompetent leaders, to protect dissenters in legitimate debates from retaliation, and to assess policy options and resolve national policy debates in a constructive fashion so that the difficult business of structural change can go forward. Without open political dialogue and debate, the probability of stalemate short of a transition to a market economy is very high. Austerity measures and so-called belt-tightening demands by ruling parties in the face of problems of inflation, debt,and unemployment prompt protests which in turn tap other sources of resentment and political dispute (e.g., ethnic differences in Yugoslavia, or opposition to Soviet domination in the Warsaw Pact countries).

If the reforms are successful in China and Hungary (i.e., if their command economies can be dismantled and a market put in their place), the similarities between the two communist-party states will fade away because of the very substantial basic differences between the two societies. Similarities will begin to disappear as the Soviet-type social system in each country is reshaped to more fully reflect the cultural, historical, and material particularities of each society. If market reforms in Hungary and China are successful, the two countries will no longer have anything much in common, except a past history of life under a Soviet-type social order.

Finally, there remains the question of whether market reforms in socialist societies will be sustained.

Are the Reforms Irreversible?

This might sound like an odd way to put the question, but it is posed in this way by reformers and radicals alike in the countries we are studying. Given the political character of the communist-party state and especially the degree to which the party truly monopolizes political power within the system, it would seem that the reforms could be reversed at any time. Moreover, the history of China's domestic development strategies shows that Beijing, for example, has made several abrupt changes in direction over the forty years since the founding of the PRC (see Chapter 7 by Van Ness and Raichur); and in Hungary, market reforms were begun in 1968 but then halted in the early 1970s before being resumed once again some six years later (see Marer in Chapter 3). Further, by Gorbachev's own admission, Moscow's previous reform efforts in the post-Stalin period failed.[60] So what basis is there for believing that the current reforms are somehow irreversible?

Clearly, the reforms are not irreversible, but there is a surprisingly strong case for expecting that they will continue. For example, the Chinese radical

Fang Lizhi, when asked if he thought Deng Xiaoping could revoke the reforms, replied: "I don't think so. The economy would collapse and also the party would disintegrate. In 1962, when millions of people in China died of hunger because of economic mistakes, the country was kept together thanks to Mao's prestige. Today, nobody has such prestige."[61]

In both Eastern Europe (including the Soviet Union) and China, there appears to be a consensus on at least two key points: No one wants a return of the terror (as in the Soviet Union under Stalin or in China during Mao's Great Proletarian Cultural Revolution), and there is a shared desire for a better material life—a better standard of living—after decades of scarcity and living with shortages. The party leadership, for its part, wants to achieve greater economic efficiency and is implementing market reforms for this purpose, as we have seen. But introducing a market mechanism means changing the fundamental structure of the economic system, and a market, if it is to achieve the intended benefits, is not something that can be turned on today and shut off tomorrow. Moreover, market operation also requires a decentralization of power (both economic and political power), and if successful, the market will create new political interests within the society that will inevitably present challenges to the party's monopoly of political power. Gorbachev, for example, argues that "the development of democracy" is the "principal guarantee of the irreversibility of perestroika."[62]

The party's reform objectives and the citizen consensus mentioned above link together in a way that can provide a substantial support for continuing market reforms. Party leaders seem to have realized that their most important resource, especially in an increasingly competitive and interdependent world, is the talent and energy of their people. In previous times of national emergency (like the Nazi invasion of the Soviet Union or the struggle against Japan in China), party leaders successfully mobilized their citizens to exert almost superhuman efforts. But daily work in a factory or on a farm, managing enterprises, or doing scientific research are much more mundane activities requiring a different kind of incentive—especially at a time when ideological incentives have largely lost their appeal because of leadership excesses of the past.

What the party leadership most needs now it cannot gain through coercion or the use of terror. The party must offer new incentives in order to gain a sustained, active, and creative participation in the productive life of the country by their citizens. When Gorbachev and Zhao Ziyang talk about "democracy" and the establishment of an effective legal system, they are promising their people political stability and restraints on both the arbitrary political power of the party and the creation of a new personality cult around another party dictator—in addition to material incentives and the promise of a rapidly improving standard of living.

In China, for example, the consumer revolution is probably the strongest popular force supporting the continuance of market reforms. During the last twenty years of Mao's rule, PRC citizens were repeatedly traumatized by mass campaigns, and the average standard of living for a Chinese household barely improved at all. As a result, when Mao died in 1976, there was both a widespread disgust with ideological manipulation by party leaders and a universal eagerness for a better material life. The market reforms introduced by Deng Xiaoping promised the Chinese people an end to ideological campaigns and an emphasis on consumption. Simultaneously, Beijing's search for foreign capital and technology and the decision to open China to the West made PRC citizens aware for the first time precisely how far behind their living standards were compared with the industrialized world. Today, in China, television advertising and news reports describing foreign lifestyles fuel consumer demand. Visiting overseas Chinese, foreign tourists and business people, and Chinese students returned from studying abroad escalate consumer standards and prompt new fashions in the changing PRC lifestyle.

Short of some future dire threat to China's national security or other national emergency, there seems to be no way that the party leadership can dissuade its people from aspirations to a higher standard of living. Given Chinese pride, how can Beijing justify PRC living standards remaining forever well behind those in the rest of East Asia, much less the standard of living enjoyed by Chinese compatriots in Taiwan and Hong Kong? In fact, Beijing, as a means of getting people to work harder, has used slogans like "some will get rich first" and "ten thousand yuan household," which obviously encourage dreams of a better life.[63]

Production efficiency and technological innovation are key factors in the competition among capitalist and socialist countries for economic growth, export markets, and advanced military capability. The Soviet-type command economy and a Stalinist political system that shuts its citizens off from regular contact with the outside world diminish the capacity of socialist countries to compete, and the result is a relative decline in performance as measured by world standards. By contrast, China and Hungary have made important gains by introducing market reforms and opening their societies to foreign contact, and now the Soviet Union is following their example.

As we have seen, these reforms challenge both orthodox Marxist ideas about socialist construction and the party's virtually exclusive hold on political power. At any point, therefore, conservatives within the top party leadership might try to halt the reforms and even attempt to overthrow the reform leadership. The problem that the conservatives would then face, however, is what to do next. What answers do the conservatives have? How could they motivate their citizens to work harder without a return to coercion or terror? If they reject market reforms, what solutions can they offer to the serious problems of declining competitiveness in socialist societies? As Nove said, "An incentive scheme seems to be the only conceivable substitute for compulsion."

Notes

1. In one day's trading, October 19, 1987, The New York Stock Exchange, for example, lost 23 percent of its value, and the Dow Jones industrial average fell 508 points. For assessments of the significance of the crash, see George Soros, "After Black Monday," *Foreign Policy*, Spring 1988, pp. 65-82; and several articles a year later in the business section of the *New York Times*, October 2, 1988.

2. Zhao Ziyang, "Advance Along the Road of Socialism with Chinese Characteristics: Report Delivered at the 13th National Congress of the Communist Party of China," translated in *Beijing Review*, November 9-15, 1987, pp. i–xxvii; and Mikhail Gorbachev's speech celebrating the seventieth anniversary of the October Revolution, November 2, 1987, and his book, *Perestroika* (New York: Harper & Row, 1987).

3. For example, the Economist Intelligence Unit, commenting on Soviet influence in the design of Hungary's economy, argued: "The years from 1949 to 1953 were the era of fully fledged Stalinism. The economic system then built up by Rakosi, who was both party leader and prime minister, was a carbon copy of the Soviet one." *EIU Regional Review; Eastern Europe and the USSR 1986* (London: Economist Publications, 1986), p. 67.

4. Richard Staar, editor of the annual *Yearbook on International Communist Affairs*, lists 25 ruling Communist parties as of 1986, but his list includes a number of doubtful cases like Congo, Ethiopia, and Zimbabwe in Africa as well as Nicaragua in Central America. These countries have Marxist governments, but ones quite different from the ten Communist-party states established during Stalin's rule: i.e., in Albania, Bulgaria, China, Czechoslovakia, East Germany, Hungary, North Korea, Poland, Romania, and Yugoslavia. All of these governments were put in power by the Soviet Red Army except for Albania, China, and Yugoslavia, where Communists won power by means of independent revolutionary efforts. With the exception of Yugoslavia (which will be discussed below), these countries plus the Soviet Union are the most comparable with respect to analyzing the impact of market reforms on a socialist command economy. For the purpose of this essay, then, the term *communist-party state* will refer exclusively to the Soviet Union, China, North Korea, and the eight socialist countries of Eastern Europe. Richard F. Staar, "Checklist of Communist Parties in 1986," *Problems of Communism*, March–April 1987, pp. 40–56.

5. See, among others, Alec Nove, *The Economics of Feasible Socialism* (London: Allen & Unwin, 1983), p. 106; Charles E. Lindblom, *Politics and Markets* (New York: Basic Books, 1977), pp. 294–299; and Robert F. Dernberger, "Economic Policy and Performance," in Joint Economic Committee, U.S. Congress, *China's Economy Looks Toward the Year 2000* (Washington, D.C.: U.S. Government Printing Office, 1986), vol. 1, pp. 15–48.

6. See Ota Sik, *Plan and Market Under Socialism* (White Plains, N.Y.: International Arts and Sciences Press, 1967), chapter 1, especially the distinction between "extensive" and "intensive" growth (from p. 49).

7. Gorbachev, *Perestroika*, p. 19.

8. This interpretation is not an analysis of political factions in the party leadership like Michel Oksenberg, "China's Confident Nationalism," *Foreign Affairs* 65, no. 3 (1987), pp. 501–523; or Susan Shirk, "The Domestic Political Dimensions of China's Foreign Economic Relations," in Samuel S. Kim, ed., *China and the World* (Boulder, Colo.: Westview, 1984), pp. 57–81. Rather, it is an identification of the principal substantive positions taken by influential

individuals in socialist countries on key issues in the debates regarding market reform. Sometimes, people change their positions (e.g., Chen Yun, in the late 1970s, was a reform leader, but by the mid-1980s, he had joined the conservative opposition to any further extension of market reforms).

9. See, for example, Nove, *Feasible Socialism*, pp. 176-177.

10. For example, General Secretary Zhao Ziyang in his report to the 13th Congress of the CCP argued that "Marxist historical materialists have held all along that the productive forces are ultimately the decisive factor in socialist development. . . . Unless the productive forces are developed, there can be no socialist society, and socialism cannot advance from one stage to another until the realization of communism." Subsequently, he added: "Whatever is conducive to this growth [of the productive forces] is in keeping with the fundamental interests of the people and is therefore needed by socialism and allowed to exist. Conversely, whatever is detrimental to this growth goes against scientific socialism and is therefore not allowed to exist. In these historical circumstances, the growth of the productive forces is the immediate and decisive criterion." Zhao, "Report," pp. xxv and xxvi.

11. Tiziano Terzani interview with Fang Lizhi in *Far Eastern Economic Review*, October 22, 1987, p. 53.

12. For a brief discussion of the concept of "totalitarianism" and the authors like Hannah Arendt, Carl Friedrich, and Zbigniew Brzezinski who developed it, see *International Encyclopedia of the Social Sciences* (New York: Free Press, 1968), vol. 16, pp. 106–113. See also Leonard Schapiro, *Totalitarianism* (London: Pall Mall, 1972).

13. The Solidarity trade union in Poland is another example of the radical position. See Lech Walesa quoted in *International Herald Tribune*, November 24, 1987, p. 6; and his book, *A Path of Hope* (London: Collins, 1987).

14. One of the key differences between reformers and radicals is their view of political reforms. In China, for example, the Zhao Ziyang reform leadership has called for separating the functions of the party and government (see Yan Jiaqi in *Renmin ribao*, November 27, 1987); decentralizing power to lower levels; strengthening the legal system; and establishing a professional civil service selected by competitive examination (Zhao, "Report," pp. xv–xxi)—all of which would be significant political reforms of the communist-party state system. The difference, however, between reformers and radicals is that the reformers want political change mainly to facilitate economic restructuring, whereas the radicals want to transform, and especially to democratize, the entire political system (Fang Lizhi interview in *Far Eastern Economic Review*, October 22, 1987, pp. 52–55).

15. There have been unconfirmed reports that Wei Jingsheng, a leader of the democracy movement in China in 1979, has died in prison (*New York Times*, reprinted in *Sydney Morning Herald*, November 16, 1987; and Geremie Barme in *Far Eastern Economic Review*, January 14, 1988, pp. 41–42). Among the most influential contemporary critics of Chinese society are some who are directing their criticism at the roots of traditional Chinese culture, not just at the contemporary political regimes in Taiwan and in the PRC: e.g., Bo Yang (Kuo Yitung), *Choulou de zhongguoren* [The ugly Chinaman] (Hong Kong: Art and Literature Book Company, 1987); and Sun Lungji, *Zhongguo wenhua de shenceng jiegou* [The deep structure of Chinese culture] (Hong Kong: Jixian She, 1983).

16. The two countries have also performed very differently in response to market reform policies. As data in the Appendix that compares nine socialist countries show, China was by far the poorest in per capita terms ($260 per capita

GNP in 1986), but has recorded much the best growth performance. In the period 1981–1985, China's rate of growth in national income was three times the average; Hungary's growth during the same period was only one-half the average of the nine countries.

17. The original formulation of the argument for market socialism was put forward by Oskar Lange in *On the Economic Theory of Socialism* (Minneapolis: University of Minnesota, 1938). See also Wlodzimierz Brus, *The Market in a Socialist Economy* (London: Routledge & Kegan Paul, 1973); and, more recently, Xue Muqiao, *China's Socialist Economy* (Beijing: Foreign Languages Press, 1981).

18. János Kornai, "The Hungarian Reform Process: Visions, Hopes, and Reality," *Journal of Economic Literature* 24, no. 4 (December 1986), p. 1715.

19. Zhao, "Report," pp. xi–xii.

20. For Maoist views on these issues, see Mao Tsetung [Mao Zedong], *A Critique of Soviet Economics* (New York: Monthly Review Press, 1977); and "Is Yugoslavia a Socialist Country?" in *Polemic on the General Line of the International Communist Movement* (Beijing: Foreign Languages Press, 1965), pp. 139–183.

21. "Any word or deed which deviates from these four principles is wrong. Any word or deed which denies or undermines these four principles cannot be tolerated." *Resolution on CPC History (1949–81)* (Beijing: Foreign Languages Press, 1981), p. 74. See also Zhao, "Report," p. vi.

22. For a trenchant criticism of the weaknesses in the Marxist paradigm as a conceptual approach to understanding contemporary socialist societies, see, for example, Nove, *Feasible Socialism*, part 1 (which will be discussed below). For an interpretation of Marxist and other radical criticism of neoclassical thinking, see Keith Griffin and John Gurley, "Radical Analyses of Imperialism, the Third World, and the Transition to Socialism: A Survey Article," *Journal of Economic Literature* 23, no. 3 (September 1985) pp. 1089–1143.

23. On this point, compare the *People's Daily* editorial of September 3, 1958 [translated in Robert R. Bowie and John K. Fairbank, *Communist China 1955–1959: Policy Documents with Analysis* (Cambridge, Mass.: Harvard University Press, 1962), pp. 459–463] with Zhao, "Report," pp. iii–vi.

24. "Breakthroughs in Traditional Economic Theory," by Wang Zhenzhong and Chen Dongqi in *Beijing Review*, September 7, 1987, pp. 15–17, provides in a nutshell some of the key theoretical changes that have been adopted since the Third Plenum of the 11th CCP Central Committee of December 1978. Taken together, they clearly show the direction of change implied by government policy in the PRC. The article points to six "new breakthroughs in economic theory."

a. "The achievements of socialism are now evaluated according to the level of the forces of production" (rather than in terms of the contradiction between relations of production and forces of production). In short, this implies that for the Deng Xiaoping leadership, socialism equals economic growth.

b. "China is still in a preliminary stage of socialism," and socialism is "a fairly stable, relatively independent socio-economic formation." Hence, China has fallen back on the road to communism and is only in a "preliminary stage" while socialism itself has been redefined as an "independent formation" which may last for a rather long historical period.

c. "Different forms of socialist ownership may coexist," meaning that private ownership of productive capacity is permitted and can even be encouraged during the socialist period, and new arrangements such as the separation of ownership and management can be attempted.

d. "A new economic pattern integrating market forces with planning has been created" which encourages the development of a commodity economy including "a consumer goods market as well as markets dealing in the means of production, capital, labour, technology and information."

e. "An open economic system involving international competition has been constructed," which encourages foreign private investment in China, the marketing abroad of Chinese labor, and membership in the principal institutions of the capitalist world economy: World Bank, IMF, and GATT.

f. "Varied methods for economic analysis have been developed," and Western neo-classical economics has increasingly supplanted Marxian political economy in university curricula in the training of China's economists.

25. For a thoughtful attempt to create such a new analytical paradigm, one that focuses on solving contemporary global problems yet still employs a Marxian theoretical perspective, see Rudolf Bahro, *The Alternative in Eastern Europe* (London: NLB and Verso, 1978).

26. Kornai, "Hungarian Reform Process," p. 1728.

27. Sik's views changed after he left Czechoslovakia following the suppression of the Prague Spring reforms in August 1968. See, for example, his *The Third Way* (White Plains, N.Y.: International Arts & Sciences Press, 1976). What is especially useful about the earlier *Plan and Market* book is that it is written from the perspective of a communist party leader and economic planner having practical responsibilities in a socialist state government, as well as that of an economic theorist.

28. For concise descriptions of the classical Soviet-type economic system and key components of the command economy in the context of analyzing Hungarian and Chinese reforms, see Kornai, "Hungarian Reform Process," pp. 1689–1693; and Dernberger, "Economic Policy and Performance," pp. 21–24.

29. Kornai, "Hungarian Reform Process, pp. 1700 and 1715.

30. Milovan Djilas, *The New Class: An Analysis of the Communist System* (New York: Harcourt Brace Jovanovich, 1957), p. 65. See also Michael Voslensky, *Nomenklatura: Anatomy of the Soviet Ruling Class* (London: Bodley Head, 1984), especially chapter 4.

31. Djilas, *New Class*, pp. 70 and 75. In 1988, Djilas was permitted to make his first public speech in thirty-four years in Yugoslavia to students at Maribor University. *International Herald Tribune*, June 4–5, 1988, p. 5.

32. Charles E. Lindblom, Politics and Markets: *The World's Political-Economic Systems* (New York: Basic Books, 1977), p. ix.

33. Ibid., pp. 116 and 299–309.

34. See, for example, Kornai, "Hungarian Reform Process"; and Jonathan Unger, "The Struggle to Dictate China's Administration: The Conflict of Branches vs. Areas vs. Reform," *The Australian Journal of Chinese Affairs*, forthcoming.

35. A hidden agenda item in this comparison of China and Hungary is the economic success of the newly industrialized countries (NICs) of East Asia. When PRC officials talk about comparisons between the PRC and "Hungary," they often seem to mean Taiwan. Clearly, Japan and the East Asian NICs (Taiwan, Hong Kong, South Korea, and Singapore) set the standard of economic performance for China. Moreover, the role of the state in the NIC economic success may provide some answers for China, despite the fact that the problems of state and market in those societies are very different from China's. See, for example, Robert Wade, "The Role of Government in Overcoming Market Failure: Taiwan, South Korea and Japan," in Helen Hughes, ed., *Achieving Industrialization in East Asia* (Sydney: Cambridge University Press, forthcoming).

36. Nove, *Feasible Socialism*, p. 20.

37. Ibid., p. 48.

38. Ibid., pp. 52 and 179–180.

39. Ibid., p. 58. For a Marxist rebuttal, see Ernest Mandel, "In Defense of Socialist Planning," *New Left Review* 159 (September/October 1986), pp. 5–37.

40. For example, Bahro, *The Alternative*.

41. Christopher Chase-Dunn, ed., *Socialist States in the World-System* (Beverly Hills, Calif.: Sage, 1982), p. 48.

42. Peter Van Ness, "Three Lines in Chinese Foreign Relations, 1950–1983: The Development Imperative," in Dorothy J. Solinger, ed., *Three Visions of Chinese Socialism* (Boulder, Colo.: Westview Press, 1984).

43. Constance Holden in *Science*, March 4, 1988, pp. 1088–1089.

44. See, for example, Lawrence J. Lau, ed., *Models of Development: A Comparative Study of Economic Growth in South Korea and Taiwan* (San Francisco: Institute for Contemporary Studies, 1986).

45. Nicholas R. Lardy (rapporteur), "China's Place and Role in the Asia-Pacific Regional Economic System, Summary of a Consultative Seminar" (Honolulu: Pacific Forum, 1988), pp. 6–7.

46. *The Guardian Weekly*, September 13, 1987, p. 15.

47. *New York Times*, April 4, 1988, p. A5.

48. For example, despite Hungary's poor economic performance in recent years (see the Marer chapter and the Appendix), Mikhail Gorbachev apparently intends to emulate Hungary as an example of structural reform. Karoly Grosz said in an interview that Gorbachev told him "it is probably the Hungarian endeavors and the Hungarian perceptions that are closest now to those of the Soviet Union." *International Herald Tribune*, July 11, 1988, pp. 1 and 6.

49. "Without reform of the political structure, reform of the economic structure cannot succeed in the end." Zhao, "Report," p. xv.

50. Theoretically, the ruling parties are re-writing the social contract of socialism between communist rulers and the citizens of the countries they govern, proposing that those who have jobs in the state-owned economy give up their entitlements (fixed salary, life tenure, retirement, housing, health care, etc.) in return for the possibility of a much improved standard of living and the opportunity to choose one's own place of employment through the establishment of a competitive labor market.

51. State Statistical Bureau, PRC, *Statistical Yearbook of China 1986* (Oxford: Oxford University Press, 1986), p. 143.

52. Reported by Constance Holden in *Science*, March 4, 1988, pp. 1088–1089. At the special CPSU nineteenth party conference held in June–July 1988, Mikhail Gorbachev seemed to be taking a different tack: putting political and social reforms first. He is quoted as having said, "I will tell you outright: If we do not reform the political system, all our initiatives, the whole massive task we have undertaken, will grind to a halt." *International Herald Tribune*, July 4, 1988, pp. 1 and 4. Perhaps this is because after 70 years of communist rule, any leader's capacity to make immediate economic benefits available to the people in the Soviet Union, is much more limited than in either China or Hungary, and therefore, he has chosen to win public support for restructuring more through social and political changes initially. Under the rubric of glasnost and perestroika, Gorbachev also appeared more determined to make the party work, rather than to work around the party, to achieve reform. See his report to the conference, "On Progress in Implementing the Decisions of the 27th Party Congress and the Tasks of Promoting Perestroika," *Tass*, June 28, 1988.

53. Vivienne Shue, *The Reach of the State: Sketches of the Chinese Body Politic* (Stanford: Stanford University Press, 1988), especially chapters 3 and 4.

54. For analysis of the general phenomenon based on the Soviet case, see Voslensky, *Nomenklatura*. Regarding China, see John P. Burns, "China's *Nomenklatura* System," *Problems of Communism*, September–October 1987, pp. 36–51; and the entire issue of *Chinese Law and Government*, Winter 1987–88, for which John Burns was guest editor.

55. The Chinese film "The Black Cannon Incident" [Hei pao shijian] presents a humorous example of conflicts between managers and party committees in enterprise management.

56. For example, when the Central Committee of the Chinese Communist Party backed down on price reform at its meeting in late September 1988, Ellen Salem commented: "But to impose an austerity programme on a society where the party is viewed as venal, cadre corruption as the norm and ideology a litany of meaningless phrases, is tantamount to political suicide. Thus, economists hold that China's leaders believe they have only one choice: buy time and placate the masses with price subsidies in the hope that the country can somehow sort out the problem of supply and demand over the next several years." *Far Eastern Economic Review*, September 22, 1988, pp. 70–71.

57. For a different interpretation, focusing on what he calls "civil society" instead of chaos and corruption, see S. Frederick Starr's analysis of the Soviet Union in *Foreign Policy*, Spring 1988, pp. 26–41.

58. Regarding the wave-like pattern of implementing the market reforms in China, see Harry Harding, *China's Second Revolution: Reform after Mao* (Washington, D.C.: Brookings Institution, 1987), chapter 4; and Penelope B. Prime, "Low Expectations, High Growth: The Economy and Reform in 1987," in Anthony J. Kane (ed.), *China Briefing, 1988* (Boulder, Colo.: Westview, 1988).

59. Conversations with Predrag Tutulic, Australian National University, Canberra, Australia, August 1988.

60. Gorbachev, *Perestroika*, p. 84.

61. Interview in *Far Eastern Economic Review*, October 22, 1987, p. 55.

62. Gorbachev, *Perestroika*, p. 63.

63. See, for example, Zhang Xinxin and Sang Ye, "Head of a Ten Thousand Yuan Household," one of the Chinese profiles from *Beijing ren*, published in *Shouhuo*, No. 1, 1985, pp. 161–163.

PART 1

HUNGARY

Each of the three substantive sections of this book contains four chapters, and the final chapter in each section is a comment. Part 1, on Hungary, includes Hungarian and U.S. perspectives on the economic reforms undertaken in that country since 1968.

Like China, Hungary is a member of the World Bank and the International Monetary Fund (since 1982); but unlike China, Hungary is also an East bloc country, a member of both the Warsaw Pact and Council for Mutual Economic Assistance (CMEA). Beginning its market reforms in 1968, ten years earlier than China, Hungary operates under constraints different from those in China, foremost of which is Soviet dominance. Hungary has had a communist-party state, the Hungarian People's Republic, about as long as China, but it came to power under very different circumstances. Unlike the Chinese Communist Party, which made its own revolution, the Hungarian Communists took power with the help of the Soviet Red Army.

One of the key features that distinguishes among communist-party states is the way that the ruling communist party came to power — that is, whether the party made its own successful revolution (like the Soviet Union, China, Yugoslavia, Albania, and Vietnam) or whether the party was put in power by the Soviet Red Army (as in the rest of Eastern Europe and North Korea). What is remarkable about Hungary, which is in the latter category, is the extent to which it has been an innovator among CMEA countries in adopting controversial market reforms.

In 1956, after Stalin's death, Hungary wanted to liberalize its Soviet-type system and attempted to leave the Warsaw Pact, but Soviet troops intervened, causing thousands of dead and wounded and forcing many Hungarians into exile. In 1987, there were still 65,000 Soviet troops stationed in Hungary. The János Kádár regime, set up by the Soviets in 1956 after their invasion, even sent Hungarian troops to participate in the Warsaw Pact intervention to destroy the "Prague Spring" reforms in Czechoslovakia in 1968, the same year Budapest initiated its own market-oriented New Economic Mechanism. Nonetheless, among the CMEA countries, Hungary is generally recognized to have "advanced farthest from the Stalinist legacy."[1]

Inevitably, events in Yugoslavia—the first socialist country to attempt market reforms after Tito's break with Stalin in 1948—influence the attitudes of policymakers in Hungary and China. But by 1988, Yugoslavia faced its most serious economic crisis since World War II: high unemployment, over 200 percent inflation, $21 billion of foreign debt, a declining standard of living, and widespread corruption.[2] The "Agrokomerc" scandal in August, for example, resulted in the resignation of the vice president of Yugoslavia, Hamdija Pozderac, who would have become the next president of the country.

Although part of the cause of Yugoslavia's problems has to do with its unique ethnic diversity, worker management system, and federal government (a confederation of six semi-independent republics and two autonomous provinces), Yugoslavia's economic crisis is a warning to all socialist countries attempting market reforms.[3] At the least, some increases in inflation, unemployment, and government budget and foreign trade deficits appear inevitable. The task is to control these potentially serious problems to the greatest extent possible while pressing ahead to fully implement the market reforms.[4]

These essays analyze the Kádár era in postwar Hungary. János Kádár, 76, head of the Hungarian Socialist Workers' Party since the Soviet intervention in 1956, was replaced at a party conference in May 1988 by ambitious Prime Minister Károly Grósz, 57; and eight of Kádár's thirteen-member Politburo were deposed, including Kádár himself. Radical Imre Pozsgay, who has called for an independent press and sharing power with the political opposition, was promoted to the new Politburo, and subsequently a non-party man, Brunó Straub, was elected president for the first time.

Budapest has authorized new economic and political reforms in combination with austerity measures in its attempts to deal with Hungary's stagnating growth and the highest per capita foreign debt in Eastern Europe (a total of $17.7 billion hard currency debt in 1988).[5] Hungary's economic problems are not as grave as those of Poland and Yugoslavia (see Appendix), but the prognosis is for several years of belt-tightening.

The Gorbachev leadership in the Soviet Union, under the rubric of glasnost and perestroika, is now taking a direction similar to that pioneered by Hungary and China—despite considerable resistance from within the CPSU top leadership.[6] Moscow's decision is a reinforcement for Hungary and other CMEA allies like Poland that are interested in undertaking market reforms. Vietnam, another example, has begun to implement what has been called "the most comprehensive economic policy change since the unification of Vietnam in 1975,"[7] and in CMEA, Gorbachev is pressing to reconstruct the East bloc economy more in accordance with market principles.[8] In a sense, Hungary is an experimental laboratory in which the CMEA can assess the viability of different kinds of market reforms on socialist command economies.

The first essay in this section, Chapter 2, by György Ránki, the late director of the Institute of History, Hungarian Academy of Sciences, analyzes the historical origins of the New Economic Mechanism reforms introduced in January 1968. Ránki decribes the establishment of the centrally planned Soviet-type economic system after the communist party took power following World War II, and he examines the problems that led to the decision to introduce market reforms—problems inherent in the Soviet-type command economy.

In Chapter 3, Paul Marer, an economist in the School of Business at Indiana University, presents an overview of Hungarian economic reforms during the past thirty years and analyzes the relationship between the reforms and economic performance. He identifies the successes and failures to date and assesses Hungary's reform prospects for the future. Like János Kornai (see discussion in Chapter 1), Marer concludes that the Hungarian system is still far short of a market economy ("about one-third of the distance from a traditional centrally planned economy to an efficiently operating socialist market economy").

In Chapter 4, János Kornai, an economist at the Hungarian Academy of Sciences and Harvard University, assesses China's market reforms from the perspective of what has been learned in Hungary, where market reforms were begun a decade earlier than in the PRC. His analysis was prepared initially for a visit to China, where he has become the most influential of the East European economic theorists, and his chapter focuses on the difficulties of successfully reforming the Soviet-type command economy.

George Barany, a historian at the University of Denver, concludes this section with Chapter 5, a comment on the discussions by Ránki, Marer, and Kornai. Barany, who thirty years ago was a refugee from Hungary but who now regularly returns to Budapest as a participant in U.S.-Hungarian scholarly exchanges, points to the ambiguous legacy of the Hungarian uprising against Soviet power in 1956. Asking if "totalitarian" systems can ever be peacefully reformed, Barany assesses the political implications of the market reforms already undertaken in Hungary and the political prerequisites of further reform.

Notes

1. Thomas Schreiber in *Guardian Weekly*, December 20, 1987, p. 16.
2. *New York Times*, October 11, 1988, p. 1.
3. Gwynne Dyer in *Canberra Times*, April 15, 1986, p. 6.
4. See "Economic Growth and Trade in China, Eastern Europe, and the Union of Soviet Republics during the Period 1986–1990," in *World Economic Survey 1987: Current Trends and Policies in the World Economy* (New York: United Nations, 1987). For a comparison of how Hungary and Yugoslavia responded to the oil shocks of the 1970s, see Bela Balassa and Laura Tyson, "Policy Responses to External Shocks in Hungary and Yugoslavia: 1974–76 and 1979–

1981," in Joint Economic Committee, U.S. Congress, *East European Economies: Slow Growth in the 1980s*, vol. 1 (Washington, D.C.: U.S. Government Printing Office, 1985).

5. *Handbook of Economic Statistics*, 1987 (Washington, D.C.: Central Intelligence Agency, 1987), p. 60; and *International Herald Tribune*; July 11, 1988, pp. 1 and 6.

6. Mikhail Gorbachev, *Perestroika: New Thinking for Our Country and the World* (New York: Harper & Row, 1987).

7. Barbara Crossette in *International Herald Tribune*, December 30, 1987, p. 2; and Murray Hiebert's cover story on Vietnam's reforms in *Far Eastern Economic Review*, July 23, 1987, pp. 26–31.

8. Jackson Diehl in *International Herald Tribune*, October 14, 1987, p. 7.

2

The Introduction and Evolution of Planning in Hungary

György Ránki

After World War II, Hungary found itself in a desperate economic situation.[1] Forty percent of the country's national wealth had been destroyed, and twenty-four percent of its industrial capacity was lost. A large part of the railway system and most bridges were destroyed, and agriculture had also suffered terrible loss. The task of reconstruction was even more difficult—stocks of raw materials had been depleted, inflation had reached unbelievable heights, and the country had to pay reparations for its participation in the war against the Soviet Union. Goods were scarce and production was far below the prewar level, all of which obliged the newly established democratic government to maintain some form of state intervention introduced during the war by the political system that had collapsed with Nazi Germany.

Despite the fact that planning is so often identified with socialist transformation and with the establishment of the Soviet-led bloc of the Eastern European countries after World War II, planning can be seen as one in a series of gradual steps of state intervention in the economy. In fact, the idea that the state had to play an important or even crucial role in a country's economic development emerged long before the socialist transformation in Eastern Europe, and even long before John Maynard Keynes suggested it as a means to overcome the economic difficulty produced by the Great Depression.

State Planning Under Capitalism

State intervention was used after World War I as the major instrument to assure national independence. The interwar years can be divided into two periods with respect to the role of the state. The years up to the Great Depression still belonged in certain ways to the pre–World War I period, in spite of increased state intervention. State involvement was motivated more by political than economic factors and was more an expression of political nationalism than of any specific economic theory. There were many measures regarded as temporary—as being the consequence only of the war and of the special circumstances of the emergency and due to be abolished after a couple of months or years when the hoped-for return to the prewar liberal era would be possible.

After the Great Depression and up to World War II, the economic approach changed. State intervention became the dominant practical economic policy in nearly every country. It soon found its theoretical explanation in Keynes's work, and it became absolutely clear that the liberal era had disappeared forever. As a consequence of the depression, state intervention not only had increased tremendously but it became official economic policy, and it opened a new phase in Eastern European economic development. New theories and almost unknown economic practices became fashionable. There appeared a marked turn toward a new kind of economic system in which the state had a very dominant role, providing what private enterprise without effective governmental help could not establish—a self-sufficient economy.

The theory of state intervention was still very vague, the practice mostly taken over from Germany, where the economic policy of Hjalmar Schacht seemed adequate to cope with the new problems faced by East European countries as well. In this sense, if the 1920s could be regarded as the epilogue of the old, the 1930s might be regarded as the prologue of the new period.

Certainly during the 1930s the idea that the state would or should play a decisive role in transforming stagnant economies into growing economies seemed to have been widely accepted. It led to the conclusions that (1) not only must state control be strengthened but state ownership ought to be extended as well and (2) after the state had control over finance and foreign trade, some kind of planning should be introduced over the whole economy, including production, for eliminating obstacles to economic development and for avoiding such catastrophes as the Great Depression. In 1938, the government accepted a program stressing Hungary's rearmament. Even if one does not regard it as a plan, one has to admit that much of its measures and scope constituted something new and had an element of planning, at least so far as financial and budgetary problems were concerned.

Later, when Hungary became involved in World War II, government intervention was greatly extended. As early as the outbreak of war, a government price commission was brought into being, a price freeze was put into effect, and any price increases required the permission of the government. Apart from government purchasing, state intervention also appeared in the efforts to solve the more serious problems of raw materials and energy supply. State direction appeared most unmistakably in the management of raw materials, for here it was easiest to estimate reserves and needs, domestic production, and available imports and to regulate the destruction of stocks on that basis. A system of state allocations replaced the free-market sale of essential raw materials. State intervention had a similar character in agriculture: distribution of existing stock through rationing, the stimulation of production to meet wartime needs, regulation of the organization of production, and obligatory deliveries on fixed prices to the state. Through military orders, allocation of raw materials, and control of consumption by rationing, the free market for a number of goods gave way to production and distribution directed by the state.

State intervention partly modified the money market as well. Bank credit was put under greater control, with the banks obliged to screen requests for loans closely in order to determine the borrowers' intended purposes for their loans. If the requests were not found to be justified, they were to be rejected. Expansion of war production was directly financed by the state through large loans to the most important companies working for war production. The share of the state budget in the national income increased from 16 percent in 1937–1938, to 33 percent in 1938–1939, to 50 percent in 1941, and to 67 percent in 1943. State intervention contributed to a temporary increase in war production; in the first years of World War II, when Hungary was not directly involved, the economy was prospering, and the balance between supply and demand was maintained. Nevertheless, serious shortages, inflation, wartime distortion of the economy, and capital depletion later clearly demonstrated the contradictions in the war program. Finally, in the last year of the war, after German troops occupied Hungary, the economy collapsed—shattered by the increasing Anglo-U.S. bombardment, the tremendous burden put on the economy by the systematic plundering by the German troops before the evacuation of the country, and the six months of fighting between the Germans and the Soviets on Hungarian territory in 1944 and 1945.

The Period After World War II

After the war, the economic difficulties all over Europe led to the idea of a state-centralized economy. Besides prolonging the activity of the earlier established institutions like the Office of Price and Raw Material Control, Hungary established a number of other committees, ministries, councils, and offices to cope with the difficulties of reconstruction. As early as March 1945, a National Economic Council was created, but more with the right of proposing than actually exercising executive power. Later a special so-called Ministry of Reconstruction was established to fulfill the task of being a supreme economic organ. But all these organizations were still unable to establish comprehensive control on the economy.

At the end of 1945, however, a Supreme Economic Council was established with exceptional powers in order to secure the process of economic activity in spite of the particular difficulty that emerged during the first winter after the war. The Secretariat of the Supreme Economic Council was actually led by the Communist Party, whose program called initially for a significant influence and partial state control and later for a fully centralized, planned economy. In order to maintain some balance in the economy where shortages prevailed, a large number of regulations were certainly necessary in various areas like prices, wages, and taxation.

The extension of state control was actually carried out in two directions: first, by the expansion of state property and, second, by state control and regulation of all types of activities regarded as crucial in the economic life of the country. The state remained the major buyer of industrial goods, but instead of armaments, goods were being produced for reparations. Because of inflation, a large part of savings and other forms of capital disappeared. Later, when stabilization was successfully carried out in 1946, a deflationary policy was introduced that meant strong government control over credit. A price and wage system was also established by the state; thus, in spite of the fact that the economy was still basically in the hands of private firms, it was closer to a mixed economy than to a completely market economy.

At this stage, state property did not go far beyond where it had been before. Legislation concerning the nationalization of the mines was very much in line with economic policy followed by the Labor Party in England and socialist parties elsewhere. The ensuing nationalization of the four major companies of Hungary did extend the state sector, but it did not yet effect a change in the dominance of the private sector.

The question was still unanswered as to whether this mixed economy would return to a liberal free-enterprise system after reconstruction was completed, as liberal political forces advocated, or would go on to introduce systematic planning, as the Communist Party foresaw it. The answer to this question was dependent on the balance of domestic and international political forces.

Nevertheless, because the acceleration of the recovery process was badly needed and because the idea of some kind of planning was very much alive everywhere in postwar Europe, an interim reconstruction plan for three years was accepted. In August 1947, when the three-year plan was introduced, the private sector was still the dominant sector in the Hungarian economy. A part of industry (coal mines, electric power stations, and the most important heavy industrial companies) had been nationalized, but this was not the majority even in the industrial sector. In banking and wholesale and retail trade, the share of state property was low, as was also the case in agriculture. Except for a few state farms, peasant plots were the prevailing form of land tenure since a radical land reform had in 1945 put an end to the old land-tenure structure under which large landholdings still survived from the age of feudalism. Although a National Planning Office had been established, its task was no more than to set some basic targets for the economy (for industrial and agricultural production and growth rates), to coordinate the most important efforts, and to influence directly or indirectly the most important investment decisions.

The three-year plan was a special combination of a mixed economy: A large but declining private sector had to work with a growing state sector, and the role of planning was combined with substantial elements of the market. Measured in terms of its achievements, the plan can be called a success. Reconstruction was more or less successfully carried out. With a suprisingly high rate of industrial growth and with state-controlled major investments, industrial production reached the prewar level as early as 1948 and largely surpassed it in 1949. National income was around the prewar level by 1949, and even the income of the working class was a bit above the 1938 level. Agriculture, however, was behind the prewar level, but it is hard to tell to what extent this was the consequence of the radical changes in the land-tenure system.

The three-year plan was still in effect when decisive changes occurred in the political structure of Hungary. These changes transformed the country's multiparty system into a one-party system, turned a mixed economy into a socialist economy, and shifted the combination of nationalized and private firms into entirely state-owned property. The Communist Party started to fight for the extension of state-owned property with the introduction of the three-year plan, and when the parliament accepted state control over the ten largest banks, the financial system and the majority of industrial production came under direct state control.

The Communist Party Takes Power

The decisive turning point came in 1948–1949, however, when the Communist Party, having achieved an absolute monopoly of political power, changed its economic strategy and demanded much greater nationalization as a prerequisite for successful planning. The change in international circumstances led the party—which had regarded the postwar maintenance of a mixed economy as a key element in its political strategy—to change its views. It gave up the concept of achieving socialism in a gradual way and decided to establish a socialist economic and social system within the shortest possible time. A key element in this strategy was the extension of state-owned property, seen as the only property arrangement adequate for a socialist economy. As private enterprise was regarded as harmful to economic growth and even as an obstacle to economic transformation, an ambitious policy was established to liquidate private firms. In March 1948, all types of firms in private hands employing 100 persons or more were nationalized. This measure, covering 594 firms and 160,000 workers, enlarged the state sector in industry to more than 80 percent of large-scale industry. Some key branches like mining and metallurgy were now entirely in the hands of the state, while the engineering and construction industries were up to 90 percent state-owned, and the textile, paper, and food industries approximately 50 percent state-owned.

Nevertheless, the nationalization process did not stop there. On December 28,1949, a new decree was codified calling for all firms employing more than 10 workers (i.e., much of small-scale industry as well as large-scale industry) to be expropriated. In some cases, for example the printing industry and pharmaceuticals, every enterprise was nationalized. This represented not only the annihilation of the private sector in large-scale industry and banking but also a rigorous effort to eliminate private small-scale industry and private ownership. The realization of this aim, however, was carried out not by acts or decrees but by administrative pressure. One has to consider that small-scale industry played a very significant role in Hungary until the mid-twentieth century. One quarter of industrial output came from this sector, which employed more than 40 percent of all industrial workers. Even in 1948, there were 180,000 artisans and they employed 188,000 workers. Most of these shops, being very small, were not nationalized; but because of taxation, price controls, materials allocation, and sometimes just by bureaucratic harassment, the number of artisans declined to 120,000 and the number of their workers dropped to 29,000 (i.e., altogether 19 percent of the industrial labor force) by the end of 1950. The same trend can be seen in the number of private shopkeepers in Budapest, which diminished from 20,000 to 1,300 between 1948 and 1952. The state sector became completely dominant in the wholesale trade in 1949 and to a great degree in retail trade as well by 1952.

With the establishment of the one-party system and the introduction of a new socialist constitution in August 1949, the political process of transformation had been completed: The state was formally proclaimed a dictatorship of the proletariat, and its main aim was stated as being to build socialism in Hungary. During 1949, serious preparations were launched to elaborate a new five-year plan. It was indicated that this was no longer to be a plan for reconstruction nor a plan with a mixed economy in which plans were merely orientation points; instead, it was to be a real "socialist" plan that would include and actually command the whole process of economic development. This type of plan existed only in the Soviet Union, and now in all fields of economic, political, and institutional life, the Soviet Union was regarded as the great example to be followed. Consequently, it was obvious that this interpretation of a state plan was nothing less than the introduction of Soviet-type planning in Hungary.

Adopting the Soviet Economic Model

The socialist reorganization of the economy began with the reorganization of the credit system. The central role of banks in a modern economy was acknowledged as early as the second half of the nineteenth century by Karl Marx. The idea that the Soviet model had to be mechanically copied prevailed mainly because Stalin was demanding this type of policy, and thus the principles for the Hungarian reorganization were based on Soviet practice in which the credit system not only financed the economy but served also as its control organ.

The Hungarian National Bank became the central organ of credit life. It not only had the monopoly to issue banknotes but it became the direct and almost exclusive source of credit. All credit institutions were bound to transfer their assets and liabilities (claims and deposits) to the National Bank. Beginning with the summer of 1948, it became the sole source of short-term commercial credits. This gave the National Bank central control over the country's whole economy and enabled it to institute a kind of national accountancy. Each nationalized undertaking was allowed to maintain but a single bank account. This account, kept with the National Bank, recorded all revenues and expenditures, a system that made it possible to have a clear financial picture of the firms concerned. By controlling their accounts, the National Bank was in a position to survey the fulfillment of the financial plan in production, marketing, and so on.

A network of specialized banks was then set up around the National Bank. The Investment Bank was formed from the former Credit Bank. It had to finance and control investments in industry, mining, transportation, and building trade. The Investment Bank, moreover, financed the investments of state and public bodies. This bank was closely connected with the Planning Board and had nothing to do with short-term credits and the business activities of industrial undertakings. Amounts assigned from state and local budgets for plan investments were domiciled at the bank. Besides, the bank was entitled to draw, for the purposes of long-term investments, on a part of the deposits accumulated in the National Bank. Finally, enterprises had to put 25 percent of their amortization fund at the disposal of the investment fund.

The Bank of Foreign Trade was formed from the Hungarian Commercial Bank of Pest. Beginning May 15, 1948, all trade connected with exports or imports had to be transacted through the Bank of Foreign Trade. Earlier, foreign exchange transactions of the National Bank and the other banks had been assumed by this bank. Its functions grew more complete after the further nationalization of commerce. The monopoly of the bank was not quite complete, however: With respect to foreign trade with the Soviet Union, it had to work in cooperation with the Hungarian Commercial and Industrial Bank, which was owned by the Soviet Union.

At the beginning, the sum total of private bank deposits was taken over by the savings department of the National Bank, which developed in 1949 into an independent credit institution, the National Savings Bank. It had the task of accepting private deposits and supplying credit for small-scale industry, the retail trade, and private enterprises. But this institution did not come up to expectations.

The beginnings of the unsound economic policy that was to become especially pervasive in the first half of the 1950s—a policy aimed at concentrating all financial means for the purposes of the state and limiting all other financial activity—can be traced to 1949. It unduly restricted savings and their practical employment. Accrued sums were used for other purposes of the National Bank, and only 10 percent of the deposits were placed as direct credits through the National Savings Bank. The National Cooperative Credit Institute became the Agricultural Credit Institute. It operated, however, only with poor results, partly because of the uncertainty of economic policy.

The new banking system served also as a main control organ for the planning authority. All state undertakings had to maintain a so-called simple account with the National Bank, and all of their financial activities went through this account.

The settlement of the financial situation was only one side of the reorganization of newly nationalized industry. Reorganization was necessary with respect to both private enterprises and the governmental organs controlling them. An appropriate form also had to be found for state enterprises. The form of the capitalist joint stock company, of course, did not suit the new situation, and neither did the old form of state enterprises with their rigid rules and their excessive bureaucracy. The creation of the new category of "nationalized undertakings" was an attempt to find a form that would ensure the necessary independence to individual enterprises (including their legal status) and that would at the same time fit into an overall organization of socialist industry. In 1948, not only the control of individual enterprises but also that of the industry as a whole had to be organized. Apart from the organs supervising the earlier state enterprises, such as the Centre of Heavy Industry and the Hungarian State Collieries, this work became the responsibility of the Ministry of Industry.

The Ministry of Industry, however, was not fit to perform the task, for it had been established under capitalist conditions and had undergone no organizational change between 1945 and 1948. Besides, the ministry could not assume responsibility for the direct control of 750 undertakings. Therefore, direct-control organs were instituted for each branch in the form of industrial directorates. Twenty-nine such bodies were set up; nineteen were directly subordinated to the Ministry of Industry, whereas the rest came under the authority of other ministries (e.g., the Ministries of Agriculture, Transport, and Construction).

These industrial directorates performed two functions: They were government authorities, but directed the concerned branch of industry at the same time. Their tasks were to have plans prepared by each undertaking, to reconcile these individual plans, to oversee their fulfillment, and to promote industrial cooperation. They were, moreover, partly responsible for the price policy and the supply of materials.

Besides supervision by the Ministry of Industry and the Ministry of Finance, the most important role in industrial control was provided by the Soviet-type planning system itself and the crucial role given to the National Planning Office. This office was established as early as 1947, but at this time its functions were still quite different. Now, by taking over the task of material control from the dissolved Anyag és Árhivatal (Materials and Prices Authority) and by taking over price control in 1949 from the short-lived Gazdasági Fötanács (Supreme Economic Council) in 1948, the Planning Office became the supreme directive organ of all economic activity.

Establishing a Soviet-Type Command Economy

What were the basic systemic features of the Soviet-type centrally planned economy? First, there was state ownership of the means of production in every branch of the economy, particularly banking, industry, and trade. In agriculture, nationalized ownership of the means of production was not regarded as a condition to central planning; nevertheless, strong pressure was exerted by the state to abolish private farms and to turn them into cooperative or state-owned farms. The state-owned farms were supposed to operate along the same principles as state-owned industrial enterprises. Collective farms were strongly controlled by state regulations, and private farms were pushed by different types of pressure (e.g., heavy taxation, extremely high compulsory deliveries of product, and continuous government harassment) to join the collective farms. Actually, with the exception of small household plots, the plan anticipated the abolishment of private property in agriculture.

The second most important feature of Soviet-type planning was a hierarchical economic organization in which all decisionmaking was concentrated at the very top. Plan targets were transmitted through administrative channels to the executors by administrative directives. This meant that decisionmaking was hierarchical, with the scope of decisionmaking authority automatically declining at lower levels. Top decisions concerning the main trends and the major targets of economic development were actually made by the supreme organ of the ruling Communist Party, which controlled all official government bodies, including the Planning Office.

Because the plan was intended to encompass all economic activity in the country, a principal role was given to the Planning Office, which would draw up a national plan that included the means and procedures for its fulfillment, a production plan for the industry, some general regulations, and a long-range plan in addition to the current plan. As the uniformity of indications seemed very important, targets were in physical units rather than in value terms whenever possible.

The plan, in the form of an order from central authority, determined the quantity and quality of goods to be produced as well as the means of implementation. Three types of means were considered: total investments, raw materials and equipment, and personnel resources. All three were rationed: total investment by the central allocation of investment funds; construction materials and the like, raw materials, and machinery by administrative orders; and personnel resources by state control of the scope of employment and wage expenditures.

Resource allocation was carried out by direct command from the Planning Office. First, material balances were drawn up for production, allocation, and consumption; then the supply plan was formulated indicating the allocation of raw materials, semimanufactured products, and manufactured products among different users. The balances and distribution plans were usually elaborated for whole years and often for quarters as well. The number of balances was constantly increasing because this was regarded as an improvement of planning methods.

Foreign trade was treated as a state monopoly, executed by a number of special firms called foreign trade enterprises. These were in some ways intermediaries, as production enterprises had no direct contact with foreign markets. A special plan for foreign trade was usually prepared, and the implementation of this plan was strictly controlled by foreign exchange controls and other means.

Personal compensation was regulated by fixed wage scales—under which rewards for differences in skill were usually low—and was related to the fulfillment of the plan directives. Plan directives included a total wage fund at the company level, and special bonuses were given for managers who met or exceeded the quantitative quotas set by the plan. Farm income, whether collective or individual, was controlled by the extremely low prices set up for compulsory deliveries and by taxation.

The price system was the weakest point in the planning system. Prices were set administratively by the Planning Office, and fixed prices came to be regarded as one of the basic elements of a socialist economy—in direct contradiction to a capitalist economy where prices change in response to market forces. Prices in a planned economy have nothing to do with market forces, but are fixed on a cost-plus basis within a sector. Enterprises that were unable to produce at the fixed price level for their product (for example, in producer-goods industries where prices were kept extremely low) were subsidized by the state. Special prices were established for consumer goods.

The Stalinist industrialization strategy formally met Hungary's requirements insofar as industrialization was needed for economic, social, and even international reasons. However, no serious consideration was allowed as to whether the Soviet model would be the proper one for Hungary or whether it could be adjusted to Hungarian circumstances. The Soviet priorities were to achieve a very high rate of investment and labor mobilization, which would rapidly build up a production structure on autarchic lines. The stress in this economic policy was laid upon energy and raw materials—both very scarce in Hungary—and all priorities, including the price system, were supposed to promote the production of goods in heavy industry.

These priorities had several particular disadvantages for Hungary. First, they absorbed an overwhelming portion of capital formation and showed very low investment efficiency. The forced industrialization assumed an unrealistically high investment rate. In the first version of the so-called five-year plan, the investment rate varied between 20–25 percent; later it was even higher. More than half of investment was allocated to industry, and more than 90 percent of the industrial investment went to heavy industry.

Besides its effect on investment, the price policy can be regarded as one of the main levers for carrying out economic policy. The basic principle of the price policy was that the cost price of the goods produced by the state sector had to be covered from the sale price of consumer products. The means of production, however, were to be sold at cost price. The cost price, therefore, bore no fixed relation to the sale price, and a great many primary industrial materials were sold at below cost with substantial state subsidies.

The situation was further aggravated by the great difference between the market price of agricultural goods and the price agricultural producers got upon delivering their goods to the state. The large-scale compulsory deliveries, forced at unrealistically low prices, were meant to draw off some of the agricultural income and make it contribute to the state's capital accumulation. Producers' prices in the state sector, on the other hand, were considered as mere technicalities—a technical means of balancing the books. The prices of basic materials were thus kept down, without regard even for the increasing cost price of later years. As a result, prices reflected real value relations less and less.

To compound this trend, foreign trade prices had no relation at all to domestic prices. The prices of export goods bore no relation to real production costs or to the domestic price level. The prices of export goods were determined first by the foreign price level and by the competitiveness of these goods on the world market. The producing company, however, sold its products at the domestic producers' price to the foreign trade company, where the often significant difference between the domestic and the world market selling price was bridged by the state's price-leveling fund. There was a marked difference between the official rate of foreign exchange and the rate used in foreign trade transactions, the latter being often four to five times higher. Similarly, the government sold imported goods and materials to the companies not at cost price but at the domestic producers' price for the same kind of product, which was usually much less than the import price.

During the Korean War (1950–1953), there was a conversion to fixed prices in CMEA foreign trade in order to eliminate the unfavorable effects of price fluctuations in the world market caused by the war boom. From then on, the rigid price system of the CMEA market became totally independent of the world market price level and price ratios. This made economic planning easier, as it eliminated the spontaneous effects of price fluctuations. As a result, the price system did nothing to stimulate economic activity and efficiency, the organic relationship between input and output (in the sense of supply and demand) having been totally done away with.

The price mechanism thus had real pricing functions only in one very limited sphere of the domestic market—consumer goods—but even here the pricing system affected only demand, not supply. The confinement of market effects to such a narrow area made the companies practically independent of the realization of their products. Marketability, cost, quality, or the technological standard of their goods played no part in the companies' economic standing.

The companies' interest in fulfilling central directives, their sole concern, was reinforced by a system of bonuses and wages. It was, however, impossible for a company to keep to the letter of such a comprehensive planning system. The companies concentrated their resources on fulfilling those plan indicators that were the most important—the most rewarding—for them. The framers of the economic policy, however, tried to ensure that this coincided with the most dynamic production growth possible. Of the 200 central bonus regulations issued between 1950 and 1955, the fundamental one of November 1, 1952, encouraged companies to achieve targets (set in both quantity and values) by making the fulfillment and even overfulfillment of the production plan the primary bonus criterion. The system of central planning, worked out in the late 1940s and early 1950s, was adequate for a maximal rate of development, one strongly concentrated on primary production, because it was from the very beginning essentially a strategy of war economy.

It soon became clear that the system of central planning (i.e., making the companies' activities independent of price and market effects and making them materially interested only in the primary objective of the quantitative growth of production) encouraged the development of a special kind of hierarchy in which all important central objectives became subordinate to fulfilling and overfulfilling the plan. Prescriptions for increased efficiency, improvement of quality, material savings, and reduction of costs were necessarily heeded less and less. Central planning thus led to a partial and somewhat contradictory realization of economic objectives. In a number of fundamental respects, the consequences were quite contrary to original intentions.

One would assume that this very strongly centralized, hierarchical economic system would be able to implement its implied strategy. However, the Soviets—and, following them, the Hungarian leaders—accepted the view that politics comes before economics. Thus, short-term adjustments were quite frequent because of political needs (e.g., war was expected) or in order to fulfill immediate economic requirements, and this in turn triggered new economic requirements. Moreover, the cyclical changes and fluctuations caused by bad methods of investment planning, wrong project selection, unfinished investment projects, accumulation of unusable inventories, and shortages were further problems. Short-term adjustment even occurred in priorities affecting the distribution of investment and capital replacement. The lack of consistency in selecting investment projects and the constant undervaluation of real costs led to an increase in unfinished projects. Because financial means—János Kornai in Chapter 4 calls it a soft budget constraint—were easily available, a waste of resources ensued that reduced productivity.

During the plan period itself, there was one drastic revision (in 1951) when the actual growth target of the national income was increased from 63 to 130 percent and the growth of industrial output from 86 to 210 percent. In other words, instead of a 13 percent annual growth rate during the five-year period, the new version embodied an increase in the yearly growth rate to 26 percent. More than half of investment was to go to industry, and 90 percent of industrial investment was to be channeled into heavy industry. Special preference was given to the production of strategic materials and to efforts to achieve economic self-sufficiency. Instead of building up multinational economic collaboration with neighboring countries, Hungary's industrialization was to be based on utilization of Soviet raw materials.

Within these priorities, increased production of basic materials received special emphasis. Two-thirds of total industrial investment was allocated to the development of mining and metallurgy. The index of metallurgical investment reflects the extraordinary dynamism of the investment policy in these branches. With 1950 equal to 100, the investment index in 1951 was already 264; in 1952, 463; and in 1943, 489. This large industrial investment, however, was not directly concerned with the needs of Hungary. It was planned for the needs of the Soviet Union—for which Hungary was to serve as an industrial workshop.

This type of economic policy, however, further reinforced the inherent deficiencies of Soviet-type planning, so well characterized by Maurice Dobb:

> Problems of economic planning seem to acquire a resemblance to the problems of military strategy, where in practice the choice lies between a relatively small number of plans, which have in the main to be treated and chosen between as organic wholes, and which for a variety of reasons do not easily permit of intermediate combinations. The situation will demand a concentration of forces round a few main objectives and not a dispersion of resources over a very wide range.[2]

The drastic application of an economic strategy of forced industrialization in a country like Hungary, poor in capital and natural resources, had led to serious difficulties by the time the first long-term plan was completed. A planned economy did make possible a rapid accumulation of capital, the concentration of material resources, and a rapid rate of development, but it did so in a way that was excessively costly. As a result of this generally wasteful system of management, about one-fifth of the increase in national income was lost again through various "leaks" in the economy. In agriculture—which had furnished most of the capital needed for industrialization through taxation and the system of forced deliveries at low prices and where administrative measures to hasten collectivization had further agitated the peasantry—the situation was extremely grave. Production declined, and by the mid-1950s, it had not yet recovered the prewar level. Serious supply problems appeared. As a result of these shortages and because of the heavy burdens placed on the population by forced industrialization in the form of strong inflationary pressures, real wages fell by more than 20 percent—instead of the 50 percent rise in the living standards called for by the five-year plan. By the middle of the 1950s, serious social, economic, and political tensions had arisen, which were to become one of the main sources of the tragic political crisis of 1956.

In agriculture, socialist ownership was still far from universal, so the government pushed hard for collectivization—for example, by pressuring individual peasant farmers to join cooperative farms. Up to the end of 1949, only 1,300 cooperatives had been established, with a relatively insignificant number of members; however, these were cooperatives actually founded on a voluntary basis. After 1950, the government used the police force and constant harassment, combined with ruthless methods, to oblige the peasants to join cooperatives. Concurrent tactics included high taxation, low prices for farm products, the elimination of private markets and the substitution of a compulsory delivery system.

Peasants grew disenchanted with the harassment, and a large number left the villages, abandoning large quantities of arable land. The number of cooperatives increased and by the middle of 1953 included more than 300,000 peasant families with about a quarter of all arable land. But the cooperatives were not successful: Economic policy gave priority to industry, agriculture failed to receive sufficient machinery and fertilizers, and cooperative farms were similarly unable to attract peasants to join them because production and income were very low. The economic policy deliberately exploited agriculture in favor of heavy industry.

From Stalin's Death in 1953 to October 1956

Political changes in 1953 following the death of Josef Stalin in the Soviet Union eased the pressure on Hungary. The tension prevailing in the country (resulting from the decline in the standard of living, shortages, decay in agriculture, and the impossible targets for industrialization) was addressed publicly in a party decision highly critical of existing economic policy. The former party leader Mátyás Rákosi was replaced by Imre Nagy as prime minister, and in 1953 an increasing amount of comprehensive criticism was permitted, with the aim of easing tension and modifying the course taken.

The first criticism regarded the basic mistake to be the forced, one-sided industrialization and the neglect of agriculture. The leadership was blamed—rightly so—for having been unable to realize the basic differences in the potentialities of factor endowments between Hungary and the Soviet Union, as they did not take into consideration the fact that the Hungarian economy was much more developed than the Soviet economy when planning started. No word was even mentioned at this stage that something might be wrong with the planning system as such.

The essence of the new course was formulated as the following:

> The economic policy of the Party (the ruling Communist Party) ought to be radically modified, the growth rate of industrialization and, first of all, the development of heavy industry had to be reduced, and all

development plans for the national economy had to be revised, particularly the investment plans.[3]

The new government program formulated by Prime Minister Nagy first tried to correct the distribution of national income, partly by increasing consumption and partly by providing more investment in agriculture. Some decrease in prices and an increase in wages contributed to a better relationship between the government and the population. To some extent, the same aim was served by decreasing the burden on the peasants and even providing them with some material incentive to increase agricultural production. Because secondary elements of the planning system, like overcentralization and the growing bureaucracy, had been mildly criticized, a decision was even accepted to decrease the number of state employees: However, no deeper revision of the system emerged.

The idea of reform at this point was far from radical. Nevertheless, even this narrow road was not an easy one. The former general secretary of the Communist Party kept a large part of his former power, and he tried to minimize errors in the former course taken, blocking every effort to carry out radical corrections. This resistance to change, even concerning the economic policy, led to serious ideological and political battles.

Partly because of this factional struggle and partly because of some theoretical articles published by economists who started to elaborate a deeper analysis of the deficiencies of the existing economic system, the differing views were sharpened. By using ideological arguments, Rákosi tried to limit the corrections of the former economic policy to slight cosmetic changes, while Nagy sharpened his criticism of past practices and demanded more radical reform. The battle was temporarily won by Rákosi, who was cleverly able to regain decisive outside support from the Soviet Union and combine it with the resistance to reform among local party leaders—meanwhile blaming the new course taken since 1953 for recently emerged economic difficulties. In the "new" program Rákosi introduced in 1955, which in every respect was a regression to the old economic policies, he stressed the development of heavy industry, urging again collectivization. All the former mistakes were explained away as the result of having been quantitatively too ambitious.

However, while the government was looking backward and defending the old line, in the economic literature criticism and more profound analysis gained ground. The first important analysis that led to a better understanding appeared as early as 1954. György Péter published an article in December 1954 in the *Közgazdasági Szemle* (Economic Review) in which he criticized the administrative-bureaucratic, overcentralized system of direction and called for the introduction of money-market relations assuring greater independence for industrial firms. State intervention in the suggested system would become more indirect, and planning would be concentrated on the "direction of the development and the structure of the economy"—that is, the proportion of consumption and investment, the balance between supply and demand, the growth rate of the different branches of the economy, and the central planning of the structure of investments. Planning, however, should not be based on compulsory directives. These would be replaced by indirect economic methods and the market.

János Kornai proved that the different shortcomings and errors of economic performance in the Soviet-type system were not accidental and independent of each other but were part of an interdependent and consistent complexity. Partial corrections thus were impossible and could not lead to real results. "A consistent and radical reform is needed"—this statement, however, wasn't publicly made until the summer of 1956.

Despite this first deep analysis, which discovered basic mistakes in the system and presented partially developed new proposals, radical reform was definitely not the intention of the government. It still maintained that the existing planning system was good (and basically the only possible one) but overcentralized. The Planning Office therefore started to prepare a certain reform focused on the "rationalization" of the command economy. A basic effort was made to limit the number of compulsory directives and give more independence to firms to enable them to decide, for example, the format of their production. A certain price reform was also prepared with the aim of creating a factory-price system closer to the cost of production, but without changing the system of fixed prices and the existing separation of factory prices from consumer prices.

The preparation and the character of the second five-year plan, which was introduced at the beginning of 1956, clearly showed the delay in implementation of real reforms and fundamental changes. The planning system basically remained as it was, a typical command economy, but a bit more moderate and flexible. Forced industrialization continued as the "leitmotif" of the economic policy, but again in more moderate form: Lower accumulation, a lower growth rate, and a more balanced structure of investment and development were all that was needed to cope with the difficulties that had emerged.

The delay in reform during 1955–1956, however, was no longer only an economic problem. It had definitely become an element of the deepening political crisis that hindered the realization of even these timid reforms. On October 23, 1956, a massive student demonstration revealed the need for radical changes to improve the implementation of socialism. That evening, armed groups attacked the Hungarian Radio building after police had unwisely fired into the crowds. An uprising swept the capital, and the army joined the revolutionaries.

The cathartic, tragic events of the autumn of 1956, after the intervention of Soviet troops, closed one chapter—and opened a new one—in postwar Hungarian economic development. The new Kádár government was under tremendous pressure and gave serious consideration to far-reaching economic reform, but from the very beginning, politics prevailed. The struggle for power required that all decisions be made first from the perspective of whether or not they contributed to the consolidation of the political situation in the country. In that sense, one of the most important and far-reaching economic changes—the abolition of the compulsory delivery system in agriculture—was decided and promptly introduced more for political than economic reasons: to regain the confidence and loyalty of the peasants for the new Kádár government. However, the abolition of the compulsory delivery system (the first such abolition among countries with Soviet-type planned economies) had a far-reaching impact upon agricultural production, and later when further reforms were introduced, it became the starting point for subsequent reform policies. Partly because of political pressure—a large number of reform proposals had appeared in the autumn of 1956—and partly because the government was determined to establish an economic policy free from the former mistakes, to improve living standards, and to build up a quickly developing and more balanced economy, an expert committee was established to elaborate the principles of the new economic and planning policy.

A New Chapter

The committee came up with a radical proposal for a comprehensive reform aimed at replacing compulsory plan directives by a controlled market mechanism and introducing real prices and profit motivation. The blueprint still retained centralized investments, financed entirely by the state budget. However, the conservative political groups supported from outside initiated a strong ideological offensive, branding this modification of the planning system as nonsocialist and blocking the road to reform. As a result, the plan was rejected. Nonetheless, corrections in economic policy were accepted, mainly along the lines of those that had been rejected in 1955 under the Nagy government, but no radical changes occurred in the economy.

Among groups of smaller or larger corrections and half measures, the most important and the most far-reaching was the change in agricultural policy. To regain the political support of the peasantry, the government canceled the former collectivization policy. Two-thirds of the members of the collective farms left, and the government made a strong pledge not to use political harassment to force them any longer to participate in collectives.

In this way, the basic pillars of the command economy in agriculture were destroyed. Between the peasantry and the state remained nothing but a market connection, instead of administrative means (direct orders and force). The state organs bought agricultural products from the peasants, and when they wanted to buy, they had to pay market prices for them. (Under compulsory delivery, it was possible for the state to pay artificially low prices because the peasants had no choice but to deliver the goods.) Instead of compulsory sowing plans, the state now had to use economic means (basically price incentives and tax differentiation) to encourage production and to influence structural changes. In one sector of the Hungarian economy, therefore, a controlled planned market economy was introduced. This was a pioneering step toward a new economic model.

However, the abandonment of collectivization did not prove to be a long-lasting policy, partly because of domestic changes but more in order to yield to foreign pressure (China's Great Leap Forward and the Soviet campaign against revisionism). Thus, in the winter of 1958–1959, mass collectivization began again in Hungary.

In the new collectivization campaign, governmental coercion and the impoverishment of the private peasant—practices of the early 1950s—were avoided. New incentives were offered for organizing cooperatives: obligatory payment of a rental on land; a new solution of the kulak (rich peasants) question that permitted cooperatives to decide themselves whether to accept well-to-do peasants (a great point of contention in earlier years); election of the cooperatives' leaders and freedom to decide how land should be cultivated; a more flexible wage system generally more favorable to the peasantry; and freedom to cultivate allotments. Another extremely important factor was the readiness of the state to provide large numbers of agronomists, financial support, and many other kinds of assistance, far surpassing that available earlier and to be provided well before the main work of reorganization was begun in order to assure the stability of the cooperatives.

The emerging collective farm, in the end, represented a new model compared with the Soviet kolkhoz type. The new income system did allow for various forms of crop sharing, and about 40 percent of the animal stock remained in private hands on the private plots (1 hectare, about 2.4 acres) that were assured to each member of the collective farms. The foundation for modern agricultural enterprise was also enhanced by allowing additional industrial activities to be established inside the cooperatives (e.g., food processing and machine repairing shops). As a result, for the first time in the history of the collectivization of agriculture, the number of livestock did not decline at all and even gross industrial production increased.

The modification in economic policy and the crucial change in agriculture, however, did not prove to be sufficient in making the Hungarian economy more effective. Certainly during the late 1950s and early 1960s, one could observe some improvement: investment decisions were made in more cautious ways; factor endowment was taken more into consideration; and particular attention was given to improving living standards and to developing agriculture. However, no radical changes occurred in the planning system, and the government still firmly believed that with small corrections, the deficiencies in the planning system could be overcome and the system made workable.

Because it was well known that one of the basic deficiencies in the planning system was the artificial price system (i.e., prices did not reflect relative scarcities, and they were distorting resource allocation), a moderate price reform was undertaken. The basic objective was to replace artificial prices with reconstituted prices based on real values. Nevertheless, the reformed prices remained fixed, and factory and consumer prices remained unlinked. In other words, changing world market prices and input relations soon made the new factory prices obsolete and artificial once again. As consumer preferences and the market could not influence and reorient production, price reform had only transitory consequences and no permanent influence on economic performance.

Another characteristic reform measure was a radical limitation of plan directives. The uniformity of plan directives was abolished; the ministries now had the right to decide the number of compulsory directives. Some of them, beginning with the Ministry of Light Industry, cut back radically, reducing their compulsory indices from several dozens down to five. However, the calculated gain to be achieved by such reductions (more flexibility and more autonomy for business enterprises) was not realized. There was no real market, and the most important activities still remained under strict central control; therefore the reduction of central directives did not result in more flexible performance but led only to a great deal of uncertainty. Even the industrial firms—reported the Planning Office in 1959—urged "the reestablishment of discipline for a better basis to fulfil their plans."

A profit-sharing system introduced in 1957 met almost the same fate. Because of the lack of both real markets and market prices, the profit incentive could play only a secondary role compared with the basic interest in fulfilling plan quotas. In the last analysis, profit sharing (equal, on average, to 7–14 days' wages) became a form of bonus and could not give an impetus to a profit-maximization orientation.

Another attempt was made to correct the planning system by introducing interest charges on capital and by curtailing the practice of using subsidies and taxes to establish priorities. Emphasis was placed on reassessing industrial organization. The existing pattern of hierarchical organization, which placed industrial enterprises under two layers of organizational authority and made the legal independence of the enterprises entirely fictitious, did not work properly. However, the proposed remedy called for removing only one layer (the industrial directories); and instead of establishing properly working horizontal linkages among the enterprises, the proposal sought to cut the number of enterprises by concentrating production in fewer, large enterprises.

Administrative management was indeed simplified as a result, and a part of the bureaucracy was eliminated. However, by urging the concentration of production (sometimes the production of a whole industrial branch and other times only one industrial product) in one huge enterprise, a new hierarchy was developed by merging small factories into large ones and creating an industrial structure unique in its high concentration of workers. (More than two-thirds of the workers were engaged in enterprises employing more than 1,000 workers.)

Enterprise dependence on higher authorities, a basic element of the planning system, changed only in form, and the elimination of the industrial directories between the ministries and the enterprises in fact kept that dependence on the ministries very much intact. The major decisions were still made by higher authorities, not at the enterprise level, and the only small difference was that the few huge enterprises were probably somewhat more successful in influencing the decisionmaking process than enterprises had been under the earlier arrangement.

It is true that the number of production indicators handed down to the enterprises were substantially decreased, and among these, the qualitative indicators gained some importance as compared with the merely quantitative ones. Yet, no radical changes occurred either in the relation among the enterprises or in the direction of production from above.

We should not fail to note the important differences overall between the structure of the classical centrally planned economy of the 1950s and the new, much more flexible revised version that slowly came into existence after 1956. Most of the linkages in the command economy had been modified, and as the indicators became more flexible, they were no longer regarded as commands. Enterprises gained more freedom of action and influence in decisionmaking, and the hierarchical relations between the controllers and the controlled became more complex. Nevertheless, the basic elements of the centrally planned economy still existed, and they had a decisive influence upon the development of the economy.

Continued disregard for market forces, the retention of obligatory directives, and the survival virtually intact of the system of prices and incentives that went with them vitiated the effect of these individual reforms. The system of obligatory directives, which had undergone no basic change, was an organic part of the earlier strategy of economic planning—a necessary means for realizing the program of forced industrialization. Its survival, despite changes in economic thinking, led to a continued stress on attaining quantitative targets within a model of extensive forced development, which resulted in a neglect of technological progress and a lack of interest in the quality and variety of goods to be marketed. Waste in investment and production remained a prominent feature of this kind of economic system. But the recognition that instead of minor corrections, a more thorough reform was needed had gained more and more ground. On July 21, 1964, the Committee on Economic Policy of the ruling Communist Party came to the conclusion that to assure the better realization of the aims of the economic policy, it was necessary to make a comprehensive analysis of the organization of the economy, including the system of management, price incentives, and the financial and institutional systems.[4] This assessment led to the New Economic Mechanism, which opened a new chapter in Hungary's economic history.

Notes

Editor's note: Paul Marer and George Barany generously assisted in editing this chapter because György Ránki did not have an opportunity to review the edited manuscript before his death.

1. This chapter is based mainly upon previous publications of the author, among them Iván T. Berend and György Ránki, *Hungary: A Century of Economic Development* (Barnes and Noble, 1974); and Iván T. Berend and György Ránki, *The Hungarian Economy in the Twentieth Century* (New York: St. Martins, 1985). I have drawn on the extremely rich literature on the topic, including Paul Marer, *East-West Technology Transfer: A Study of Hungary 1968–1974* (Paris: OECD, 1986); János Kornai, *Overcentralization in Economic Administration* (Oxford: Oxford University Press, 1959); M. C. Kaser and E. A. Radici, eds., *The Economic History of Eastern Europe, 1919–1975*, three volumes, (Oxford: Clarendon Press, 1985); and a recently published and most comprehensive book by Iván Pető-Sándor Szakács, *A hazai gazdaság négy évtizedének története 1945–1985* [Four decades of Hungary's economic history, 1945–1985] (Budapest: Közgazdasági és jogi kiadó, 1985), hereafter cited as *Four Decades*.

2. Maurice Dobb, *Soviet Economic Development Since 1917* (London: Routledge & Kegan Paul, 1948), p. 6.

3. Pető-Szakács, *Four Decades*, p. 243.

4. Iván T. Berend, *Gazdasági útkeresés, 1956–1965* [Searching for an economic path, 1956–1965] (Budapest: Magvetö, 1983), pp. 448–461.

3

Market Mechanism Reforms in Hungary

Paul Marer

This chapter deals with three topics.[1] The first section presents an overview of Hungary's reform process during the last thirty years. This is followed by a discussion of the relationship between system reforms and economic performance. The chapter concludes with an assessment of the reforms and prospects.

Evolution of the Economic System Since 1956[2]

Impact of the Revolution of 1956

The revolution of 1956 was a shock to the system's directors and triggered consideration of far-reaching economic reforms. Right after the revolution the party appointed an expert committee, its membership dominated by reform-oriented economists. In June 1957 the committee proposed radical reforms that contained most of the reform measures introduced in 1968.[3] But the comprehensive reform plan was not implemented, owing to the faster-than-expected consolidation of the Kádár regime's economic and political power, which reduced the urgency of the reform, and the considerable domestic and foreign opposition to reforms, for political-ideological reasons.

Significant Reforms in Agriculture (1957–1968)

During the early 1950s the majority of peasants were forced to join collective farms in a brutal campaign drive modeled on the collectivization of Soviet agriculture during the early 1930s. During and immediately after the revolution of 1956, two-thirds of members left the collectives and during the next few years did better as private farmers. In 1957 the government made an important decision to abolish compulsory production and delivery obligations, replacing them with voluntary contracts at more favorable prices. The abolition of compulsory deliveries in agriculture later had a parallel in the abolition of compulsory plan targets in industry in 1968.

In 1958 the decision was made to recollectivize agriculture, accomplished during 1959–1962. Its method, however, was different from that of any previous collectivization drive in a centrally planned economy (CPE). Instead of relying only on coercion, persuasion and incentives were used also. For example, those who joined received lifetime annuities for the land and token payment for the other assets contributed and were allowed to retain a household plot and a number of animals. After a few years well-to-do peasants could be chosen for leadership posts in the collective, and many were elected. A further distinctive aspect was the government providing inputs and substantial investments, including grants and loans, and later canceling a good portion of the repayment obligation. Agricultural prices were raised for all types of farms, with prices paid for deliveries by collective farms set higher as an incentive to join.

During the quarter of a century since recollectivization, reforms in this sector continued, although in a stop-and-go fashion. Examples of reforms include the following: Pioneering personal incentive mechanisms were introduced; production and marketing by private, collective, and state farms became integrated; and collective and state farms were gradually permitted to set up entrepreneurial ventures in industry, construction, and the services. The reform initiatives often came from below, from the management of the collective and state farms. Depending on the political climate, the authorities sometimes enthusiastically endorsed, sometimes tolerated, and at other times vetoed or reversed the reform initiatives. But each time significant restrictions were placed on producers, a stagnation or decline in output was triggered, prompting the lifting of the restrictions.

Reforms in agriculture have made important direct and indirect contributions to Hungary's overall reform process. The sector's success in terms of increased yields and output has facilitated the introduction—from above—of reforms in other sectors also. Agriculture has remained in the vanguard of Hungary's reform movement.

Industry: Modest Reforms and Counterproductive Mergers (1957–1965)

In the decade after the revolution of 1956 the reforms introduced in industry were much more modest than those implemented in agriculture. The number of centrally prescribed indicators for enterprises was reduced, and profit sharing with workers was introduced. The domestic prices of imports and depreciation rates were set at more realistic levels. However, enterprises continued to have little difficulty recovering costs. Thus, although the price measures may have improved the decisions of planners, they did not advance greatly the efficiency of enterprise operations.

During the the late 1950s and early 1960s, many industrial enterprises were merged and large trusts established to "improve" the functioning of the traditional centrally planned system. These large units were given additional power to make decisions, thus in effect implementing limited administrative decentralization without changing the planning mechanism in any fundamental way. The merger movement created an exceedingly high degree of industrial concentration that impeded subsequent attempts to establish horizontal, market-oriented relations between firms.

The New Economic Mechanism: Blueprint, Implementation, Assessment (1965–1972)

Background. During the mid-1960s, deteriorating economic performance outside agriculture and the example of reforms introduced in the Soviet Union and elsewhere in Eastern Europe generated a wave of discussion on economic reforms. These factors led to the introduction of the New Economic Mechanism (NEM) in 1968, just before the invasion of Czechoslovakia by Warsaw Pact forces in August of that year, which ended a set of political and economic reforms in that neighboring country.

Blueprint. In the NEM concept, central planning was not abandoned, but its scope was to be reduced and its instruments changed. Whereas in a traditional CPE, the center plans both macro and micro decisions, planning under the NEM focused mainly on macro issues. Direct planning in the micro sphere was to be limited to investments in infrastructure, large investments in high-priority sectors, the administrative regulation of defense industries, the supervision of domestic supply responsibilities for key products such as basic consumer goods, and the fulfillment of CMEA trade obligations. To fulfill macro objectives, the center would rely on a combination of market forces and government-adjusted "economic regulators" like prices, exchange rates, interest rates, taxes, and subsidies. The uniform application of the regulators was to be achieved gradually, over a period of five to ten years.

One feature of the NEM blueprint was to be the "open" character of the plans. In recognition that unforeseen domestic and external events require flexible adaptation, plan targets would be given as ranges and could be revised during implementation. Instead of compulsory plan directives to enterprises, firms were to formulate their own plans in the context of the national economic plan and the regulators they faced and discuss them with their superiors, but plan fulfillment would not be compulsory.

Implementation. The NEM was introduced on January 1, 1968. Further reform steps were implemented during the next four years, approximately as scheduled. Enterprises became more profit-oriented. Current production decisions by enterprise management became more flexible. Management was told to maximize profits, but controls remained in many areas, such as price and wage determination, foreign trade, and investments. Firms had to allocate profits to a sharing fund to finance wage increases, to a development fund to finance some investments, and to a reserve fund for contingencies—each fund taxed at varying rates. Productive investments outside agriculture that could be initiated by enterprises (approximately 50 percent of the total) were regulated closely. Detailed rules controlled the creation and replenishment of enterprise development funds. The central allocation of some key inputs continued, as did the licensing of imports and administrative guidance regarding credit and investment decisions. For example, the granting of credits under guidelines specifying central objectives became an increasingly important instrument for determining the level and direction of enterprise investments. The interest charged played only a minor role. Although enterprise proposals had some bearing on the granting of credits for investment projects, the proposals themselves were usually drafted to fit the monopoly credit-granting institutions's guidelines.

In sum, the reform devolved to enterprise managers many decisions regarding inputs and outputs and some decisions concerning personal compensation and investments. However, strategic business decisions remained subject to strict central guidelines and intervention.

An assessment. The NEM is often labeled a comprehensive reform. This term is justified by the simultaneous introduction of a large set of interrelated reform measures. But from a different perspective, the NEM was not a comprehensive reform: The institutional framework of a traditional CPE—the basic organs of central planning, the branch and functional ministries, the monopoly positions of many enterprises on the domestic market, and the concentration of all banking functions in a single institution—had remained unchanged.

Creating a real market mechanism requires the operation of real market forces. No economy allows all resource allocation and income distribution decisions to be made only by market forces, but for an economy to operate efficiently, government intervention has to remain below a certain threshold. Although a more or less genuine market mechanism has been operating in Hungary since 1968 in agriculture and (outside agriculture) in the private and cooperative sectors, in the dominant state industrial, construction, and service sectors, government regulation has remained decisive. One reason has been that as long as the institutional structure remained unchanged, genuine market forces could not be unleashed.

Many reform economists recognized this structural constraint when the NEM was drafted, but there was insufficient political support at the time to reform the institutional structure also. This lack of support was not just a question of vested interests but a general unwillingness to effect such a radical break with the past. In the economy's key sectors certainly, decisionmakers did not want to relinquish central planning to market forces; rather, they wanted to employ market-type instruments to guide enterprises to fulfill central objectives. Thus, in the view of some reform supporters, the purpose of the "regulators" was to exert the will of the planners (more effectively than could be done through administrative directives) rather than to simulate what the market would do if it existed.

Several other considerations were involved also. In 1968 Hungary did not (and today still does not) have in place the kind of industrial organization and competitive conditions that are essential for an efficiently operating market mechanism. Prices, wages, and so on cannot be allowed to be freely market-determined if most producers are monopolistic sellers or monopsonistic buyers on the domestic market and face no import competition.

Another reason for setting and controlling the regulators administratively was that skewed economic development and the arbitrary price, wage, tax, and subsidy policies practiced for nearly two decades before the NEM was introduced had created all kinds of imbalances in the economy. These included large excess capacity in some sectors and insufficient or outdated capacity in others, many shortages and some surpluses in certain services and products, and arbitrary product and factor prices. Therefore, even if competitive conditions would have been assured, allowing the regulators immediately to be market-determined would have caused large initial economic dislocations, including inflation and unemployment, which were unacceptable for social and political reasons.

Still another reason for centrally controlling the regulators was that in some cases the politically determined preferences of the planners differed from the outcomes that would be generated by efficiently operating market forces, even in sectors where there were no major disproportions. Most important was the unwillingness to allow employment dislocations and enterprise bankruptcies— that is, the budget constraint had remained "soft," to use János Kornai's well-turned phrase.[4] This meant insufficient pressure—and incentives—for producers to respond to market-type signals, causing a large segment of the economy to remain rigidly inflexible.

A key point in understanding the NEM is this: What the Hungarians call "economic regulators"—prices, exchange rates, interest rates, rules for setting wages and profit sharing and allocating credits—are determined in the West largely by market forces, although government policies do affect them. In a traditional CPE, prices, exchange rates, and so on play little if any resource-allocation role. But how such "regulators" are set and the role they play under Hungary's NEM are not clear. Many observers in the West have the impression that since the NEM was introduced, prices, exchange rates, interest rates, and other economic matters are determined and operate more or less in the same fashion as their counterparts do in the West. But this parallel does not really exist—even in the NEM blueprint much less in practice. The regulators are shaped and adjusted by the center, often after explicit or implicit bargaining with the enterprises that will be affected by them. On what basis the regulators are set and adjusted is not transparent. There is a great deal of uncertainty also about their economic consequences, given the environment in which they function. Moreover, if the outcomes are not what the planners want, or if political or economic circumstances change, the regulators are modified. For all these reasons, there is much uncertainty about how the NEM influences enterprise decisions. Large state enterprises are subject to stricter controls than smaller ones or those in the collective and private sectors.

Increased Administrative Interventions (1973–1978)

Beginning in late 1972, domestic and international political and economic developments led to a retrenchment in the implementation of the NEM, although the NEM principles were not formally abandoned. Large industrial enterprises reacted to the deterioration in their relative economic positions and to the decline in the prestige of their managers and workers by criticizing the impact of certain reform measures. Small and medium-sized firms, and agricultural producers generally, were better able to take advantage of the opportunities opened up by the NEM. Trade unions did not like that the relative income positions of workers in state industry deteriorated vis-à-vis those employed in agriculture and in the private and cooperative sectors and therefore lined up with the reform's opponents.

Further weakening the reform momentum was the deterioration in Hungary's terms of trade in the wake of the explosion of world market prices of energy and the subsequent Western recession. Foreign trade difficulties played into the hands of those who favored a more centralized model of economic decisionmaking as the authorities tried to protect the economy from external economic shocks. The scope of quantitative regulations increased. Higher taxes were levied, on a firm-by-firm basis, on "unearned" profits, and more and more enterprises bargained for and received subsidies. Because producers had few incentives to become cost-conscious, the energy- and material-intensive pattern of production continued.

The Pressure for New Reform

Background. The rapid deterioration in Hungary's convertible currency balance of payments is detailed later in this chapter. It is sufficient to state here that the economic situation convinced the authorities that significant long-term improvements could come only if the economy was returned to the reform path.

Alternative Concepts. Although a consensus was reached that the first step should be to implement the NEM blueprint more consistently than during the 1973–1978 period and that further improvements would have to be made in the blueprint, there was no consensus on what precise economic mechanism should be created because the reforms were now entering uncharted waters. My understanding is that the reformers were divided. One group believed that the reform effort should concentrate on "perfecting" the regulators, all of which should continue to be centrally determined in a way best suited to exert the will of the planners. Others argued that the reforms should focus on creating the conditions under which the "regulators" could be increasingly market-determined; until then, the regulators should be set to simulate what the market would do if it existed. The latter group believed that enterprises should be allowed to enjoy or suffer the consequences of how well they could adapt to the regulators and eventually to market forces. It is my impression that the former group had the upper hand in the late 1970s and early 1980s, but as the realization grew that it was not possible to simulate a market mechanism through bureaucratic rules, the latter group gained adherents.

In any event, the series of reform measures introduced from 1979–1988 represented something of a compromise between the two groups. The reforms actually introduced mirrored not only the reform debate itself but also changes in domestic and external economic and political circumstances that helped determine the substance of new reform measures—and whether and when—they were introduced.

New Reform Measures (1979–1988)

During this decade, two kinds of reform measures were introduced: partial reforms in the structure and functioning of economic institutions and further reforms in the economic regulators. The main *institutional reforms* were cutting the size of the central bureaucracy; breaking up several trusts and large enterprises into smaller units; establishing new or easier procedures for founding small and medium-sized business ventures in the socialized sector; enlarging the scope of and easing restrictions on the legalized private sector; introducing some competition between Hungarian firms in foreign trade; creating new financial intermediaries and instruments; and establishing new methods for appointing or selecting enterprise managers. The principal *reforms in the economic regulators* involved changes in the price system, in the wage system, and in the regulation of enterprise income. The reform measures are briefly summarized next.

Cutting the size of the central bureaucracy. In 1980 three industrial ministries were merged into a single Ministry of Industry to reduce the opportunities for direct supervision of enterprises. Total personnel was cut by about half. The main responsibility of the new superministry became industrial policy. To be sure, some of the supervisory functions of the old ministries were turned over to other national organs, the most important being the National Material and Price Office, which—as its name implies—has responsibility not only for designing and enforcing the new price rules but for "material supply" also.

Selective breakups of large producing units. Many of Hungary's large trusts and mammoth enterprises were huge not because they were modern, large-scale producers but because formerly independent firms were merged to facilitate central planning. In industry especially, the organizational structure combined the disadvantages of small numbers, which limited competition; relatively small plants, which meant foregoing economies of scale; and lack of a network of subcontractors, which contributed to high costs. Many large producers thus became monopolists and behaved as powerful lobbies. From 1979 to 1983, 14 of 28 trusts and a significant number of mammoth enterprises were broken up and their components set up as independent firms. Some 300 new enterprises were thus created by reorganization.

New enterprise forms in the socialized sector. Since 1982 it has become possible (or easier) to establish various types of small enterprises, such as subsidiaries, domestic joint ventures, and small cooperatives. Their main purpose is to complement the activities of large enterprises—that is, to let small, independent firms perform those tasks that in a market economy large firms typically subcontract. Small enterprises were always regulated somewhat more flexibly than the large ones, and in 1982 their flexibility was increased further. Earlier restrictions regarding the type of activities a small firm might engage in and the number of persons it might employ were eased, and regulations concerning pricing, bookkeeping, and taxation were simplified.

Enlarged scope and eased restrictions of private activities. Certain activities that previously may not have been fully legal (and thus were carried out "underground") became legalized. The authorities also began to move from an adversarial to a more cooperative posture concerning the relationship of the cooperative and private firms to state enterprises. These reforms have followed the example in agriculture, where giving greater scope to private initiatives and incentives and integrating small and large producers yielded good results.

Foreign trade. The NEM gave direct foreign-trading rights to a few large enterprises and made it possible for foreign trade enterprises (FTEs) to become partners or agents of firms producing exports. The trend to decentralize foreign-trading decisions was accelerated after 1980, and the idea that some FTEs should face domestic competition was introduced. Accordingly, several FTEs were authorized to trade in any product; in other cases the product lines assigned to FTEs overlapped. By 1988, several hundred partnerships were operating between FTEs and one or more producing enterprises.

New financial intermediaries and instruments. Under the NEM, Hungary retained its highly centralized banking system. The National Bank of Hungary was simultaneously the central bank, fiscal agent of the government, and the country's principal commercial and investment bank. As such, it continued to play more of a supervisory than business-partner role vis-à-vis enterprises. In 1987, a decision was made to separate the central and commercial banking functions of the National Bank, the first step in the envisioned creation of a full-fledged commercial banking system. Since 1983, enterprises, cooperatives, and financial institutions have had the right to issue and purchase bonds, some of which can be sold also to the population. Furthermore, a series of reforms since 1979 have created about a dozen small—but in their totality modestly important—new financial intermediaries to provide financial backing for promising inventions, export projects, and other ventures. When developed more fully, these new institutions and instruments of financial intermediation should help mobilize and channel in an improved way the voluntary savings of enterprises and the population.

New methods of selecting enterprise management. Since 1983, top managerial positions of important enterprises have been announced in public tenders, inviting applications from qualified persons, who must propose a long-term business plan. Directors are appointed for an agreed-upon three to five years, not indefinitely, as earlier, and performance is reviewed every few years. A reform step of great potential significance was introduced in 1985 and implemented by the end of 1986. All state firms are divided into three categories: (1) At "key" enterprises, top management is designated by the ministry, as before. (2) At other large firms, an "enterprise board"—composed of the directly elected representatives of the work force (50 percent) and the designated representatives of management (50 percent)—was created, which in turn confirms or appoints the director. The state, and thus implicitly the party, retains the right of veto. (3) In smaller enterprises—generally those employing fewer than 500 persons—the general assembly of all employees or a council elected by them became the top decisionmaking body.

The price system. Hungary's reforms face the dilemma that in the absence of significant domestic and import competition, most prices cannot be allowed to be freely determined by supply and demand (assuming that that is the intention of the authorities). There is agreement, however, that the domestic prices of tradable inputs should be adapted continuously to changing relative prices on the world market and that the automatic recovery of costs should not be allowed for all producers. In 1980 a complex "competitive" price system was introduced: a set of rules for forming producer prices by industrial enterprises accounting for about 70 percent of industrial output. (Pricing in the remaining 30 percent remained unchanged and is essentially cost-plus.) Competitive pricing means that the prices of energy, raw materials, and selected semimanufactures are set equal to Western world market prices (converted to forints at the prevailing exchange rates), regardless of costs or import prices actually paid to CMEA partners. In addition, *changes* in the domestic prices of manufactured goods are governed by a series of rules that take cognizance of a firm's export performance on convertible currency markets, the extent of competition the firm faces domestically and abroad, and the actual or hypothetical import price of same or similar products. The pricing rules are complex, often are subject to bargaining between enterprises and the authorities, and are frequently changed.

The wage system. Wage and income regulations are complex and have been altered frequently since 1968. Like price regulation, wage regulation is influenced strongly by how the overall economic system functions. As long as enterprises have monopoly power on the domestic market and management is not motivated strongly by profitability, there will be insufficient countervailing power at the enterprise level against wage-push pressures. Wage regulations thus in part substitute for the absent countervailing power, just as the complex price rules substitute for absent or weak market forces. Labor income has two main components: (1) wages and salaries determined by enterprise managers within a range (generally widening as a result of the reform process) set by the authorities for each category of skill and effort; and (2) profit-sharing distributions. The essence of the wage system is that complex rules determine how large of an increase in a firm's average annual compensation will be tax-exempt; increases beyond those levels are taxed at steeply progressive rates to prevent rapid wage increases.

Enterprise income regulation. The price and wage regulation systems summarized above are two of the main instruments of enterprise income regulation. Incomes are further regulated by two other mechanisms. First, enterprises must compute revenues and expenses in a prescribed sequence, and taxes are levied not once, on profits, but at several places in that sequence. Second, enterprises must allocate after-tax profits into three enterprise funds, each taxed at varying rates. The rules and regulations on pricing, wage determination, taxes, and the allocation of after-tax profits are changed frequently, which creates uncertainty and a great deal of bargaining between individual enterprises and the authorities.

Economic Reforms and Economic Performance

Conceptual Issues

Performance trade-offs. Economic performance is multidimensional. Economists use the following indicators to measure the performance of a country over time or to compare the performances of countries: growth rates of aggregate output; production efficiency (i.e., how much output is produced per units of input); the standard of living; distribution of income, including consumer price inflation; the level of unemployment; export competitiveness; and the balance of payments.

One difficulty in assessing performance is that a comparatively good performance in one area of the economy may be achieved at the expense of a concurrent or postponed weaker performance in some other area. For example:

- Borrowing large sums from abroad can accelerate a country's growth rate over a certain period. But servicing the debt later can slow the growth rates of a later period, especially if the borrowed resources were not invested wisely.
- The easiest way to achieve zero inflation is to impose and maintain state controls over prices. But such a situation often creates or perpetuates shortages, which will cause bottlenecks, queues, and the expansion of gray- or black-market transactions at prices significantly higher than those fixed on the official markets. These results have been precisely the experience of many CPEs. But even if there were no shortages, keeping prices fixed for a long time tends to cause problems because it prevents the needed adjustments in relative prices to reflect changing relative prices on the world market or changing supply-and-demand configurations on the domestic market. If relative prices are incorrect, production and investment decisions will be distorted.
- One way to achieve zero or low unemployment is to permit nearly all employed persons to keep their jobs irrespective of individual performance or enterprise profitability. But this social achievement involves a high economic cost: Improvements in productivity will be held down, and the economy will become less flexible.

Establishing causation. A further conceptual difficulty is identifying convincingly the causal factors that explain economic performance. In my conceptualization, there are four sets of variables (each composed of a large number of component factors): the initial domestic environment, the economic system, the economic policy, and that part of the external environment that impacts on the domestic economy's performance.

The initial *domestic environment* concerns the size, the level of development, the resource endowment, and the cumulative historical, cultural, and social experiences of the population at the beginning of the period for which performance is to be assessed. *Economic system* is defined as the set of institutions and arrangements through which the economy makes the traditional decisions of what, how, and for whom to produce. *Economic policy* is a set of linked decisions by policymakers about the relative importance of certain economic objectives and the ways to achieve them. If policy objectives can be quantified, they become targets—for example, rates of growth of consumption, investment, and the military; the direction of state investment; the commodity and geographic composition of foreign trade; or the desired level of unemployment or inflation. The *external environment* refers to economic and political developments outside the borders of the country that affect its economy. Examples include changing relative prices and demand-supply patterns on the world market; increases or decreases in the liberalization of trade and capital flows by trade partners; the attitude of governments, businesses, and banks toward economic cooperation with the country; and so on.

It is exceedingly difficult to hold constant the environmental and policy variables in order to measure the impact just of the economic system. One reason for this is that the four sets of variables are not independent. For example, a CPE system tends to be associated with certain economic policies, such as ambitious growth rates and import-substitution industrialization, that affect economic performance. The variables are linked in other ways also. For example, a country's terms of trade (changes in the ratio of export to import price indices over time) are usually taken as exogenously determined. But over a period of years, the prices of a country's manufactures exports will be determined largely by how quickly and ably its producers and consumers adapt to changing demand-and-supply conditions on the world market. But adaptability is largely a function of the economic system and of economic policy decisions.

Measurement Problems

Assessing a country's economic performance requires some standard of evaluation. One standard frequently employed is comparing performance with those of other countries.

Assessment of a CPE's economic performance must rely on statistics published by its central statistical office. But meaningful international comparisons are hindered by differences between CPEs and market economies— and also within CPEs—in conceptualizing and measuring performance. For example, CPEs report net material product (NMP), market economies use gross domestic or national product (GDP or GNP). For CPEs there are notably serious problems with measurement accuracy, especially of such key performance indicators as the growth rates of output. It has been convincingly documented that the growth rates of most CPEs are calculated with distorted prices and according to methods of index number construction that yield varying degrees of upward bias.[5] This hinders not only the comparison of the performances of CPEs with those of market economies, but those of one CPE with other CPEs also. For example, experts agree that Hungary publishes the most comprehensive and reliable (though by no means flawless) set of economic statistics, while the officially reported performance indicators of Romania and Bulgaria are the most distorted.

A further consideration that hinders linking Hungary's economic reforms with economic performance is that the positive impact of the reforms has been more qualitative than quantitative. As one observer put it:

> Hungarian economic policy . . . has been clearly focused not on spectacular growth rates but on balanced development with concomitant increases in real incomes of the population, again rather without

spectacular jumps in statistical indices but with the purchasing power of the population relatively well covered by the supply of consumer goods on the market.[6]

Economic Policies and Performance

Before discussing the relationship between reforms and performance, I will suggest the impact of domestic economic policies and external developments from 1968 to 1987 on Hungary's economic performance.

The span of two decades can be divided into four periods: the golden age (1968–1972), the period of illusions (1973–1978), the period of realism (1979–1985), and the "caution-to-the wind" years (1986–1987).

During the *golden age*, the economic policy targets were by and large realistic. The economy was growing at a good tempo, there was no open unemployment or inflation (though not all consequences of this were positive, for the reasons noted), and both the convertible currency and transferable ruble trade flows—with the West and the East, respectively—remained approximately in balance. Although the NEM could not solve many of the economy's problems, it did release the creative energies of many individuals, cooperatives, and small firms. Agriculture especially flourished. The external environment was favorable, which contributed positively. Economic growth rates averaged about 5 percent per annum, approximately the same on a per capita basis because Hungary's population was not increasing.

The *period of illusions* refers to the policymakers' response to the external shocks Hungary suffered after 1973: rising energy and raw material prices, large deterioration in the terms of trade, and increased difficulties of exporting to the recession-plagued countries of the industrial West. Policymakers' illusions were revealed by their actions, which were based on the belief that the shocks were temporary, that the economy could be insulated from their effects, that investment and trade should be oriented toward the CMEA partners, that the rate of economic growth should be accelerated, and that the economic reform process should be halted. The relatively good performance of the economy during the 1968–1972 period probably contributed to the overambitious nature of the plans.

The policies pursued after 1973 had exceedingly unfavorable consequences. Their key manifestation was the rapid rise in the convertible currency debt, from about $1 billion in 1970 to $9 billion by 1980. On a per capita basis, Hungary's debt became larger than Poland's.

The economy could not be insulated from external economic shocks. Energy, raw materials, and intermediate products dominate imports, and their acquisition costs are tied to prices on the world market even if sourced in the CMEA. Hungary must purchase a rising share of all kinds of inputs and much of modern technology on the world market; those purchases require convertible currency. Accelerating the growth rate required a more than proportionate increase in convertible currency imports, especially because the growth spurt of the 1970s was investment-led. Major industrial projects with long gestation periods were undertaken at pre-1974 factor and product prices (themselves distorted), with much of the planned output intended for the CMEA.[7]

External causes also contributed to the substantial trade deficits in convertible currency: deterioration in the terms of trade with the West (before 1975 and again in the mid-1980s) and a much larger and continuous deterioration with the East through 1986—though shortcomings of the economic system and mistaken policies contributed to the *extent* of the deterioration, for the reasons noted. Deteriorating terms of trade with the East, together with supply limitations on the CMEA market, forced Hungary to increase rapidly purchases from the West, where sluggish demand, increased protectionism, and Hungary's weak ability to adjust to changing demand patterns limited its export growth.

The *age of realism* refers to the policymakers' belated response after 1978 to the unsustainable increases in the convertible currency debt. By the late 1970s, policymakers realized that unless the trend of running large trade deficits with the West was reversed, Hungary would be unable to meet its payment obligations in a few years. An austerity program was therefore introduced that gave a high (but not yet the highest) priority to improving the convertible currency trade balance. But the improvement was insufficient. After 1979, Hungary suffered a series of new external shocks—the second explosion of energy prices; rapid increases in the real rates of interest on external debt; and the reduced availability of external finance to the CMEA countries after the Soviet invasion of Afghanistan, the imposition of martial law in Poland, and the forced debt reschedulings by Poland, Romania, Yugoslavia, and many less developed countries. Thus, in 1982 the austerity program had to be tightened considerably. Economic austerity continued until 1985, when political pressure prompted the leadership to relax it.

At this point, let us take a small detour and explain the rationale and consequences of economic austerity.[8] Why and how long austerity is necessary can be explained as follows: Assume that Hungary is unable or unwilling to increase the level of its total outstanding convertible currency debt, although it is able to refinance the repayment of any principal when it comes due. Under this scenario, Hungary must generate a surplus on goods and services trade sufficient to pay the interest on its total outstanding debt. Because of its debt level and world interest rates, the surplus required was $1.1 billion in 1981, which declined to about $700 million during 1983–1985.

A trade surplus can be generated by some combination of export expansion and import limitation. Regrettably, much of Hungary's (and other East European countries') surplus has been and continues to be generated by restricting imports rather than by expanding exports. The basic reason for this is inability to produce on a sufficient scale the kinds of manufactures that can be sold on the world market readily for convertible currency and at a good price.

Comparing Hungary's trade performance with that of a reference group— middle-income oil-importing countries—shows that during 1978–1984 the *volume* of manufactures exports of the comparator group increased by 11.5 percent per annum, but Hungary's rose only 3 percent per annum.[9] This indicates Hungary's loss of market share in world manufacturing trade. The main reasons for insufficient export competitiveness are domestic: mistakes in economic policy (some of which still continue); the many remaining shortcomings of the economic system (see next section); and the persistent import shortage, which in turn can be traced to policy and systemic shortcomings in the economy. The secondary reason was adverse external developments, to which Hungary's inflexible economy had not been adjusting quickly.

To achieve and maintain a sustainable current account position in the face of unsatisfactory export performance has forced policymakers to rein in severely convertible currency imports. During 1978–1984 imports of Western machinery and equipment declined by 2–3 percent per annum, whereas those of the comparator group increased by about 6 percent per annum. Forced cuts in imports year after year have not only weakened the growth rate of output, given the economy's high dependence on imports from the West (and of course the East also), but have also contributed to the declining export competitiveness of the country's manufactures.

The restrictive policies in effect since 1979, and especially between 1982– 1984, created pent-up demand throughout the economy—for investment, consumption, imports—and growing political pressure to satisfy it. The leadership gave in to these pressures during 1985–1987 and pursued *caution-to-the-wind* policies: increasing the money supply at a rapid rate; permitting substantial deficits in the state budget; and easing somewhat the restrictions on consumption, but especially on investment and imports. The result was that the supply side of the economy increased very little (largely because during 1981– 1987, total factor productivity stagnated) while domestic demand expanded at a rapid rate. This led to growing macroeconomic imbalances, whose net effect was large increases of borrowing from the West in each of the three years. This moved Hungary, once again, to the brink of having to reschedule. To avoid such an outcome, a new Stabilization and Economic Reform Program was adopted for 1988–1990, which places the brunt of the adjustment on consumption, by allowing the rate of inflation substantially to exceed wage increases. During the first six months of 1988, real wages declined by 9 percent; if the published rate of inflation (17 percent) were to understate the real rate of inflation (as some economists think it does), then the decline in real wages reached double-digit levels. This explains in part the increasingly difficult political situation in the country, one manifestation of which was the retirement of János Kádár.

Reforms and Performance: An Interpretation

My conclusions regarding the relationship between economic reform and performance can be summarized in four statements:

First, some of the improvements attributable to economic reforms cannot be readily quantified. They include a general reduction of the shortage phenomenon so prevalent in traditional CPEs; the improved availability, quality, and assortment of certain goods in the consumer sector, especially of foodstuffs and certain services; and somewhat greater economic flexibility and manifestations of entrepreneurship, primarily in Hungary's private, cooperative, and certain small-scale state-owned businesses.

Second, in terms of the readily quantifiable economic indicators, Hungary does not appear to have performed significantly better since 1968 than what may be considered "average" for all of Eastern Europe. To be sure, intra-CMEA performance comparisons are fraught with difficulties, owing to the varying degrees of bias in the official statistics of these countries.

Third, serious mistakes in economic policy and adverse external developments in the regional and world economies have weakened considerably Hungary's economic performance, especially since 1979. At the same time, however, it must be recognized that economic policy and the ability to parry the adverse consequences of external shocks are not independent of a country's economic system.

Fourth, although since 1968 Hungary's economic system can no longer be described as a traditional, Soviet-type CPE, it has yet to become an efficiently operating regulated market economy toward which it has been evolving, albeit much too slowly. The reforms so far have not been able to overcome several of the most fundamental shortcomings of a traditional CPE, namely, insufficient improvements in total factor productivity, lagging technological and new product development, and declining export competitiveness.

Assessing the Reforms and Prospects

Why Has Hungary Been in the Reform Forefront?

The revolution of 1956. That event in 1956 so discredited the political and economic aspects of the system in place during the first half of the 1950s that the party has been guided ever since by a strong desire to avoid a possible repetition of 1956.[10] That fear in turn has required changing certain features of the political and economic system. The party realized that if it attempted to push society too far, the reaction could undermine its ability to govern.

János Kádár assumed political power in 1956 and spent the next few years consolidating it. Once that objective was achieved, Kádár—joining the leaderships of several other East European countries—decided to ease political tensions, following Nikita Khrushchev's own more liberal policies in the USSR during the early 1960s. Hungary is unique in the CMEA not so much because it has pursued a course of political liberalization and economic reform but because it is the only CMEA country where the relatively liberal political climate introduced throughout the region in the 1960s has continued—though the movement has not always been forward.

Political personalities. Of considerable importance has been the coincidence of the right person being at the right place in certain crucial periods to effect some milestone decisions. Kádár has of course been of key importance. His role in 1956 has probably guaranteed him the lifelong trust of the Kremlin, placing him in a uniquely strong position to manage the foreign policy aspects of the reform. Much credit for promoting the reforms is deserved by others also. For example, reformist Politburo member Lajos Fehér was responsible for agriculture at the time recollectivization was decided in the late 1950s and implemented in the early 1960s. Leading conservative economist and party functionary István Friss became a reform supporter in the mid-1960s, out of conviction that a change in the economic mechanism was needed. Friss's conversion helped to diffuse political-ideological opposition to the idea of introducing the NEM. Of key importance also was the appointment of reform supporter Rezső Nyers to the Politburo (for reasons largely independent of his position on the reform), where he was put in charge of the economy when crucial reform decisions were made during the second half of the 1960s.

Foreign trade dependence. Hungary's unusually heavy dependence on foreign trade is probably also a reform factor. Foreign trade demands economic rationality, especially for a country that must increase its export of agricultural products and manufactures on the world market to pay for imports of the many items not available—at least in the right quantities or quality—from domestic or Eastern-bloc suppliers.

Political Liberalization and Economic Reform

Political liberalization was an essential condition for market-oriented economic reforms. It is a prerequisite because economic decentralization requires a substantial reduction of direct political interference in economic decisions. But there are other reasons also. A comprehensive reform like the NEM is an intricate mechanism. Because it has no precedent—no blueprint—it takes a great deal of expertise to design and implement. Expertise can be developed only through a relatively free and open debate in which all sides can be heard and logic, not rhetoric, prevails. The remarkably free and open discussion of economic problems and reform options during the 1960s was critically important for the reform and was made possible by the relatively liberal political climate.

A further important reason why political liberalization must precede meaningful economic reform is the need for reliable and publicly available economic statistics. Although there are still gaps, the set of economic statistics Hungary has published since 1956 is the most comprehensive and reliable in Eastern Europe. The importance of economic understanding and good data cannot be overemphasized. In many countries economic reforms are stifled by an absence of sophisticated economic understanding and lack of opportunities to debate the issues freely. This situation is made worse by glaring shortcomings in the statistical systems that often fail to disclose facts and that provide an inadequate basis for the kinds of economic computations needed to design a feasible reform blueprint.

Economic Reforms: A Summary Assessment

Hungary has pioneered reforms in the CMEA. This is impressive, considering the difficult domestic and regional political environment in which the reform measures have had to be introduced. Nonetheless, the criterion of assessment here is not political feasibility but the impact of reforms on economic performance.

Although the reforms have been responsible for certain notable economic achievements, the overall conclusion is rather negative: The reforms so far have not been able to solve the most fundamental problems they have tried to address—namely, to improve significantly total factor productivity and export competitiveness on the world market. This negative conclusion remains even if mitigating circumstances are taken into account: that certain economic improvements attributable to the reforms cannot be easily quantified; that Hungary's economic statistics reveal a more truthful picture of performance than those of the other East European countries with which it is most often compared; and that adverse external developments and mistakes in economic policy are responsible for some of the negative aspects of performance.

Why have the reforms—so far—fallen short of achieving their intended purpose?

The most fundamental lesson of the Hungarian experience is to reveal how difficult and time-consuming it is to transform a traditional CPE into an efficiently operating socialist market economy. If such a transformation is to take place through evolution (that is, through incremental changes in the system), even under the most favorable circumstances the process will take decades to complete. So far Hungary has traveled about one-third of the distance from a traditional CPE to an efficiently operating socialist market economy, although in the agricultural sector the distance traveled may be closer to two-thirds. The examples of Hungary and (more recently) China show also that market- and incentive-oriented reforms work better—and yield results more quickly—in agriculture than in the economy's other sectors. This advantage results because there are no monopolistic producers in agriculture, much of output is standard so that product innovation and market research are less important, viable price and incentive systems are easier to introduce, and investment decisions tend to be simpler. Partly for these reasons, the authorities are also more willing to release their bureaucratic grip on agriculture than on the state industrial sector.

In the economy overall, the reforms have decreased significantly the scope and details of central planning and correspondingly enlarged the room for enterprises to maneuver. Yet, the reforms have not been able to create an environment in which enterprises would be able—and motivated—to make good, long-term economic decisions. The basic problem, in my view, is that much of the economy is not operated by an actual market mechanism. The authorities and not the market mostly establish and manipulate the "regulators"—prices, wages, exchange rates, interest rates, credits. Hungary's cumulative experience of many years shows that the outcomes in such a system are not very efficient. It is utopian to believe that the operation of a market can be efficiently simulated by the planners, instead of allowing a real market to develop.

What Should Be Done?

In my view, Hungary needs a substantial program of further reform to attack several problems simultaneously. A great deal remains to be done to build a competitive market in basic, intermediate, and finished products and services. That would require, first and foremost, that the economy be "opened up" to more domestic but especially to import competition. For all practical purposes, import competition today is almost completely absent. It is a folly to say that imports cannot be allowed in more freely because of the tension in the balance of payments. The causation runs rather the other way: Because so many producers cannot obtain the right kinds of imports and do not face import competition, they cannot remain or become competitive on the world market. This is especially the case in manufacturing, a sector that requires timely access to sophisticated technology and components.

Another area that requires substantial further reform is investment decisionmaking. Most large investments are still made or approved somewhere in the bowels of a large central bureaucracy, with no one having clear responsibility for the outcome. The typical attitudes of a traditional CPE still dominate many levels of decisionmaking about investments: "Whatever can be produced will be sold." The starting point is still not market research, and in reality, no hard-headed financial assessments are made. During periods of economic austerity, investments tend to be cut across the board; selectivity based on long-term profitability is not yet the basic practice.

Good investment and production decisions require meaningful prices, not only of inputs and products but of factors of production also. Today the price of capital is high and that of labor too low for enterprises relative to the country's factor endowments. This imbalance is perhaps one reason why rate-of-return computations on proposed investments remain formalistic. The price, wage, credit, and tax systems are too complex, often seem arbitrary, are subject to bargaining between enterprises and the authorities, and there have been much-too-frequent rules changes.

There is a need also for a mechanism to value realistically—and to revalue when necessary—the prices of productive assets, based on their expected future earnings potential. Revaluation is essential for improving the price system and ridding the slate of past mistakes as far as earnings and rate-of-return computations are concerned. If the authorities decide to maintain unprofitable operations for some economic or social policy reasons, at least the cost to the economy would become transparent. A meaningful revaluation of assets presupposes the existence of an institution something like a stock market with many buyers and sellers, though the shares need not be predominantly privately held.

Substantial further financial reforms are needed also to create an independent, profit-oriented commercial banking system. Various instruments of financial intermediation also are needed.

The CMEA trade mechanism is another obstacle to efficiency. Because Hungary can neither cut its economic and political ties to the East nor wait until its CMEA trading partners implement compatible reforms in their economic systems, there is a need to create a bridging mechanism between Hungarian firms and the state trading agencies of the other CPEs. Today, Hungarian firms have insufficient incentives to produce world-class goods for the CMEA markets, where they face no real competition, engage in no real marketing, and do not control the prices and quantities of the goods traded. This certainly is one reason why Hungarian firms have been losing competitiveness on world markets with their manufactures. A possible solution would be to set up one or several large trading trusts to negotiate deals with CMEA partners and then invite Hungarian firms to "bid" for contract implementation. Such a mechanism may not work well immediately in all sectors, but the scope of the system could be enlarged as the economy is opened up to more domestic and import competition.

Economic policy would have to be changed also. There is an urgent need to restructure Hungary's industry, whose current pattern does not correspond to the country's potential comparative advantage and is becoming increasingly outmoded. Instead of concentrating on how to secure the largest amounts of energy and raw materials needed to utilize the existing and excessively energy- and material-intensive production capacity, priority should be given to upgrading manufacturing.

A key building block of Hungary's industrial strategy should be to try to serve as a bridge between the West and the East in selected sectors and products (excluding those the West would consider strategic). Today, it is Hungary's new official policy to try to attract the capital and expertise of multinational corporations on a large scale. I am not sure whether policymakers realize that under the prevailing economic mechanism and intra-CMEA trading arrangements, Hungary has comparatively few attractions to offer to multinationals for joint venture arrangements. In my view, the prime potential "asset" Hungary could offer to multinational corporations is its geopolitical position to help them penetrate the markets of the CMEA—the USSR's first and foremost. If through joint ventures with Western firms Hungary would be able to offer world class goods in the CMEA, perhaps it could negotiate payment from its CMEA partners, if not in convertible currency at least in convertible goods. To succeed, Hungary would have to demonstrate that with Western participation it could supply to its CMEA partners goods that they would otherwise have to obtain directly from the West for convertible currency. The essential condition for this is substantial further improvements in Hungary's economic system.

Are Significant Further Reforms Feasible?

The feasibility and the likelihood that the kinds of reforms sketched could or would be introduced are separate issues.

Regarding feasibility, the essential questions would seem to be the following: Would the kind of economy just sketched still be a socialist system? If so, would it be the kind of system that could survive politically in the prevailing regional alliance structure? I would venture a "yes" on both counts.

A single-party political system could be preserved, but with the plurality of economic and political interests much better represented and their conflicts much more openly resolved than now. Central planning over the main directions of the economy would be maintained, although its scope would be limited to macroeconomic policy issues, the direct allocation of some large investments, public-utility-type arrangements to maintain infrastructure and defense capability, and the fulfillment of commercial obligations to CMEA partners. The predominately nonprivate ownership of the means of production could be preserved also, but with considerably greater scope for private entrepreneurship and property rights than found in a traditional CPE or in the prevailing Hungarian system. The rise in income inequality could be kept within limits by progressive taxation.

What about outside political pressures? Gorbachev's moves to introduce economic and political reforms in the USSR have given the Hungarian leadership much greater room to maneuver. Certainly, pressure to eliminate a particular undesirable consequence of the reforms or to postpone a reform step may still be present and could intensify if Gorbachev's policies are reversed. However, not one country—certainly not the USSR—can point to a clearly superior alternative to the Hungarian model, and thus foreign critics do not have strong arguments to sway the Hungarian decisionmakers.

The key to the feasibility of substantial further reforms is to be found in Hungary. If the post-Kádár political leadership of Károly Grósz were to unite and strongly support a reform program, it would appear to be feasible to implement it.

Prospects

What are the chances that Hungary will move expeditiously with further reforms, in the direction sketched? At least in the short run, prospects are uncertain. Although strong pressures are exerted for further reforms by the economy's serious problems and by a consensus that returning to a traditional CPE would certainly not solve them, a series of constraints make it exceedingly difficult to make the major moves forward.

There is no consensus yet on the part of economists, bureaucrats, and policymakers that the kinds of far-reaching reforms sketched are really needed. In scanning the Hungarian economic literature and pronouncements of the authorities, one is struck by a paradox: The problems are identified accurately and discussed openly, but there is no "vision"—and little meaningful action—of how to overcome them. Economic decisionmaking in Hungary seems to be "drifting." The following reasons may explain this indecisiveness.

Economic reforms have become increasingly unpopular since 1979 because the new wave of reforms has coincided with deep and prolonged economic austerity. Many persons associate economic reforms and austerity; even if reforms are not seen as the cause, perpetual "reforms" do not have a large constituency. One of the most visible aspects of the reform has been the increased scope and legalization of private-sector activities; in fact, the majority of the population probably equates economic reform with increased privatization. Given the many imperfections in the economic mechanism, some persons are able to make a great deal of money quickly, much of which goes into conspicuous consumption because too many constraints and uncertainties limit their opportunities and the will to invest it in business. Growing income inequalities at a time when the majority's standard of living is declining or stagnating fuel antireform sentiments. This public reaction contributes to the paralysis of the political leaders, who since 1956 have been careful not to disregard the mood of the citizens. The solution to this dilemma would appear to be for the authorities to identify correctly not only the problems (which the public knows full well) but also their real causes and be willing and able to educate the public. Required would be a consensus among experts, their ability to convince the authorities, and of course imaginative leadership.

In addition to what might be called the political mood of the public, there is domestic opposition from three organized groups: those who are against market-oriented reforms on ideological-political grounds, those who fear its adverse economic consequences, and those who represent vested interests. Membership in the three groups is overlapping.

There is, furthermore, uncertainty about the long-term direction of Soviet reforms: What will be the fate of Gorbachev and his policies?

The following scenario would appear to be the most favorable for a major new reform push: an economic crisis that galvanizes the leadership and the public into a conviction that meaningful actions must be taken; reasonable consensus among economists on what must be done, with a detailed blueprint;

consensus in the top leadership that the advice of reform economists must be followed and the presence of good leadership skills to implement it; Soviet policies that continue to pursue pragmatic experiments with reforms in the economic mechanism (as opposed to "campaigns"); continued economic reforms and successes in China; and a sustained improvement in East-West political relations.

Notes

1. Much of this chapter represents a synthesis of my previous work on the Hungarian economy. My books, chapters, and articles cited in the following notes contain extensive documentation, including footnotes and references to English and Hungarian sources. Readers who would like to check facts or consult original sources will find full documentation in the sources cited.

2. This section is based on Paul Marer, "Economic Reform in Hungary," in Morris Borstein, ed., *Comparative Economic Systems: Models and Cases*, 5th ed. (Homewood, Ill.: Richard D. Irwin, 1985). For further details, see Paul Marer, "Economic Reform in Hungary: From Central Planning to Regulated Market," in Joint Economic Committee, U.S. Congress, *East European Economies: Slow Growth in the 1980's*, vol. 3, Country Studies on Eastern Europe and Yugoslavia (Washington, D.C.: U.S. Government Printing Office, 1986) and Paul Marer, *East-West Technology Transfer: Study of Hungary, 1968–1984* (Paris: OECD, 1986).

3. Iván T. Berend, *Gazdasági útkeresés 1956–1965* [Searching for an economic path, 1956–1965] (Budapest: Magvetö, 1983).

4. János Kornai, *Ellentmondások és dilemmák* [Controversies and dilemmas] (Budapest: Magvetö, 1983).

5. Paul Marer, *Dollar GNPs of the U.S.S.R. and Eastern Europe* (Baltimore and London: The Johns Hopkins University Press for the World Bank, 1985).

6. Wlodzimierz Brus, "Political System and Economic Efficiency: The East European Context," *Journal of Comparative Economics* 4, no. 1 (March 1980), p. 49.

7. See chapter 5 of Marer, *East-West Technology Transfer*, for a detailed discussion and documentation.

8. See Paul Marer, "Hungary's Balance of Payments Crisis and Response, 1978–84," in Joint Economic Committee, *East European Economies*; and Paul Marer, "Hungary's Foreign Economic Relations in the Mid-1980's: A Retrospective and Predictive Assessment," in *The Economies of Eastern Europe and Their Foreign Economic Relations* (Brussels: Economic Directorate of the North Atlantic Treaty Organization, 1986).

9. *World Development Report* (Washington, D.C.: The World Bank, 1986), pp. ix and 213–215.

10. Ellen Comisso and Paul Marer, "The Economics and Politics of Reform in Hungary," *International Organization* 40, no. 2 (Spring 1986, pp. 422).

4

Some Lessons from the Hungarian Experience for Chinese Reformers

János Kornai

For the proper understanding of this chapter,[1] a personal introduction is needed. I am a Hungarian economist who has had a keen interest in the reform of the socialist economy for thirty years.[2] I am a researcher working in academic institutes and universities. Sometimes my advice is sought by governmental authorities, but I have never participated in actual decisionmaking. This position gives me a certain combination of closeness to, yet distance from, policymaking in Hungary. I am a convinced supporter of reform ideas and at the same time a rather critical observer of the present situation. I will try in this chapter to give a balance of appreciation and criticism and to do so as objectively and frankly as possible.

Since the beginning of the reform process, there have been many discussions among Hungarian economists, from time to time even very vehement disputes. Even today opinion remains divided on many issues. Therefore, I do not put forward here a generally accepted "Hungarian opinion"— only my individual views.[3] I am sure that for each paragraph of the chapter, one could find Hungarian readers who agree and some others who disagree.

When I wrote this chapter, I had not yet been in China, and I am not an expert on Chinese affairs. I used only secondhand information collected from books and articles. I have done my best to focus on issues that in my perception might be relevant for the Chinese reformers. My choices are, however, a mere guess, and the experts might not agree with my selection of topics. Perhaps some of the lessons are already well known in China. Nevertheless, I do hope that something can be learned from this collection of Hungarian experience.

There are, of course, very great differences between the two countries. China is a giant with a billion people, Hungary a tiny country with only one percent of the population of China—that is, 10 million inhabitants. China is a fully autonomous great world power. Hungary is a member of the multinational integration of the Warsaw Pact and of the Council for Mutual Economic Assistance (CMEA, or Comecon). China is at a lower stage of development, agriculture being the largest sector; Hungary is semi-industrialized at a medium stage of development. The two countries have totally different political, social, and cultural history, and even the more recent political background of the reform process is rather different. The list of differences could be continued for a long while; nevertheless, there is sufficient similarity to make the present analysis meaningful.

The point of departure for the reform process is rather similar in both cases: the traditional classical form of a highly centralized economy, with a very powerful central management of economic affairs, tight control over inputs and outputs, a hierarchical-bureaucratic structure of administration, and a forced, accelerated growth pattern. In any case, because of the significant differences, much caution is needed in applying the experiences of another country. This chapter is not a cookbook with recipes to be followed word for word. My aim is much more modest: I would be happy if some of my comments stimulate thinking and careful consideration. The text is written in the inevitable style of "recommendations." I did not add to each paragraph the above words of caution. However, the reader should raise repeatedly the question: "Is this Hungarian experience applicable in my country—if not fully, perhaps only partially or not at all?" Either uncritical acceptance or prejudiced rejection would be a mistake.

The reform is a manifold process, and there are hundreds of important issues that could be discussed. The chapter is selective, but still it covers a rather wide set of problems. Therefore, each issue will be discussed briefly, almost in a bulletin style.

In spite of my efforts to be comprehensive, the special problems of agriculture will not be discussed in great detail. The agricultural reform took place in China several years ago, and it is closely studied by many Chinese and foreign scholars. In contrast, the reform of the rest of the economy gained new momentum only recently; it is in this area that the fresh yet unresolved questions lie. Therefore, I will focus partly on the nonagricultural sectors and partly on economywide macro problems (like prices and monetary policy) that affect both the agricultural and the nonagricultural sectors.

In the following two sections, I will discuss the two main subdivisions of the changes in Hungary: changes in the state-owned sector, which produces the larger part of total national output, and changes in the rest of the economy—that is, in the non-state sector. The public's support of the reform and the strategy of the reform will be discussed in the last two sections of this paper.

The State-Owned Sector

A brief historical overview will be helpful to an understanding of the reform. In Hungary, nationalization of large and medium firms began in the late 1940s. The organization of centralized planning and management started at the same time, following rather closely the Soviet model. This well-known form of highly centralized bureaucratic-hierarchical economic administration prevailed in the period 1949–1956.

The first reform proposals were put forward by Hungarian economists in 1954–1955, and the first actual changes in the system were introduced in 1956–1957. The first deep change with genuine historical significance was the abolishment of mandatory delivery in agriculture, right after events in 1956. Accordingly, the reform process has a history of more than thirty years.

The term *process* must be emphasized. There were important peaks—certain times when a large package of important measures was introduced in one stroke. The most relevant peak was in 1968, when the mandatory short-term plans for state-owned firms were abolished. But there were influential changes both before and after 1968. (Specific dates of the different changes generally will be omitted in this chapter because it concentrates on the lessons of the whole three-decade reform period, with special attention to the present state of affairs.)

Conceptual Framework

Some conceptual clarification is needed in order to discuss the Hungarian experience. For the sake of exposition, I will do that in a highly simplified manner.

The activities of state-owned firms (acquisition of inputs, productive transformation of inputs into outputs, and the transfer of outputs to the users) can be controlled and coordinated by two alternative basic mechanisms: *bureaucratic coordination* and *market coordination*.

In Mechanism 1 information flows in a vertical direction from the center to the firm and from the firm to the center. This is a representation of bureaucratic control. In Mechanism 2 the information flows in a horizontal direction from one firm to the other, from the buyer to the seller and from the seller to the buyer. This is a representation of coordination by the market.

In Mechanism 1 there is super- and subordination; the center has power over the firm. In Mechanism 2 there is no super- or subordination, the firms have equal "rank" and they voluntarily agree about the input-output flows of goods.

There are two main variants of Mechanism 1. Mechanism 1A represents *direct* bureaucratic coordination and Mechanism 1B *indirect* bureaucratic coordination. The difference lies in the means of vertical regulation. In the case of direct bureaucratic coordination, the center gives commands to the firm: detailed mandatory output targets and input quotas. The firm is obliged by law to follow the commands. Those who do not follow them can be punished. In the case of indirect bureaucratic coordination the center does not give commands to the firm. Instead, the center holds a set of "levers"; the center can actually regulate in an indirect way the conduct of the firm. Thus, the impulses triggering certain reactions of the firm come vertically—from the center—and not horizontally from the other firms and other economic units, which buy from and sell to each other.

It must be understood that the three schemes presented here are abstract and theoretical. Coordination mechanisms of actual socioeconomic systems are never as pure, but rather are mixtures and combinations of these abstract schemes.[4] Nevertheless, within the mixture typically one or the other pure mechanism is predominant and the others play an auxiliary role.

Before the reform, Hungarian state-owned firms were mainly coordinated by Mechanism 1A—direct bureaucratic control. There was some Mechanism 1B indirect bureaucratic control, and Mechanism 2 market coordination also had some influence, but these mechanisms performed only supplementary functions.

As a result of the reform, Mechanism 1B—indirect bureaucratic control— became predominant. The Type 1A role was severely cut back, although it has not been completely abolished. The influence of Mechanism 2—market coordination—increased significantly even within the state-owned firms, but it still plays a secondary role.

Many proponents of the reform suggested a transition from Mechanism 1A to Mechanism 2, and in fact the first resolutions in the mid-1960s led some to expect that such a shift would be accomplished. It took some time and it required deep analysis to recognize that this expectation did not materialize.

Many foreign observers, after superficial observation of the Hungarian economy, assert that it became a "market socialism." In my own perception— shared by many Hungarian economists—this analysis is not accurate. The system could be regarded a "market socialism" only if the state-owned sector (producing the largest part of national output) would be coordinated basically by Mechanism 2, leaving Mechanisms 1A and 1B to play only an auxiliary role. However Hungary does not follow this model.

Next I will describe Hungary's shift from Mechanism 1A to Mechanism 1B. This discussion will include an explanation of the differences between the actual situation (Mechanism 1B) and a potential situation of "market socialism" (Mechanism 2).[5]

Some Aspects of the Reform

As briefly mentioned previously, the most important change was the 1968 measure: the abolition of short-term central commands. From the time the first reform ideas emerged in Eastern Europe and the Soviet Union, there were economists who advocated a partial measure: a smaller number of mandatory plan indicators instead of the large number prescribed before. In addition, there was also the suggestion to apply only more aggregated indicators instead of the very disaggregated, detailed ones. There were economists who suggested a change in the content of the mandatory indicators—for example, having the target refer to net output or sales instead of gross output, or perhaps prescribing a mandatory profit target. Some economists proposed another compromise: Abolish short-term commands in certain sectors and continue their use in other sectors. Another variant was to give a mandatory output target that would capture only a part of total capacity and allow the firm to manage its remaining capacity autonomously. In Hungary, all these compromise suggestions were finally rejected, and a radical, consistent solution was accepted in 1968: the total abolition of all formal short-term commands. After Yugoslavia, Hungary was the second country to adopt this measure. As far as I know, no other socialist country has since followed suit.

It turns out that the change was viable. The economy has not collapsed in "anarchy," as the advocates of the command system predicted, and it is still running smoothly in this respect. The detailed command system had many drawbacks. The adjustment of production to changes in technology and in demand was slow and rigid. The attention of managers was focused on bargaining over the tightness of the production plan with higher authorities; thus they were motivated to distort information—to overestimate input requirements and underestimate output capabilities. They had a personal interest in holding back some unused possibilities as a "reserve." If they mobilized all their resources and overfulfilled their plan, they would get a tighter target next time; thus it was advantageous to keep production close to the mandatory target's level. These kinds of flaws of the rigid and bureaucratic command system have been eliminated by the drastic reform measure.

There are many economists in Hungary who are not satisfied with the present state of the economic system. But there is practically nobody who would seriously propose a return to the Mechanism 1A direct bureaucratic control. This lesson drawn from Hungarian experience could be applied unhesitatingly anywhere.

Introduced jointly with the abolition of short-term commands were other changes. Following is a concise list of the most important ones:

- There are financial rewards to increase profit: bonuses for managers; welfare funds within the firm, linked to profitability; and profit sharing for the employees.
- Some prices (but not all) are determined by free contract of the seller and the buyer. In other words, in cases of trade between state owned firms, the seller and buyer get partial autonomy in price setting. This area of autonomy has increased since the initial reforms.
- Producer goods (material, parts, semifinished goods, machinery, equipment, construction service, and so on) are not "rationed" by central authorities, nor are they allocated by an instruction determining which producer must deliver what product under what terms to which user. Instead, the allocation is coordinated either by the agreement of the producer firm and the user firm or by a state-owned wholesale company acting as an intermediary. These companies buy certain producer goods and sell them to users on a commercial basis.
- Firms can retain a part of their profits for investment purposes. Before the reform, the overwhelming part of investment was financed from the

state budget. Now a large part of financing comes from the retained profit of firms and from bank credits.

• Firms have more autonomy in setting wages; the change of the wages in each firm is linked partly to the change in profitability. There are no administrative quotas of employment; the firm is autonomous in hiring and firing.

This list of changes gives the impression that a great leap occurred from Mechanism 1A, the command system, to Mechanism 2, the market coordination system. A deeper analysis, however, suggests a somewhat different conclusion; many qualifications must be added.

Management. Even without mandatory short-term plan targets, the dependence of the firm on superior agencies remained very strong. The most important vertical linkage remained the selection and appointment of the state-owned firms' top managers. Until some very recent changes, the three leading executives of all state-owned firms have been appointed by the superior authority, in most cases by the ministries. Successful managers are not limited to being promoted only within the same firm; they can be transferred to other firms or to ministries or state agencies. For example, a manager might start with a medium position in a more important firm, move on to become an officer in the ministry, later be appointed to a top position in a large firm, and so on. There is no "job market" for managers; their careers depend to a large extent on the opinion of the leading people on the top of the bureaucracy. Therefore, it is quite understandable that one of the main objectives of a manager is still—after the reform—to please the superiors. That is more important than to please the customer, which would be a central objective in a market system.

As a consequence, the superior official in the bureaucracy need not rely on giving explicit commands; it is usually sufficient to make a polite request or a suggestion. In theory, the firm can follow or reject these proposals; but this legal autonomy notwithstanding, it is in the personal interest of the firm's manager to fulfill the request and to follow the suggestion of the superior officials. This pressure is a very important and quite common component of Mechanism 1B, the indirect bureaucratic coordination mechanism.

New rules have recently been introduced with respect to choosing managers. In many enterprises, the manager will be selected in a process in which both the superior state agencies and the employees participate. (In public utilities and other key firms, the managers will be appointed in the former way by the superior authorities.) The new rules, if applied in a consistent manner, may lessen the dependence of the managers on the ministries and other parts of the bureaucracy. However, more experience will be needed before conclusions can be drawn about their usefulness.

Profit incentive. Profit incentive has been mentioned previously as an important reform. Unfortunately, there are many factors weakening the influence of profit.

There is a large array of nonuniform tax arrangements (additional taxes or tax exemptions) and subsidies that have a decisive impact on post-tax profit. Actually, post-tax profit serves as the basis of individual and collective incentives linked to profit. On the one hand, a state-owned firm in serious financial trouble will usually be rescued from its distress: It might be given tax exemption or subsidies or the administrative price of the output might be raised or credit granted to overcome insolvency and assure the survival of the firm. On the other hand, if a firm earns high profits, the financial authorities will levy extra taxes to skim them away. The solemnly declared requirement that state-owned firms must be profitable and must pay expenditures out of the proceeds of selling their output thus becomes a mere illusion. The budget constraint—the financial and profitability constraint of the firm—is not effectively binding on the activities of the firm.

This phenomenon is what I call the "softening" of the budget constraint. Ultimately, the financial position of the firm is not determined by success or failure in production and on the market but more by the arbitrary decisions of state officials. If they desire (perhaps under the pressure of the firm), they can make a firm suffering great financial loss seemingly "profitable," but they can also shift a highly profitable firm to medium or low profitability. Under such circumstances, profit is not an objective criterion of efficiency in production and on the market but only a reflection of the attitude of the higher authorities vis à vis the firm. Profitability depends more on success in the vertical bargaining with higher authorities than on the horizontal bargaining with the buyer and the seller. In my own appraisal, this situation is the main reason the outcome of the reform process in the state-owned sector cannot be regarded as a transition to Mechanism 2, the market system. It is only a transition to Mechanism 1B, indirect bureaucratic coordination.

Prices. In spite of the efforts made to improve the price system, many Hungarian economists (myself included) are dissatisfied with the present situation in this field. Their view is that there is no genuine market mechanism without effectively operating price signals—and such signals are far from existing. The problem must be divided into two parts: price *determination* and price *responsiveness*.

In Hungary, four main types of price determination are used. At one end of the spectrum are genuine market prices, set by the contract of the seller firm and the buyer firm without any bureaucratic interference. At the other extreme are genuine administrative prices, set by the price control office without being influenced by the pressure of the producer or the user firm. Then there are two intermediate types. There is the contract price under bureaucratic restrictions which is a price seemingly set by the contract of seller and buyer but actually made under the influence of some bureaucratic rules and/or ad hoc interventions of different authorities. Finally, there is the pseudo-administrative price, set by the price control office but under the effective pressure of the seller or the buyer (usually the former is more forceful). Typically, this price is determined by the producer and rubber-stamped by the price control office.

Some advocates of the present system of price determination hoped for a good combination of market forces and central control. This hope materialized only partially. There is also a lot of confusion, lack of transparency, distortion, and conflicting forces that mutually extinguish each other's beneficial impacts. Administrative prices are very rigid; it is difficult to change them. Many of the administrative prices inherited from the prereform era are arbitrary, far from reflecting the true situation on the market. Bureaucratic interventions lead to distortions when market forces would otherwise determine the price. It is well known that because all input-output flows are mutually interdependent, all prices also are mutually interdependent. One cannot have "good" prices in some parts of the economy and "bad" prices in some other parts. If a serious distortion enters the cost calculation of many users, it will influence their output prices, these prices will in turn affect the costs of their users, and so on. There are criss-cross, spillover effects. If some important components of the price system are distorted from the outset, inevitably the whole relative price structure will be distorted. The final outcome is a relative price system full of arbitrariness. Profit under such circumstances does not have a clear economic meaning. This factor is one (though not the only) motivation for the redistributive interventions into profit formation.

There have been repeated partial price reforms in Hungary.[6] Some of them had reasonable objectives—for example, they were intended to bring the domestic prices of energy, raw material, and exportable and importable goods closer to world market prices. Unfortunately, measures that attack only one or the other part of the price system—as these measures did—are ineffective. Between two attacks, everything is meanwhile changing outside the reformed segment: costs, technologies, external and internal demand and supply, and so on. The spillover of the partial reform flows into the "unreformed" rest of the price system. There is no evidence, either on the theoretical level or in practical experience, that a sequence of such partial "segmental price reforms" would converge to a solution—to a reasonable price system free from at least the gross distortions. It seems that Hungary is more or less floating from one set of arbitrary prices to another set of arbitrary prices. A much more circumspect and consistent strategy of price reform is needed.

The state-owned firms' responsiveness to prices is rather weak, although it is somewhat stronger on the output side than on the input side. In many cases, the producers are enjoying a seller's market—that is, there is a shortage of the goods they are producing. Therefore, the producers are in a stronger position than their buyers. Multiproduct firms may prefer to produce those products that are more profitable. (Even with a soft budget constraint and a weak profit incentive, it is uncomfortable to ask for subsidies or tax exemptions in case of financial loss. Enough profitability is not a matter of life-and-death, although it is not negligible.) When deciding on the product mix, producers consider relative profitability, which means a kind of response to the output price signal. However, this factor is not a very decisive criterion. In any case, because relative prices are rather distorted, this responsiveness does not really help in adjusting supply to demand.

On the input side, the producer is much less selective. As mentioned before, there are shortages rather frequently; thus the main criterion in purchase is availability and not the relative price of alternative inputs. In the case of inputs in short or unreliable supply, the user is willing to pay a higher price, which can be a source of inflationary trends. The permissive behavior on the input side might lead to cost increases. Nevertheless, the producers are not overly afraid of increases because in case of serious financial trouble, they can count on the assistance of the state.

In summary, the phenomenon I call the softening of the budget constraint and weak profit incentive leads to a weakening of the impact of prices on supply and demand. Added to that distortion are the interventions of higher authorities in the production: It is more important to listen to the telephone call of the ministry than to the muted signal of prices. In addition, the two issues of price determination and price responsiveness are mutually interacting. The fact that relative prices are arbitrary and distorted harms the prestige of price and profit signals. Everybody knows that relative prices do not reflect relative scarcities—that differences in profitability do not reflect the true differences in efficiency. The lack of respect for prices and profits contributes to the weakness of price responsiveness. The converse is that because firms are not terribly interested in profits (although they are not quite indifferent either), they do not fight hard for correct prices—there are more important issues to fight for. They are more or less reconciled to the existing distorted price system. Any solution will require two inseparable tasks: the improvement of the price system and the strengthening of price responsiveness.

Production. The essence of the 1968 measure was the abolition of mandatory output targets and input quotas. In addition, the market contacts previously mentioned were established between seller and buyer firms to assure a flexible flow of goods between the producer and user.

In practice, however, there are events that hinder these endeavors of the reform. Ministries intervene in the determination of production targets, putting pressure on the firm to produce one item and not another. There are input quotas, licenses, and rationings again and again, usually in a disguised form. Methods of the abolished command system are "smuggled back."

The most frequent excuse for the return to administrative-bureaucratic methods is to refer to difficulties in foreign trade: Imports must be cut and exports must be promoted by all means. The excuse is, in my opinion, not acceptable. With an effectively operating market mechanisn, with undistorted relative prices (including reasonable exchange rates), and with strong price responsiveness, the economy would adjust to the requirements of foreign trade in a more flexible and more efficient way. Bureaucratic ad hoc interventions can help in overcoming momentary bottlenecks, but at the same time they disrupt a better-founded adjustment process.

Investments. The reform measure of partial decentralization of investment decisions seemed to hold great promise. However, the outcome was less favorable than hoped for.

Investment projects are mostly large, indivisible actions. The retained profit of the firm is not enough to cover the expenditure, and therefore the firm must ask for additional bank credit and/or state subsidy. In that case, the bank (which is under central supervision) and other central authorities will have a say in the decision, though the project was initiated and partly financed by the firm. In fact, a rather small fraction of total national investment is truly decentralized—that is, decided and financed exclusively on the firms' level. The larger part is determined by decisions that involve the consent of higher authorities; the result is a return to the lengthy and rigid bureaucratic decision processes. There are so many state agencies, so many levels of the administrative hierarchy participating in the choice, that in the end everybody—and nobody—is responsible. In case of failure, everyone can point elsewhere. All participating agencies are interested in covering up the mistakes.

The aim of profit retention was to create a strong linkage between profitability and investment. The more profitable the firm, the more possibility it would have to grow and to modernize. Unfortunately, the expectation has not been fulfilled. Firms earning and retaining little or no profit can receive government-subsidized investment resources or investment credits. Other firms earning high profits can be heavily taxed and thus be unable to finance their investment projects. Ultimately, the allocation of investment depends much more on the will of the authorities than on the profits the firms make. This additional factor contributes to the weakening of the profit incentive.

An important source of financing investment projects is bank credit. The real interest rate is very low, considering the large excess demand for investment credit. But if interest rates were much higher, they would not seriously restrict demand for investment credit, for reasons discussed before. The investment budget constraint is soft. In case of cost overrun in the completion of the project, the additional costs will be covered by the state. Similarly, if the finished new plant operates without making profits or perhaps making losses, it will be compensated by some means (tax exemption, subsidy, higher administrative price, and so on). If the firm is unable to repay the investment loan, the debt can be rescheduled. In any case, an investment failure does not lead to serious consequences in the reputations and careers of those who made the wrong decisions. This situation perpetuates superficial and even ill-founded selection of projects; promotes waste and protraction of construction and installation; and leads to inefficiency in operating the new plant.

Thus, the selection of investment projects did not become a part of the overall horizontal market processes, where firms with the highest expected profitability would lead the way in accumulation and modernization. Instead, allocation of investment remained to a large extent a part of the direct and indirect vertical bureaucratic coordination—Mechanisms 1A and 1B.

An important issue is the use of retained profit of the state-owned firms. For a long time, the Hungarian firms could choose only between two alternatives: either reinvest it in the same firm where the accumulated profit was earned or deposit it into a bank account. The bank was not very attractive because the interest rate was low and because higher authorities sometimes constrained the use of the deposit. Therefore, a firm was almost forced to use its saving for its own expansion—even if it was clear that investing in other firms' expansion would be much more efficient and profitable. The only instrument of capital reallocation was the vertical-bureaucratic way through the governmental budget and through the central bank.

Quite recently, the first opportunities for horizontal reallocation have been created. Some firms raise capital by issuing yield-earning bonds that can be bought by other firms (and some bonds also by the individual citizens). There are now a few financial intermediary institutions that organize the transfer of one firm's retained profits to another firm for investment. The first firm will in some ways be a co-owner of the second firm. Only the first modest experimental steps have been taken to arrange more flexible ways of capital reallocation and financial intermediation. It will be worthwhile to go further in this direction.

Wage setting and employment. A great virtue of the present Hungarian situation is flexibility in the labor market. There are practically no restrictions on the workers in their choice of professions and jobs. Workers are not assigned to a particular workplace, but can freely choose it. They are allowed to quit, their only risk being to lose some fringe benefits attached to the workplace they leave. There are impediments to labor mobility—a housing shortage, for example—but administrative legal restrictions do not interfere with a change of workplace. There is little unemployment, on the contrary, a rather general labor shortage exists, which also puts the worker in a strong position.

As for the decisionmaking on the firm's side in the issues of employment and wages, there is certainly a higher degree of autonomy than before the reform. As mentioned before, the firm does not get obligatory employment quotas— upper or lower bounds—on employment. However, there is still a significant degree of central control in wage determination. Administrative rules allow wage increases in each firm only in accordance with the improvement of profitability. This restriction sounds reasonable, but unfortunately it is again partly an issue of negotiations and bargaining; the rules are not strictly uniform formulas valid for longer periods. In my opinion, a certain degree of wage control is really needed—without it, the danger of runaway inflation would be greater. But it seems that a better compromise between a firm's autonomy and flexibility in wage determination on the one hand and centrally enforced wage restraints on the other hand perhaps could be found. New wage rules would be all the more advisable because they are relatively easily enforced in the state-owned sector and much less enforceable in the non-state sector. As a result, cooperative and private business can offer better wages quite often and thus entice only the best workers away from the state-owned sector.

Conclusions

The preceding survey of several of the reform changes leads now to a summary of the main conclusions concerning the state-owned sector. My initial proposition was that the Hungarian state-owned sector shifted from a situation in which Mechanism 1A, direct bureaucratic command, was predominant (1B and 2 playing only an auxiliary role) to a situation in which Mechanism 1B, indirect bureaucratic control, became predominant (1A and 2 only supplementing it). The observations presented in this section support this proposition. However, these observations merely record the state of affairs; the question remains of how to evaluate the situation that arises from the long reform process.

In my assessment, there is great improvement compared with the prereform conditions. The autonomy of the firm and its flexibility and adaptability increased. There always were (and still are) ongoing negotiations between the higher and the lower levels of decisionmaking. In this exchange of views and in the search for compromises, the bargaining power of the firm (especially of the large firm) increased a good deal. In addition, more signs of market orientation—Mechanism 2—appeared; shortages have been eliminated in some segments of the economy, and the producer firm must pay more attention to the requirements of the buyer. The firm is not more indifferent toward profitability.

Is the change sufficient? Here the views of Hungarian economists are divided. Many of them, both in governmental offices and in the academic area, would give an affirmative answer. They find the combination of central management and market mechanism as it prevails right now in the state-owned sector satisfactory. They have great confidence in the use of "economic levers"—the economic regulators. They regard the determination of administrative prices and pricing principles, the granting of credit, the levy of taxes, and the handing out of subsidies as "economic levers" firmly in the hand of the center. They feel this control allows the center to steer all units of the system in the direction desired by central policy. Of course, they are not completely satisfied with the present state of affairs; they would like to see further improvement in the use of economic levers, but they do not favor far-reaching further changes.

I do not share this view, and many of my Hungarian colleagues would agree with the rejection of it. A fifty-fifty compromise between two conflicting mechanisms is not necessarily the optimal solution, although it may attract those who are looking for compromises. Unfortunately, the situation presents a mixture in which the best properties of both components get lost in the combination.

There are illusions concerning the "economic levers." Some aggregate measures (discussed later in the chapter) can and should be applied. But to use "indirect" methods for the sake of specific, concrete, detailed interventions—and to use them not only in exceptional circumstances but all the time in all details—is simply not feasible. As the prereform stage showed, it is impossible to give reasonable, well-founded, efficient commands for all details of outputs and inputs. But it is no more viable to intervene in an efficient way in a million cases of price setting, in the selection of all investment projects, in tax and subsidy manipulations. Disaggregated, detailed intervention in the operation of the market does not assure that the market will be "subjected" to the plan. But it does disrupt the effectiveness of prices, does undermine the responsibility of the managers, and does weaken the profit incentive.

Many Hungarian economists (myself included) support further steps in the direction of Mechanism 2, with preservation of an important supplementary role for Mechanisms 1A and 1B. I am not sure whether in the Hungarian case the transition from 1A to 1B was an indispensable phase before progressing to Mechanism 2—history cannot be repeated for the sake of experiments. But if a system arrives at the phase in which Mechanism 1B is predominant, it should be stressed that the phase is a provisional one. It would be highly desirable if reformers could have a long-term strategy to complement their envisaged long-term goals for achieving the transformation of the economic system.

Finally, a discussion of the problems of the state-owned sector would be incomplete without mention of the "spatial" aspects of centralization and decentralization. This is a very important dimension of the reform: What are the decisions to be taken on the central level, and what must be delegated to lower-level regional-local governments, like counties or districts? A closely associated question is the financial autonomy of the regional-local governments: In what proportions should the central and the regional-local governments share the revenues (taxes and the profit of state-owned firms), and in what proportions should they contribute to the expenditures, especially for investment projects? A further issue related to both of these questions is the distribution of ownership of state-owned firms between the different regional levels of government.

Hungary took several important steps in the direction of decentralization. In the present chapter, I cannot address this issue. However, I do want to draw attention to the distinction between the mechanism shift previously described and decentralization. There is no automatic correlation between these separate kinds of changes. For example, a country can move toward decentralization without abandoning Mechanism 1A—central command over state-owned firms. It is simply that the command will now be exercised by a regional or local government rather than by the central government. In any case, an emphatic word of caution is needed: Decentralization is not a substitute for the abolition of the bureaucratic command system (Mechanism 1A) and for the broader scope of market coordination (Mechanism 2). All the disadvantages and inefficiencies of the overcentralized Mechanism 1A can be preserved even after decentralization.

My recommendation for reform is that a close and positive association between the two dimensions of the reform be established: increase regional-local decisionmaking power and autonomy, and at the same time move forward from the direct bureaucratic mechanism (1A) in the direction of more indirect control (1B) and the market mechanism (2).

The Non-State Sector

Considered next are all sectors of the economy not in the exclusive ownership of the state—the non-state sector for short. In my appraisal, the changes in the non-state sector went much further than did those in the state-owned sector.

Before the reform process started, the non-state sector was small; the "vision" of the future was that this sector would wither away completely. Progress meant moving toward complete state control: all people working in state-owned organizations controlled by governmental administration; almost no activity in the private domain, not even in the household; and almost all activities transferred to huge institutions under the direction of the bureaucracy. The reform halted—and to a certain extent reversed—this trend. This shift is one of the most remarkable features of the Hungarian reform.

As a point of departure, a classification of the non-state sector is needed.

- *Formal private sector.* Here activities are pursued with means of production in private ownership. The owners, perhaps together with family members and employees hired by the owners, do their work as a "first job"—as their main income-earning activity. The formal sector is legal: Business is done under legal licenses, and the businesses pay taxes.[7] In terms of Marxian political thought, economic activity in the formal private sector can be small commodity production (no employee) or small-scale capitalist production (hired labor) or on the borderline of these two pure cases. Because there are strict limits on employment even after the reform, medium- or large-scale capitalist production does not exist in Hungary. (Activities of foreign capitalist firms operating in Hungary are not considered in this discussion.)
- *Informal private sector.* Activities here are not pursued by private individuals as their main source of income. People have a "first job" in the state-owned or cooperative-collective sector, but also engage in second and third (sometimes more) activities. This work can be unpaid (for example, to serve the needs of the family or friends), or it can be done for financial compensation. The informal private activity can be

legal or *illegal*. Some activities lie on the borderline—for example, they are prohibited but the prohibition is not enforced.[8]

- *Cooperative-collective sector*. There are different legal forms here, but they have common attributes. The means of production are in group ownership, although it may be de facto (not necessarily legal) ownership. Remuneration of the members depends not only on individual but also on collective performance. Managers are not appointed by the state, but are elected by the members.
- *Mixed-combined sector*. These forms are combinations of private and nonprivate (state or cooperative-collective) ownership and private and nonprivate activities. For example, a state-owned catering enterprise leases a restaurant to a private individual. The building and the equipment are state-owned, and working capital is provided by the private individual. The individual's family and a few hired employees work in the business. Further examples will follow in the pertinent section below.

Formal Private Sector

One of the most visible changes in Hungary is the widening of the formal private sector. There are areas where private business was strictly excluded before the reform but is allowed now: taxicabs, restaurants, fashion shops, and so on. Areas where there was a very small formal private sector before the reform (handicraft, retail trade) have been significantly extended. Yet in spite of this expansion, the total weight of the formal private sector must not be overrated. Its contribution to national output is still minor—only a few percent of the total. There is a low upper limit on employment: A private business unit cannot hire more than seven employees.

In my personal view, it would be advisable to go further in this respect. If 2–3% contribution to total national output is compatible with socialism, why would 6–10% be incompatible? If the employment of seven workers can be tolerated, why would the hiring of ten or twenty workers be intolerable? There are no unquestionable axioms that put a strict a priori limit against experimentation in that direction. I think efficiency should be the main criterion in judging these experiments. There is no reason to give extra support, subsidy, or tax exemption to any kind of private business. But as long as a private economic unit is able to compete financially, it should be allowed to survive.

There are important areas where—at least in the Hungarian experience—the formal private sector is able to show impressive efficiency. A few examples are construction, personal service (cleaner, tailor, barber), intellectual service (lawyer, architect, foreign language teacher, translator), repair (clothing, equipment, car), transport (taxi, truck), retail trade, restaurant and hotel, production of parts for factories, and so on.

Given the very nature of these types of activities, the entry of private business into them leads to profit seeking and to the differentiation of earnings. There is quite an understandable aversion to that among people educated in a socialist tradition. This hostility leads to peculiar reactions: Officials in charge of granting licenses keep the number of legally licensed businesses low because they do not want too many high-earning people. The result, however, is just the opposite: It gives the artifically small number of legally licensed private businesses a privileged—often almost monopoly—position, which in turn drives up their prices and ultimately their income. The reasonable conduct is to grant more licenses and allow as many entries as the market can bear. This would lead to competition and to lower prices and ultimately to less high income in the formal private sector.

Private business is often only tolerated by government officials—not really accepted as an organic part of the economic system with full rights. It is frequently almost forced into illegal actions: to try to get material or other productive inputs by bribing the seller, or to get credit from private individuals on usurious terms. At the same time, there is widespread tax evasion. I suggest fair terms both in rights and in obligations. The formal private sector should have the same legal chance in the acquisition of inputs and in receiving credit as does the nonprivate sector. On the other hand, the tax laws must be consistently enforced.

The most important change needed is to give a clear, stable framework both to private business and to the government officials who deal with the private sector. It must be clear what is permitted and what is prohibited. Rules must not be changed capriciously. Hungarian experience shows that ambiguity, improvisation, and unpredictable steps forward and backward create the feeling of uncertainty in the formal private sector, which is hypersensitive because of earlier prereform experience. As a result, many individuals in private business have a very short-term horizon. They want to get rich as soon as possible because they do not feel secure that their businesses will be allowed to continue for extended periods. They have no patience to build up customer goodwill and thus assure a better position in competition. They do not make serious accumulation in fixed assets with long lifetimes because they are afraid of confiscation. To change these attitudes and to establish confidence, different actions must be taken, including the introduction of legislation clearly regulating the rights and the obligations of the formal private sector as well as some ways of allowing the articulation of the interests of this sector.

Informal Private Sector

Legal activity. There is a remarkable improvement and extension of the informal legal private sector in Hungary. Perhaps the most important change is in the "social climate" surrounding this kind of activity. It is no longer regarded as an almost shameful *petit-bourgeois* occupation pursued because of greed. On the contrary, nowadays people who work in addition to their prescribed "first jobs" are highly respected as diligent and productive citizens. In fact, some material assistance (though not enough) is given to informal legal private activities.

The most important informal legal activity in the private sector is the work on the private household plots of agricultural workers. This was legally permitted in the prereform period, but then it did not get genuine support. This situation has changed completely. The household plot is regarded not as an "antisocialist" competitor to the socialist (that is, state-owned or cooperative) sector but as an organic part of the system, complementary to large-scale farming in the big state-owned or cooperative units. The division of tasks is based mainly on efficiency criteria. Intensive agriculture relies heavily on small-scale production and extensive agriculture on large-scale production. Small-scale private and large-scale nonprivate farming should mutually help each other. It must be emphasized that large-scale agricultural production has not been abandoned in Hungary; it can have great advantages if it is well organized and the workers have sufficient labor incentives. At the same time, the small-scale household plot is assisted in many ways: The household members can acquire seeds, fodder, and use of large machinery like tractors and transport, and they get expert advice from agronomists. The members of a typical agricultural family share their total working time between work in the state-owned or cooperative farm and in the household farm.

Many people whose main occupation is outside agriculture do some agricultural work on their own small plots. They grow fruit and vegetables and breed poultry, pigs, and rabbits. People were strongly discouraged from doing that before the reform but are very much encouraged to do so now.

The result of the two types of informal private agricultural activities described is that they account for almost half of total Hungarian production of meat, fruits, and vegetables. The country is now very well supplied with food.

Building homes also became much more important in the private sector. Future owners of the homes work on the houses together with family and friends and can also hire private or nonprivate contractors. However, the conditions could be much improved by providing a larger supply of building material, by allowing the entry of more private contractors, and by granting more credit to the individuals building private homes.

Finally, there are different arrangements that allow legal "moonlighting"— doing informal private work after the regular working time or on weekends. This work can be done individually, with the intermediation of a cooperative, or in special partnerships (called "economic working teams" in Hungary). Some workers do repair jobs in households (plumbing, electricity); others do domestic service (window or carpet cleaning). Some professional people do consulting or translation, secretaries do typing, economists and mathematicians have contracts for operations research commissioned by firms, and so on.

There is one danger in this trend toward increased informal activity: extreme "self-exploitation"—overwork up to the limits of exhaustion. But at the same time, people do this work voluntarily. They want to earn more, or they want to get a dwelling sooner than they could if they waited their turn in the long queue for public apartments. Thus they work perhaps ten to thirty hours per week in addition to their official "first jobs." This increased activity is one important source of the fast increase of real consumption in Hungary.

Illegal activity. There exist informal illegal private activities: black marketeering, earning taxable income but evading taxes, unlicensed private work, and so on. One way of fighting such activities, of course, is law enforcement by the police, prosecutors, and courts. But what is remarkable in the Hungarian situation is that legal enforcement is not the only means applied—it is complemented by a careful and pragmatic reconsideration: Is the law overly restrictive? If there are shortages and bureaucratic rationing, black marketeering and corruption are unavoidable. If people want very much to work more for the sake of earning more, they will find some way to do so even if the work is prohibited. The main method to diminish illegality of this kind is to legalize all socially useful work; prohibition by law must be restricted to the genuinely harmful criminal activities.

Private Saving

A special problem of the private segment of the economy is private saving. As income is rising, the total amount of saving is increasing. There are unresolved issues. The inflation rate went up, exceeding the normal rate of bank deposit interest. In other words, the real interest rate is negative: Money deposited in the bank is losing purchasing power year by year. This factor provides incentive for individuals to avoid bank deposits and hold savings in other forms that promise a more stable or perhaps increasing value: foreign currency, land, private houses, gold, jewelry, and objects of art. The increased demand drives up the price of these commodities, but it also diverts financial resources that could be used by the banking system for the financing of more urgent "productive" investment.

This restricted investment availability leads to a more general problem. Well-to-do people are allowed to spend their money as they want, provided they spend it on consumption goods or services (including the purchase of a private home). But until recently they were not permitted to invest their money in a "productive" manner (unless they wanted to become self-employed in private business).[9] This prohibition and the negative real interest rate on bank deposits provide a stimulus for wasteful consumption. The problem is widely discussed. There are now a few municipalities and state-owned enterprises that issue bonds paying a slightly higher interest rate than does the saving bank. The idea came up to introduce dividend-earning stocks issued by state-owned firms to the public, but the suggestion has not yet been accepted. There also is a related question: Can private individuals legally invest their savings in the businesses of other private individuals, and not actually work in the business? These investors would expect to get interest on their investment or a share in the profit. Such transactions do exist, but the contracts are not unambiguously protected and enforced by law; therefore, such a private financial investment can be rather risky.

In my opinion, the state-owned bank should pay a reasonable positive real interest rate on bank deposits. Different financial institutions must be established to channel private savings into the financing of productive nonprivate and private investment. Appropriate legal regulation is needed to protect the private investor and to eliminate ambiguities in this important area.

Cooperative-Collective Sector

An important part of the Hungarian reform is the increased role of the cooperative-collective sector. This change occurred first in agriculture, but has moved to the rest of the economy. Following is a brief survey of changes.

Effective incentive schemes have been introduced in the agricultural cooperatives, and more responsibility has been delegated to the teams and working groups. Coexistence and cooperation between the collective and the household farm has been mentioned previously. It must be emphasized, though, that large-scale production in the cooperative has not been abandoned; it is only complemented by the small-scale production on the household plot. There are many production lines, including in grain production, where large-scale methods are more efficient than the small-scale ones. A reasonable division of labor is needed between large-scale and small-scale operation—not a one-sided predominance of one or the other.

Agricultural cooperatives concentrated exclusively on agricultural production before the reform. As a result of the reform process, many of them became more diversified, extending their profile into such areas as construction, food processing, food retail trade, and restaurant business in nearby cities. Some of the cooperatives went further and started to produce parts, perhaps also equipment and machinery, usually in cooperation with state-owned factories. Diversification helps to protect the members of the cooperative against seasonal fluctuation in employment and uncertainties in earning created by random weather conditions, ultimately increasing profitability and income.

The autonomy of agricultural and nonagricultural cooperatives is much more respected now than in the prereform era. The cooperatives are not given obligatory output targets and input quotas, but can decide on input-output plans on their own. They have more independence in selecting and hiring the leading personnel. Still, more consistent autonomy is needed, mainly in the process of selection and appointment; there are interventions by individuals at higher levels that could be avoided.

The cooperative sector is still heavily dependent financially on the central authorities and the central banking system; in my opinion, the dependence is too great.

Finally, there has been a slight expansion of the nonagricultural cooperative sector, but in this respect the reform process did not go far enough. I believe this sector could play a much more extended and decisive role.

Mixed-Combined Sector

There are different mixed-combined forms of nonprivate and private ownership and activity, and with ingenuity and free initiative, other such forms may emerge. Three types will be mentioned here.

One combined form is the leasing of a state-owned productive unit to a private individual or a group of individuals. The fixed capital remains in the ownership of the state; the lease contract determines whether working capital will be provided by the state-owned firm or by the leaseholder. The leaseholder has full responsibility for running the business and must pay the rental plus taxes; any profit made on top of those obligations may be retained. In addition, the leaseholder has the right to hire the employees in the unit. These leasing arrangements started in different areas—restaurants, retail trade, gasoline stations—but they could be spread much wider.

Typically the leaseholder is selected by auction: The person with the highest bid will get the lease. That is a useful selection process, but some precaution is needed. The would-be leaseholder can be irresponsible in bidding—for example, by offering a rental price that will be too high compared with the true revenues. If deep financial trouble later developes, the leaseholder will be tempted to apply adverse remedies—spoil the quality of service, neglect maintenance of fixed assets, seek postponement of due payments, and so on. In such a case, the leaseholder ultimately goes bankrupt, and somebody else must be found to continue the business. Appropriate procedures must be worked out. One solution would be a legal framework in which the leaseholder guarantees the observation of the contract even at the cost of the person's personal wealth.

However, there is the other side of the coin: Sometimes the state-owned enterprise is too greedy, demanding an unrealistically high price and almost hounding the lease candidate into financial trouble. It requires some learning and experience to arrive at contracts assuring reasonable terms to both partners, but then the contract should be strictly enforced.

A recent experiment in Hungary is the establishment of "economic working teams" within the state-owned firm. For example, a group of manual workers will do repair for households or computer experts will do programming for other firms—after they have fulfilled their obligations at their "first job" in the state-owned firm. They may even do overtime work at their first job in the framework of the working team for extra payment.

The activity of the working team is not hidden or disguised. Employees need the permission of their supervisors in their first jobs to join a team. The membership is a privilege granted only to those who do their first job properly. Those employees with whom the supervisor is satisfied may get permission to earn additional money in the working team. In other words, this opportunity is complimentary work and payment, based on voluntary participation and on the consent of the supervisor in the first job. This peculiar dependence on the supervisor is questioned by some Hungarian scholars. In any case, it is an experiment worthy of attention.

A third type of mixed-combined activity is a revival of outwork (homework) by private individuals (mainly women) for state-owned or cooperative-collective firms. This arrangement is a combined form because there is mixed ownership: The material typically is provided by the state-owned or cooperative-collective enterprise, but the workers own their tools and perform the work at home.

Conclusions

I briefly mentioned that a new way of selecting managers has been introduced in the smaller state-owned firms recently. According to the new rules, the manager will be elected by the employees of the firm. The change brings the position of these firms very close to the situation of a cooperative: They will be on the borderline of state ownership and cooperative ownership—formally still in the domain of the former, but in reality closer to the latter.

Hungary is experimenting with a large variety of forms of ownership. The leadership does not dictate what must be the right proportions of the different sectors and subsectors based on different forms of ownership—the determination of proportions is left to an evolutionary process over a long period spanning several decades. That approach is commendable. I would add a further suggestion: It is advisable to rely heavily on the "natural selection" that genuine competition on the market brings. Those forms that prove their efficiency will survive. Those forms that can be kept alive only with the aid of artificial state support might be sheltered transitionally but not forever; they ultimately must go out of business.

Currently, the Hungarian system does not allow a genuine competition between the different forms of ownership. On the one hand, the state-owned sector has privileges in input-supply, access to credit, investment subsidy, imported material and machinery, and so on. On the other hand, the state-owned firms are much more handicapped than the non-state units by a host of bureaucratic regulations, administrative constraints, and open and disguised interventions. In this respect, the non-state sector has more room for flexible maneuvering. For the sake of healthier competition and natural selection, it would be very useful to diminish both the privileges enjoyed and the extra burdens suffered by the state-owned enterprises.

The increased level of private activity described in the preceding sections raises a question: Does the application of these new ways and forms lead to abandoning socialism and adopting capitalism? My answer is no. First, such a transformation will have certain limits. Even if all these forms were to become more widespread than they are in Hungary today, they would still encompass only the smaller part of total social activity and produce only the smaller part of total national output. Most means of production in the dominant sectors of the economy would remain in nonprivate ownership. Second—and this is the more important consideration—ownership is not the main criterion when determining whether a system deserves the name "socialism." In the normative sense, socialism should be a system in which production is efficient and the standard of living and quality of life are improving. Justice prevails; equal chances are given to everyone. Society helps the disabled, the sick. Economic planning plays an important role in the rational allocation of resources. All these desiderata are fully compatible with some domain of private activity and private ownership.

The Popular Support for Reform

Reform is not a purely economic matter, limited to some changes of prices, taxes, incentives, decisionmaking rules, and so on. It is an issue of utmost political significance. It touches upon highly sensitive politicized problems: the distribution of income, wealth, property rights, and power among different social groups. Nobody in society remains unaffected and indifferent.

This chapter is an examination of political economy, but it is not a study in political science and political sociology in the stricter, narrower sense. I cannot go into the political aspects of the reform process in great depth, but perhaps a brief summary of a few experiences will be helpful.

Leadership in socialist countries is often inclined to use the following rhetoric: "It was perfectly all right to follow policy A up to now, but from now on the only acceptable thing is to follow policy B." This rhetoric is explained by the endeavor for continuity, but it does not inspire the population to undertake all the risks and sacrifices connected with the transition from policy A to B.

In Hungary, the transition from the prereform to the postreform system has been accompanied by a thorough critical analysis of the "old mechanism"—the bureaucratic command system. The old system has been discredited in the eyes of many people, and the criticism helped in understanding what went wrong. This denunciation was made on different levels: Books and scholarly articles were aimed at the more skilled audience—economists, managers, and officials, for example—but the same critical ideas have been repeatedly explained in more popular forms as well. In any reform, there is a permanent danger of reversal; without thorough criticism of the old mechanism, the danger of reversal would be greater.

The critical attitude toward the past is a strength of the Hungarian process.

The weakness is the lack of clear perspectives for the future. People are willing to work harder and make sacrifices for great ideals, but this kind of enthusiasm is weak or missing in Hungary. Questions remain that have not yet been answered by the analysts of Hungary: Is it possible at all to have a pragmatic approach in the renewal of the system—and at the same time project an inspiring and mobilizing picture of the future? Hungary has not really been able to do both. Perhaps other countries—and Hungary too—will have more success in the future.

In Hungary, all indicators of the standard of living—among them real consumption per capita—have shown high growth rates from 1957 until 1979. Unfortunately, after that the rapid growth came to a halt; the 1980s have been characterized by slow improvement, stagnation, and/or decline—the characterization depending on which indicator of general welfare is analyzed. The slowdown and the decline have many causes. External conditions worsened: After the oil shock, the terms of Hungarian foreign trade deteriorated. It became more difficult to get the most-needed imports within Comecon and at the same time more difficult to export to the convertible currency markets. High interest rates increased the burden of debt service. These troubles caused by unfortunate external circumstances have been aggravated by mistakes in Hungarian economic policy—namely, delayed and unsatisfactory adjustment to the external changes and stubborn continuation of overambitious growth and investment up to 1978, followed by an abrupt cessation of growth and investment that disrupted all economic processes.

What is the relationship between the present troubles and the reform? Opinions differ. I agree with those who believe that the troubles are not because of the reform, but that deeper reforms may have prevented some of them. The Hungarian response to outside changes was too slow and inefficient because Hungary did not go far enough in the reform process. In the language used earlier in this chapter, Hungary barely evolved from Mechanism 1A—direct bureaucratic control—to the overly complicated, insufficiently adaptive indirect control of Mechanism 1B. The country did not proceed toward implementing Mechanism 2, market coordination. A more decentralized economy—with more complete autonomy for the producers, more flexible prices, and fewer protections cushioning the economic agents from the consequences of external changes–would have stimulated a much more effective adjustment.

This is not the place to go into further detailed analysis of the Hungarian situation; the purpose in this section was to discuss some political implications. The average person does not do a sophisticated study strictly separating external misfortune from internal mistakes and does not make a distinction between "too much" or "too little" reform when analyzing the mistakes. To the regret of the adherents of the reform, there is a wrong—but very convincing—thought at hand: Because troubles and reform coincide in time, reform must be the *cause* of the trouble. The present economic difficulties in Hungary do not help the reform process.

Thus there is an important lesson for other countries: It is better to be cautious in goal setting, striving only for modest growth of output and standard of living—and to keep this pace consistently. An unsustainably fast increase at the beginning followed by a slowdown or decline undermines the popularity of the reform. The "moral capital" built up in the good years can be easily eroded in the bad years.

The first beneficiaries of the Hungarian reform process were in the agricultural population. Farmers gained in different ways: from the abolition of low-priced obligatory delivery, from the increases of agricultural producer prices, from wider opportunities to produce on the private plot and sell on the free market, from the increase of wages paid by the cooperative, and from earnings in the nonagricultural side activities.

Improvement of the urban standard of living was slower and less spectacular than the agricultural development. The gap between urban and rural income diminished rapidly. This made the population in the rural areas more satisfied, but caused bad feelings among the urban population, which felt that the reform favored the peasant and slighted the industrial worker. Antireform demagogy tried to make use of these sentiments in the early 1970s.

It later became clear that the urban population has also been gaining. Not only have some disparities in nominal income been corrected, but there has been the major gain of a good food supply. The urban population has recognized that in a period when many other Eastern European socialist countries have experienced serious troubles in food supply—sometimes real food crises—the average Hungarian household is well supplied with all kinds of food, including meat, dairy products, fruits, and vegetables.

In any case, there is an important lesson to be drawn: The relative proportions of agricultural versus industrial wages and of rural versus urban standards of living must be carefully and constantly monitored to avoid potential tensions.

One of the main risks of the reform process is that it may open the door for inflation. The prereform system was less prone to inflation for a variety of reasons. First, prices and wages were fixed and tightly controlled. This had the many drawbacks previously discussed, but it surely repressed inflationary tendencies. Second, because profit incentives were weak, firms did not press hard enough for higher prices. The reform may change this situation by leading to more autonomy in price and wage setting. Given a strengthened profit incentive, the firm—if monetary policy is lax and other conditions allow it—will try to increase profits by raising prices.

Hungary in the mid-1980s presents a medium case of inflation: There is not runaway inflation, but there is no stable price level either. The official consumer price index has been in the upper bracket of single-digit inflation for the past few years. Monetary and fiscal policy, strong restriction on investment activities, and various ceilings on wages were able to hinder further acceleration toward double-digit inflation.

Nevertheless, inflation can pose a serious dilemma for the reform. The restructuring of the distorted relative price and wage system can be implemented by making overall increases in price and nominal wage levels. However, because both prices and wages are rather rigid downward, corrections are more easily implemented by keeping some prices or wages stable or allowing only a small increase, and permitting larger increases for other prices and wages. But behind the advantages of this flexibility lie dangerous drawbacks. Just when the impact and the reputation of the price signal should be reinforced in the economic sphere, inflation makes the signal weaker.

The situation produces harmful effects on income distribution. People selling their individual products on the market are able to keep up with inflation by raising their prices. Some groups may even gain from inflation. As for the larger mass of industrial workers, their position will of course depend on wage policy—the extent to which they are compensated by regular increases of nominal wages. Typically, the main losers are those who have fixed wages and salaries: teachers, clerks, pensioners, the sick and the handicapped living on welfare payments, students living on stipends, and so on. The more active members of the population can try to complement their earnings from their first jobs in the formal economy with additional earnings from the informal economy. But people who for some reason are unable to do that will suffer the most from inflation.

Inflation weakens confidence. It is a risky undertaking to implement inflationary policies because inflation has a self-reinforcing mechanism—once started it tends to accelerate. If not kept under control, it may disintegrate popular support for the reform.

The proponents of the Hungarian reform usually referred to the requirements of higher efficiency, flexibility, innovation, technical progress, and better adjustment to consumer demand. Of course, it was constantly emphasized that the ultimate goal was the improvement of the life of people, but it was argued that the main instrument for achieving the ultimate goal was to make production more efficient.

However, the greater emphasis on incentives leads to increases in income differentiation. There are people who for various reasons cannot keep up with competition: the sick, the handicapped, the aged, and those who earn for many dependent family members. Some of them are suffering from multiple disadvantages and therefore feel their chances for improvement are almost hopeless. These are social strata that deserve extra attention and care. Unfortunately, in the first period of the reform there was no sufficient consideration of this kind of social policy. As a result, some people—those who were more concerned with the issues of fairness and social justice, with helping the poor and the disadvantaged, and with the goal of equal opportunities and other ethical and political desiderata—drifted to the side of the reform's opponents.

Advocates of Hungarian economic reforms are becoming increasingly aware of the disenchantment among some people and are promoting some kind of rapprochement. The problem is very complex and a more elaborate discussion exceeds the limits of this chapter. Deep conflicts and contradiction may occur between the requirements of efficiency and the postulates of social justice, equity, and security. In many cases, tough choices must be made—abandoning some requirements, compromising on others. There is no general recipe to resolve the dilemmas. At this point, I want to draw attention to only one consideration: It would be wrong to evolve a one-sided, purely "technocratic" approach to the reform. Improvement of social policy must become an organic part of the reform process.

The Hungarian reform is not driven by a spontaneous, forceful mass movement. This is not the first time in human history that a "reform from above" has occurred. In retrospect, this fact will explain many of the successes and also many of the failures and limitations. Those individuals who are propelling the reform are mostly "cadres"—high- or middle-level officials in the party, in the government bureaucracy, and in economic life. At the same time, those who are resisting the reform are also "cadres" in similar positions. Phases of quick progress, stagnation, and reversal are alternating according to the relative power of proreform and antireform forces. The speed and the direction of the process depend to a large extent on the attitude of people in the government apparatus and ultimately on the will and determination of the top leadership.

There are different roots of the resistance. Ideological orthodoxy is one of them. The idea of a wide scope for market forces is rather alien to the traditional blueprint of a socialist system. This source of resistance can be weakened by patient, enlightening education.

A deeper root of resistance is people's anxiety about power. It would be dishonest to deny that genuine decentralization means that some power is transferred from a higher level of decisionmaking to a lower level. Those individuals whose exclusive goal and passion is to wield power will inevitably lose something valuable. But there are many cadres who have other goals and aspirations as well. If they possess good managerial and administrative abilities and if they are intelligent and have good contacts with their subordinates, they will be eagerly awaited in important positions of the more decentralized economic mechanism. They do not have to fear the progress of the reform. Many Hungarian ministerial officials became top managers in enterprises and enjoy their new responsibilities. There are many ways of reallocating the staff of economic management. The explanation of these opportunities may help in overcoming resistance.

Economists working in research institutes, universities, and in the economic analysis sections of governmental offices have played an extremely important role in the Hungarian reform. They provided the criticism of the old mechanism, and most of the initiatives and proposals for change came from this circle. Research economists regularly participated with practitioners in the committees in preparing the new resolutions.

A significant contribution of economists is the continuous critical appraisal of the state of affairs. This criticism is not always warmly received by the officials responsible for the delays and imperfections—it is sometimes ignored or even sharply rejected. Nevertheless, there are economists who repeatedly have the courage and integrity to come forward with their criticism and new suggestions. Such kind of independent monitoring by critical minds should be encouraged because it is an indispensable condition of the reform's progress.

Strategy of the Reform

The following discussion requires some conceptual clarification of the term "planning." In the usage of most socialist countries, including Hungary and China, this word has a double meaning. First, it refers to an *ex ante* exploration of possibilities and coordination of human activities. A plan sets targets and assigns the instruments to fulfill the targets. The "product" of the planners' work is the plan itself—that is, a document accepted by political and legislative bodies that later serves as the working program of the government. Second, the term "planning" is also used to denote what this chapter has called "central control" or "bureaucratic control"—coordination Mechanisms 1A and 1B. It means a permanent flow of instruction, recommendations, and incentives from a higher level of regulation to a lower level. It means central management and administration of economic affairs and thus an unceasing flow of interventions. The governmental official acts as a "dispatcher" in a firm—urging firm number 1 to deliver a specified amount of goods to firm number 2, commanding firm number 3 to introduce the use of another kind of raw material, and so on.

I prefer to use the term "planning" only in the first meaning and call the second phenomenon "central control" or "bureaucratic control." I apply this separation of concepts throughout this chapter to avoid possible confusion about the true ideas of the reform.

Under this terminology, therefore, the reform means a change in the scope and the methods of central control: A part of discretionary power is transferred from higher- to lower-level decisionmakers, and the role of commands is narrowed. At the same time, reform does not mean any reduction in the influence and significance of planning (in the term's first sense). On the contrary, after being freed from the nuisances of "dispatcher" work, the planner finally has time and intellectual energy for the genuine task: to explore the possibilities of the country, compare alternative solutions, assign targets, coordinate programs, and so on.

The frequently disputed dilemma of "plan versus market" is partly a false dilemma—false because of conceptual confusion. The true rival coordination mechanisms are "bureaucratic coordination" and "market coordination." With some simplification, it can be said that the more active the bureaucratic control, the less vigorous will be the market. Thus, these two types of coordination systems have to share control duties, because their overlapping activity can lead to many disturbing effects. But there is no such contradiction between planning (in its first sense) and the market. Circumspect planning can help the market work more smoothly and at the same time assist the remaining elements of bureaucratic control in finding their right place and working more efficiently.

Hungary is searching for the best planning methods under the circumstances of the reform, but has not yet arrived at a satisfactory solution. There are remarkable efforts to elaborate long-term plans, but the linkage between these plans and the actual regulation of economic affairs is rather weak. Further improvement of planning methodology is much needed.

The language in the Hungarian economic literature makes a distinction between issues of "economic policy" and "economic mechanism." Instead of a general abstract definition, I give a sample of problems belonging either to the first or to the second group. "Economic policy" issues include the share of investment and consumption in total output, growth rates of total output and its main components, the proportions of the main sectors, and general price and wage levels. These issues apply to what Western economist would call "macropolicy," plus some "meso-policy" issues as well. With respect to future plans, "economic policy" can be described by a set of quantitative indicators. By contrast, "economic mechanism" refers to phenomena like incentives, rules of price and wage setting, the correct distribution of decisions between different authorities and economic units, the organizational structure of economic administration, and so on. Although some aspects of the "economic mechanism" can be characterized by quantitative indicators (for example, relative proportions of sectors based on different types of ownership), the bulk of describing the mechanism requires verbal analysis of institutions, organizations, formal-legal rules, and informal conventions.

For most Hungarian economists, the term "reform" is associated with the second set of issues—with changes in the economic mechanism. Those are the changes I have discussed in this chapter. It was not my intent to address the important changes in Hungarian "economic policy" in the past three decades (although the interaction between "economic policy" and "economic mechanism" is mentioned at the end of this discussion).

Direct bureaucratic control—Mechanism 1A—is closely associated with a certain economic policy that Hungarian economists call "forced growth." (I once used the term "rush" as a synonym.) The main characteristics of forced growth can be summarized as follows:

- The investment rate is very high. Growth targets are overambitious and frequently unattainable. Priority is given to industrial investment, especially the accelerated growth of heavy industry. Not enough resources are allocated to agriculture, transport, telecommunication, commerce, housing, and other services. Infrastructure and environmental protection are neglected. Within industry, light industry is disproportionally pushed into the background.

- Permanent expansion takes the form of establishing new productive units, to the neglect of the proper maintenance and technical renewal of existing capital.
- The focus is on very large projects. Not enough resources exist for the millions of minor improvements and fine adjustments needed.

The consequence of these factors is that the objective of a permanent increase in the standard of living does not get high priority in allocation. In case of economic troubles, the cutting of consumption serves as the first buffer.

The highly centralized command system is in the service of forced growth. It enforces by administrative means the high saving and investment rate; it sets taut output targets for each sector and for each firm; it adopts the outlined priorities through the centralized allocation of investment resources. The command economy is called by some authors a "mobilization economy" because it is able to mobilize by all means (even with the aid of drastic administrative measures) both labor and capital for the sake of accelerated growth.

There is an alternative economic policy more congenial to a reformed economic mechanism. Called balanced or harmonious growth, its main characteristics can be summed up as follows:

- There is a more moderate investment rate, allowing a larger share of consumption.
- Growth targets are modest but surely feasible.
- At first, investment resources are shifted into sectors formerly neglected: light industry, agriculture, transport, telecommunication, commerce, housing, other services, infrastructure, environmental protection, and so on. Later, when the backward sectors catch up, sustained and balanced sectoral proportions are mandated.
- Equal attention is given to maintenance, technical renewal, and expansion.
- Sufficient resources are allocated for small projects and minor fine adjustments in addition to the necessary large projects.

The consequence of this balanced economic policy is that growth becomes consumption-oriented. In case of trouble, reduction of consumption serves only as last resort.

Hungary made significant changes both in policy and mechanism. This chapter discussed the development of the economic mechanism in detail, but here I should add that there was also a remarkable shift from the path of forced growth in the direction of a more balanced growth pattern. Unfortunately, neither change was quite consistent, and there were vacillations, cessations, or reversals more than once. The two basic processes—the transformation of economic policy and the reform of the economic mechanism—were not fully coordinated. In some cases one proceeded, the other ceased—and vice versa.

Small wonder that there were contradictions between the two basic processes. For example, in the early 1970s, economic policy reverted partially to the old habits of forced growth. Investors went elsewhere when more moderation was needed in the difficult times after the oil shock. Later, excessive acceleration was followed by drastic slowdown, executed mainly with the aid of administrative means. Forced growth provokes a return to command methods.

The lesson from Hungarian experience is this: The more consistent the shift from forced to balanced, harmonious growth policy, the more favorable are the conditions for the reform of the economic mechanism. Even the rectification of former mistakes and imbalances must come gradually because excessively fast changes lead to harmful side effects similar to those created by the original mistaken economic policy—that is, forced growth.

One of the most complex problems is the time schedule of the reform. It is certainly impossible to make all the changes in one giant stroke—a series of successive steps is needed. The difficulty is that interaction among different measures is very strong. Any serious change introduced into an unchanged political and economic environment will perhaps be unable to deliver all the expected results. Allowing a firm to retain profit but not yet having financial intermediaries or a capital market established prevents the firm from making the best use of the profit. Such types of inconsistencies cannot be avoided. "Perfectionism"—insistence on having completely consistent sets of interdependent measures or otherwise doing nothing—would lead to total passivity.

There are no generally applicable rules for the best time schedule for reform measures, but some Hungarian experiences are worthy of consideration. Hungary introduced a large package of far-reaching measures in 1968. The core of the set of changes was the abolition of obligatory plan indicators for the state-owned firms, and this was associated with a large number of other new regulations. The new rules were carefully prepared by special committees, then translated into the form of new laws and government regulations, and finally were all made effective on the same day (January 1, 1968).

Such "packages" can be very effective—they help to assure consistency between the different dimensions of the reform process. It is debatable whether the Hungarian leadership made the right decision in avoiding a similar "package solution" of an overall price and wage reform (instead of making partial price and wage corrections successively protracted over three decades). My feeling is that a heroic "surgical operation" of the price system could work better. If the extreme change could be made politically tolerable (for example, through compensations assuring the maintenance of the average real income), the population could more likely adjust after the one great shock. The other alternative—a protracted series of piecemeal changes—leads to recurrent tensions and to the acceleration of an inflationary process. Of course, such a sweeping price and wage reform has great risks and requires careful political and economic preparation. Still, it is worth serious reflection because of the great disadvantages and costs of successive partial price reforms.

Another typical dilemma is the following: How frequently should the rules be changed? Reform is a process of trial and error. The status quo is never perfect, and there are always critics who are urging further amendments. Yet a collection of good rules alone is insufficient; people—officials, managers, decisionmakers—must be able to *adjust* to these rules. New incentives are introduced in the expectation that people's behavior will be shaped by exactly those incentives. But such adjustment means learning, and that takes time, perhaps a few years. What happened quite often in Hungary was that people barely had time to get accustomed to a set of regulations before these were changed—and changes came repeatedly. Perhaps the new rule *is* better than the former one, but it has no impact if the whole system is permanently in a state of flux. Some degree of stability is needed. It is better to keep an imperfect but workable set of rules for a while.

Finally, it is highly desirable to have a long-term plan for the institutional changes—an all-embracing strategy of the more important measures and a blueprint of the system that should be created at the end. This long-term strategy of the reform should be associated with the long-term plan for economic policy. The Hungarian reform did not have and still does not have such a strategy and blueprint; the various individuals and groups have rather differing visions of the future. I am not quite sure such a common plan can be achieved—agreement is largely a matter of constructive discussions that explore the alternative solutions and eventually lead to common understanding. I am not so naive as to believe that all differences can be eliminated by argumentation that appeals to nothing but rational considerations; there are conflicting social forces, different interest groups, and political power struggles to consider. Still, the outside observer who does not know the Chinese circumstances well cannot exclude the optimistic scenario of a wide national consensus supporting a common plan of reform.

Notes

1. This chapter is the product of research during the period when I was F. W. Taussig Research Professor of Economics at Harvard in 1984–1985. The research work was supported by the World Bank. The assistance of both institutions is gratefully acknowledged.

2. Readers interested in my views in more detail are referred to the following works: *Overcentralization in Economic Administration* (Oxford: Oxford University Press, 1959); *Mathematical Planning of Structural Decisions* (Amsterdam: North-Holland, 1967); *Anti-Equilibrium* (Amsterdam: North-Holland, 1971); *Rush Versus Harmonic Growth* (Amsterdam: North-Holland, 1972); *Economics of Shortage* (Amsterdam: North-Holland, 1980); "The Dilemmas of a Socialist Economy: The Hungarian Experience," *Cambridge Journal of Economics*, vol. 4, no. 2, (1980), pp. 147–157; "Some Properties of the Eastern European Growth Patterns," *World Development*, vol. 9, nos. 9–10, (1981), pp. 965–970; "Comments on the Present State and the Prospects of the Hungarian Economic Reform," *Journal of Comparative Economics*, vol. 7, no. 3, (1983), pp. 225–252.

3. My views were of course influenced by the work of other Hungarian

economists. Without implying completeness, following is a list of Hungarian economists whose ideas had a significant impact on my thinking: László Antal, Tamás Bauer, Iván T. Berend, Zsuzsa Dániel, Andrea Deák, Zsuzsa Ferge, István R. Gábor, János M. Kovács, Mária Lackó, Tamás Nagy, Rezsö Nyers, György Péter, Miklós Pulai, Attila K. Soós, and Márton Tardos. This general acknowledgement substitutes for later references: I do not want to burden the reader with tracing one by one the sources of each observation and proposition.

4. Mechanism 2 can be broken down further into Mechanism 2A, a "pure" market economy where any kind of state intervention is excluded, and Mechanism 2B, where the market mechanism is predominant but governmental macropolicy has an impact on the economy.

5. Mechanism 2B "market socialism," to use the more precise distinction introduced in the previous footnote.

6. Here I am discussing only interfirm prices—the price paid by one firm to the other firm. The problem of prices paid by the household will be elaborated later in the chapter.

7. The other formal sectors are the state-owned firms, cooperative collective organizations, and governmental and other nonbusiness institutions. Their common property is to offer a full-time "first job," i.e., a main income-earning job in a formalized legal framework.

8. The literature uses the term "secondary economy" in an ambiguous way. it may mean the illegal informal private activities, all informal activities, or both formal and informal private activities. Because of this ambiguity, I will not use the term.

9. As mentioned, there has been an important change: Individuals are permitted to buy interest-yielding bonds. The total quantity of bonds is, however, rather small up to the mid-1980s.

5

Problems and Perspectives on Market Reforms in Hungary: A Comment on Ránki, Marer, and Kornai

George Barany

"By comparison with the rest of Eastern Europe, the life-style in Hungary can be very fine. . . . Ambitious reforms freed Hungary from many of the stifling restrictions that are built into Soviet-style economies. . . . It is the only net food exporter in the Warsaw Pact, though crop sales were interrupted this year by the Chernobyl nuclear accident in the Soviet Union. Hungarians enjoy broad personal freedoms, so long as they do not cross the lines of outright political dissent."

These are excerpts from an article, which precedes an interview with János Kádár, general secretary of the Hungarian Socialist Workers' Party, in *Time* magazine on the eve of the thirtieth anniversary of the Hungarian revolution of 1956.[1] They suggest that in spite of the slowdown of Hungary's economy in recent years and concomitant problems of inflation and threat of unemployment, the Hungarian "experiment" is still seen as a masterstroke in the West.

The foregoing sophisticated essays by a "troika" of distinguished authors thoroughly scrutinize the genesis, successes, shortcomings, and perspectives of Hungary's experimentation with centralized Stalinist planning and the country's partial return to market-type mechanisms and encouragement of individual entrepreneurship under a more relaxed command economy. The three analyses represent a diversity of aproaches and emphases, reflecting differences in the contributors' field of specialization and geopolitical perspectives. Yet taken together, the contributions by Professors György Ránki, Paul Marer, and János Kornai supplement each other to give the reader a sense of a certain "unity in diversity" and a feeling that the squaring of the circle labeled "market socialism" might become a tangible historical reality and not merely a speculative intellectual tour de force.

Chronologically, Ránki's study serves as a historical background for the other two. Beginning with an important introductory section on the origins of the theory and practice of economic statewide planning between the two world wars, Ránki describes the establishment, growth, and ultimate failure of an increasingly centralized, state-controlled, and bureaucratic-vertical command economy, developed first in the shadow of the German-sponsored war machine and later forcibly patterned after Stalin's Soviet model. The two-pronged central question to which Ránki's paper offers an answer is why central planning was introduced into the Hungarian economy and why it was radically changed— twice—after the national tragedies of the German occupation of Hungary in 1944 and after the Soviet suppression of Hungarian dreams of neutrality between power blocks a dozen years later.

Ránki's account, which revolves around the problem of national planning mechanisms, demonstrates the historically justified and recurrent need for radical reform, even within the context of a socialist economic system. It only peripherally touches on the attempted reforms themselves. Marer and Kornai in turn present a critical overview of the reappearance of market forces in the wake of the mass upheavals in Poland and Hungary in 1956. Both authors tend to use the events of that revolutionary year as a point of reference; but the focus of their attention is directed at trends that developed after 1968, when a drastic revision of Hungary's economy first obtained the Kádár regime's official approval and the New Economic Mechanism was first spelled out and set into motion.

At the opening of his concise analysis of the evolution of state intervention and central planning in Hungary, Ránki implies rather than stresses the significance of Germany's economic expansion in southeastern Europe during the years of the Great Depression and the consolidation of Nazi power. After the Austrian *Anschluss* ("annexation") and the absorption of Czechoslovakia's developed economy into its *Lebensraum* ("living space") in 1938, Germany's will became fiat in the entire region for the duration of the war. It was the transfer of defeated Germany's economic assets to the Soviet Union, in addition to war reparation payments stipulated by the postwar peace treaties, that enabled Moscow to redirect the economies of especially Hungary, Romania, and Bulgaria even before the political Sovietization of these countries. Soviet or jointly owned mining, industrial, and commercial enterprises and financial institutions constituted a potent economic lever during the three-year plan of reconstruction, which was still geared to a mixed economy. Not unlike in the case of Germany, Soviet political *Gleichschaltung* ("forcible incorporation") of the area followed on the heels of economic domination.

Another footnote that may be added to Ránki's sober references to the interlocking aspects of striving for autarchy, war preparations, and the stepped-up reckless industrialization pursued during the first five-year plan beginning in 1949 relates to the "New Course" announced by Prime Minister Imre Nagy in July 1953. Ránki correctly emphasizes the parallelisms if not causal relationship between the rigidity of the price system of the CMEA "market" and the failure of central planning in both domestic industrial and agricultural production, also manifest in a distorted policy of investment in major unfinished projects. In careful nuances, he points out the connection between the post-

Stalin thaw in Soviet attitudes and the cautious but significant efforts aimed at the redistribution of Hungarian resources during the first prime ministership of Imre Nagy. Sabotaged by Rákosi and the entrenched apparatchiks, the idea of controlled reform to be led by a yet to be rejuvenated communist party nevertheless regained momentum when detente continued under Khrushchev. If Georgy Malenkov's elimination from the Soviet party leadership was used by Rákosi to have Nagy expelled from the Hungarian party, Khrushchev's "secret" speech at the 20th Party Congress in February 1956 and his partial reconciliation with Belgrade led to Rákosi's fall and the reluctant official restoration of the increasingly popular Nagy's authority within the party. At the same time, the gradual release of former communist and non-communist political prisoners, begun under Nagy's tenure as prime minister, shocked the public into the realization of the horrors and human misery inflicted on the country by Stalinist misrule. It became clear even to the less sophisticated youth educated under communist auspices that the cause of economic reform was inseparable from that of individual and civil liberty. The beginning and end of the Hungarian armed uprising in the autumn of 1956 also showed that the effectuation of interlocking radical political and economic reform depended largely on the balance of forces in Eastern Europe, above all on the willingness of the Soviet Union to tolerate it—not for Hungary's sake but in the interest of its own grand strategy.

Hence this analysis explains the limitations—and opportunities—of János Kádár's policies of reform in the last three decades. Of the two learned studies dealing with Kádár's Hungary, Marer's seems more concerned with the limitations, while Kornai's reveals more of the opportunities. This diversity is perhaps natural: An "independent outsider," however knowledgeable, is more inclined to apply value judgments developed *extra-Hungarian* than is an "independent insider," who however widely traveled lives the life of the natives and is keenly aware of their daily struggle to "overcome."

In his meticulously researched and tightly organized survey of Hungarian market reforms, Marer stresses the shock effect of the revolution of 1956, a per se political event enhanced by widespread economic dissatisfaction. It was the revolutionary experience of 1956 that propelled Hungary into the forefront of political liberalization and economic reform during the 1960s. Of particular significance is Marer's description of agricultural reforms, which in his words "remained in the vanguard of Hungary's reform movement." It is in the agricultural sector of the economy that a "more or less genuine market mechanism" has been operating since 1968 with considerable success. Although Kornai does not deal with agriculture in any detail, his observations regarding the agricultural cooperatives reinforce Marer's contention. The negative reaction of workers and trade unions to the relative improvement of the position of agricultural producers in the wake of the NEM during the 1970s tended to strengthen bureaucratic and conservative opposition to the cause of reform in general, especially because it coincided with a simultaneous explosion of world market prices of energy that led to a deterioration of Hungary's terms of foreign trade. Thus global economic trends far beyond the control of small, energy-starved Hungary combined with rigid Marxist-Leninist doctrine stipulating that in a "people's democracy"—a euphemism for dictatorship of the proletariat—the industrial working class must be the leader of the body politic and its authority and economic well-being must reign supreme.

Inherently, then, the cause of reform in a fragile economic system such as Hungary's, which a priori depends on foreign suppliers of energy and raw materials to turn the wheels of its industrial enterprises, is bound to face recurrent crises—no matter how skillfully managed—in an unstable if not outright unpredictable world economy vulnerable to embargoes, military conflicts, and nihilistic fanaticism of a variety of extremes. In addition to a lucid periodization of different phases of the reform movement in the economic field, Marer's assessment reflects the coherence of a broad spectrum of economic factors and their interdependence with political liberalization. His analysis is a key to the understanding of Hungary's relative success in economic reform, so far sustained for a quarter of a century in spite of occasional reversals and an erosion of momentum far from unique to Hungary in recent years.

It is noteworthy, however, that in his summary, Marer assesses Hungarian achievements not on the basis of their political feasibility but measured against "the impact of reforms on economic performance." Whether the two criteria are separable at this particular juncture of history is open to question. Ironically, the penultimate section of Marer's chapter—"What Should Be Done?"—presents a set of exclusively economic desiderata, containing, no doubt, much useful stimuli for a market-oriented economy functioning independently of countervailing regional "environmental" forces. But the author knows—and herein lies the irony—that the rhetorical question to which he gives a purely economic answer was first formulated by two Russian revolutionary intellectuals, N. G. Chernyshevsky (1862) and V. I. Lenin (1902). While the former advocated an agrarian populist transformation of czarist society, the latter became the leader of the Bolshevik adaptation of Marxism to rural Russia; would it be possible that the certainly consciously formulated distant echo of the title of two classic pamphlets could evoke a nonpolitical remedy to Hungary's economic ills?

Be that as it may, Marer himself returns to the problem of political feasibility through the back door in the concluding sections, exploring the prospects for future reforms. He rightly points to the uncertainty of expeditious further reforms, considering in his evaluation both an ideologically-politically motivated organized domestic opposition and a lack of enthusiasm for major initiatives of a political leadership headed by an aging Kádár. In this respect, Marer is again right in underlining the correlation between the types of economic reforms to be implemented in the Soviet Union under Mikhail Gorbachev and, more specifically, Soviet reaction to new Hungarian initiatives for reforms. Indeed, Marer ends his discussion by mentioning the need for "improved East-West political relations and continued economic reforms and successes in China"—a wish that brings us to Kornai's chapter.

A brilliant overview of the "lessons" of Hungarian economic reform in its current stage, with short retrospective flashbacks, Kornai's interpretation of what he calls "the reform process" was written with an eye on China—hence its de-emphasis on agriculture, which was collectivized in China in 1953–1954 and decollectivized twenty-five years later. In contrast, Hungarian agricultural cooperatives, disrupted in 1956, were (as indicated by Marer) recollectivized in 1959–1962. Kornai, of course, is also aware of other vast differences between China and Hungary; hence his analysis may serve for the edification of comparative studies scholars, especially in Eastern Europe.

The first half of the paper deals with the state-owned sector of the economy. Kornai disagrees with those who think that the Hungarian economy has been transformed along the lines of "market socialism." Indirect bureaucratic control continues to dominate in the state-owned sector, which produces the largest part of the national output; and "horizontal"—market—coordination predominates only in the non-state-owned part of the economy, which contributes at most 17-19 percent to it.[2] To be sure, centrally mandated short-term plan targets were abolished, and except for Yugoslavia, Hungary is the only socialist country that took this step. The autonomy of firms has increased considerably vis-à-vis state agencies since 1968, and workers can essentially choose their professions and jobs. (In fact, many are allowed to work in foreign countries such as West Germany or Austria if they can prove that they received a job offer.) But despite these and other improvements, bureaucratic-administrative coordination persists in the spheres of price formation and the selection of investment projects, at the expense of the principles of supply and demand and profitability, even when regional decentralization of enterprises is attempted.

The "classification" of the non-state sector, the growth of which has been "one of the most remarkable features of the Hungarian reform," starts with a scrutiny of the economic, legal, and even psychological conditions in which private entrepreneurship functions. In this second part of Kornai's contribution, fascinating questions abound. "If the employment of 7 workers can be tolerated [in private business], why would the hiring of 10 or 20 workers be intolerable?" "Can a private individual invest his savings into the business of another private individual, without actually working in his business," so he can share in the latter's profit? These questions and the description of numerous other "ways and forms" applied in the private economy raise the crucial point of whether all this means "abandoning socialism and adopting capitalism." The author's answer is in the negative; he insists that "such a transformation will have certain limits. . . . Most means of production in the dominant sectors of the economy would remain in nonprivate ownership." Moreover, he argues,

> Ownership is not the main criterion when determining whether a system deserves to be called "socialism." In the normative sense, socialism

should be a system in which production is efficient and the standard of living and the quality of life are improving. Justice prevails; equal chances are given to everyone. Society helps the disabled, the sick. Economic planning plays an important role in the rational allocation of resources. All these desiderata are fully compatible with some domain of private activity and private ownership.

To achieve this "socialism with a human face," the author visualizes "an evolutionary process over a long period spanning several decades" and reliance on the "natural selection" guided by "genuine competition on the market." Is Hungary—is mankind—going to have such a leisurely respite of peaceful progress?

This question brings us to the last two sections of Kornai's chapter, which examine the popular support for reform in Hungary and the desirable strategy for reform. According to the author, "only some political implications should be discussed" here, and Kornai largely sticks to his word. But beyond the impressive array of sober economic arguments, there are psycho-political realities such as "anxiety concerning power," which he also considers "a deeper root of resistance" to reform at the level of individuals as well as groups, including political cadres.[3]

Kornai sees no a priori contradiction between his preferred concept of planning—"exploration of possibilities and coordination of human activities" (as distinct from "central control" and "bureaucratic coordination of economic mechanisms")—and the functioning of the market. In his discussion, he elects to focus on the "economic mechanism" operating in Hungary since 1968 and to refrain from discussing the important changes in "economic policy" during the same period. Naturally, he knows very well the significance, if not primacy, of the latter. As Soviet scientist Andrei Sakharov said in 1987 in reference to General Secretary Mikhail Gorbachev: "Without democratization, all of his goals in the economic sphere, in the industrial sphere, in the international sphere, cannot succeed."[4]

Hungarian economists are aware of the dilemma. As Kornai repeatedly says, they are divided on both technical issues and the politics and international overtones attached to them. Without ignoring these problems, Kornai presents them in fair understatements. Aside from many interesting and informative nuances and insights, this is the forte of his study.

Meanwhile, the discussion goes on in Hungary—and not only in scholarly journals. A 1986 article under the telling title "Further Reform, Whither?" in *Magyar Nemzet* (the daily of the People's Patriotic Front) pointed to the interrelationship of political and economic conditions initiated by the economic reform of 1968. Accordingly, many advocates of the reform considered "the economy only as a *breakthrough* toward wider democratization, decentralization and an opening for a public forum of society." The article also claimed that the sociopolitical institutional framework failed to respond to the challenges of economic reform. Yet without accountability and further democratization of the party and government apparatus and public debate—that is, political reform—no nationwide consensus can be built. In a follow-up article on "The 'Cursed-Blessed' Bureaucracy" three weeks later, also published under the heading "Regenerating Economy" by the same newspaper, the author (a sociologist) warned that in the so-called nonproductive fields of education, public health, culture, and sports, centralized administrative and hierarchical controls continue to survive in institutionalized form, as they had in the economy prior to 1968. According to the article, it was at the end of the 1970s that attention began to turn to the malfunctioning of the nonproductive infrastructure of the service sector, which revealed the symptoms of waste and low-quality performance common in the economy prior to the reform.[5]

Clearly, the malaise cannot be confined to the economy, nor is economic reform a cure-all for society's manifold ills. Even economists who are satisfied with the progress of economic reform and think that it has reached its limits—and who argue for the maintenance of the centralized control mechanism in the state-owned sector to avoid endangering its socialistic structure—admit the timeliness of carefully designed political and social reforms, including a better demarcation of the purview of party and economic agencies.[6] An article in the December 1986 issue of *Valóság*, the monthly of the Society for the Dissemination of Scientific Knowledge, explores "Alternate Roads to the Reform of the Political System," conceding that attempts at invigorating the parliamentary system have failed so far and that whatever pluralism exists prevails only behind the scenes in the form of the tug-of-war of competing administrative agencies and to the exclusion of the public at large. One recommendation set forth tentatively suggests the strengthening of the office of the prime minister to exert effective control over individual ministries; another favors corporate representation of interest groups, perhaps in the form of a second chamber, to broaden public participation in the debate of issues. New institutionalized and independent constitutional guarantees of individual citizens and of private organizations are also deemed necessary.[7]

Thus, the question of further economic reform in today's Hungary has grown inseparable from reforms in the political arena. Although the two topics are not always considered together, the debates run parallel. The same issue of *Valóság*, which considers alternatives of political reform, examines in its leading article the problem of comprehensive economic reform in Hungary against the background of trends in the world economy. Describing Hungary as one of the countries on the "semi-periphery"—that is, in the category of states whose national income reaches only 10–30 percent of that of the most advanced nations—the article argues that in recent years, Hungarian economic backwardness increased not only compared with the most industrialized economies of the world but also in comparison with a number of Third World countries, such as Taiwan, South Korea, or Singapore. Similar caveats appear, in a different context, in the leading article of the preceding issue of the journal.[8]

Although both articles last mentioned tend to dwell on the serious and precarious status of the Hungarian economy, they should not be considered as sure signs of imminent radical reform. In this respect, Marer's conclusions are important to remember. In addition, recent events in China may strengthen the hand of those advising caution, although the impact of the momentum of Gorbachev's *glasnost* is bound to be more immediate. Yet one must also bear in mind that it may take years before the new waves of significant reforms in the Soviet Union attain the level of those reverberating in Hungary since 1953–1956.

Today's Hungary—where there are no political prisoners and where there is relative freedom of expression and movement across international borders—can hardly be decried as a country under a harsh totalitarian dictatorship. Nevertheless, the Communist regime in power rests on an authoritarian one-party system put in place by the Soviet Union, and there are limits to political dissent and to the writer's freedom to challenge the official party line. Consequently, along with the rest of the world, Hungarians follow with utmost attention the renewal of the efforts to come to grips critically with Stalin's ghastly legacy in the Soviet Union, attempted by Khrushchev three decades ago. Skeptics doubt that Gorbachev can achieve lasting success where Khrushchev failed. But fickle Clio at times resorts to tricky ways. The demolition of the Stalinist totalitarian regime in Hungary began with Rákosi's abrupt removal from power upon Moscow's direct command in the spring of 1953; it was completed three years later via revolutionary means in the wake of Khrushchev's "secret" speech at the Soviet Communist Party's Twentieth Congress and a deepening crisis in both Poland and Hungary. Despite Soviet armed intervention in November 1956, subsequent reprisals, and the execution of Imre Nagy and his three close coworkers in 1958, Hungarian Stalinism has been subdued and the Soviet party leadership has not insisted on its restoration.[9]

Is then the democratization of a totalitarian system possible? The answer lies not so much in political theory but rather in historical experience.

Less dependent on the Soviet Union than Hungary, Marshal Tito's Yugoslavia, which had the most Stalinist of all East European Communist governments after World War II, managed to extricate itself from the grips of totalitarianism following the protracted Cominform crisis of 1948. In addition to astute political leaders and domestic stability manifest in popular support against Moscow's pressure, West European and U.S. assistance on the international scene contributed significantly to the gradual transformation of the Yugoslav state along more democratic lines and to its assertions of independence in the realm of foreign policy. Patient and flexible Western diplomacy seems to have also helped in Spain, where the Falangist regime—conceived in the spirit of the totalitarianism of the Right, which prevailed fifty years ago—was peacefully replaced by a democratic parliamentary system. Yet two of the three major totalitarian states of the interwar period, Nazi Germany and Fascist Italy, had to be crushed militarily to establish functioning democracies in their place.

Whether Lenin's party-state—born in war, civil strife, and foreign intervention and consolidated on the twin principles and practice of class struggle and terror—is susceptible to "radical" internal reform directed by a rejuvenated and more enlightened party elite, many doubt. They argue that the Stalinist brand of Marxism-Leninism in which the incumbent Soviet leaders have been raised is too heavily burdened with the tradition of czarist despotism and Muscovite slavery to set a historical precedent for the development of a totalitarian police state of the Left into a system of Communism "with a human face." Other observers, however, contend that "Gorbachev's rise to power represented the victory of the Westernizers in the Soviet elite, people with a positive attitude toward the West and many of its organizational forms . . . [who] are open to introduction of markets into the Soviet economy, to the relaxation of cultural restrictions, to greater freedom of travel and contact with the outside world." Some even believe that due to his "almost reckless commitment to technological change," the general secretary "has already launched society on a course from which there can be no turning back." These analysts insist that because of the inner logic of this commitment that takes "precedence over existing institutions and practices . . . Gorbachev has already embarked on a course akin to the Hungarian route of reform, perhaps without yet realizing how far and how fast he wants to go."[10]

To this writer, such predictions seem premature. In a huge empire such as the Soviet Union with its enormous variety of inhabitants, it may take years before a thoroughgoing reform movement develops its own momentum and asserts itself even under "normal" circumstances—that is, without shake-ups in the leading elite, basic structural changes in society, or unanticipated major disasters such as Chernobyl or war. Essentially, such conditions prevailed during the nearly half-century-long relatively stable period between the Crimean and Russo-Japanese wars. Whether the chances for a per se awesome "systemic reform" are better in the post-Stalin Soviet state today is hard to tell.

Even if the Soviet political leadership knew what kind of systemic reform should be effectuated and was ready to support it without reservation or dissent (which does not appear to be the case), two circumstances would make the enterprise very difficult. One of these is the challenge of the U.S. "high-tech" weapons build-up and the unpredictability of U.S. foreign policy in recent years, which "must be perceived as provocative" from Moscow's point of view. The Soviet Union's influence on U.S. foreign and armament policies is, understandably, indirect and limited; yet these factors contribute to the Soviet sense of urgency and determination to modernize the economy.[11]

Although U.S. behavior and actions are beyond Soviet control, neither Gorbachev nor any other Soviet leader can yield dominating influence over the Council for Mutual Economic Assistance (CMEA) to an outside power in the foreseeable future. Yet this Soviet-created organization for the close coordination of the economies of the USSR and its East European allies[12] has declined during the last few years. Even if the Soviet Politburo were interested in market-based reformism, which is far from certain, and Hungary's "economic experiment" were permitted to continue, "the requirement to partake fully of CMEA's non-market-based integration limits the possibility for that country or other East European states to move further away from centrally determined economic parameters."[13]

Of the governments represented in CMEA, those of Hungary, East Germany, and Romania have repeatedly indicated that maintenance of ties with the West contributed to their domestic stability.[14] But the leaders of Czechoslovakia and Bulgaria show no signs of distancing themselves from the Soviet-type centralized command economy, and the Polish and Romanian economies—for different reasons, to be sure—are in shambles.

All this means that not unlike de-Stalinization some thirty years ago, Gorbachev's catchwords of *glasnost* and *demokratiia* may not be received with equal enthusiasm in all parts of Communist-dominated Eastern Europe. Although Hungarians will probably greet them with open arms, even their hopes may be dampened by the knowledge that in the Soviet Union de-Stalinization has had its ups and downs too. The sounds of the bells in the Kremlin have yet to be tuned to the ringing of the Bell of Liberty.[15]

Notes

1. *Time*, August 11, 1986.
2. István R. Gábor, "Reformok, második gazdaság, 'államszocializmus'" [Reforms, second economy, "state socialism"], *Valóság* (Budapest) 29 (1986), p. 45, n. 29.
3. For a splendid analysis, see Tamás Kolosi, "Strukturális csoportok és reform" [Structural groups and reform], *Valóság* 29 (1986), pp. 19–31; and Kolosi, "A megvivatlan ütközet" [The battle not fought], in the Budapest daily *Magyar Nemzet*, September 9, 1986, p. 5.
4. Cited by Philip Taubman in the *New York Times*, as printed in the *Denver Post*, February 12, 1987, p. 2A.
5. László Lengyel, "Merre tovább a reformmal?" [Further reform, whither?] and László Belley, "Az 'átkozott áldott' bürokrácia" [The "cursed-blessed" bureaucracy], both in *Magyar Nemzet*, Budapest, August 12 and September 2, 1986, p. 5 (both), respectively, emphasis in the original.
6. Gábor, "Reformok," pp. 40–41; for a critique of this article, see Gyula Bock, "Milyen messze vagyunk a reform határaitól?" [How far are we from the limits of reform?], *Valóság* 29 (1986), pp. 86–91.
7. Béla Pokol, "Alternativ utak a politikai rendszer reformjára" [Alternate roads to the reform of the political system], ibid., pp. 32–45.
8. Béla Csikós-Nagy, "Az uj gazdaságnövekedési pályáról" [About the new course of economic growth], *Valóság* 29 (1986), pp. 1–9; and Sándor Kopátsy, "Egy reformkoncepcio világgazdasági háttere" [The roots of a conception of reform in the world economy], ibid., pp. 1–16. For the utmost seriousness of Hungary's economic situation and its expected further deterioration, see András Tábori, "The Economy in 1985–86—A Situation Report" and Béla Kádár, "Structural Policy Dilemmas," *The New Hungarian Quarterly* 27 (Winter 1986), pp. 33–42 and 43–60, respectively. According to Tábori, the actual budget deficit

reached 15.7 billion forint in 1985 instead 2.5 billion, a more than sixfold increase over the plan. Kádár claims that theoretical debates tend to become irrelevant "at a time of the changing of tides in the world economy" that "may especially harm the smaller countries with their narrow elbow room." In his provocative piece, he traces Hungary's current economic difficulties to the outdated "specialization patterns" developed in contradiction to the technology-intensive trends unfolding in the world economy during the last quarter of a century and suggests that "Structural therapy must not rely on 100 per cent proof theoretical solutions deduced either from the market-mechanism or from the central-planning idea."

Given the present stage of shock in the world economy because of the transformation of the United States into the world's largest debtor nation and Japan's into the foremost creditor on the international scene, could it be that the formulation of the question of market economy versus centralized bureaucratic planning systems has lost much of its earlier significance? Or could it be that insofar as it maintains its relevance to socialist and Third World economies, the Soviet answer to it may come via an ideological somersault by a return to the "foundations" laid by the NEP period of the early 1920s to be rediscovered as a true Marxist-Leninist road to socialism and not a mere tactical detour as claimed during the Stalinist period of Soviet history? Could economic de-Stalinization mean—and be justified as—a modernization of classical Marxian theory of socialist reproduction reinterpreted by Lenin in an endeavor to adapt it to postczarist Russia following the failure of "war communism"? Such implications appear, at least in an embryonic form, in a theoretical article by István Herédi, "A klasszikus és a modern szocialista ujratermelési mód" [The classical and modern way of socialist reproduction], *Valóság* 30 (1987), pp. 88–101.

9. For further reference, see Charles Gati, "Imre Nagy and Moscow, 1953–56," *Problems of Communism* 35 (1986), pp. 32–49.

10. *The 27th Congress of the Communist Party of the Soviet Union: A Report from the Airlie House Conference* (Abraham Becker, Seweryn Bialer, Arnold Horelick, Robert Legwold, Marshall Shulman), published under the auspices of the RAND/UCLA Center for the Study of Soviet International Behavior and Columbia University's W. Averell Harriman Institute for Advanced Study of the Soviet Union (Joint Notes Series-01, December 1986), pp. 8–9 and 14–15.

11. Ibid., pp. 61–63 passim.

12. Cuba, Mongolia, and Vietnam are also member-states of the CMEA.

13. Vladimir V. Kusin, "Gorbachev and Eastern Europe", *Problems of Communism* 35 (1986), pp. 39–53.

14. *The 27th Congress of the Communist Party of the Soviet Union*, p. 70.

15. The changes that occurred in Hungary during the eighteen months since the writing of this chapter in early 1987 have further enhanced the ambivalence of Hungarian reform. The policy of severe austerity officially announced on July 1, 1987—manifest in steep price increases, a rise in unemployment, introduction of a graduated income tax, calculated depression of the population's real income, inflationary pressures, and devaluation of the currency—has led to a crisis that is both political and economic, as indicated by the replacement of Kádár and others in the top leadership of the party and government. Analyzing the background of a situation bordering on economic chaos, recent debates stress the resistance to reform that prevailed on the domestic scene in the years 1972–1978 despite reiterated lip service to the New Economic Reform of 1968 and that was encouraged by attacks on the Hungarian experiment in the Soviet, East German, and Czechoslovak press until Gorbachev launched his *perestroika* and expressed a favorable attitude toward it. These debates also point out the breakdown of CMEA

in the wake of "Polish events" and the futility of expecting miracles from Hungary's admission to the International Monetary Fund and benevolent treatment by the World Bank unless the country's economy undergoes a long-overdue radical structural change enabling it to compete more effectively on the world market. The success of such a major enterprise, however, depends on the lasting improvement of climate and conditions of East-West trade, and this improvement in turn implies institutional changes in the political system not only in Hungary but in the Soviet Union as well. Whether in either case the process of pluralism, just barely begun, will be permitted to go beyond the open discussions of a single ruling party remains to be seen. In Hungary, the demand for political reform *and* a scrutiny of the role of individual freedom in socialist systems— articulated in János Kornai's presidential address at the European Economic Association's Copenhagen Congress of August 1987 (for its text, see *European Economic Review*, March 1988, pp. 233–267)—arose simultaneously as a culmination of years of piecemeal economic reforms that, after partial success, were followed by stagnation. In the Soviet Union, political "democratization" and radical change within the party seem to be prerequisites for economic dynamism. In both instances, a quantum leap forward appears to be needed to reach a higher plateau. The historian can only await developments in awe.

PART 2

CHINA

This section analyzes market reforms undertaken in the People's Republic of China since Mao Zedong's death in 1976. It includes Chinese and U.S. perspectives—four essays by economists and political scientists.

The market reforms undertaken by Deng Xiaoping are certainly as revolutionary a departure from established practice as were Mao's innovations of the 1950s and 1960s, and they have been considerably better received by the Chinese people. In the ten years since market reforms were first introduced in China in 1978, Beijing has decollectivized agriculture, encouraged private enterprise and foreign investment, and extended domestic consumer goods markets. Provoking even more controversy among conservatives, the Deng Xiaoping leadership has also begun to permit markets for producer goods (i.e., "means of production"), labor, and equities (ownership shares in companies)— all of which, from a Marxist point of view, raise serious questions about a potential exploitation of labor through the private ownership of means of production.[1]

The results to date have been impressive despite problems of inflation and growing international debt (estimated at $30 billion[2]). For example, the PRC currently leads the communist world in rate of economic growth and increase in food production (see Appendix),[3] and China has climbed in world trade rankings: During the period from 1973 to 1985, it moved from twentieth to fifteenth place in exports and from twenty-third to eleventh in imports.[4] Moreover, according to official figures, China during the five years 1983–1987 attracted $24 billion in foreign investment.[5] However, the reforms introduced so far have created a situation in which price adjustments "find it easy to move upward and hard to move downward," causing, by 1988, the highest inflation rate in China in forty years, and for many of China's urban population, a decline in living standards.[6] After a decade of averaging 9 percent growth in GNP, China in mid-1988 was attempting price reform, one of the most sensitive and difficult tasks in implementing market reforms. Already, one-third of the prices of *agricultural products and retail commodities were determined by supply and demand.[7]*

The 13th Congress of the CCP, held in Beijing from October 25 to November 1, 1987, chose a new party leadership headed by General Secretary Zhao Ziyang and comprised principally of younger reformers. Deng Xiaoping and several older leaders, many of them conservatives like Chen Yun, Peng Zhen, Hu Qiaomu, and Deng Liqun, retired from their posts, but Deng kept the key party-army post of chairman of the Military Affairs Commission.[8] Subsequently, the National People's Congress elected Li Peng premier, replacing Zhao Ziyang. Despite the sacking of Hu Yaobang (who had been general secretary and a major proponent of reform) in the campaign against "bourgeois liberalism," market reform policies were reconfirmed by the party; and Zhao Ziyang's report, endorsed by the congress, laid out an elaborate theoretical justification for the reforms, which included the proposition that China is currently in the "primary stage of socialism."

Market reforms and the opening to the West, taken together, are now claimed by the Chinese Communist Party to be one of the two most important strategic innovations made by the party since its founding in 1921. The first innovation was Mao's concept of "new democratic revolution," a design for making socialist revolution in a semicolonial and semifeudal Third World country, which was the theoretical basis for the CCP's successful strategy to overthrow the Kuomintang government in 1949.[9]

Both Mao's and Deng's innovations have been departures from classical Marxist-Leninist doctrine and justified on the basis of the need to apply theory to concrete conditions in order to produce a "socialism with Chinese characteristics." CCP General Secretary Zhao Ziyang, in his report to the 13th Party Congress, put it this way:

> *The integration of Marxism with practice in China has been going on for more than 60 years. During this time there have been two major historic leaps. The first took place during the new-democratic revolution, when the Chinese Communists, after repeated experimentation and learning by trial and error, found a way to make revolution based on China's particular conditions and led the revolution to victory. The second took place after the Third Plenary Session of the 11th Central Committee [in December 1978], when, having analyzed both the positive and negative experience of more than 30 years since the founding of the People's Republic and studied the experience of other countries and the world situation, the Chinese Communists found a way to build socialism with Chinese characteristics, thus ushering in a new period of socialist development in the country.[10]*

The implication of Zhao's argument is that just as Mao had to reject dogmatism and innovate in order to discover a way to make a successful revolution in China before 1949, so too must the CCP leadership now reject

Marxist-Leninist orthodoxy ("we shall not let ourselves be bound hand and foot by treating isolated theses from books as dogmas")[11] and carry out its controversial market socialist strategy in order to develop Chinese society. Similarly, both innovations came only after years of trial and error. Just as the CCP, after its founding in 1921, took twenty years to formulate a successful revolutionary strategy, so too was the correct line for socialist construction in China only discovered after three decades of trying inappropriate (the Soviet model) and even disastrous (the Great Leap and the Cultural Revolution) development strategies. But since initiating market reforms in 1978, the party has taken the correct path, according to Zhao; the strategic line of the Third Plenary meeting of the 11th Central Committee in 1978 has proven to be the right one.

This section on China opens with a chapter by Jiasheng Chen, a Chinese economist from Liaoning University, in which he presents an overview and a general evaluation of the history of market reforms in the socialist world. Chen begins with a brief history of market reforms attempted in different socialist countries, including the Soviet Union and Yugoslavia, and then focuses his analysis on China. He spells out the imperative for reform, in his view, identifying both the rationale and key dimensions of the structural changes undertaken in China.

Chapter 7 is an analysis of alternative strategies of socialist development, written by the late Satish Raichur, an economist, and Peter Van Ness, a political scientist, when they were colleagues at the University of Denver. Their objective is to assess the implications of the three main developmental approaches to socialist construction that have been attempted by Communist leaders so far. Using China as a case study, they first describe theoretically the three developmental strategies and then evaluate them as implemented in the PRC.

Stephen C. Thomas, author of Chapter 8 on human rights, is a professor of political science at the University of Colorado, Denver. Treating human rights broadly in terms of their social, economic, and political dimensions, Thomas evaluates China's performance with respect to established international standards and compares the PRC empirically with other developing countries. His analysis graphically demonstrates the implications for the individual citizen of the leadership's choice of developmental strategy and links changes in economic policy to social and political life.

Finally, Su Shaozhi was director of the Institute of Marxism-Leninism and Mao Zedong Thought, Chinese Academy of Social Sciences, when he wrote Chapter 9, but he was attacked during the campaign against "bourgeois liberalism" in 1987 and has since lost his directorship. Su analyzes the history of reforms in Hungary from the perspective of Marxist theory and comments on their successes and failures, paying special attention to lessons to be learned for China from the Hungarian experience.[12]

Notes

1. For discussion of the merits of establishing a stock exchange in socialist China, see two articles from *Wenhui bao*, translated in *Inside Mainland China*, December 1987, pp. 26–28; and *Beijing Review*, October 5, 1987, pp. 22–25.

2. *International Herald Tribune*, May 16, 1988, p. 9

3. For a brief analysis of China's economic performance since 1949, including the reforms since 1978, see Robert F. Dernberger, "Economic Policy and Performance," in Joint Economic Committee, U.S. Congress, *China's Economy Looks Toward the Year 2000*, vol. 1 (Washington, D.C.: U.S. Government Printing Office, 1986).

4. *International Trade 1985–1986* (Geneva: General Agreement on Tariffs and Trade, 1986), pp. 23–24.

5. *Beijing Review*, June 6–12, 1988, p. 26.

6. *Zhongguo shehui kexue*, 1987, no. 4, pp. 66–68, translated in *Inside Mainland China*, November 1987, pp. 28–30. China's retail price index (the best measure of inflation) increased an average of 7.3 percent annually during the period 1985-1987, and reached 11% in the first quarter of 1988. Louise do Rosario in *Far Eastern Economic Review*, March 10, 1988, pp. 53–55; and May 15, 1988, p. 12. Subsequently, the inflation rate went even higher. At the end of 1988, Robert Delfs reported: "China's inflation rate is expected to reach 20% by the end of the year. The cost of living for urban workers in 32 major cities is already 31% up on a year ago, the highest annual gain yet reported. On December 3, price controls were reimposed on 36 different food and consumer goods in Peking, and similar measures are anticipated in other major cities." *Far Eastern Economic Review*, December 15, 1988, p. 12.

7. Louise do Rosario in *Far Eastern Economic Review*, June 30, 1988, pp. 50–52.

8. Robert Delfs and Bob Hu in *Far Eastern Economic Review*, November 12, 1987, pp. 35–42. For an interpretation of political maneuvering behind the scenes in preparation for the congress, see Luo Bing in *Zheng ming*, November 1987, pp. 6–9.

9. The original version of Mao's "On New Democracy" is *Xin minzhuzhuyi lun* (Liberation association, 1940). Later versions, such as the one translated into English in the official *Selected Works of Mao Tse-tung* (Beijing: Foreign Languages Press, 1975), vol. II, have been substantially changed.

10. *Beijing Review*, November 9–15, 1987, p. xxv.

11. Ibid., p. xxvi.

12. See Nina P. Halpern, "Learning from Abroad: Chinese Views of the East European Economic Experience, January 1977–June 1981," *Modern China*, January 1985, pp. 77–109. Su Shaozhi also published in Chinese a series of articles on Hungarian reforms of the political system in *Shijie jingji daobao* (World Economic Herald), May 12, May 19, May 26, and June 2, 1986.

6

China's Market Reforms in Comparative Perspective

Jiasheng Chen

Overview of the Prereform Period

The 1960s and 1970s marked the beginning of a new era of economic reform in the Soviet Union, the Eastern European countries, and the People's Republic of China. Until this time, in almost all of these countries, the planning activities had been highly centralized, and production decisions were passed down to the industrial enterprises. Thus, one of the important features of economic reform was that it sought to decentralize the process of economic decisionmaking, and decentralization involved making restricted use of the market mechanism in the planned economy. However, the degree of decentralization varied among the socialist countries. Some that were either heavily dependent upon foreign trade or were already industrially advanced—like Hungary and Czechoslovakia—went furthest in the use of indirect economic levers. Others, like the Soviet Union, reduced the number of planned indicators to be used by enterprises, but made restricted use of the market mechanism.

The highly centralized Soviet economic system served as a model for all the newly emerged socialist states. This system played a positive role in the postwar or postliberation periods, allowing for quick economic rehabilitation and development, and in the socialist transformation of the private ownership of the means of production. Under the prereform model, once the plan targets had been fixed by the planning authorities, individual enterprises merely had to carry out the plan directives. All the plan indicators (gross output, assortment of goods, price, number of persons to be employed, the total wage bill, etc.) were fixed by the planning body. Raw materials and other immediate goods were also centrally allocated to individual enterprises.

But defects in the conventional socialist economic system became increasingly apparent after the basic completion of socialist transformation and the initial expansion in economic construction. Overcentralization was a major problem. Industrial enterprises lacked sufficient power to handle their personnel, financial, and material resources and also lacked guidance in production, procurement of supplies, and the marketing of products. Production and business operations were subjected to direct orders from administrative agencies, which controlled all the administrative measures. The ministries provided them with all their means of production and guaranteed purchase of all their products. It took almost all their income and paid for all of their expenses. Thus, the enterprises were appendages of the government administration. This put the enterprise in a passive position, fettering the initiative and creativity of both the enterprise managers and the workers. As a result, producers often overlooked the needs of consumers, with some products chronically in short supply, others overstocked, and enormous wastage.

Egalitarianism was another major defect, particularly in the Chinese case. In emphasizing mass equality—called "eating from the same big pot" in China—worker productivity and cost efficiency were ignored, with workers all paid almost equal wages. Such a practice, which seemed to be equal, in fact promoted inefficiency, laziness, and general apathy toward work. A basic principle of socialism is distribution according to work. Egalitarianism dampens workers' initiative and hinders the growth in production.

Overcentralization and misguided egalitarianism were the two most glaring defects in the prereform economic system. They demonstrated that a managerial reform implemented in a methodical way was essential for a socialist country's economic development.

The Soviet Union

Economic reforms in the post-Stalin period were introduced on an experimental basis in the consumer goods sector, especially in the clothing and footwear industries. Commenting upon the success of the experiments, the Soviet government indicated that the new system of planning and economic stimulation increased the workers' interest in the results of their work. In 1965, following the successful experimental reforms, the Soviet premier, announced a comprehensive set of economic reforms.

The main thrust of the reforms was aimed at the reduction in the number of enterprise targets and the replacement of gross output by sales as the prime indicator of an enterprise's success. An enterprise manager was now issued eight targets or indicators, compared with twenty or thirty in the pre-1965 period.[1] The eight targets given to an enterprise were as follows:

1. The volume and the value of goods to be sold
2. The main assortment of goods
3. The enterprise's wage funds
4. Its rate of profits and the level of cost accounting
5. Its payments into and allocations from the state budget

6. The volume of centralized capital investments and the putting into operation of production capacities and fixed assets
7. The main assignments for introducing new technology
8. The indices of materials and technical supplies

All other indices of economic activities were to be independently planned by the enterprises without endorsement from higher authorities.

The other important feature of the reform was that in matters of financing the enterprise investment, the importance of the state budget was reduced and that of the bank was increased. The bank now provided investment funds at differential rates of interest, a step taken primarily to reduce the role of budgetary grants as a source of investment finance and also to reduce the role of subsidies. The bank also sought to establish a production development fund, which was to consist of profits, depreciation, and returns from the sale of redundant equipment. An important departure from the previous practice was that the profitability of an enterprise was now calculated in relation to the efficiency of its use of capital and labor.

Along with managerial reform, came revision of industrial prices upward to allow many enterprises to be profitable under normal circumstances. A number of enterprises had been suffering losses because of the average branch cost pricing system set by the government. Thus, the industrial prices after 1967 were fixed to ensure a normal profit of 12–25 percent[2] on fixed and working capital and to fully cover the average branch cost of production. Though profits have always been a part of the Soviet managerial system, they were now given prominent position along with other indicators. For the enterprise managers, profit now became an important source of decentralized investment.

The new economic reforms were not without their shortcomings, however. These were mainly related to an unduly large share of bonus funds received by managerial personnel, lack of attention to labor productivity and product quality, and the unwillingness of managers to economize costs. Thus, between 1971 and 1973 the economic reforms were further revised.

The more flexible system of the enterprise incentive fund was replaced by a somewhat rigid one. The ministry, within the limits set by the state planning body, determined the size of the enterprise incentive fund by fixing its target. Thus, the actual size of various incentive funds was now dependent upon the fulfillment of output targets.

Strict controls were also placed over the distribution of incentive funds. Limits were placed on the rate of growth of managerial bonuses. Average wages were not to increase at a rate of growth faster than that of labor productivity. Bonus differentials among different branches were also regulated. Bonuses paid to the manager cadre were now tied to the fulfillment of sales and profitability plans and the material balance plan. The managers' control over the size of the production development fund was also curtailed, and six more indicators were added to the centrally planned targets. These related to labor productivity, gross output, material, fuel economy, quality targets, and consumer goods targets.

The initial impact of the economic reforms on the industrial enterprises was good. Many industrial units recorded increases in profits and sales turnover after adopting reforms. But during their implementation, many problems were encountered. For instance, many enterprises that adopted the new system, now had production plans consisting of fourteen indices instead of the previous eight.[3] These shortcomings are now being overcome through mergers of enterprises—called "associations"—under which a number of similar enterprises are combined and a single management team used for all. The major decisionmaking powers are vested in the socialist associations, the new middle level of management between the ministries and enterprises. The powers given to the enterprises under the 1965 reform are shifted to the associations. The main idea behind the mergers is that the associations will be better qualified than central planners and ministries to make planning and resource allocation decisions at the enterprise level because the associations will be closer to the source of information on which these decisions are based. However, very little information is available on this aspect to pass any judgment at this point.

Available data shows that the economic reforms have not enabled the Soviet Union to recapture the growth rates of the 1930s and 1940, and the Soviets are attempting to check the economic slide.

Under the rubric of *glasnost* and *perestroika*, even more fundamental reforms have been proposed. The momentum of the Soviet reform—which Soviet leader Mikhail Gorbachev has referred to as a "revolution without shots"—is unlikely to be reversed, even though its final outcome is as yet unclear.

Needless to say, the Soviet reform has prompted China to push ahead with its own structural changes. Undeniably, there remain between these two socialist countries conspicuous differences in economic conditions that would prevent China from simply copying what the Soviets do. But the Soviet comprehensive reform undoubtedly will give fresh impetus to China's reform effort because Soviet successes as well as failures have consequences for China.

First, the general plan for reform revealed at the 19th party conference of the CPSU in June–July 1988 indicates that the current reform is the most comprehensive ever attempted in the history of the Soviet Union. Although emphasis during the mid-1980s was mainly on deliberating reform policies and building public opinion to support the changes, the pace of reform has since quickened. In light of this, China should speed up the reorganization of its own economy to avoid being surpassed by the Soviet Union, a latecomer to reform.

Second, the Soviet leadership seems to have adopted a prudent and systematic approach toward the reform. Special attention is being attached to increasing production of agricultural items and consumer goods so as to ensure that the reform brings immediate material benefits to ordinary people, who in turn will voluntarily support the reform. This strategy is instructive for China, which has suffered from double-digit inflation, particularly in agricultural products.

Finally, the CPSU and especially Gorbachev, who masterminded the reform, enjoy prestige among the Soviet populace. An increasing number of administrative officials who have undergone professional retraining in management, science, and technology have sided with the reforms. China should parallel this experience by giving priority to investing in human capital. Only in this way can China continuously support its reform in the long run.

Yugoslavia

In Yugoslavia, reform has come in three distinct phases. The first period of reform (1950–1963) was initiated after the Yugoslav leadership recognized the inherent problems of the Soviet centralized model. In addition to inefficiency, mismanagement, and bureaucratization, the Yugoslavs were confronted with a unique cultural problem: Yugoslavia is a country of many nationalities, many of which traditionally have been at odds with one another. Therefore, overcentralization or overemphasis on one minority to the detriment of another were problems the government sought immediately to correct. Apart from these problems, the deterioration of the Soviet-Yugoslav relationship accelerated the course of the reform.

During the first period of reform, the policies were multifarious. The planning system and pricing system were both reformed, as was the management of income of enterprises. From 1954, enterprise income was no longer an item in the government financial budget.[4] Instead, a social investment fund (SIF) was created. It operated at the state, republic and district levels, channeling investment funds and bank loans to enterprises. Profits earned by the enterprise had to be divided between it and the district in which it was located. In 1958, a progressive income tax was assessed on enterprise income, with the remainder being used for accumulation and employee income. In 1961, a new income distribution system went into effect,[5] eliminating the progressive tax and replacing it with an income tax paid according to 155 different categories across and within industries. It became the enterprise's responsibility to support the social investment fund and the common reserve fund and to pay extra income tax. Remaining profit could be used at the enterprise's discretion. These reforms greatly elevated morale and subsequent productivity: the decade from 1953 to 1963 was the fastest development period in Yugoslav history.[6]

The second period of economic reform, from 1963 to 1971, brought an enlargement of autonomy and a release of financial power. Bank loans now became more important and were of a greater dollar amount than the social investment funds. Each republic was responsible for funding culture, education, sanitation, and so on. There was a simplified tax system, and no income tax or funds were turned over to the central government.[7]

Foreign trade and the foreign exchange control system were reformed. Foreign trade was emphasized, and Yugoslavia became an active participant in international organizations like the International Monetary Fund (IMF) and the World Bank. To promote exports, the devaluation of currency was necessary.

Price reforms were essential for the assignment of actual product value. Before price reforms took place, historical planned price—which provides an inaccurate reflection of enterprise management—was used for product valuation. After the unification of the exchange rate and a price freeze, the Yugoslavian government began to readjust the domestic price and abolished many kinds of price subsidies. The new price system was characterized by state supervision of prices set by autonomous enterprises—prices based on the principle of supply and demand. Finally, there was a restriction of consumption and an attempt to control inflation.

The third period of economic reform (since 1971) has established Yugoslavia's position as an effective and autonomous socialist economic system. There have been four major developments since 1971:

1. There was a revision of economic law and regulation. A new federal constitution act was unanimously adopted. Additionally, social plan law, labor law, and laws concerning banking, price, foreign exchange, and international trade were promulgated.
2. Combined and autonomous labor organizations were established.
3. The social autonomous planning system was adopted. The social plan was developed on the basis of an autonomous agreement signed by the producer, combined labor organizations, parliament, and other affected departments. The five-year plan (1981–1985) was established in this manner.
4. The final phase was the implementation of the stablized economic policy and the readjustment of the economic system.

Despite the reforms, problems still exist. There are weaknesses in the macroeconomic adjustment to decentralization. Mutual agreement, difficult to obtain, is needed to establish the autonomous social agreement and contract. Recently, with an increase in economic nationalism, each republic wants to become self-reliant. If implemented, this could have an adverse impact on commodity circulation. Another major problem is the disequilibrium of the economic structure. The present system is too dependent upon the importation of energy and raw materials; Yugoslavia must better utilize its abundant natural resources. Additionally, the growth rate of consumption and accumulation exceeds that of the national income. So far, Yugoslavia has been unable to procure sufficient capital to meet investment needs. Finally, there exists a need to reduce Yugoslavia's dependency on foreign trade, which accounts for 33 percent of national income. In fact, the country has a severe deficit in its balance of payments.

China

The crux of the reform lies in choosing the proper model to build a socialist economy, and the current economic management system needs a thorough reorganization and readjustment. This innovation has captured the attention of not only the Chinese people but also of their foreign friends.

Why Reform Was Necessary

The system of economic management in China is highly centralized, relying primarily on administrative methods of management. It was basically copied from the Soviet Union during the latter period of Stalin's leadership. China's experience over the past 35 years has revealed many defects in this model. These can be summed up in four separate aspects:

- Enterprises have become mere extensions of administrative organs at different levels, and their relative independence has been negated. Enterprises lacked initiative and were treated almost as abacus beads that could be moved to and fro by the central ministries and the administrative organs of the localities. It is not that the enterprises do not wish to have initiative, but rather the system restricts their initiative.
- Because the government manages the economy through administrative systems and divisions, intrinsic market relations within the economy were cut off. For example, the enterprises were administrated by the responsible governmental organs at the central or local levels, resulting in a predominance of vertical relationships and few horizontal relationships. This imbalance has been the cause of much irrationality.
- Too many targets in the economic plan are rigidly set by the higher authorities and handed down in the form of directives, so that producers and consumers do not contact each other directly. Production is not coordinated with marketing and is divorced from the consumers' needs. As a result, there is overstocking of many products that cannot be sold, while many other products in great demand are always in short supply.
- The enterprises have to turn over all revenues to the state, which also subsidized losses. Thus, the enterprises did not feel any economic responsibility and do not pay attention to economic results. As a result, egalitarianism is prevalent among the employees of enterprises—they are assured of their "iron rice bowls" and can "eat from the same big pot."

These defects made the economic structure wholly ineffective in mobilizing the enthusiasm and creativity of enterprises' workers and staff members. In addition, these flaws were detrimental to the goal of achieving modernization and to the effective management of Chinese economy. Under such a system, practically everything was included in a unified plan of the national economy, with the state having a monopoly on the purchase and marketing of commodities. The state is also responsible for arranging jobs for the labor force and was in charge of all revenues and expenditures.

This heavy involvement on the part of the state requires a highly centralized form of management that relied mainly on administrative means instead of economic means. With such an economic structure and managerial methods, socialist commodity production cannot develop rapidly. The sluggishness of the economy and the poor economic results are very much related to the defects in the present economic structure.

China has practiced this management style for such a long time because of an incorrect understanding of the nature of the socialist economy. In particular, China failed to consider the socialist economy as a planned economy in which commodity production and circulation exist. An essential characteristic of a socialist economy is a planned economy that is based on public ownership of the means of production. Emphatically, I hold that it is in a planned economy that socialist commodity production and exchange should be actively developed. The regulatory role of the market acts as a supplement that is brought into play in order to actively develop commodity production and exchange.

The Nature of Commodity Production in Socialism and Capitalism

Capitalist commodity production is established on the basis of private ownership and is unplanned; moreover, labor is considered to be a commodity, which leads to the existence of exploitative relations of production. A socialist economy, on the other hand, is established on the basis of public ownership of the means of production; commodity production and exchange are planned. But the question of commodity production under socialism has been a major subject of discussion for over a century and also a topic of debate among Marxists. In *The Critique of the Gotha Program*, written in 1875,[8] Marx referred to socialism as the initial stage of communism with vestiges of the old society still remaining. By the phrase "vestiges of the old society," Marx was mainly referring to the system of distribution of income according to work done. Marx at that time conceived of socialism as having no commodity or monetary relations because it would be established on the basis of a highly developed capitalist economy. Marx did not then foresee that countries with a moderate degree of capitalist development—or even a country such as China in which capitalism was only in its initial phase of development and the natural economy was still predominant—could also successfully carry out socialist revolution and build socialism. Socialist construction in an economically underdeveloped country requires that commodities and money be fully utilized. In other words, a socialist economy is a planned one that should actively develop commodity production and exchange.

In 1917, Lenin also advocated the abolition of commodities and money in a socialist society. After the victory of the October Revolution, the economic system known as war communism was adopted in the Soviet Union. It was related to the guiding theory of abolishing commodities and money. The attempt to abolish commodities and money during the period of war communism failed, and Lenin summed up the lessons of this experience. He put forward the New Economic Policy based on the fact that the Soviet Union's economy at that time was made up of five economic components, predominant among which was the small-commodity economy and small-scale production. The New Economic Policy was aimed at utilizing commodity and monetary relations to develop commerce and to promote the rehabilitation and development of the socialist economy. Unfortunately, Lenin died soon after transformation was completed under the leadership of Stalin, and only the socialist economic component remained. Under such conditions, the question was whether there should still be commodity production and exchange.

After the completion of agricultural collectivization, Stalin pointed out that two kinds of public ownership existed side by side,[9] that is, ownership by the whole people and collective ownership, and that there existed two classes, the workers and peasants—hence the need for exchange. But for a very long time after the completion of agricultural collectivization, Stalin did not clearly explain or prove whether the exchange between these two kinds of public ownership was commodity exchange or whether the law of value played any role. As a result, these questions were debated throughout this period in the Soviet Union. It was not until 1952, in his later years, that Stalin recognized that relations of commodity production and exhange existed between these two kinds of public ownership; he also held that the law of value should be utilized. But he maintained that the means of production are not commodities under the socialist system. IIc also emphasized time and again that commodity production and the role of the law of value should be restricted. One can say, therefore, that Stalin never considered the socialist economy to be a planned economy in which socialist commodity production and exchange should be actively developed.

In view of such a theory and understanding, the structure of economic management put into practice during Stalin's time was not designed to meet the requirements of the planned development of commodity production and exchange but rather the requirements of a "seminatural economy." The economic management system of the Soviet Union at that time did not treat products as commodities, nor was the principle of exchange at equal value implemented. Implemented instead was a system of mandatory planning that completely excluded the regulatory role of the market and a highly centralized system of management that relied principally on administrative methods. This system of planning by decree treated the national economy as if it were one big factory. But as things stand now, the economy is more complicated than a factory. It was found that viewing the whole national economy as one big factory gives rise to a multitude of problems. A highly centralized system of economic management has negated the relative independence of enterprises. The theory and practice of Stalin had a tremendous impact on China's socialist construction.

The system of economic management that has been implemented in China up to the present time has basically been patterned after Stalin's model, though there have of course been some changes. A number of aspects have been mentioned: a virtually all-inclusive state economy plan, state monopoly in the purchase and marketing of commodities, state responsibility for assignment of jobs, state responsibility over all revenues and expenditures, and the practice of "eating from the same pot." All these are basically a part of Stalin's model. If China can change this model, it should break through the trammels of erroneous or outmoded ideas.

The Chinese have already achieved a theoretical breakthrough in recognizing that not only the means of livelihood but also a large portion of the means of production are commodities under socialism. In addition, commodity exchanges occur both between state-owned enterprises and collectively owned establishments and within the state-owned sectors. China's recognition of these factors should be considered a significant achievement. Without such an understanding, ideas for how to reform the system cannot be developed.

Direction of the Reform

Economic reforms in China must proceed from the vantage point of wanting to develop China's productive forces and in the light of the characteristics of its socialist economy. To set the direction of the reform, let us focus on some major issues facing the economy and then draw on the experiences of foreign countries.

The salient features of the Chinese economy are its massive land, gigantic population, weak industrial foundation, low productivity, backward technology, imbalance among economic sectors, underdeveloped commodity production, and poor transportation and communication facilities. Because of this state of affairs, the reforms should focus primarily on the development of that part of the economy in which the state sector is to play a dominant role while coexisting with the other sectors, which include collectively owned enterprises and the individual economy. The following nine directions cover all the major issues:

1. First, in order to run such a system, one should integrate economic planning with the market, that is, rely primarily on the economic machinery and economic means to serve genuinely the interests of the state, of the collectives, and of the broad masses. For such a reform, an enterprise should be free from rigid state control and be treated as an independent economic entity that assumes responsibility for profits and losses. Enterprises should carry out their activities according to both social needs and the guidelines laid down in state plans

(although there is obviously a contradiction between making firms responsible for their own profits and losses, on the one hand, and expecting them to meet social needs, on the other).

2. National, regional and interregional economic organizations should be set up according to the principles of the division of labor and industrial interdependence. This will improve the shortcomings in the current economic system, in which enterprises are mutually exclusive, fragmented, and poorly coordinated.

3. China should expand the sector of commodity production and circulation and establish a unified market in which capital goods and consumer goods will be traded as commodities, except for a few necessities that will be rationed according to state plans.

4. Economic and trade centers should be set up where activities will be carried out according to intrinsic industrial interdependence, which is dictated by "expanded social reproduction" rather than according to administrative functions or geographical distribution.

5. China should reverse the existing planning practice that arbitrarily imposes production targets from the top and replace it with a planning system that integrates both the upper and the lower levels. Mandatory directives should be tempered by flexible guidelines.

6. Instead of relying on administrative control, China should use price, taxation, and monetary policy and other means to regulate economic activities.

7. Work discipline should be strictly enforced, economic legislation strengthened, and supervision tightened.

8. The party and the state organs should be relieved of their routine functions so they can focus on policy. Leave operations and decisionmaking to the enterprises with no party or state interference.

9. State control should be relaxed and some of the economic power should be delegated to regions that under state unified leadership are to be responsible for planning, implementing, and supervising economic activities. The factory management should be responsible to the worker's congress rather than to the factory party committee.

These nine factors constitute an organic whole. If and when they are incorporated and carried out in the reform, the economic system will encompass both the virtues of socialist planning and the merits of a market economy, for it will be primarily a centralized system and yet have no rigid control. Such a system can develop a socialist commodity economy and enhance the socialist productive forces.

How the Reforms in China Began

What has China done in the past years since the beginning of the economic reform? In the third plenary session of the 11th Central Committee of the

Chinese Communist Party, convened in December 1978, the Four Modernizations policy was initiated.

The reform began in the field of agriculture. The Third Plenum proposed a series of guidelines for changing the managerial system in the rural areas, including[10]

- respect for the property rights and decisionmaking powers of production teams
- adherence to the principle of "to each according to his work"
- restoration and protection of the commune members' private plots and household boundaries
- reopening of rural bazaars or free markets
- increase in state purchasing prices for farm and other agricultural by-products.

These measures were followed by introduction of the household responsibility system and other agricultural production contract arrangements.

Reforms in the managerial system in industry were also introduced, focusing on expanding the decisionmaking powers of the enterprises. The reforms were tried out on a limited number of enterprises and were then extended to others. Basically, these pilot enterprises were no longer required to turn over all their profits to the state,but by the same token they could not rely on the state to cover their expenses or even losses. Retaining a portion of their profits gave incentive to the staffs and workers, making them more conscious of the level and effectiveness of management, the market conditions, and the quality of their work. In 1979, the enterprises starting the experiment produced about 60 percent of the total industrial output value and delivered about 70 percent of the total profits.[11] The experiment brought about an increase in the income of the state, the enterprises, and the workers and better goal congruence among all three parties.

In an expanded pilot experiment, decisionmaking power was delegated to many enterprises. By the end of June 1980, the pilot enterprises in provinces and municipalities throughout the country had increased to 6600.[12] According to the statistics of 84 local enterprises in Sichuan Province, the output value for 1979 rose 14.9 percent and profit increased 33 percent compared with the previous year.[13]

Since the reinstatement of the market under state guidelines, the means of production traded as commodities have gradually found their way to the market, and more channels have opened up for consumer goods. In the past, capital goods were produced and distributed according to state plan; now they are freely produced and marketed after the planned target has been fulfilled. For example, steel turned out in 1979 over and above the planned target of 20 million tons was sold in the market. In 1979 alone, there were 600 new enterprises and 60 new trade centers that manufactured, marketed, and shipped capital goods for other enterprises.[14] It is estimated that capital goods worth over 3.5 billion yuan were traded in 1979.[15] Enterprises were even more active in producing and marketing consumer goods. According to these statistics, over 35 percent of the consumer goods were produced for and channeled through the market.

A new public finance system has been put into effect recently, according to which the state and the local government must delineate their respective revenues and expenditures, as well as their allocation of investment funds. This delineation of financial responsibilities between levels of administration, together with the profits retention incentive, has aroused the enthusiasm of both enterprises and local governments, cut expenditures, and raised revenues. The favorable development stems from separating the financial management of the different levels of administration and from retrenching expenditures while augmenting revenues. Many local governments took the initiative and transformed or closed down enterprises that long had incurred losses. All these improvements have strengthened financial management and enhanced the reform.

Some enterprises have begun to specialize while maintaining coordination with various affiliated factories and with the head office. In keeping with the principle of the division of labor, a number of provinces and cities have formed specialized corporations and multifunctional enterprises. Statistics from 17 provinces and cities indicate that from 1979 to 1982, over 1,000 specialized corporations were established.[16] This change has not only improved economic efficiency, but it has also fully tapped the potentials of individual provinces or cities.

On a trial basis, capital construction is being financed by bank loans rather than by free state appropriation. Construction projects in the experiment include light industry, commerce, and tourism. In the past, funds for capital construction were directly appropriated by the state, and neither the appropriating department nor the recipient department was responsible for profits or losses. As capital funds were freed, local government and enterprises competed for more funds, but they paid little attention to economizing in using the capital. Now, because investments are financed by bank loans, capital efficiency has been enhanced, and enterprises that borrow from banks are subject to the latter's supervision and auditing. For instance, the Shanghai Non-ferrous Rolling Metal Works, with a planned annual processing capacity of 10,000 tons of copper, applied for 6.85 million yuan to expand its capacity to 40,000 tons; the amount applied for was three times the actual need.[17] When bank loans replaced free state appropriation, the mill manager, concerned about the cost of the loan, took merely 2 million yuan. The planned capacity was met by technical innovations and a better utilization of the existing facilities.

Multitrade models have been developed and resources of different economic sectors have been pooled. Agricultural policy has been liberalized to suit the conditions of individual localities, especially the poor remote mountainous areas where production quotas were formerly fixed down to the production team or even to the individual household. The individual private economic transaction is now permissible. Collectively owned handicrafts, retail stores, restaurants, repair shops, and transportation and construction teams have been revived in cities. In addition, the reinstatement of individal handicraftsmen and peddlers has created many jobs, enlivened the market, and improved the people's livelihood.

In short, although the experiment only started in 1978, it has already broken loose from the shackles of the existing economic ststem, galvanized and stimulated the initiative of people in many areas, and motivated enterprises and workers to improve management and increase production. It has achieved favorable economic results, revived the whole economy, and paved the way for further reform.

Reform Possibilities in the Immediate Future

A comprehensive overhaul of the economic management system is an intricate and complex task. Chinese and foreign experiences suggest that reform can be carried out step by step only when the conditions are ripe. The current reform, which may last several years, should not be too hastily implemented. There were extensive and far-reaching initiatives attempted in China during the Great Leap Forward (1958–1960) the Cultural Revolution (1966–1976), but neither achieved satisfactory results. One of the reasons for the failure was a lack of preparation and planning. The old system was discarded before the new one was fully planned; thus reform was hastily put into effect. History teaches that a successful reform calls for great resolution, clear direction, good coordination, and phased-in progress in the right sequence. In the late 1980s, the economic reform in China has entered a crucial transition period. China should promptly set up the main objectives of the reform, identify the means to achieve this objective, and then persistently push the reform forward.

One objective of reform for the immediate future should be to continue improving the initial reforms. A major issue is how to coordinate the new measures, that have already been begun. So far, the experiment has been confined to delegating decisionmaking power to the enterprises—primarily the power to dispose of a portion of earned profits. From now on, an enterprise should be allowed to draft its own plan, market its product, and purchase materials and equipment, as well as develop the restructured and reoriented enterprises in light of the reform policy. It is necessary to create jointly operated enterprises and to encourage trades such as handicrafts, restaurants, repair shops, and other services, whether under collective ownership or private ownership. Correspondingly, China should open up more channels of circulation for both capital and consumer goods according to market supply and demand. Some of these goods should be under state uniform purchase and sale, some under planned trade, some under preferential treatment, and others freely traded.

China also should stress reforms of the price system, fiscal and monetary policy, and employment. The objective should be that they become economic levers so as to perform regulatory functions. Finally, state planning should be strengthened.

Pricing system. The prices of the means of production call for extensive readjustment. For example, some enterprises have earned profits because of efficient management, but others have earned profits as a result of irrational state pricing. To remove the cause of the unfair distribution of profits between enterprises and to encourage competition, a multitiered price system may be necessary.

Once reform of the economic management system is started, especially after market regulation occurs, the existing deviation of prices from actual values will not last for long. Therefore, the question of how China should manage the relation between price stability and price adjustment is central in pricing reforms. China must expedite the formulation of a series of specific policies to ensure that, provided prices for major livelihood means are basically stable, prices for other products (especially producer goods) can be adjusted accordingly. The price adjustments should not be handled exclusively by price departments. Experience shows that this task cannot be handled by such departments alone.

In addition, it is felt that price stability is very hard to maintain. The overall movements of prices after adjustments may be upward. Fluctuations in prices depend mainly on production development and the balance between money supply and social demand for money—that is, the balance between money supply and social supply of commodities. During the period 1958–1962, for example, the state's planning management was greatly strengthened, but because of declining agricultural output since 1959 and the 40 percent increase in the money supply, prices of agricultural products shot up. As a result, the state had to resolutely control prices over eighteen categories of major consumer goods. With the rise in agricultural output in 1962, prices in agricultural products fell back to normal.

Price adjustment is by no means an easy task. The deviation of prices from actual values has been accumulating since the mid-1950s. The extent of the needed price adjustment is very large. To a large degree, certain price adjustments will adversely affect the people's livelihood and the budgetary balance. Therefore, it is imperative that there must be a clear direction of price adjustments, and it is important to proceed gradually with the adjustments—starting with those that pose the least disruption to the people's livelihood and the budgetary balance.

Adjustments of producer goods prices affect the national economy and the people's livelihood most. These must be done very cautiously. For producer goods like coal or timber, the effects will be apparent in the production costs of most enterprises and most consumer goods. Coal is China's most important source of energy. Prices for coal in China are about 50 percent lower than the world market prices, and the coal industry as a whole manages only to cover costs or, at most, to turn a marginal profit. Close to half of the coal mines have experienced losses. It is imperative that the price of coal be raised.

But the steps toward increasing prices must be carefully arranged so as to avoid massive requests for general price increases. For lumber, the negotiated prices are so much higher than planned prices that lumber producers are reluctant to deliver lumber to the state for unified allocation. They want to sell it on their own. If the government forbids negotiated transactions, China will have problems obtaining wood furniture, building materials, and packaging for export products. These problems must be carefully handled by phasing in price adjustments.

Fiscal and Monetary Policy. Instead of continuing the earlier practice that required enterprises to turn over their revenues to the state, China should identify and impose an appropriate rate of profit taxes. This change will not only assure an enterprise a reasonable return on investment under normal conditions, but also provide the state and local governments with a steady and reliable flow of revenues. In addition, regarding monetary policy, China should maintain overall control but let banks finance an enterprise's capital investment, instead of the present direct allocation of construction funds and working capital by the state free of costs. In that case, banks would perform some functions of economic regulation.

Employment. China should adopt every measure feasible to create jobs, including projects to be organized by labor unions or labor departments and by self-employed individuals. Within the framework of the state plan for the work force, enterprises should be allowed to hire and discharge employees freely and thus foster competition.

To promote a market-oriented economy in socialist China, labor mobility is very important. In the past, the idea was forbidden, and nobody was comfortable mentioning it for fear of being criticized as an advocate of capitalism. However, various kinds of labor mobility have sprung up like mushrooms. Workers are anxious to be transferred from one post to another in search of different opportunities; this is beneficial to the reallocation of the productive factors that remain obviously scarce in China.

Before the introduction of the current economic reforms, China implemented a mandatory plan for the allocation of labor in different sectors according to the state's employment plan. Under such a system, once hired by a state-run enterprise, one became a permanently hired worker who could rely on the state for everything, including wages, medical care, pension, and even jobs for one's children. This primary characteristic of the traditional employment system, which was based on the highly centralized system, had a detrimental effect on the nation's economy. First, it caused the cost of production to rise and productivity to be lowered. Second, overstaffing weakened workers' motivation to work, dampening their willingness to upgrade their work skills. And third, an egalitarian income distribution among workers hindered the use of an incentive mechanism.

Under the nationwide reform program now under way, which has prompted demands for worker mobility, there is a chance to reorganize the labor assignment system in order to build a new reward structure better suited to a market-oriented economy in socialist China. The increase of workers hired on a contractual basis (rather than permanent employment) in state-run enterprises represents a first step in this reorganization. It helps improve enterprise management and greatly increases labor mobility. The contract system provides a choice for both workers and enterprises.

The introduction of competition accompanied by a contract system in state enterprises will require an overhaul of the employment system. Competition in the employment system will mean enterprises can select high-quality workers, and workers can choose to work for well-managed firms. Therefore, both management and the operation of enterprises are greatly enhanced. It is believed that the contract labor system adds to greater efficiency of the enterprise and will promote greater labor mobility and personnel management reform. Even the permanent workers who used to enjoy the benefits of egalitarianism are supposed to be subject to the new managerial rules designed for contract workers.

Theoretically, employment on a contract basis can motivate workers and create a labor force that best fits the needs of well-managed enterprises. For example, enterprises having inferior working conditions often find it hard to enlist workers, but with a contract system, they could attract high-quality workers by increasing wages. In contrast, contract workers in a poorly managed enterprise can either reasonably demand their contracts be renegotiated or decide to leave the factory once their contracts expire. This kind of mobility encourages managerial efficiency and improves working conditions. In practice, however, there is a juxtaposition of two employment systems (permanent employment as well as contract workers) within China's economy, and thus friction does occur.

To erase the distinction between the two types of labor, some factories began to manage contract workers much in the way permanent workers were treated. This was a step backward. In other factories, however, things were reversed: All of the contract and permanent workers were assigned to work posts strictly according to their skill level, and both types of workers awaiting assignments would have to measure up to the standard required for the job. Therefore, rewards and penalties were meted out to all. In this way, both contract workers and permanent employees must continuously upgrade their work skills.

The tremendous surplus of labor in China is a big obstacle to labor mobility. Surplus labor in urban enterprises has constituted the main obstacle to achieving labor mobility. There are some 30 million surplus workers in the urban areas—twice the total population of Australia. It is difficult to estimate the magnitude of the economic loss caused by such a situation. Apart from impeding productivity and efficiency, overstaffing in factories has been a major factor in preventing labor mobility from being put into effect. Unless the number of surplus workers is reduced, greater mobility will be impossible.

Solutions to such a problem are available. Surplus workers could be advised and encouraged to move into other business undertakings or acquire more professional training to upgrade their expertise. Only through such an arrangement will these workers be in a position to change themselves from being "extra" productive factors into qualified ones. The core of the problem lies in a sharp contradiction between overstaffed and understaffed industries. While millions of workers have nothing to do in some factories, other factories are suffering from a severe shortage of qualified employees. The sharpening of this conflict is most acute. In the final analysis, adjustment of workers among factories should be implemented. Obviously, surplus workers must be transferred to understaffed companies and firms, and practical ways to encourage such a flow of personnel should be developed.

I believe there are several feasible solutions for achieving a balanced work force distribution. The first is by creating—or expanding—differences in wages and benefits. For example, people who are employed by factories requiring heavy labor should be paid more than those working in other trades. They should have more bonuses, more subsidies, shorter hours, and more holidays. The second method would be to set up improved coordination among factories. Workers should not be hired on a permanent basis, and some should be induced to leave for more challenging jobs elsewhere when factories become obviously overstaffed. Third, more power should be given to factory managers to adjust the number of workers by themselves or through coordination with their counterparts. In short, the Chinese authorities must realize that it is high time to stimulate labor mobility and to stop using arbitrary measures in the handling of workers. Otherwise, how to promote worker mobility will remain a problem.

Strengthened state planning. With the expansion of a horizontal coordination of economic activities, a mandatory fulfillment of planned targets—the former vertical coordinator—will be reduced. Nevertheless, planning as a guide for economic activities will need to be strengthened in order to meet the demands of socialist large-scale production, to ensure proportional growth among various sectors of the economy, and to prevent anarchy in production and construction.

The state should focus its attention primarily on key objectives, such as attaining a comprehensive and overall balance in long-range plans, setting priorities for major construction projects, defining the scope and scale of capital investment, maintaining an adequate ratio among the different sectors of the economy, and raising the people's standard of living. In drafting short-run annual plans, four principal balances should be stressed: state budget, material supplies, bank credit, and foreign exchange. Using various economic measures, the state should provide guidance to enterprises so that they can carry out their activities within the planned framework. Once a long-range plan is drawn up, individual enterprises can each work out their annual plans on a contractual basis, from low levels all the way to the top, striking a balance on every level and reaching out for vertical integration. This system will certainly lead to a better integration between economic planning and the market.

Simultaneously, China should strengthen its statistical system, setting up information centers, creating data banks, and making accurate economic forecasts. Moreover, China should establish adequate machinery to better coordinate economic activities. All these aids are bound to strengthen, expand, and improve China's economic planning.

Conclusion

A proper handling of the relationship between economic planning and the market mechanism is crucial to China's managerial reform. To give full play to the supplementary role of the market as a regulator of the economy within the framework of a planned economy, different forms of management will be adopted. These will be based on the importance of different enterprises to the economy and to people's livelihood, the system of ownership, and the importance, variety, and specifications of their products.

Generally, some key enterprises and major products that are vital to the economy (like coal, steel, and machine building) should be maintained under mandatory state planning. Their output value accounts for the greater part of China's GNP, but the types of goods are limited. On the other hand, many other commodities are made by a large number of small enterprises and individual producers, but their output value is only a small percentage of GNP; it is therefore impossible to include all these goods under mandatory planning. Thus, the reformed system should combine mandatory planning for key industries with guidance planning for the rest, seeking to encourage the initiative of the smaller enterprises. Such a system would be different from both the rigid conventional system and the ideal-type market economy under capitalism.

Economic reform in China is an enormous task because of the large population, uneven economic development, and complications of a wide range of economic and political interests. However, the Chinese people are engaged in socialist modernization through experimenting and by reviewing their experiences. China's reforms are designed to develop the productive forces while maintaining the advantages of socialism.

Notes

1. *Sulian wenti yanjiu* [*Soviet Union Studies*], August 1983.
2. Li Zhong, "Managerial Reform in the Soviet Union," *Shijie jingji* [*World Economy*], July 19, 1982.

3. *Sulian wenti yanjiu*, August 1983.

4. *Studies on Economic Reformation in Yugoslavia* (Beijing: Foreign Languages Press, 1984), translated by Chang Dong Ming.

5. Ibid., p 79.

6. Ibid., p. 86.

7. Ibid., p. 95.

8. Karl Marx, *The Critique of the Gotha Program* (Beijing: People's Press, 1954), Chinese edition, pp. 86–88.

9. Josef Stalin, *Socialist Economic Problems in the Soviet Union* (Beijing: People's Press, 1955), Chinese language edition, pp 37–42.

10. Ren Tao et al., *Modernization—The Chinese Way* (Beijing: Beijing Review, 1983), p. 85.

11. Yu Guanyuan, ed., *China's Socialist Modernization* (Beijing: Foreign Language Press, 1984), p. 120.

12. Ibid., p. 323.

13. Ibid., p. 327.

14. Xu Dixin et al., *China's Search for Economic Growth* (Beijing: New World Press, 1982), pp. 77–84.

15. Ibid.

16. Li Yung, "The Strategy for China's Economy," *Jingji guanli* [*Management Review*], July 1983.

17. "Correspondence in Shanghai's Industrial Development," *Jingji pinglun* [*Economic Review*], March 1984, pp. 36–38.

7

Dilemmas of Socialist Development: An Analysis of Strategic Lines in China, 1949-1981

Peter Van Ness and Satish Raichur

. . . how to build this future—which is not something to be received by men, but is rather something to be created by them.

—Paulo Freire

The end is the means by which you achieve it. Today's step is tomorrow's life.

—Wilhelm Reich

Chairman Mao has been officially laid to rest, and the process of leadership transition begun at his death in 1976 appears to be largely completed. The Central Committee of the Chinese Communist Party at its meeting in June 1981, on the 60th anniversary of the Party's founding, both chose a new Party Chairman, Hu Yaobang, and approved a 35,000-word resolution evaluating Mao Zedong's contributions and mistakes during the period of his rule.[1] The new Deng Xiaoping leadership, comprised principally of Mao's opponents from the Cultural Revolution, has adopted a new design for development in China and has proposed new methods for achieving socialist construction. The time seems ripe for an evaluation of socialist development to date under the People's Republic of China.[2]

The purpose of this article is to identify, to describe, and to analyze the implications of the principal alternative strategic lines of socialist development which have been attempted in China during the first thirty-two years of the People's Republic, from 1949 to 1981. In our view, there have been three such

With the permission of the *Bulletin of Concerned Asian Scholars*, we reprint this essay by Peter Van Ness and Satish Raichur, drafted before Raichur's death in 1980, to place the analysis of market reforms within the context of Marxist debates about strategies of socialist development. The essay is an examination of Marxist theory and socialist practice in China up to the early years of the post-Mao reforms.

lines (*luxian*), each of them a distinctly different approach to socialist development conceived in terms of its own particular logic and basic theories, and implemented in China during a particular historical period. We have labelled them: Strategy A (the strategic design for the First Five Year Plan, 1953–57); Strategy B (the Great Leap Forward, 1958–60); and Strategy C (so far only partially implemented under the Four Modernizations, 1978–present).[3]

Each strategic line is familiar to students of comparative socialist development. Strategy A is the Stalinist model which emphasizes centralized bureaucratic planning and resource allocation, or what Western economists have called "command economy." Strategy B is a social mobilization approach, based on Party-directed mass movements to create a communist "new man." And Strategy C or "market socialism" is an effort to build a market mechanism into a socialist planned economy in order to increase productivity, to achieve greater economic efficiency, and to stimulate the initiative of workers and managers through material incentives.

In our judgment, the first two strategies have failed for different reasons as systematic attempts to achieve socialist construction in China, and the third is fundamentally flawed. We will try to explain how and why.

In the theoretical and comparative literature on socialist development, a number of authors, both Marxists and non-Marxists, have identified alternative strategies of socialist development approximately in terms of what we are calling Strategies A, B, and C. For example, Sweezy in his debate with Bettelheim[4] describes three alternative roads very similar to what we have found in the case of China. Another example is Eckstein.[5] Eckstein died before the Chinese leadership began systematically to implement a market-socialist strategy in 1978, but he, like Sweezy, identified the same three alternative approaches. Eckstein recognized, even in the readjustment and recovery from the Great Leap period in China, 1961–65, how decentralizing decision-making to production units, emphasizing material incentives, and increasing the scope of the market all seemed to fit together as one potential approach to socialist development—a market socialism approach (our Strategy C) which was later adopted by the Deng Xiaoping leadership in 1978 under the so-called Four Modernizations.

Clearly there are a number of parallels between the Chinese experience and that of other socialist countries. For example, the Soviet Union under Stalin attempted to impose Strategy A, the Stalinist model, on virtually all socialist countries that Moscow could influence; and, therefore, most socialist countries have had a significant experience with that strategic line. Regarding Strategy B, the social mobilization model, there are some striking parallels, for example, between Cuban policy during the period 1966–70 and China during the Great Leap Forward, 1958–60.[6] And, finally, the present Chinese leadership has been studying and emulating certain aspects of the Strategy C, the market socialism model, drawing on the experiences of Yugoslavia and Hungary.[7]

In order to maximize opportunities for cross-socialist country comparisons, when analyzing the Chinese experience, we will describe the three models which have been attempted in China in terms which could be applied to any other socialist society. See, for example, our Figure 7.1 and Table 7.2 below.

Franz Schurmann provides the best clue to the historical relationship among these three approaches to building socialism when he characterizes them as: centralization (Strategy A), decentralization II (Strategy B), and decentralization I (Strategy C).[8] As Schurmann's labels suggest, Strategies B and C—two different kinds of decentralization—are both reactions to an initial experience with Strategy A, the centralized Stalinist model. They are micro answers to problems created as a result of the macro preoccupations of Strategy A (stifling of initiative and enthusiasm at the production unit level, economic sector imbalance, low productivity of labor and capital, etc.). Strategy B, by means of social mobilization, proposes a more political solution to these problems; Strategy C, through use of the market and material incentives, suggests an economic solution. To our knowledge, the best descriptions of each of these general strategic lines which are available in English are: for Strategy A, Stalin's *Economic Problems of Socialism in the U.S.S.R.*;[9] for describing Strategy B, Mao Zedong's *A Critique of Soviet Economics*;[10] and, finally, with regard to Strategy C, a book by the Czech economic theorist of the "Prague Spring" in 1968, Ota Sik, *Plan and Market Under Socialism.*[11]

As an interpretation of China's development history, our analysis differs markedly from interpretations that have characterized PRC history in terms of "pendulum swings" alternating between radical and pragmatic phases, or, for example, from the Skinner and Winckler model (1969) which has interpreted PRC history as essentially cyclical, involving little or no qualitative change.[12] Our analysis also differs from those who interpret the Cultural Revolution period, 1966–76, as reflecting a significant departure in development strategy.[13] Instead, we argue that the Cultural Revolution is better understood as a struggle in the realm of so-called "superstructure," an intra-Party leadership conflict which became a mass movement in the years 1966–69 but which did not involve important innovations in development strategy.

Definition of Terms

We use the term strategic *line* to mean a conceptual model for development. It is a systematic design which spells out both the ends and the means for purposeful action. Strategic lines, if adopted by a ruling communist party, are implemented by specific development *policies*. If the policies are thought to be successful and if they are sustained over time, they create a particular *social system*, a social order and way of life which has its own characteristic division of labor, culture and social values, and form of political rule. Thus, the Strategy A line was successfully implemented in terms of the policies of the First Five Year Plan, which in turn created a social system in China characterized by a centralized, bureaucratic command economy. Subsequently, the mass mobilization line of Strategy B was attempted during 1958–60 under the policies of the Great Leap Forward and the communes, but it was never successfully implemented. In 1961–62, the basic policies were changed in order to reverse the economic downturn of 1959–61. Finally, the third alternative, Strategy C, the market socialism line, to date has only been partially implemented under the policies of the Four Modernizations, and the results so far are mixed.

The term *socialism* has been used in many different ways. For the purposes of this analysis, socialism is understood to be a process of basic societal transformation, a historical period of planned transformation from capitalism to communism, undertaken in a society ruled by a communist party. We assume that the various communist party leaders and planners will often have very different notions about what socialism in concrete terms means and what the central characteristics of socialism as a process of transformation should be, but they all agree that communism is the end and that all of them are trying to achieve it. Hence, proponents of different strategies of socialist development may disagree about the means, socialism; but we assume that they agree about the end, communism. Quite frankly, we feel that much of the debate concerning which communist party–ruled countries are "socialist" and which are not has been unproductive. One of the main reasons for our decision to define socialism as a process is to emphasize the importance of focusing on the direction of social change produced by the implementation of each of the three strategies as a basis for evaluating the different approaches.[14]

There is no textbook definition of *communism* in the classical Marxist literature. Here, we assume that the proponents of the various strategies of socialist development would all agree on a definition limited to three characteristics: ownership of the means of production, the process of production, and distribution—the less ambiguous characteristics of communist society. Hence, we define a communist society as one in which: 1) the means of production are owned by the whole people (e.g., in Mao Zedong's terms, the means of production have been redistributed to all the people); 2) the production process is fully socialized; and 3) distribution of that which is produced is on the basis of "need" rather than an individual's "work"—commodities are no longer produced for exchange but rather products are allocated on the basis of need. We will limit our definition to these characteristics. Communist party leaders and planners might well disagree about other defining characteristics of communism: for example, what level of social output in production is essential to provide the material basis of support for communist society; what the disappearance of social classes might mean in concrete terms; or what procedures would replace the state and perform the continuing necessary functions of organizing production, allocating that which is produced, and regulating social interaction in a communist society.

Finally, the debate—or, more accurately, the struggle—among proponents of the different strategic lines of socialist development is carried out within the conceptual context of Marxist economic theory. The advocates of all three different strategies of socialist development similarly conceive of the process of achieving communism as one requiring the concurrent development of both *forces of production* and *relations of production* in order to create the material conditions required for a transition from socialist to communist society. They identify the main contradictions in the socialist historical period as those between the forces of production and the relations of production, and between the superstructure and the economic base.[15] The forces of production have been defined as "the relation of society to the forces of nature, in contest with which it secures the material values it needs," and relations of production as "the relations of men to one another in the process of production."[16] The forces of production include labor, the means of production (land, tools or machinery, and raw materials), and technology. Relations of production essentially comprise the ownership of the means of production, the social organization or administration of production, and the distribution of that which is produced. In terms of Marxist theory, the two together (the forces of production and the relations of production) constitute the *economic base* or material foundation of any society. The *superstructure* of society, which includes government and other social institutions, legal systems, culture and ideology, is usually conceived of as a reflection of the economic base—i.e., the economic base of any society is thought largely to determine the structure of classes, government, and prevailing ideology.

Preliminary Comparisons: Theoretical and Historical

Figure 7.1 depicts the three strategies of socialist development in China in terms of the contradiction between relations of production and forces of production. Forces of production constitute the horizontal axis and are specified in terms of a continuum indicating changes in capacity to produce "use values" (i.e., the productive capacity of the economy) running from subsistence to affluence. Changes in relations of production, indicated on the vertical axis, are specified on the basis of the main characteristics of different kinds of societies: feudal, capitalist, and then classless society under communism. The northeast corner of Figure 7.1, toward which all three strategies are directed, is "communism."

The three strategies are compared in Figure 7.1. The pattern depicted for each strategic line represents *the logic* of the strategic design, *not necessarily the actual performance* of the strategy when it was implemented in China. Strategy A, implemented during the First Five Year Plan, 1953–57, conceived of a fairly linear relationship between the development of forces of production and relations of production. An initial period of sharp changes in relations of production (e.g., the takeover of state capitalist enterprises, the establishment of joint state-private enterprises, and the collectivization of agriculture) would be followed by

Relations of Production

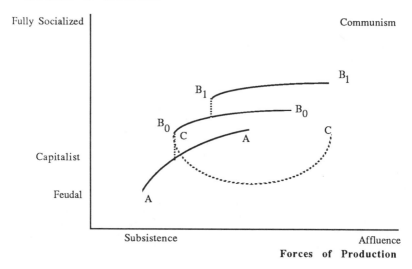

Figure 7.1   Strategies of Socialist Development: Compared in Terms of Relations of Production and Forces of Production

a consistent pattern of planned incremental changes—initially intended to cover three five-year plans, 1953–67—in both relations of production and forces of production moving toward communism. By contrast, Strategy B, Mao Zedong's design for the Great Leap Forward, 1958–60, sought to achieve qualitative leaps in relations of production as a part of a dialectical process leading to more rapid development of both relations of production and forces of production. During 1958, for example, the hope was often expressed that this approach could significantly shorten the road to communism. Finally, Strategy C, the present Four Modernizations development strategy, places great emphasis on the development of the forces of production or economic capacity through retrenchment with respect to relations of production (e.g., by seeking to combine market with plan, encouraging foreign private investment in China, and emphasizing individualized material work incentives). Although the characteristics of Strategy A and Strategy C are very different, the two strategic lines are similar in envisaging a continuous pattern of incremental change, rather than the dialectical pattern described by Strategy B.

Table 7.1 places the three strategies within the thirty-two year history of the People's Republic. It is our contention that the alternative approaches which we have labelled Strategies A, B, and C were the principal strategic lines of socialist development attempted during this time in China.

Table 7.1   Periods in PRC Economic History & Strategies of Development[18]

	Policies	Strategies
1949–52	Rehabilitation of the economy	
1953–57	First Five Year Plan	Strategy A
1958–60	Great Leap Forward and communes	Strategy B
1961–65	Readjustment and recovery	
1966–76	Great Proletarian Cultural Revolution	
1976–77	(CCP leadership transition: deaths of Zhou Enlai, Zhu De, and Mao Zedong; and defeat of the "Gang of Four")	
1978–present	Four Modernizations	Strategy C

The first period in the economic history of the PRC, 1949–52, was essentially a time of rehabilitation. For over a century (since the first Opium War in 1839–42), China had experienced the agonies of foreign invasion and domestic turmoil. Worst of all had been the Japanese invasion of China (1937–45) and the subsequent four years of civil war between the Guomindang government of President Chiang Kai-shek and the revolutionary movement led by the Chinese Communist Party. Once victorious in 1949, the CCP's principal tasks were to establish order under CCP rule, to resume production in industry and agriculture, and to carry out a basic land reform in the rural areas of China. As the prominent Chinese economist Xue Muqiao pointed out in a recent interpretation of the PRC's economic history, "By the end of 1952 the work of agrarian reform and economic recovery had been successfully completed."[17]

Having consolidated their regime and achieved a level of production comparable to pre-1949 peak years, the CCP leadership in 1953 was prepared to launch its first major effort to achieve socialist construction in China. This was the First Five Year Plan, 1953–57, and Strategy A. Although the Chinese leadership never completely copied the Stalinist strategic line (especially with regard to the collectivization of agriculture), many aspects of Strategy A were borrowed from Soviet theory and the U.S.S.R.'s development experience. Moreover, Soviet economic support and technological assistance were central factors in the design and success of the First Five Year Plan. Xue Muqiao, in his review of Chinese development, comments:

> In the First Five Year Plan we emulated the Soviet Union and implemented a policy of giving priority to the development of heavy industry. With the help of the Soviet Union, China carried out the construction of 156 key projects (mainly heavy industries) to lay the initial foundation for socialist industry, and the achievement was colossal.[19]

Although there was continuing debate in China regarding many aspects of this first effort at socialist development, it seems that all of China's top Party leaders agreed that it was the correct approach. Mao Zedong as well as the comrades with whom he would later disagree profoundly (e.g., Liu Shaoqi, Deng Xiaoping, and Peng Dehuai) all favored the Strategy A approach at that time.

By 1956, however, Mao with his speech, "On the Ten Major Relationships," began to press for an alternative approach. The Great leap Forward, 1958–60, and the people's communes constituted his design for achieving a faster transition to communism by employing an approach, Strategy B, built upon ideas proven to be successful during China's struggle against the Japanese during the Yan'an Period. Rejecting reliance on heavy industry, Mao called for simultaneous development of agriculture and industry to be combined with a massive social mobilization to release the productive energies of the Chinese people. A new kind of social organization, the people's commune, would be the vehicle for resolving the contradiction between China's two economies (the collective agricultural economy and state-owned industry) and serve as the institutional basis for the transition from socialism to communism. For Mao:

> The characteristic of the people's commune is that it is the basic level at which industry, agriculture, the military, education, and commerce are to be integrated in our social structure. . . . The commune is the best organizational form for carrying out the two transitions, from socialist (the present) to all-embracing public, and from all-embracing public to communist ownership. In the future, when the transitions have been completed, the commune will be the basic mechanism of communist society.[20]

The Great Leap failed. Publicly, three reasons were given: 1) natural disasters; 2) the abrupt cutoff of Soviet aid and the withdrawal of all Soviet technicians in the summer of 1960; and 3) a rather ambiguous category of organization and administrative problems having to do with the implementation of the Great Leap approach. During 1959–61, China experienced a decline in output comparable in magnitude to the American Great Depression of the 1930s—but in a country having a material standard of life which was only a fraction of that enjoyed in the United States. CIA economists estimate that China's agricultural production dropped thirty-one percent from the peak year of

1958 to the bottom of the economic decline in 1960. Industrial production is estimated to have dropped forty-two percent in just one year, from 1960 to 1961.[21] Such sharp economic reverses caused great hardship throughout China. Party policies sought to equalize food consumption among the population in order to avoid large-scale starvation.

The party leadership divided over its interpretation of what went wrong and what should be done. Most courageous among those who opposed Mao Zedong was Peng Dehuai, Defense Minister and longtime associate of Mao, who circulated a "letter of opinion" criticizing the Leap at the Lushan plenum of the CCP Central Committee in July 1959.[22] Mao subsequently attacked Peng, and the meeting passed a resolution dismissing him from office.

By 1961–62, the Party had agreed upon a number of expedient measures to readjust the economic system in order to halt the decline and to restore economic growth. These measures constituted a substantial retreat in relations of production from the surges in a communist direction attempted during the Great Leap Forward.[23] For example, in agriculture, the 25,000 large-scale communes of 1958–59 were reorganized into 75,000 smaller communes (about the size of the *xiang* or administrative village); the production team (approximately the size of a small village) was made the basic accounting unit; and peasants in the collective economy were once again permitted "private plots" on which to raise crops for household consumption and even for sale.[24] This structure of collectivized production has remained largely the same since 1962, in spite of efforts at different times during the decade from 1966 to 1976 to alter it.

The policies of readjustment during 1961–65 were successful, and economic recovery and the beginning of a general pattern of growth of output ensued. However, the consensus within the Party leadership that expedient policies should be undertaken in the short run to deal with the economic decline began to break down once a pattern of substantial economic growth had again been restored. Many CCP leaders had opposed Mao's Strategy B concept of development as early as 1955–56 when he first pressed for its implementation. After the collapse of the Great Leap and the extreme price that the Chinese people paid for its failure, presumably many others were determined not to permit another such experiment in social change in China. But Mao would not remain content with the status quo. Precisely at the time that the policies of economic readjustment were being formally adopted as Party doctrine, Mao Zedong sought to reverse the retreat from socialism in the relations of production and superstructure in China by launching a Socialist Education Campaign. By means of education and propaganda, the campaign was designed to build on the poor and lower-middle peasants in the countryside, revitalize the class struggle, and to press Chinese society once again in a communist direction.

Differences about the correct road for China's future came to a head in 1965 and 1966. The Great Proletarian Cultural Revolution became a struggle over policy and power, each side convinced that its approach to socialist construction was the best for China, and that the opposition's strategy would lead to disaster. In June 1966, Mao Zedong and Lin Biao, frustrated by Party obstruction and sabotage of their initiatives, turned the Cultural Revolution into a mass movement to remove their opponents from power. "Bombard the Headquarters" was their motto as student Red Guards besieged government and party offices. Mao, Chairman of the Chinese Communist Party, had gone to the streets to recapture control of his own party organization. Cadres at all levels were thrown out of office between 1966 and 1969, and head-of-state Liu Shaoqi and CCP General Secretary Deng Xiaoping were singled out as the most prominent "persons in authority taking the capitalist road." The Cultural Revolution focused largely on superstructure, and it had surprisingly little effect in reshaping the economic base of Chinese society.[25] It was a struggle which remained unresolved for ten years, 1966–76, and which resulted in no fundamental and consistent new direction with respect to Chinese development. Hence, for the purpose of this analysis, the Cultural Revolution does not represent a separate strategic line of socialist development.

The Ninth Party Congress in April 1969 seemed to signal at least a limited victory for the cultural revolutionaries, but it was followed by further struggles—especially between Mao and Lin Biao. Ultimately, Lin died under mysterious circumstances in a plane crash in September 1971, and was charged with having attempted a military coup d'etat.[26] Struggles within the Party over policy and power continued until Mao's death in September 1976.

Looking back over the period from the beginning of the Cultural Revolution in 1966 to Mao's death in 1976, the present leadership tends to lump together the entire decade as ten years lost to Cultural Revolution. The inconsistency of the policies implemented during this ten years is explained by some as due to virtually continuous struggles within the top Party leadership resulting in no agreement about a clear new strategy, and by others as reflecting popular resistance to policies that did not make any sense. In autumn 1979, Ye Jianying, in his speech celebrating the thirtieth anniversary of the founding of the People's Republic, analyzed the impact of the so-called Gang of Four and concluded: "In everything they did they set themselves against the overwhelming majority of the people in the Party and country." The ten years, according to Ye Jianying, were "an appalling catastrophe suffered by all our people."[27]

The traumatic year for China was 1976. First, in January, came the death of Premier Zhou Enlai, and later, in April, the Tian An Men demonstrations (sometimes called the April 5th Movement) in support of Premier Zhou and against the policies and power of Jiang Qing (Mao's wife), Zhang Chunqiao (a Deputy Premier), and others in the group which would later be called the Gang of Four. During the summer the old veteran and acting head-of-state Zhu De died, and one of the most destructive earthquakes in history killed 240,000 people in Tangshan. Finally, in September, Chairman Mao died, and the final stage in the process of leadership succession began. In October, the Gang of Four was arrested, and during the following year, a new leadership was formed around Hua Guofeng, supposedly chosen by Mao to succeed him; Ye Jianying, a veteran cadre closely linked to the military; and Deng Xiaoping, once again rehabilitated to become the mainstay of the new regime.

After the new leadership had consolidated its power in 1977, a new strategy of socialist development began to take shape. The Four Modernizations—a plan to turn China into a powerful socialist country with modern agriculture, industry, national defense, and science and technology by the year 2000—had its roots in Premier Zhou's report to the First Session of the Third National People's Congress in 1964 (before the Cultural Revolution) and the Fourth National People's Congress of January 1975. But the Four Modernizations as an approach to socialist construction was not duly adopted as policy until after the First and Second Sessions of the Fifth National People's Congress and the Third Plenum of the Eleventh Central Committee of the CCP—meetings held in 1978 and 1979. Even today, certain aspects of the strategy are still being debated in China, and much of what apparently had been decided has not yet been fully implemented.

Nonetheless, the general patterns of the new strategy are fairly clear. The Deng Xiaoping leadership has proposed a combination of market mechanism with state plan, more autonomy for production units, a strategy which overwhelmingly emphasizes the development of productive forces, and an appeal to workers based on greater material rewards and consumer benefits. In 1979, Zhao Ziyang, more recently elevated to the Standing Committee of the Party Politburo and the position of Premier, defined socialism as having two central principles: 1) public ownership of the means of production, and 2) distribution on the basis of "to each according to his work." "With these two principles as the prerequisites," Zhao Ziyang asserted, "we should adopt whatever system, structure, policy and method are most effective in promoting the development of the productive forces."[28] In other words, according to Zhao, if those two principles are kept inviolate, almost anything else might be attempted in China in an effort to develop the economy.

Logic and Implementation

Table 7.2 identifies the key differences among the three major strategies of socialist development which have been attempted in China. Our analysis will focus on comparing Strategy B and Strategy C, but let us begin with a brief description of Strategy A to set the scene in concrete terms for the subsequent discussion of the other two strategic lines. Rather than analyzing the separate dimensions of the strategies (i.e., reading Table 7.2 horizontally, across the three alternatives), we will emphasize the integration logic and how the separate dimensions fit into a logical whole as a strategy of development (i.e., reading down the three columns).

Table 7.2 Strategies of Socialist Development: Dimensions

	Strategy A	Strategy B	Strategy C
1. strategy focus:	social system (country-wide infrastructure)	individual ("new man")	production unit (management of enterprises)
2. structural point of policy emphasis:	center	intermediate level (commune in China)	production unit
3. economic base/superstructure emphasis:	relations of production & forces of production together	relations of production & superstructure	forces of production
4. economic sector emphasis (assuming that "balance" and integration of sectors is always important):	heavy industry	simultaneous development of industry & agriculture	agriculture and light industry (consumption emphasis)
5. strategy implementation:	plan	social mobilization within plan	plan-market combination
6. work incentive emphasis:	individual, material incentives	moral plus material incentives on group basis	individual, material incentives
7. international economic relations:	integration with Soviet Union and socialist camp economies	self-reliance[29]	integration into the world market economy
8. role of the communist party:	centralized rule from top down	social mobilizer in process of "continuous revolution"	contradiction between economic decentralization and party political power

Strategy A

The Chinese never fully adopted even those ideas that were proffered by the Soviets during the First Five Year Plan, so Strategy A in its implementation was always a mixture of Soviet advice and the dynamic of the CCP experience up to that point. Soviet influence was greatest in the heavy industry sector during the first ten years of the People's Republic, and pervasive as well in military organization and science and technology. However, in agriculture (from which seventy per cent of output was derived in 1949), the CCP kept its own counsel, and the success of the collectivization of Chinese agriculture between 1953 and 1956 was in no sense due to Soviet advice but was rather the result of tried and tested CCP mobilization strategies from pre-1949 and the initial land reform program.

As has been mentioned, the First Five Year Plan was originally intended as the first of three five-year plans, to be implemented in connection with a comprehensive program of Soviet economic and technological assistance to China. Soviet aid commitments were part of a combination of military security and assistance pacts negotiated by Chairman Mao himself in Moscow from December 1949 to February 1950. These negotiations came at a time when the Cold War was reaching fever pitch and only shortly before the outbreak of the Korean War in June 1950. Chinese intervention came in October-November to help defend North Korea after the United Nations forces crossed the 38th parallel in an American-led rollback operation. Already in June 1949, Mao Zedong had put forth the policy of "leaning to one side," cooperating with the socialist countries against the imperialists. By the end of 1950, the CCP had little alternative since the American reaction to the outbreak of the Korean War included efforts to clamp a global embargo on trade with the People's Republic and to isolate it diplomatically. The CCP had no choice after 1950 but to rely on their Soviet and East European comrades.

In this sense, Strategy A for China was an imposed system, especially as it affected heavy industry. The Soviet Union provided approximately $1.5 billion in credits to China during the 1950s, and thousands of Russians and East Europeans worked in China as technical advisers in positions critical to China's economic modernization.[30] Soviet planning concepts, patterns of industrial and scientific organization, and a wide variety of technologies had important influences in China during these years. Strategy A—a "command economy"—gave clear priority to developing central planning; it emphasized heavy industry in an effort to build a country-wide industrial infrastructure; and the strategic design was one which seemed to assure a roughly proportional concurrent development of relations of production and forces of production in the direction of communism (see Figure 7.1).

Initially, Strategy A was tremendously successful as a design for achieving economic growth and modernization. For example, during the five years from

1953 through 1957, industrial production increased by 128.6% and agricultural production by 24.8%. Heavy industry increased an annual average of 25.4% during these years, and light industry an annual average of 12.9%.[31]

Strategy B

By the mid-1950s, the international situation had changed. Stalin had died in March 1953, and a negotiated conclusion of the Korean War had been reached soon thereafter. Gradually China had broken out of the American-imposed diplomatic isolation, especially after the successful Bandung summit conference of Afro-Asian states in 1955. Domestically, the First Five Year Plan had been successful in laying the material foundations for socialist construction in China, and internationally, conditions were shifting, it seemed, in favor of the socialist camp. Prompted by the Soviet launching of the first earth satellite in October 1957, Sputnik I, Mao Zedong put forward a new interpretation of global politics using the metaphor of East Wind over the West Wind.[32]

By 1955–56, Mao had apparently concluded that the time was ripe for building socialism—socialism on a Chinese design fitted to China's concrete conditions—and that the Soviet-style First Five Year Plan should not be continued. Indeed high rates of economic growth and an immense development of heavy industry had been achieved, but at the same time, differences between mental and manual labor, city and countryside, and worker and peasant were growing greater. Building socialism for Mao was a dynamic, mass-participant process, not simply the imposition of a centralized social system which gave directions to the populace. It has been a working assumption among many American political scientists, especially since the Cultural Revolution, that the state system in China is fundamentally unstable. On the contrary, for Mao in the mid-1950s, the PRC state system was seen to be too stable, too centralized, too rigid, and too given to running the country by issuing commands from the center.

The logic of Strategy B, which in our view is best represented in the approach attempted during the Great Leap Forward, begins with a particular epistemology and emphasizes transforming individual citizens as both the means and the end of socialist construction. For example, compared with the logic of Strategy C or market socialism, Strategy B as a concept of socialist development is different in many fundamental ways, especially regarding epistemology or how one attempts to understand the world, assumptions about human motivation, and theories about how societies change.

The Strategy B approach, which is conceptually founded on dialectical materialism, begins with the proposition that contradictions exist in all things and that life should be understood as a dialectical process. There are "laws" which govern the evolution of human affairs, but these laws are different for the various countries because of the particularities of the concrete conditions of each. Thus, a strategy for socialist development (like a struggle for national liberation or any other purposeful collective action) must be undertaken as a process of discovery. No one knows in advance what the objective laws are. Hence, the correct strategy must be discovered through experience. According to Mao:

> At the beginning no one has knowledge. Foreknowledge has never existed. If you want to know the objective laws of the development of things and events you must go through the process of practice, adopt a Marxist-Leninist attitude, compare successes and failures, continually practicing and studying, going through multiple successes and failures; moreover, meticulous research must be performed. There is no other way to make one's own knowledge gradually conform to the laws. For those who see only victory but not defeat it will not be possible to know these laws.[33]

For Mao, "Human knowledge and the capability to transform nature have no limit."[34] We are limited only by our capacity to understand. Therefore, those who aspire to achieve socialist construction must work in the unknown to discover those laws of transformation which apply in the particular conditions of any country. Socialist transformation is not achieved by anyone's imposing a system. Transformation, by definition, is anti-system.

In Mao's view, the Chinese Communists would have to be as inventive and imaginative in designing strategies for socialist construction in a non-industrialized country as, for example, Marx was original in his analysis of capitalism in the middle of the 19th century. They would have to find ways of doing what had never been done before.

People must liberate themselves, Mao insisted—they must transform themselves. For example, land was not given to peasants in China during the period of land reform. Rather, under the leadership of the Party, they waged a class struggle to take the land away from the landlords. Mao argues that contradictions are the motive force in the development of socialism, and that "a thoroughgoing socialist revolution must advance along the three fronts of politics, economics, and ideology."[35] In his view, "no line of development is straight; it is wave or spiral shaped. . . . The development of all things is characterized by imbalance."[36] According to Mao Zedong, in a process of socialist construction, changes in relations of production must be closely linked to changes in forces of production, and the impact of superstructure is also important in creating the ideological and political bases for initiatives in the transformation of the economic base of the society.[37]

The Great Leap approach clearly draws on an analogy with the successful mass mobilization strategies of the Yan'an Period during the war against Japan. In socialist construction, as in waging revolutionary war, Mao assumes that the key to success is a motivated population. Party-led efforts to mobilize and to sustain support should be designed to tap the basic enthusiasm of the people through the implementation of the "mass line." It is not a matter of moral *versus* material incentives for Mao Zedong, but rather political mobilization to achieve greater collective efforts in which all will benefit. In terms of the logic of Strategy B, those who "serve the people" also serve themselves as the collective effort moves forward both relations of production and forces of production at an unprecedented rate. At a micro level, as has already been mentioned, the commune was for Mao the basic social unit of socialist transformation, and the creation of the "new man" in China was in a sense both the means and the ends of Strategy B. The success of the Maoist concept of socialist development during the Great Leap depended on individual Chinese making a commitment to work selflessly and energetically for the collective good. If such mass attitudes could be inculcated and such behavior sustained, both the productive energies needed to develop productive forces and the ideological and political prerequisites for communist society could be attained simultaneously.

Strategy C

Finally, let us turn to Strategy C, the market socialism approach.[38] Although there are a number of different thinkers contributing theory to the Four Modernizations strategy of socialist development (e.g., Chen Yun, Hu Qiaomu, Xue Muqiao, Deng Liqun, and Ma Hong) and there are some disagreements among them, it seems to us that the strategy as a general line is fairly clear and consistent. Moreover, Chinese economists confirm that the ideas underlying the Four Modernizations are largely in agreement with the theoretical argument made in Ota Sik's *Plan and Market Under Socialism*. Therefore, Sik can also be helpful in illuminating this approach.

The Strategy C concept seems to assume that the laws for the development of socialism are fairly well understood. Unlike Mao, who calls for *discovering* laws of development, Hu Qiaomu has written an important article calling upon the people of China to *observe* economic laws.[39]

In the minds of the theorists of Strategy C, these laws call for an overwhelming emphasis on the development of forces of production. They condemn the policies of the Great Leap as utopian and conceived on the basis of idealism rather than concrete materialist analyses of the potentialities of Chinese society. Unstated in their arguments—but clearly implied—is the understanding that to reconsolidate Chinese society after the ten lost years of Cultural Revolution, 1966–76, Chinese development strategy must make a short-term retreat from socialism in relations of production (see Figure 7.1) in order to get the economic system running efficiently after such prolonged dislocations—attributed to the Gang of Four (and Mao Zedong).

In order to increase efficiency and economic output, Strategy C calls for the combination of a market mechanism with state plan; the competition of production units within a given industry; much greater autonomy to be permitted to individual enterprises; and appeals to Chinese workers to produce more and better quality products in return for individual material rewards. The production unit is the focus of this strategy, and improving enterprise management is one of its principal tasks.

The pattern of development envisaged by Strategy C is continuous and incremental, not wave-like as in Strategy B, on the assumption that after certain levels in the development of productive forces are achieved, somehow changes in the relations of production moving sharply in a more communist direction would take place. One problem here is that there is no theory as yet spelling out how or why that would take place. On the contrary, Xue Muqiao, for example, is theorizing about how the collective economy should be expanded as one way of dealing with unemployment, rather than designing ways to transform the collective economy into the more socialist form of ownership by the whole people.[40]

Underlying Strategy C is the assumption that human beings are basically motivated by individual material interests, and that the best way to increase efficiency and productivity is to encourage competition among workers and enterprises through promises that those which produce most will be rewarded most. This, it would seem, is the main intended function of the market and the concept of distribution on the basis of "to each according to his work."[41] In evaluating the Four Modernizations approach as it is implemented in China, some of the central theoretical and empirical questions which should be considered, we think, are: 1) the role of "law of value" in both circulation and production; 2) treating means of production as "commodities" and what implications follow from that for the principle of public ownership of the means of production (especially in light of Mao's notion of the redistribution of the ownership of the means of production as one of the key elements in a process of socialist transformation); and 3) greater enterprise autonomy combined with distribution based on "to each according to his work" and their influences on worker income differentials, social stratification in Chinese society, and the politics and socialist consciousness of a socialist society.[42]

Finally, with regard to international economic relations, Strategy C calls for China to become integrated with the world market system for the purpose of gaining access to foreign capital and technology—in a manner parallel to international economic relations under Strategy A which call for integration with the economies of the U.S.S.R. and the socialist camp. Strategy A, "leaning to one side," is based on economic integration with the East; Strategy C, leaning toward the other side, seeks integration with the West. Both differ markedly in this regard from the "self-reliance" policy of Strategy B.[43] At year end 1981, international economic policies that were anathema under Mao Zedong's rule were being pursued by the Four Modernizations leadership: establishing joint ventures in China with multi-national corporations;[44] joining the International Monetary Fund and the World Bank, the two key multilateral institutions linking the capitalist industrialized countries with the Third World; accepting long-term foreign loans; building a tourist industry;[45] importing foreign consumer goods for sale to Chinese citizens; and sending thousands of Chinese students and scholars abroad for academic training in capitalist countries.

Implications and Evaluation: Dilemmas of Socialist Development

Only one of the three approaches to socialist construction considered here, Strategy A, has ever been completely implemented in China in the sense of a strategic *line* being translated into public *policies* which ultimately transform the structure of society into a particular kind of *social system*. In fact, in terms of its fundamental characteristics, the social system of China in 1982 was still that which was created during the First Five Year Plan, 1953–57: i.e., a centralized command economy, under the political regime of a "dictatorship of the proletariat." Hence, the evidence available is only sufficient for an empirical evaluation of Strategy A. With regard to Strategies B and C, we must rely more on the implications of the conceptual design and on evidence from the experiences of other socialist countries. For example, "market socialism" strategies have been implemented for a number of years in both Yugoslavia and Hungary. Evidence from the economic history of these two countries can suggest implications for the implementation of the Four Modernizations approach in China. To our knowledge, Strategy B, the mass mobilization line, has never been successfully implemented in any country. We will return to this point.

Strategy A

The successes of the Stalinist model in China were: 1) establishing an infrastructure for industrial development; 2) achieving high rates of economic growth, especially in heavy industry; and 3) bringing about significant social change, principally the nationalization of industry and the collectivization of agriculture.

With regard to the shortcomings of Strategy A, probably the most telling criticisms are those made by Mao Zedong and Ota Sik, both proponents of alternative development strategies.[46] Critics find that, economically, Strategy A: 1) produces economic sector imbalances and bottlenecks through its emphasis on heavy industry; 2) leads to irrational resource allocation and production priorities, because of the inefficiencies of administered allocation; 3) stifles the enthusiasm and initiative of workers and enterprise managers; and, over the long run, 4) leads to low rates of capital and labor productivity.

Politically, the critics say, the social system created by Strategy A becomes a dictatorship by the ruling communist party in the "new class" sense of Milovan Djilas[47] or what some Poles during the strikes of 1980–81 were calling the "red bourgeoisie."[48] Applying Lenin's *State and Revolution* to the analysis of socialist societies under Strategy A, one can argue that the communist party having established a "dictatorship of the proletariat" does not *own* but comes to *control* the means of production and emerges as a new ruling class, enjoying tremendous power through their centralized bureaucratic direction of the economy under state planning, and their formal monopoly of political power. As a result, the initial process of social transformation toward communist society begun under a Strategy A-type social system *stops*, because of the vested interest developed by the "new class" in the established order. In addition, it would seem that such a system has a tendency to stratify into privileged and less privileged groups, and to rigidify under bureaucratic rule.

If socialism is understood as we have defined it in this paper—i.e., as a process of basic societal transformation and a historical period of planned transition from capitalism to communism—then, under Strategy A, the term "socialist state" becomes a contradiction in terms. "Socialism" calls for basic social transformation, but the "state" stands for defense of the established order. Empirically, in contemporary history, it seems that the principal function of *any* state has been to preserve the established order, and those leaders who hold state power (including revolutionaries who have won state power by force) develop an interest in preserving that order which sustains them in power. From this perspective, it should not be surprising to find that in socialist societies, state officials and economic planners do not write theory of socialist transformation. Instead, they write designs for the development of productive forces—strategies to achieve wealth and power which do not threaten the established order. One wonders, therefore, how under a Strategy A social system there can ever be a successful *socialist* state in the sense of those who hold state power directing a process of basic social transformation which must ultimately undermine their own power.

Strategy B

In these terms, however, Strategy B is an exception. Of the three strategic lines, it is the only one designed to produce repeated attempts to achieve social transformation toward the communist-society ideal. Significantly, the communist party leaders who write Strategy B theory and call for mass mobilization strategies of development are the original leaders of the struggle for state power, men like Mao and Castro, who apparently retain in their minds a vision of the ideals for which the revolution was made in the first place, and for whom, unlike most of their Party comrades, achieving state power and the privileges that go with it are not enough.

Mao Zedong believed that the two objectives of social transformation (continuing fundamental change in the relations of production) and economic modernization (the rapid development of productive forces) were congruent objectives which could both most rapidly be achieved through strategies of social mobilization. Unlike the theory of Strategy C which conceives of a trade-off relationship between the two objectives at least in the short run (see Figure 7.1), Strategy B theory argues that the key to socialist development is to achieve both goals simultaneously by means of social mobilization.

In fact, however, the Great Leap line in China, 1958–60, failed to achieve *either* sustained social transformation *or* economic modernization. Instead, the Great Leap Forward resulted in a sharp economic downturn and widespread hardship for the Chinese people. Moreover, social mobilization strategies have never been successful in achieving both objectives over a sustained period of time in any other socialist country either.

In China after Mao's death, the prevailing view was obviously that the theoretical design of Strategy B was fundamentally wrong, that it was an "idealist" notion inappropriate to the objective conditions (the present stage of the development of productive forces) in China,[49] or even that it was a theory contrary to human nature. At least one senior member of the CCP has concluded that Mao Zedong "was never a Marxist."[50] Yet, Mao's concept of mass mobilization did indeed succeed as a strategy during the struggle for state power before 1949. Why did it fail as a design for socialist construction in the late 1950s?

In the critics' view, the Great Leap failed because the Chinese people would not support it. For example, some argue that the Yan'an analogy, which Mao invoked, was at best inappropriate. During the Yan'an Period, the Chinese people were fighting for their lives against invading Japanese, and later fighting to overthrow a corrupt and rapacious Guomindang government before it exterminated them. Radical solutions, they argue, were appropriate to the radical problems of the time. But by the later 1950s, conditions were very different. The people of China felt relatively secure from foreign attack and had become concerned with the more prosaic problems of increasing their material living standard, planning careers, and aspiring to brighter futures for their children. Radical policies of mobilization and continuous remobilization failed, therefore, to gain necessary popular support.

Another way of trying to understand the contrast between Mao's success during the struggle for state power and his failure during the Great Leap Forward might be to compare the importance of popular support for the CCP leadership before and after 1949. During the struggle for state power (both against the Japanese and the Guomindang government), the Party's survival was at stake. If the Party's mass mobilization policies were not successful in winning the support of the Chinese people, the CCP leadership as well as its followers would be destroyed. However, after gaining state power, the Maoist Party, although it still needed the support of the people it governed like any modern state leadership does, no longer depended to such a great extent on popular support for its own survival. Popular support as the critical test of the success of Party policies was no longer so important. Perhaps inevitably, Mao and the Party leadership became less responsive to the desires and demands of the Chinese people, and more likely to engage in "commandism"—ordering things done, rather than designing policies responsive to the people's concerns and requirements. In China today, people joke that Mao's approach after the mid-1950s was not so much based on the "mass movement" (*qunzhong yundong*), as "moving masses" (*yundong qunzhong*)—i.e., Party leaders manipulating the Chinese people for their own selfish purposes.

The actual reasons for the failure of the Great Leap and other Strategy B attempts remain, in our view, an open empirical question—a question of critical significance for the hope of socialist transformation under any of the established socialist systems in the world today. Empirical research in China and Cuba, for example, will have to determine the reasons for the failure to implement successfully the Strategy B approach to socialist development. We suggest, however, that the answer to this question should be sought not only in investigations of the appropriateness of the theory to existing conditions and the willingness of citizens to support policies of radical transformation, but also in research on the resistance and possible sabotage by a communist party "new class" fearful of losing its privileges and power.

Strategy C

As we have seen, advocates of the Strategy C approach criticize the inefficiencies of centralized state planning and the emphasis placed by the Stalinist model (Strategy A) on achieving rigid output quotas, arguing that such a system does not produce what is needed and desired by consumers and that the system stifles both workers' enthusiasm and managerial initiative. By combining socialist planning with a competitive market system, they say, a Strategy C approach can inspire enthusiasm among workers and managers, and reverse the pattern of low productivity and inefficiency. Enterprises should be required to compete against each other within the market, and they should earn material rewards on the basis of comparative efficiency and profitability. Workers, similarly, should be compensated for the quantity and quality of their work as measured by the market, thus directly linking production performance to material reward.[51]

The market is the heart of this design for socialist development. Moreover, a market is not something that can be turned on today and off tomorrow. It is a structural phenomenon which must be permitted to function according to its own dynamic in order to produce the promised economic benefits. The market mechanism is intended to reshape individual and institutional expectations and behaviors, and ultimately, the success or failure of Strategy C is dependent upon the implementation of a market mechanism.

Politically, it seems, especially from the experience in Yugoslavia, that under Strategy C, there arises an almost inevitable contradiction between the communist party's formal monopoly of political power and the economic power enjoyed by production units under this kind of decentralized economic system. Hence, the implementation of Strategy C would seem to challenge the customary notion of the communist party's leadership role under the "dictatorship of the proletariat." At the same time, however, Strategy C may provide the best available means to date of democratizing the Stalinist social system—the economic power of worker-managed enterprises increasingly cutting into the centralized political power of the Party. The struggle over implementing market socialism reforms in China during 1980 and 1981 seems to have been principally a struggle between Strategy A and Strategy C adherents—the advocates of Strategy A fearful, among other things, of the threat to the power of the Party and state center represented by Strategy C efforts to decentralize economic decision-making.[52]

Economically, market systems do seem, through competition, to force upon production units requirements for greater efficiency, and therefore, we should expect a fully implemented Strategy C to result in higher rates of productivity.[53] However, the incorporation of a market mechanism in a socialist planned economy can also lead to new problems for communist-party planners—especially inflation and unemployment. For example, Yugoslavia, the socialist country having the longest experience with market socialism, illustrates some of these problems. Yugoslavia registered a record balance of payments deficit in 1980, and was suffering from significant unemployment and a perennial foreign trade deficit. Furthermore, the September 1980 cost-of-living in that country was 35.8% higher than the 1979 average.[54] Reports from China in early 1981, where Strategy C has thus far only been partially implemented, indicate that the Deng Xiaoping leadership is reevaluating China's economic reforms because of similar problems: government budget deficits, inflation, overcommitment in contracts for major purchases of plant and equipment from abroad, and failure to complete successfully foreign plants in China or to bring them into production as designed.[55]

Ultimately, the central problem regarding Strategy C as an approach to socialist development, in our view, is that no matter how economically successful it may turn out to be, market socialism inevitably involves a serious reversal in the relations of production. It leads away from development toward communist society without offering any immediate prospect that these trends will be changed. To be blunt, Strategy C in both its domestic and international characteristics amounts to "taking the capitalist road."

Once implemented by government policies, the strategic line of market socialism creates its own particular kind of social system, through reshaping both the social structure and people's way of life. For Mao Zedong and many communists, the heart of socialist culture is the collective spirit represented in the slogan "serve the people." By contrast, the culture of a market system enjoins each to "serve thyself." Strategy C in its practical implications is not a design for socialist construction but rather a formula for restoring the central structural characteristic of a capitalist economic system, the market.

Notes

We are grateful to the following for their criticisms and suggestions for revision of earlier drafts of this paper: to members of the University of Denver's FGOD Seminar, especially Xu Ming and Huang Fanzhang; to participants in the Center for Chinese Studies Regional Seminar at the University of California, Berkeley, to which this paper was presented in March 1981, especially Irma Adelman and Laura Tyson; and to the reviewers for the *Bulletin of Concerned Asian Scholars*. In addition, we would like to thank the students over the years in our seminar on the Political Economy of the PRC with whom we have investigated most of the central problems addressed in this paper.

1. *Renmin ribao*, June 30 and July 1 and 2, 1981.
2. For comprehensive data on economic performance under the PRC, see the following sources: Joint Economic Committee, Congress of the United States, *Chinese Economy Post-Mao*, Vol. 1. (Washington, D.C.: U.S. Government Printing Office, 1978); the nine-volume study by the World Bank, *China; Socialist Economic Development*, June 1, 1981 (Report No. 3391-CHA) (*The Economist*, June 20, 1981, pp. 44–45 summarizes and comments on the World Bank report); and the annual reports of the PRC State Statistical Bureau on the economic performance of the previous year (e.g., "Communique on Fulfillment of China's 1981 National Economic Plan," *Beijing Review*, May 17, 1982, pp. 15–24).
3. Those years since 1949, other than the time periods specified here as representative of Strategies A, B, or C, were, as we will argue below, years of rehabilitation, readjustment, or intra-Party struggle. See Table 7.1 below.
4. Paul M. Sweezy and Charles Bettelheim, *On the Transition to Socialism* (New York: Monthly Review Press, 1971).
5. Alexander Eckstein, *China's Economic Revolution* (Cambridge: Cambridge University Press, 1977). For a somewhat different but provocative perspective, see also Charles E. Lindblom, *Politics and Markets* (New York: Basic Books, 1977).
6. See Carmelo Mesa-Lago, *Cuba in the 1970's* (Albuquerque; University of New Mexico Press, 1978), pp. 2–3.
7. For example, Luo Yuanzhen, Deputy Director of the Institute of World Economy of the Chinese Academy of Social Sciences, is head of a national society in China for the study of Yugoslav political economy, *Nansilafu Jingji Yanjiu Hui*.
8. Franz Schurmann, *Ideology and Organization in Communist China* (Berkeley; University of California Press, 1968 edition), pp. 175–178.
9. Beijing: Foreign Languages Press, 1972 (first published in 1952 in Russian).
10. Translated by Moss Roberts; New York: Monthly Review Pres, 1977. This is a collection of translations from *Mao Zedong sixiang wansui* (Long Live the Thought of Mao Zedong), 1967 and 1969. For concepts related to Strategy B, see also Mao, *On the Correct Handling of Contradictions Among the People* (Beijing: Foreign Languages Press, 1957); Mao, *Four Essays on Philosophy* (Beijing: Foreign Languages Press, 1966); and Stuart Schram (ed.), *Chairman Mao Talks to the People, Talks and Letters: 1956–1971* (New York: Pantheon, 1974).
11. Translated by Eleanor Wheeler; White Plains, New York, International Arts and Sciences Press, 1967. Regarding Strategy C and its justification and implementation in China, see also Xue Muqiao, *China's Socialist Economy* (Beijing: Foreign Languages Press, 1981).

12. G. William Skinner and Edwin A. Winckler, "Compliance Succession in Rural Communist China: A Cyclical Theory," in Amitai Etzioni (ed.), *A Sociological Reader on Complex Organizations* (New York: Holt, Rinehart, and Winston, 1969). See also, Andrew J. Nathan, "Policy Oscillations in the People's Republic of China: A Critique," and Edwin A. Winckler, "Policy Oscillations in the People's Republic of China: A Reply," both in *China Quarterly*, December 1976.

13. For example, see Suzanne Paine, "Balanced Development: Maoist Conception and Chinese Practice," *World Development*, 1976, No. 4, pp. 277–304; and David Mamo, "Mao's Model for Socialist Transition Reconsidered," *Modern China*, January 1981, pp. 55–81.

14. For a contemporary Chinese notion of treating socialism as a process, see Xue, *China's Socialist Economy*, p. viii.

15. For example, *ibid.*, pp. v–viii.

16. Stalin, *Economic Problems of Socialism in the U.S.S.R.* p. 64. Marx in *Critique of Political Economy* writes:

> In the social production of their life, men enter into definite relations that are indispensable and independent of their will, relations of production which correspond to a definite stage of development of their material productive forces. The sum total of these relations of production constitutes the economic structure of society, the real foundation, on which rises a legal and political superstructure and to which correspond definite forms of social consciousness. The mode of production of material life conditions the social, political, and intellectual life process in general. It is not the consciousness of men that determines their being, but, on the contrary, their social being that determines their consciousness. At a certain stage of their development, the material productive forces of society come in conflict with the existing relations of production, or—what is but a legal expression for the same thing—with the property relations within which they have been at work hitherto. From forms of development of the productive forces these relations turn into their fetters. Then begins an epoch of social revolution. With the change of the economic foundations the entire immense superstructure is more or less rapidly transformed.

David McLellan, *Karl Marx: Selected Writings* (London: Oxford University Press, 1977), p. 389.

17. Xue Muqiao, "Thirty Years of Hardship in Building Our Country," *Hongqi*, 1979, No. 10, p. 40.

18. See footnote number 3.

19. Xue, "Thirty Years," P. 44.

20. Mao, *A Critique of Soviet Economics*, p. 134. For further discussion of Chinese hopes for the commune during this period, see the documents collected in Robert R. Bowie and John K. Fairbank, *Communist China 1955–1959: Policy Documents with Analysis* (Cambridge: Harvard University Pres, 1965), pp. 389–529. See also, "Sixty Points on Working Methods—A Draft Resolution from the Office of the Centre of the CCP," (London: Oxford University Press, 1970), pp. 57–76. And, finally, for internal criticism of the communes and the Great Leap, especially from Peng Dehuai, and the discussion surrounding it, see Union Research Institute, *The Case of Peng Teh-Huai 1959–1968* (Hong Kong: Union Research Institute, 1968,.

21. Joint Economic Committee, Congress of the US, *Chinese Economy Post-Mao*, p. 208.

22. Union Research Institute, *Case of Peng Teh-Huai*, pp. 7–13.

23. See the seventy articles regarding industrial policy and the sixty

regulations for the people's communes in *Documents of the Chinese Communist Party Central Committee, September 1956–April 1969* (Hong Kong: Union Research Institute, 1971), pp. 689–725.

24. James Townsend, *Politics in China* (Boston: Little, Brown, 1980). Table 1, pp. 120–121.

25. However, the Cultural Revolution did have some impact on the economic base in some parts of China in the following ways: some factories were sent to the countryside; some collectives in the cities, especially in service industries (e.g., restaurants and laundries), were put under state ownership; in some rural areas, attempts were made to make the brigade rather than the team the basic accounting unit; and the policies of "politics in command" in both industry and agriculture sometimes reshaped the organization of production and patterns of distribution. For example, Parish and Whyte in their study of rural Guangdong Province found significant changes undertaken beginning in 1968–69 due to implementation of the Dazhai work-point system and a different system for the distribution of grain. William L. Parish and Martin King Whyte, *Village and Family in Contemporary China* (Chicago: University of Chicago Press, 1978), pp. 63–66.

26. See Michael Y. M. Kau (ed.), *The Lin Piao Affair: Power Politics and Military Coup* (White Plains, New York: International Arts and Sciences Press, 1975); and, more recently, *Beijing Review*, December 22, 1980, pp. 19–28.

27. *Beijing Review*, October 5, 1979, p. 19.

28. *Beijing Review*, November 23, 1979, p. 3.

29. The Great Leap Forward did not begin with an emphasis on self-reliance in 1958. Self-reliance was only adopted as policy later, after 1960 when the Soviets cut off their aid to China. Nonetheless, theoretically, self-reliance fits very well the general logic of a Strategy B approach to socialist development.

30. John Gittings, *Survey of the Sino-Soviet Dispute: A Commentary and Extracts from the Recent Polemics, 1963–67* (London: Oxford University Press, 1968), pp. 130–132.

31. Xue Muqiao, "Thirty Years Of Hardship," p. 44.

32. Donald S. Zagoria, *The Sino-Soviet Conflict, 1956–1961* (Princeton: Princeton University Press, 1962), Chapters 4 and 5.

33. Mao, *Critique of Soviet Economics*, p. 72.

34. *Ibid.*, p. 137.

35. *Ibid.*, p. 48.

36. *Ibid.*, p. 80.

37. *Ibid.*, pp. 67–68.

38. It should be noted that a number of socialist countries are presently experimenting with varieties of the Strategy C model, including Vietnam. See, for example, *Far Eastern Economic Review*, February 27–March 5, 1981, pp. 28–34; and June 19, 1981, pp. 56–57.

39. "Observe Economic laws, Speed Up the Four Modernizations," (a three-part article) appearing in *Peking Review*, November 10, 17, and 24, 1978. Some other useful Chinese-language sources for identifying the basic ideas of Strategy C in China are: Xue Muqiao, *Shehuizhuyi jingji lilun wenti* (Theoretical Problems of Socialist Economy) (Beijing: People's Publishers, 1979); Ma Hong, "The Reform of the System of Economic Management and the Expansion of Enterprise Autonomy," *Hongqi*, 1979, No. 10, pp. 5–58; and Deng Liqun, *Tantan Jihua tiaojie he shichang* (A Discussion on Planning Regulation and Market Regulation) (Beijing: People's Publishers, 1979).

40. *Renmin ribao*, July 20, 1979, p. 2.

41. See, for example, "Implementing the Socialist Principle 'To Each

According to His Work,'" *Peking Review*, August 4 and 18, 1978. One Chinese economist, Huang Fanzhang, has suggested that the market mechanism and "consumers' sovereignty" should be central elements in a socialist economy in order to mediate the different economic interests which inevitably would develop among different enterprises and individuals. The market, according to Huang, would permit those who serve China's consumers better to earn more, and those who serve badly to earn less. Moreover, such a mechanism would encourage Chinese producers in the aggregate to be more productive and efficient. Huang Fanzhang, "Comment on 'Consumers' Sovereignty,'" *Jingji guanli* (Economic Management), 1979, No. 2, pp. 25–27.

42. Irma Adelman, for example, has commented that based on her investigations of other economic systems, she could not see how a successful implementation of Strategy C could avoid increasing income inequality at least in the short run (comment at the Center for Chinese Studies Regional Seminar, University of California, Berkeley, March 21, 1981).

43. See Peter Van Ness, "China and the Third World," *Current History*, September 1974, pp. 106–109 and 133.

44. *Beijing Review* of April 5, 1982 (p. 11) reports: "More than 1,000 joint ventures and co-operative and compensatory trade items with foreign businesses, totalling 2,900 million US dollars in investment, have been approved by the Chinese Government since the adoption of the open-door policy and the promulgation in 1979 of the Law Governing Joint Ventures with Chinese and Foreign Investments."

45. China's State Statistical Bureau reports that during the year 1981: "The total number of foreigners, overseas Chinese and Chinese compatriots from Xianggang (Hong Kong) and Aomen (Macao) coming on tours and visits and for trade, sports, scientific and cultural exchanges reached 7,677,000, a 36.2 percent increase over the previous year. Included were 675,000 foreign tourists, a 27.6 percent rise over 1980. Annual foreign exchange income was 1,380 million yuan Renminbi, 49.7 percent increase over 1980." *Beijing Review*, May 17, 1982, p. 22.

46. Ota Sik's *Plan and Market Under Socialism* contains the most thorough critique of the economics of the Stalinist model that we are aware of. However, it is important to note that given certain historical conditions, Strategy A does seem to provide very substantial economic benefits for a time. See, for example, Sik's distinction between "extensive" and "intensive" development of production (pp. 49–51).

47. Milovan Djilas, *The New Class: An Analysis of the Communist System* (New York: Praeger, 1957).

48. *New York Times*, September 5, 1980.

49. For a parallel critique of Strategy B in general terms, see Ota Sik, *Plan and Market*, pp. 361–364.

50. Personal conversation in Beijing, December 1980.

51. For a good example of Strategy C reforms in both theory and practice, see the articles describing changes undertaken in 417 enterprises in Sichuan Province, in *Beijing Review*, April 6, 1981, pp. 21–29. See also: Nicholas H. Ludlow, "Who's the Boss? After Ten Years They Still Don't Know," *China Business Review*, January-February 1981, pp. 14–16; and Thomas H. Pyle, "Reforming Chinese Management," *China Business Review*, May-June 1981, pp. 7–19. Regarding agriculture, see David Bonavia, "China Rediscovers the Family Farm," *Far Eastern Economic Review*, June 19, 1981, pp. 56–57.

52. See, for example, Martin Weil, "The Collapse of Construction Projects," *China Business Review*, January–February 1981, pp. 9–13.

53. Xue Muqiao writes that in China, "Six times more workers are needed in light industry and 11 times more in heavy industry to produce the same quantities of goods as in developed capitalist countries" (*China's Socialist Economy*, p. 201). Xue argues that "The transition from socialism to communism requires a level of productive forces much higher than what is already attained in developed capitalist countries. . . . If we fail to develop the productive forces or raise our labour productivity much higher than that under capitalism, the final victory of communism will be out of the question" (p. 307).

54. Associated Press in *Rocky Mountain News*, October 31, 1980, p. 75.

55. By the end of 1980, Strategy C reforms had been undertaken in 6,600 enterprises in the state-owned economy in China which together in 1980 accounted for sixty percent of total industrial output value and seventy percent of profits turned over to the state. However, because of problems arising from the effort to implement a Strategy C model, the Deng Xiaoping leadership decided at a December 1980 work conference of the CCP Central Committee not to extend the reforms. Instead of "reform," it was decided that "readjustment" would be the central task of the Sixth Five Year Plan (1981–85). For a summary, see *Beijing Review*, May 11, 1981, p. 3.

8

Market Reforms and Human Rights in China

Stephen C. Thomas

Beginning in 1979, three years after the death of Communist Party Chairman Mao Zedong and the end of the Cultural Revolution, post-Mao leaders of the People's Republic of China initiated new economic and political policies that constitute the most comprehensive reforms in China since 1949. Economic reforms include establishing a "responsibility system" that effectively decollectivizes agriculture, permitting small-scale free enterprise, emphasizing consumer goods, opening China to foreign technology and investment, and establishing market reforms—the subject of this book. China has also developed significant political reforms in support of its economic reforms: writing a new constitution (1982), passing new criminal and legal procedure codes, reopening and expanding law schools, and re-establishing a key role in Chinese society for scientists and intellectuals.

What have been the effects of market reforms on China's human rights policies? To answer, I will first describe China's human rights performance until 1979, using the categories set forth in the 1966 International Covenants on Social, Economic and Cultural Rights and on Civil and Political Rights. Next, I will describe how Chinese human rights policies and practices have been affected by China's efforts to achieve market socialism. Finally, I will suggest directions that Chinese human rights policies may take in the future.

The two 1966 covenants each contain separate areas of human rights. The Covenant on Civil and Political Rights, of most interest to non-socialist countries, include freedom of the press, freedom of speech, freedom of association, freedom to travel, freedom from arbitrary detention, and the right to equal treatment before the law. The Covenant on Social, Economic and Cultural Rights is most often focused on in socialist countries; it includes the rights to health care, education, employment, housing, and a cultural life. In the next section, I will describe China's performance in social and economic rights before and since the market reforms of 1979.

Social and Economic Achievements, 1949–1978

In 1949, China was one of the poorest countries in the world with a per capita income of about U.S. $50 and a life expectancy of about 36 years.[1] Chinese Communist Party leaders came to power committed to providing at least minimum levels of health, education, housing, and access to employment. They also established a relatively egalitarian distribution of income and a pricing structure that placed basic needs within the economic reach of most Chinese.

To carry out socialist development and pay for social and economic programs, China's leaders adopted a Soviet-style centrally directed economy aimed at rapid development of heavy industry through high levels of investment. They also carried out land reform, moved toward creation of socialist relations of production, and worked to raise China's levels of science and technology to world standards. The World Bank reported that by 1979, despite fluctuations in policy and major disasters such as the Great Leap Forward (1958–1959), the average annual growth of China's gross national product was about 5 percent, 3 percent per capita, from 1957 to 1979.[2] By 1979, China had achieved a level of income of about $256 per capita.[3]

China's per capita growth rate compared favorably with most of the least developed countries in the world, particularly large and complex societies such as India.[4] Also, although almost all other poor Third World countries had accumulated soaring and burdensome foreign debts in the course of their economic development efforts, until 1979 China had developed without foreign investment or long-term foreign debt. China had even granted foreign aid to other less developed countries, mostly in Africa. China's economic development policies were all the more impressive as they were based on agricultural production in a country with one of the world's lowest cultivated land to population ratios. At about 0.12 hectares per capita, China had one-third the per capita cultivated land of India, one-half of Japan's, and less even than that of Bangladesh.[5]

China's Social and Economic Rights Performance

Article 6 of the 1966 International Covenant of Social, Economic and Cultural Rights lists the first right—the right to work. The Chinese constitution, like that of the Soviet Union and virtually every other socialist country, guarantees everyone the right to work, but also requires it. From 1949 to 1978, China's urban underemployment and unemployment were greatly reduced through jobs created by high levels of investment in industrialization and controlled urban migration. In the countryside, collective work organizations such as the communes included all rural dwellers.

Article 7 contains the rights to enjoyment of just and favorable conditions of work, to equal remuneration for work of equal value, to a decent standard of living, and to rest and leisure, including reasonable limitation of working hours and periodic holidays with pay. Labor rights seem to have been well protected from 1949 to 1978, with wages of urban workers supported through subsidization of basic needs (food, housing, heating, clothing, medical care) and consumption levels of the much poorer rural peasants protected by collective structures that assured access to at least a minimum level of food (through the "basic consumption grain" allotment) and to other basic needs.

Chinese in urban areas worked a six-day week, not counting time spent in political meetings. They were guaranteed a daily rest period of one to two hours and they had seven vacation days per year (Labor Day on May 1, National Day on October 1, two days for Chinese New Year, and three days for Spring Festival). Although equal pay between the sexes was guaranteed, in practice women were often denied more-skilled and higher-paying jobs and therefore had lower wages as a group. Although salary scales varied as much as 100 percent between different provinces, the central government adjusted prices of industrial goods and agricultural products to decrease inequalities. Interprovincial and urban-rural inequalities were also reduced through subsidies and allocation of new investment to poorer provinces and rural areas.

Article 8 sets out trade union rights. Trade union membership was available for Chinese workers except during the 1966 to 1976 Cultural Revolution, when unions were virtually abolished. Although Mao Zedong allowed for the right to strike in the 1975 Chinese constitution (a right lost in the 1982 Constitution), membership in trade unions in socialist countries including China was more for labor mobilization and for management of employment benefits than for improving labor conditions.

Article 9 provides the right to social security. In theory, all Chinese had a form of social security based on membership in their *danwei*, or work unit. In practice, peasants have depended mostly on their families because children were obligated by law to support their parents and because peasants were expected to depend only minimally on the commune or government. Peasants could receive help in food, housing, clothing, medical care, and burial—the "five guarantees"—only if they were childless and infirm. Urban dwellers working for state-run industries or institutions, however, did receive social security through a universal retirement system that paid 70 percent of retiring salary at 60 years for men and 55 years for women.

Article 10 provides for protection of the family. The general availability of basic social benefits in China led to very low infant mortality rates for a poor developing country[6] and seems to have met the requirements of Article 10. Families who had unplanned children, however, particularly in the early 1970s when population policies began to be more stringently implemented, could lose increased social benefits associated with having only one child: for example, a larger apartment, an increased food allowance, a child subsidy, and job advancement.

Article 11 recognizes the right to an adequate standard of living (including adequate food, clothing, and housing) and to the continuous improvement of living conditions. The rights in Article 11 are among the broadest, and performance is hard to evaluate. Nevertheless, some judgments can be made about Chinese performance for Article 11 rights from 1949 to 1978. Even though farm production barely kept up with population until 1977, almost all Chinese had enough to eat through a combination of price controls, rationing, and government subsidies. Simple but adequate clothing was available through rationing. Because of a government policy of concentration on heavy industry and of a high (around 35 percent of net national product) accumulation rate for heavy industry, little capital was left for other investments such as housing. Although housing was therefore scarce, particularly in the cities, it was reasonably equally distributed. As previously mentioned, social security–type programs were available for retired urban cadres and workers. Modest welfare programs were also available to urban and rural residents who were widowed, disabled, or suffering from other severe circumstances beyond their control.

In short, for most of the period from 1949 to 1978, China's social guarantees, though minimal, were sufficient to overcome past patterns of massive famines and severe maldistribution of food. The exception, a major one, was the "three hard years"—1960 to 1962—that came in the wake of the 1958–1959 Great Leap Forward, when a massive famine caused the normal number of deaths to be exceeded by an estimated 20–30 million.[7]

Article 12 calls for the highest attainable standard of physical and mental health. In terms of health and well-being, government policy was to provide basic medical care to all so that past public health threats such as venereal disease, yellow fever, diphtheria, polio, and smallpox would not continue to ravage the population. The Chinese government also tried to provide a healthy living environment for mothers and children. These two policies resulted in tremendous improvements in life expectancy and infant mortality from 1949 to 1978 (see Table 8.1). It is again worth noting, however, that past progress was radically reversed for several years during and immediately after the 1958–1959 Great Leap Forward when life expectancy was lower and infant mortality was even higher than China's pre-1949 level (Table 8.1).[8]

Articles 13 and 14 guarantee educational rights. China tried to increase literacy among its people and to assure that everyone had the right to at least primary school education. China did not, however, make primary education free, and the tuition plus fees that even a poor peasant family had to pay were a major disincentive to enrolling a child for even primary education. Nevertheless, basic literacy reached about 65 percent by the late 1970s.[9]

Article 15 guarantees the right to take part in cultural life. Chinese were encouraged to take part in culture but the government narrowly circumscribed the limits of acceptable art and literature, particularly during periods of high political mobilization. During the 1966–1976 Cultural Revolution, for example, the government permitted only proletarian or "people's" art.

Table 8.1 Reconstruction of Social Data on China, 1953–1982

Year	Midyear Population (millions)	Crude Birth Rate (per thousand)	Crude Death Rate (per thousand)	Natural Population Increase Rate (per thousand)	Total Fertility Rate	Expectation of Life at Birth (years)	Infant Mortality Rate (per 1,000 births)
1953	584.2	42.2	25.8	16.5	6.06	40.3	175
1954	594.7	43.4	24.2	19.2	6.28	42.4	164
1955	606.7	43.0	22.3	20.7	6.26	44.6	154
1956	619.1	39.9	20.1	19.8	5.86	47.0	143
1957	633.2	43.3	18.1	25.1	6.40	49.5	132
1958	646.7	37.8	20.7	17.1	5.68	45.8	146
1959	654.3	28.5	22.1	6.5	4.31	42.5	160
1960	650.7	26.8	44.6	–17.8	4.02	24.6	284
1961	644.7	22.4	23.0	–.6	3.29	38.4	183
1962	653.3	41.0	14.0	27.0	6.03	53.0	89
1963	674.2	49.8	13.8	36.0	7.51	54.9	87
1964	696.1	40.3	12.5	27.8	6.18	57.1	86
1965	715.5	39.0	11.6	27.4	6.07	57.8	84
1966	735.9	39.8	11.1	28.7	6.26	58.6	83
1967	755.3	33.9	10.5	23.4	5.32	59.4	82
1968	776.2	41.0	10.1	30.9	6.45	60.3	81
1969	798.6	36.2	9.9	26.3	5.73	60.8	76

1970	820.4	37.0	9.5	27.4	5.82	61.4	70
1971	842.5	34.9	9.2	25.6	5.45	62.0	65
1972	863.4	32.5	8.9	23.6	4.99	62.6	60
1973	883.0	29.9	8.6	21.3	4.54	63.0	56
1974	901.3	28.1	8.3	19.8	4.17	63.4	52
1975	917.9	24.8	8.1	16.7	3.58	63.8	49
1976	932.7	23.1	7.8	15.2	3.23	64.2	45
1977	946.1	21.0	7.7	13.4	2.85	64.6	41
1978	958.8	20.7	7.5	13.2	2.72	65.1	37
1979	971.8	21.4	7.6	13.8	2.75	65.0	39
1980	983.4	17.6	7.7	10.0	2.24	64.9	42
1981	994.9	21.0	7.7	13.3	2.69	64.8	44
1982	1,008.2	21.1	7.9	13.2	2.71	64.7	46

Source: The table was prepared by Judith Banister, Representative of the Bureau of Census, for her testimony before the Subcommittee on Human Rights International Organizations and the Subcommittee on Asian and Pacific Affairs, U.S. House of Representatives, October 31, 1985. For further detail see Judith Banister, "Analysis of Recent Data on the Population of China," *Population and Development Review,* vol. 16, no. 2 (June 1984), pp. 241–271; "Perspectives on China's 1982 Census," in *Proceedings of the International Seminar on China's 1982 Population Census,* ed. by the State Statistical Bureau, People's Republic of China, and *China's Changing Population* (Stanford, Calif.: Stanford University Press), 1987.

In summary, China's respectable economic growth rates and social policies allowed for at least minimum levels of health, education, housing, and employment to be gradually extended to most Chinese. Health and housing costs averaged 5 percent or less of a worker's salary. Primary education was extended to most school-aged children at little cost. Secondary schools charged a small tuition while colleges and universities were tuition-free and usually provided students with a modest stipend. Although agricultural communes and even whole Chinese provinces were expected to be as self-sufficient as possible, the national government provided subsidies to extremely poor areas.

The Chinese government also provided an "iron ricebowl"—a commitment to employment for all. As many as 100 million peasants who were not needed in agricultural production were still employed. While many of these redundant agricultural laborers were probably among the estimated 200 million people that lived below China's poverty line,[10] and while their employment was not economically efficient, the alternative could have been the situation in other comparable countries where the poorest 40 percent often lack employment and therefore the means to afford basic health care, education, shelter and food, leading to a shortened life span.

The overall results by the late 1970s of China's social polices can be seen in a radically reduced infant mortality rate (down from 175 deaths per 1,000 in 1953 to 37 per thousand in 1978), and a major improvement in life expectancy (from 36 to 64 years) and literacy (from about 20 percent to about 65 percent).[11] China's record at meeting basic human needs has been described in a 1981 World Bank report:

> China's most remarkable achievement during the last three decades has been to make low-income groups far better off in terms of basic needs than their counterparts in most other poor countries. They all have work; their food supply is guaranteed through a mixture of state-rationing and collective self-insurance; most of their children are not only at school, but being comparatively well taught; and the great majority have access to basic health care and family planning services. Life expectancy—whose dependence on many other economic and social variables makes it probably the best single indicator of the extent of real poverty in a country—is (at 64 years) outstandingly high for a country at China's per capita income level.[12]

Until 1978, China's progress in social and economic rights also did not seem to have inhibited its economic growth rate. According to the same 1981 World Bank Report: "Per capita GNP appears to have grown at an annual rate of 2.0–2.5% in 1957–77 and 2.5–3.0% in 1977–79. Even the former rate is significantly above the average for other low-income developing countries (1.6% in 1960–1978)."[13]

*Application of the Physical Quality of Life Index (PQLI)
to China, 1949 to 1978*

Despite having no formal policy on social and economic rights, China's record of meeting the basic social and economic needs of its people (based on its performance in the rights categories enumerated in the International Covenant on Social, Economic, and Cultural Rights) seems, at least descriptively, to be quite respectable. But it would be helpful to be able to measure China's social and economic rights performance and to compare it with that of other developing countries.

Several approaches to measuring basic human needs have been suggested by scholars and practitioners. As mentioned above, the authors of the 1981 World Bank report on China believe that the best single indicator of the level of basic social needs is life expectancy.[14] A more complex approach is the Physical Quality of Life Index (PQLI), developed by Morris D. Morris,[15] which combines life expectancy, infant mortality, and literacy into one indicator on a scale of 1 to 100. Various authors have offered criticisms of the PQLI. The most challenging criticisms are that the three measures (life expectancy at age one, infant mortality, and literacy) correlate so highly as to be redundant and that the index itself correlates so highly with GNP as to be unnecessary.[16]

The case of China raises several additional problems for the PQLI that are probably typical of developing countries. First, the index depends on statistics provided by the country, statistics that can be unreliable. China in particular has been plagued with questionable statistics since at least the Great Leap of 1958–1959. At present, however, Chinese and foreign analysts believe that they have reasonably good figures for the 1949 to 1978 period.

A second problem is that the PQLI may mask both particular problems in a country as well as country-specific variations in the three areas of scaling that could make comparing different countries more difficult. For example, as mentioned earlier, the PQLI does not hint at the very serious implications of China's current population control program— a program that may have resulted in increased infant mortality, particularly for female babies, and perhaps also in decreased life expectancy for women. The PQLI also does not permit examination of whether certain groups (such as dissidents) are severely restricted in their access to basic social needs. Politically based denial of rights could be masked if the affected group (such as the hundreds of thousands of Chinese branded as rightists or counterrevolutionaries in 1957 and during the Cultural Revolution of 1966 to 1976) are a small enough percentage of a population.

Despite its limitations, the PQLI does permit an assessment of efforts to meet basic social needs that has sufficient representational accuracy to evaluate roughly a country's performance over time. The PQLI is also useful for making crude comparisons of social needs performance between countries with different social, economic, or political systems but similarly low levels of economic development. The Overseas Development Council, for example, has used

Morris's index for more than five years in its annual publication, *U.S. Foreign Policy and the Third World.*

Comparison with Other Poor Developing Countries

According to the Overseas Development Council, by the early 1980s, China had a per capita income of about $310, a life expectancy of 67, an infant mortality rate of 71 per thousand, and a literacy rate of 69 percent. Based on an equal weighting of China's life expectancy at age one, infant mortality, and literacy rate, China's PQLI was 75 on a scale of 1 to 100. From the data in Table 8.2, China had a PQLI higher than almost all countries at a comparable economic level and even higher than many countries with up to five times the per capita GNP. Pakistan, with a GNP of $380 ($70 more than China), was the most comparable to China in terms of GNP. However, Pakistan had a life expectancy of 50, an infant mortality rate of 123 per 1,000 live births, and a literacy rate of 24 percent, for a PQLI of only 39, a little more than half of China's.

In East Asia, the area of fastest industrial growth in the 1970s, China's record was also comparatively impressive. Indonesia, for example, with a per capita income of $580, almost twice that of China ($310), had an infant mortality rate of 92 deaths per 1,000, a life expectancy of 53, and a literacy rate of 62 percent, giving it a PQLI of 58, which is 17 points below China's PQLI of 75. The Philippines had a per capita GNP of $820, about two and a half times that of China, but a life expectancy of 63, an infant mortality rate of 54, and a literacy rate of 75 percent, for a PQLI of 75, equal to China's. Even Malaysia, with a per capita GNP of $1,817, or some 6 times that of China, had a lower PQLI.[17]

In fact, in the late 1970s China had a PQLI that was 15 points higher than the PQLI average for the rest of the world's low-income countries ($400 or less per capita) and 10 points higher than the PQLI average for lower middle-income countries ($400 to $999 per capita). China was comparable in PQLI with the average of countries with 5 to 6 times its GNP per capita (upper-middle-income countries with an average GNP of $2,000 and an average PQLI of 72). China's record from 1949 to 1978 was all the more impressive because it was (and still is) a primarily agricultural country that has nearly the worst arable land-per-capita ratio in the world (0.12 hectares of cultivated land per person), a ratio that is less than one-third of India's (0.42 hectares), and less even than those of Egypt (0.15), Indonesia (0.16), or Bangladesh (0.15)[18] Only Sri Lanka, a country that had a slightly lower GNP level and a commitment to meeting basic social needs, surpassed China with a PQLI of 85 in the late 1970s.

Of historical interest is the case of India. In 1952, both China and India were reasonably comparable in terms of GNP and in meeting basic social needs—and therefore of PQLI. From 1952 to 1978, however, India achieved slower GNP growth rates and even slower increases in PQLI, such that by the late 1970s, India was 29 PQLI points behind China. Translated into human

Table 8.2 PQLI Index for Selected Lower and Lower-Middle Income Asian Countries

	Population mid-1984 (mil.)	Physical Quality of Life Index (PQLI) 1970-1975 Average	Physical Quality of Life Index (PQLI) 1981	Per Capita GNP 1982 ($)	Per Capita GNP (Real) Growth Rate 1960-1982 (%)	Population Growth Rate (%)	Life Expectancy at Birth (years)	Infant Mortality per 1,000 Live Births	Literacy (%)	Per Capita Public Education Spending 1980 ($)
ASIA										
Low Income (12)	2,133.3	n.a.	60	280	3.2	1.8	59	97	53	11
Afghanistan	14.4	18	17	220	n.a.	2.5	37	205	20	5
Bangladesh	99.6	35	37	140	0.3	3.1	48	135	26	2
Bhutan	1.4	n.a.	25	120	n.a.	2.3	44	149	5	n.a.
Burma	38.9	51	59	190	1.3	2.4	54	98	66	3
China, People's Republic	1,034.5	69	75	310	5.0	1.3	67	71	69	17
India	746.4	43	46	260	1.3	2.0	52	121	36	7
Kampuchea	6.1	40	33	120	n.a.	1.9	43	201	48	n.a.
Laos	3.7	31	39	80	n.a.	2.4	43	126	44	n.a.
Nepal	16.6	25	30	170	-0.1	2.5	45	148	19	2
Pakistan	97.3	38	39	380	2.8	2.8	50	123	24	5
Sri Lanka	16.1	82	85	320	2.6	1.4	69	43	86	8
Vietnam	58.3	54	75	190	n.a.	2.4	66	99	78	6
Lower-Middle Income (7)	277.9	n.a.	65	665	4.0	2.2	57	79	68	13
Indonesia	161.6	48	58	580	4.2	2.1	53	92	62	10
Maldives	0.2	n.a.	57	440	n.a.	3.0	48	120	82	n.a.
Mongolia	1.9	n.a.	77	780	n.a.	2.8	64	54	80	60
Philippines	54.5	71	75	820	2.8	2.5	63	53	75	11
Thailand	51.7	68	79	790	4.5	2.0	63	53	86	23
Yemen, Arab Republic	5.9	27	28	500	5.1	2.7	43	160	21	19
Yemen, People's Dem. Republic	2.1	33	38	470	6.4	2.9	45	143	40	18

Sources: John W. Sewell, Richard E. Feinberg, and Valeriana Kallab, eds., U.S. Foreign Policy and the Third World: Agenda 1985–86, Overseas Development Council, (New Brunswick: Transaction Books, 1985), pp. 218–219; Morris D. Morris, Measuring the Condition of the World's Poor: The Physical Quality of Life Index, Overseas Development Council, (New York: Pergamon Press, 1979), pp. 128–131.

terms, that meant that in 1979 the average Indian lived 15 fewer years, had a 70 percent higher chance of losing a newborn child, and was only a little more than half as likely as his Chinese counterpart to be literate (see Table 8.2).

China's Civil and Political Rights Performance, 1949–1978

Civil and political rights levels from 1949 to 1978 were influenced by Chinese traditions, the Leninist-Stalinist Soviet political system adopted by China, and the effects of Chinese Communist Party Chairman Mao Zedong's periodic political campaigns. During China's long history of dynastic rule, there were few legal rights and little political freedom. Most legal conflicts were settled informally at the local level. The individual enjoyed what rights the person had as a part of a societal grouping: the family, the clan, and the village.

China's traditional ruling class, the emperor and his exam-recruited officials, had enough political legitimacy to prevent successful challenges to the dynastic system and its Confucian ideology for over 2,000 years. It was not until the nineteenth century that Chinese intellectuals became interested in Western-style individual rights. Even after China's 1911 revolution and adoption of a republican form of government, many Chinese intellectuals harbored a deep ambivalence toward Western conceptions of law and individual rights—fostered by callous Western disregard of Chinese national rights during the 100 years of foreign intervention in Chinese affairs from the 1840s to 1949.

In 1950, China signed an agreement with the Soviet Union to receive technical aid and loans. By 1952, China had adopted a Soviet model of economic development and made major advances in industrialization during its first five year plan from 1953 to 1957. China also borrowed heavily from Soviet social and political institutions, such as the Soviet educational system, the Soviet legal system, and the Soviet party structure. The Chinese Communist Party (CCP) embraced a Leninist-Stalinist variation of Marxism that assigned the party a monopoly on political power, exercised through the "dictatorship of the proletariat."

From 1949 to 1957, Leninism-Stalinism led to very low levels of civil and political rights as defined by the International Covenant on Civil and Political Rights. For class enemies such as landlords and capitalists, the civil and political rights listed in the covenant, rights such as freedoms of speech, publication, assembly, and political mobilization, were denied by the CCP through its dictatorship of the proletariat. Even members of the ruling classes—that is, the peasants and workers—were not granted the freedom to organize institutions separate from the party, let alone to challenge the monopoly rule of the CCP or to criticize its top leadership. Writers and artists were expected to follow Mao's 1942 Yan'an Forum policy of subordinating their work to the needs of party policy. To protect their political monopoly of power, China's leaders established public security bureaus and neighborhood committees and developed dossiers on all Chinese.

China's post-Stalin Soviet-style political system did not permit workers, peasants, and intellectuals to make basic criticisms of the party, its monopoly of political power, its top leaders, or the socialist road for China. Still, until 1957, Chinese leaders agreed that China should have a level of civil and political rights comparable to that in the post-Stalin Soviet Union—what I would call "passive" civil and political rights. Individuals could hold private dissenting views, as long as they did not try actively to propagate them through public forums or demonstrations or through publication or media dissemination. Also, individuals usually would not be criticized simply for their class background or that of their parents. Important members of society, such as research scientists who contributed to increased production, could offer "constructive" criticisms, as could cultural intellectuals, as long as they did not publicly challenge political leaders or socialist orthodoxy.

Although before 1957 Chinese leaders opposed Western-style civil and political liberties, they did favor an established legal system such as was being set up in 1954. Under the 1954 legal system, most Chinese were to enjoy the right to formal and predictable court procedures and other civil and legal rights. There also was discussion of the importance of equality before the law for both party and non-party citizens.

Beginning in 1957, however, under the influence of Chinese Communist Party Chairman Mao Zedong, an "anti-rightist campaign" was begun that established a pattern of politics through tactics that undermined or denied even the modest levels of civil and political rights previously permitted. China's more pragmatic leaders (for example then–Vice Premier Deng Xiaoping) had compromised socialist legality during earlier campaigns such as land reform, when "speak bitterness" meetings and ad hoc "people's courts" had supplanted regularized legal processes. But the 1957 anti-rightist campaign was the first large-scale reduction of civil and political rights to levels well below post-Stalin Soviet levels. After 1957, human rights policy moved from a traditional Leninist position of simply suppressing public criticism to a Maoist (and Stalinist) policy of actively searching out and repressing or punishing real or imaginary class enemies.

It is not clear why the 1957 anti-rightist campaign targeted China's intellectuals, although one factor was Mao's historical suspicion of intellectuals. During debates in the Yan'an period of the early 1940s, Mao had attacked Chinese intellectuals such as writer Ding Ling for being too critical of party activities. Writer Wang Anzhou was executed. Mao's distrust of intellectuals was reinforced by his judgment that during the 1956 100 Flowers Campaign, many Chinese intellectuals had overstepped the limits of permissible debate.

Whatever its causes, the 1957 anti-rightist campaign soon expanded to include virtually any person who had a "bad" class background, pre-1949 foreign study experience, contacts with foreigners, or who had made criticisms of government policies between 1949 and 1957. Although those attacked probably did not exceed five percent of the intellectuals (anyone with a high school education), the campaign eventually engulfed about 400,000 teachers, researchers, writers, and artists, most of whom lost their responsible positions in Chinese society without trials or even formal charges. Many were sent to labor camps for several years and although most were eventually rehired in the early 1960s, few were rehabilitated until 1978. As a result, the victims and their family members suffered discrimination and other hardships for over 20 years. Among the 400,000 were thousands of lawyers and four of China's Supreme Court justices. By 1959, China's new legal system and its just-developing legal protections and procedural guarantees were nearly destroyed.

In the next campaign, the 1966 to 1976 Cultural Revolution, the scope of attack expanded to nearly everyone. The entire class of intellectuals became the "stinking ninth" bad element and were "sent down" to the countryside to "learn from the poor and lower-middle peasant." The Communist Party itself was also attacked. Former Vice Premier Deng Xiaoping and then-President Liu Shaoqi were forced from power. Liu died of abuse and medical neglect in prison. Violations of civil and political rights, though not as systematic as in state terrorist regimes sometimes found in the developing world, were widespread and heinous. According to evidence presented at the trial of the "Gang of Four," most of China's current leaders suffered personally from persecution, as did at least 2.9 million other Chinese citizens. Other estimates place the number who suffered persecution at up to 100 million. As many as 1 million Chinese may have died as a result of beatings, neglect or suicide.[19]

In summary, Chinese Communist Party leaders deserve high marks for their dramatic improvements in the social and economic lives of most Chinese between 1949 and 1978. But in terms of civil and political rights, even the very modest levels enjoyed from 1949 to 1957 were nullified during the two major periods of Maoist campaigns, 1957–1958 and 1966–1976. Maoist campaign-style politics had led to political and social disaster, even by the reckoning of the party. By 1979, pragmatic leaders such as Deng Xiaoping were arguing that China had achieved pre-1979 economic growth despite Mao's political campaigns. Also by 1979, many Chinese officials believed that China was on the verge of social and economic collapse and that the party needed to institute major political and economic reforms to save the economy and to regain the trust of the Chinese people.

Post–1979 Economic and Political Reforms

Since 1979, Chinese leaders under Deng Xiaoping have repudiated Mao's campaign-style politics and initiated significant reforms in both economic and political spheres. The reforms were intended to rebuild China's agricultural and industrial economies, particularly through such innovations as the market mechanisms discussed in this book. The economic and political reforms are interdependent and probably mutually reinforcing. Some of the reforms represent a return to the more pragmatic policies of the 1949 to 1957 period and the 1960 to 1965 period, whereas others represent innovations unique for post-1949 China.

Chinese leaders have revitalized China's legal system, reformed the government bureaucracy, and strengthened participatory institutions such as the National People's Congress. The general goal of political reforms has been to provide more checks and balances within the political system and to reduce the possibility of a return to politics by campaign. Economic and political reforms have so far, however, carefully avoided undercutting the primary role of the Communist Party, as reinforced in the "four cardinal principals"—i.e. the dominant roles in Chinese society of socialism, of the party, of Marxism/Leninism Maoist thought, and of the dictatorship of the proletariat. In the next section, China's post-1979 market reforms will be examined.

Market Reforms

By 1979, China's development strategy had developed serious limitations that current reforms have tried to address. First, China's average annual food production and GNP growth rates, though reasonably impressive compared to most other poor countries, left little food for increased consumption. Chinese per capita food consumption increased little from 1957 to 1976 and may actually have slightly decreased. Second, pre-1979 economic development strategy was comparatively inefficient and growing more so, both in terms of levels of investment required and in energy consumed. Investment had reached 31 percent of gross domestic product by 1979.[20] High investment levels contributed to keeping consumption levels relatively constant after 1957. Neither factory wages nor peasant incomes had risen much from 1957 to 1976. Energy consumption was extremely inefficient and growing more so.[21]

A third problem was that pre-1979 economic policies such as the "iron ricebowl" made it hard to stimulate workers to be more productive. Emphasis on full employment made firing workers virtually impossible, leading to labor redundancy. Wage increases were based only on seniority and Chinese workers therefore had little incentive to work regularly, diligently, or efficiently. Finally, even with "make-work" employment, China's economy by the late 1970s was not providing jobs for growing numbers of unemployed (as many as 20 million), sufficient food for the roughly 100 million without enough to eat, or ways to improve the living standards of the 200 million Chinese living below China's poverty line.[22]

The post-Mao leadership addressed the problem of levels of consumption in 1978 market-style reforms by establishing a "responsibility system" to stimulate agricultural production. To address China's pre-1979 problems of industrial inefficiency and slower-than-hoped-for growth rates, reform leaders agreed on China's need for an infusion of advanced industrial and agricultural technologies from the West and increased emphasis on science and technology within China.

Agriculture has been effectively decollectivized through the introduction of the responsibility system. Individual and family units are able to make a contract with the state for up to fifteen years to pay a certain level of taxes, to sell a certain amount of produce at a set price, and then to sell the surplus in free markets.

In industry, Chinese leaders have tried to develop reforms designed to promote more efficient allocation of capital and other resources. They have placed emphasis on production, not politics, and have tried to structure tax and banking regulations to reward profitable enterprises and punish the inefficient. Changes have been even more dramatic in the foreign sector. New laws allow foreigners to participate in joint Sino-foreign partnerships, build factories in Special Economic Zones (SEZs), and even own 100 percent of some factories making products needed by China's domestic economy. Many of the policies being followed are reminiscent of late-nineteenth-century imperial Chinese efforts to industrialize.

There also has been a major increase in small-scale privately owned service enterprises, such as repair facilities, general stores, restaurants, and even private inns. The private enterprises promise to alleviate some of China's unemployment problems, plus provide many of the valued goods and services that were scarce before 1979.[23] Small private enterprises have also permitted rural and even urban individuals to be free of the all-encompassing involvement with a *danwei*, or unit. Traditionally, the unit was the allocator of salaries, housing, clothing and consumer rations—and even permission for a couple to have a child. Increased individual employment, combined with other economic, social, and political reforms, can enable people to develop income and pay for goods and services themselves.

The results of reforms in agriculture have been impressive. Per capita production has increased, as have peasant incomes.[24] Though the results in industry have been slower, they have still been impressive. Both agricultural and industrial production expanded at over 7 percent per year from 1979 to 1984, and the rate for agriculture is a major improvement over pre-1979 levels.[25]

Although the full effects of the market reforms on social and economic rights performance are still uncertain, some observations are already possible. On the negative side, reforms in the countryside, particularly the dismantling or privatization of the commune clinics, may be having a negative effect on the ability of poorer peasants to meet their basic social needs.[26] Since 1978, crude death rates, infant mortality rates, and (therefore) life expectancy rates have all been moving against past progressive trends—the first such negative movement since the disasters of the 1958–1959 Great Leap Forward.[27] Although the regression is modest and the time period short, the direction is disturbing and the figures should be carefully watched during the coming years (see Table 8.1).

On the positive side, current reforms appear to have improved economic performance. Since 1949, only economic crises, such as the 1958–1959 Great Leap Forward, have had adverse effects on Chinese access to basic social needs. Although few would characterize 1978 as a time of economic crisis, some analysts[28] feel that it was a crucial decision year when political and economic problems—including an increasingly inefficient industrial structure and stagnating levels of consumption—demanded major reform. If current reforms are able to prevent future economic crises through increased agricultural productivity, raised levels of consumption for the vast majority of Chinese peasants, and increased efficiency in industry, then current negative movements in crude death rates, infant mortality, and life expectancy may be no more than temporary economic setbacks on the road of major economic improvement. South Korea, although it has a different political and economic system, suffered a slight decrease in its equality of distribution of income during some stages of its recent impressive economic growth; its example offers some support for a more positive view of recent downturns in China's efforts to address basic human needs.[29]

Effect on Social and Economic Rights

So far, post-Mao economic reforms do not appear to have greatly harmed China's social and economic rights record. Workers are still rarely being fired, and bonuses are often awarded to everyone in a unit. Chinese authorities have raised agricultural producer prices while still holding down prices to urban consumers—though that required a state subsidy that in 1987 consumed about 20 percent of the national budget.[30] The approximately 100 million Chinese peasants considered to be superfluous laborers appear to be no worse off than before. In fact rural wages have risen suggesting that there is increased rural demand for labor as well as increased opportunity for productive economic activities in the rural sector.

Although health care services are still available to peasants, there are fewer local health workers and services probably cost more because they are no longer being subsidized by the now defunct communes. In one case, a former barefoot doctor was reported to have purchased a clinic and provided medical services, but at higher fees.[31] Schools continue to be supported and other necessary public expenditures continue to be financed, but out of funds from townships, whose tax base is uncertain. In poor areas, access to medical care, housing, education, and food may be more expensive and therefore in practice less available. However, the post-1978 figures in Table 8.1 demonstrate that the changes are not yet so large as to be alarming.

Based on China's social and economic rights record from 1949 to 1978 under both moderate and radical leaders, the current moderate leaders will probably continue to address problems that might threaten the overall health, education, or welfare of the vast majority of China's workers and peasants. Government willingness to provide subsidies and to readjust policies when they appear to threaten social or economic rights is indicative.

The following discussion assesses the status of post-1979 China in achieving progress toward the social and economic rights set forth in Articles 6–15 of the International Covenant of Social, Economic, and Cultural Rights.

Article 6, Right to work. Employment opportunities have been increased through the establishment of small individually owned businesses, particularly in needed services, and through increased construction activity throughout China. New types of employment have been particularly important in providing jobs for formerly rusticated youth who have returned to cities and towns, reducing the number of urban-dwellers "waiting for employment" from 6.9 million in 1978 to 4.1 million by 1982.[32] Increasing jobs for young people is important because over 92 percent of unemployment in cities and towns is concentrated in the 15 to 24 age bracket,[33] the baby boomers of the early 1960s.

Despite China's post-1949 and particularly post-1978 progress in meeting employment needs, 4.7 percent of China's 546 million work force, or 26.5 million, remained unemployed in 1982. Underemployment is also a problem, created in part by the Chinese government's policy of trying to provide work for everyone. Labor redundancy is currently as high as 40 percent in the countryside. Without continued economic reforms, this figure could increase to 60 percent by the year 2000.[34]

Article 7, Labor rights. Post-1978 reforms aimed at increased economic efficiency have placed some stresses on worker guarantees, particularly the concept of the "iron ricebowl" that makes it difficult to fire an employee. Reforms have so far, however, basically left existing guarantees to workers in place, although there has been an increased use of temporary contract laborers. It remains to be seen what effects the 1986 labor-contracting regulations will have on labor rights.

Article 8, Trade union rights. China's 1982 constitution rescinded the right to strike. Current Chinese leaders are trying to discourage the "Polish Disease" of independent labor unions. Since 1978, victims of past political campaigns have been somewhat compensated for their losses, with many given back pay and compensation for their losses. The tactic of depriving political victims of their basic social and economic rights is now no longer commonly practiced.

Article 9, Right to social security. As mentioned, the post-1978 reforms have begun to reduce access to needed social services, particularly health care, for poorer peasants. At the same time, steps have been taken to strengthen social security benefits for the peasants. So far, increased benefits have been carried out mostly to facilitate the one-child family policies.[35]

Article 10, Protection of the family. Particularly since 1982, the government's policy of one child per family has demanded that a second pregnancy, if beyond the state quota, be terminated. If there is a second pregnancy that is permitted by the quota system, one of the two parents is to be sterilized after the birth of the child.[36] Such harsh measures would not be popular in any country and have caused much controversy both in China and in the United States. For the in-quota child, there are services such as paid maternity leave, child care, increased food allocations, and medical care. Although seen as necessary because of an already almost incomparable population pressure on a dwindling base of arable land,[37] population control may still prove to be too destructive of popular support for the government to sustain. Harsh population control measures have also led to some negative world public opinion.

Article 11, Adequate standard of living. So far, post-1979 problems seem to have been addressed by the positive effects of economic reforms and by continued government subsidies and local willingness to take on welfare responsibilities from the communes. Recent inflation in the cities has, however, begun seriously to threaten the living standards of relatively fixed-salaried urban workers and intellectuals, as well as retirees on fixed incomes, despite increased government subsidies to both groups.

Article 12, Health care. Health care has already progressed through the relatively inexpensive changes. China now must both protect the progress that it has made and work on a second health care revolution, one that addresses the types of diseases that now take the greatest toll in developed countries: heart disease, stroke, and cancer. Chinese health officials are also working to develop universally available potable water and to provide universal inoculation against the most common and easily treatable serious diseases such as polio, hepatitis, and tuberculosis.

Articles 13 and 14, Educational rights. Of workers over 15 years of age, 28 percent are still illiterate or semiliterate: 48.9 percent of female workers (who are a smaller percentage of the work force than men) are semiliterate or illiterate; compared with 20.8 percent of male workers.[38] Agricultural reforms will probably increase illiteracy in the countryside by putting pressure on peasant households to withdraw able-bodied workers from school.

Article 15, Cultural rights. Social reforms have permitted access to a wider range of art, literature, music, and popular culture. Despite several small campaigns against foreign influence, most Chinese are now much freer to enjoy various forms of cultural life than before 1979.

Post-1979 Civil and Political Reforms and Rights

Civil and Political Reforms

Since 1979, Chinese leaders have begun political reforms whose major impetus is found in three areas. First is the horrific experience of the Cultural Revolution, both for the masses and for China's current leadership. Chinese reform leaders describe the Cultural Revolution as a period of "feudal despotism married to 20th-century fascism."[39] As victims of the Cultural Revolution, most post-Mao leaders are eager to avoid campaign-style politics and to restore enough socialist legality to prevent a repetition of the level of chaos and terror—"beating, smashing, and looting"—that they experienced.

Second, re-emphasis on science and technology requires a greatly increased role for scientists and economists and therefore the development of new policies that can win the support of intellectuals and increase China's intellectual resources. Third, implementation of a more pragmatic economic development model demands the re-establishment of a regularized legal system, one similar to what was being developed during the successful first five year plan of 1953 to 1957. Contracts need to be enforced, property needs to be protected, and a more regularized bureaucratic society needs to be built to support China's modernization efforts. Also, China's economic relations with the West require a legal system that protects foreign economic rights.

An important limit on the scope of political reform, however, should be pointed out. Some foreign observers, noting the major changes that have occurred since 1979—and perhaps reacting to uncharacteristic public admissions of the tragedies of the Cultural Revolution—have begun to describe post-1979 reforms as a major turning point in modern Chinese history, a "quiet revolution,"[40] a move from a society based on ideology to one based on economic performance, and a "bold departure from previous political practices and assumptions."[41] One observer has suggested that the reforms add up to a major move toward democratization.[42] Current Chinese leaders have indeed made major changes that have affected China's social and economic, as well as civil and political, rights levels.

But there is also a continuity that may be overlooked: The changes are still solidly within a Leninist-socialist context as defined by the "four cardinal principles." Political reforms have not expanded to include Western conceptions of civil liberties, as described in the International Covenant on Civil and Political Rights and proposed by China's 1978–1979 movement and as most recently criticized in the campaigns against spiritual pollution (1982–1983) and bourgeois liberalization (1986–1987).

Civil and Political Rights

Although China's current leaders have not fashioned their political reforms to meet human rights criteria, they have made progress in the area of civil and political rights as defined in the Covenant on Civil and Political Rights. A recommitment by current leaders has been made to the more pragmatic and bureaucratic socialist road that was left in 1957. This move has led to at least four important changes in China's political and legal systems that will probably increase the protection of civil and political rights in China.

First, there probably will not be any more of the type of mass campaigns, such as the 1957 anti-rightist campaign and the 1966–1976 Cultural Revolution, that could again result in the widespread persecution of Chinese intellectuals and party members. The tameness and quick termination of both the spiritual pollution and the bourgeois liberalization campaigns offer evidence of a changed attitude.

Second, legal codes and judicial procedures are being reformed to increase protection from political persecution and arbitrary arrest. A legitimate role for lawyers has been re-established. Law schools have been reopened and expanded and the study of law is currently in vogue. China plans to have trained several hundred thousand "legal personnel" by the year 2000. The courts and procuracy have been substantially expanded and strengthened, and 2.9 million past victims of rightist purges have been rehabilitated. The 1982 constitution provides many of the features of the developed socialist legal system of the Soviet Union. There also is debate over questionable provisions still in Chinese law, such as administrative detention, punishment by analogy (the use of laws that outlaw vaguely similar actitivies to expand prosecutorial scope), and a lack of presumption of innocence.

Third, the 1982 constitution provides a major role for the National People's Congress, a body that is not necessarily synonymous with the party or the government. In part because of their personal suffering in past campaigns, current leaders, in the absence of Mao Zedong, have tried to reinforce rule by regular legal bodies such as the People's Congress rather than by mass mobilization or political campaigns.

Fourth, the economic reforms themselves provide a greater lattitude of freedom by allowing individuals more independence from the *danwei*. Before 1979, access to social and economic programs was totally in the hands of the leaders of one's *danwei*. Any conflict with those leaders, whether personal or political, could lead to losses in rights of all kinds. During both the anti-rightist campaign of 1957 and the 1966–1976 Cultural Revolution period, persons condemned as rightists or counterrevolutionaries, particularly intellectuals, regularly suffered major degradation of their social and economic rights. Politically condemned individuals and families might be moved into the smallest living dwellings available, lose housing altogether by being sent to the countryside for re-education, find their salaries reduced to the barest minimum, and even be denied basic medical care. Although it does not appear to have been official policy to deprive those politically criticized of their social and economic rights, many did lose these rights. Now, individuals can avoid many of the potential abuses by *danwei* leaders by contracting for their own land in the countryside under the responsibility system or by setting up small-scale individual enterprises in the city.

Although post-1979 levels of civil and political rights and legal protections are much higher than during the anti-rightist campaign and the Cultural Revolution, there is little indication that a level of civil liberties will be allowed that would permit any organized challenge of the dominance of the party as described in the four cardinal principles. Reform leaders are committed to making socialism work better, not changing China's basic political system.

Chinese leaders have reissued the old labor reform provisions allowing for administrative detention for up to four years without trials or even formal charges. They have been using these provisions to place dissidents and others in China's labor reform camps, which are still populated by a number of political prisoners. When Chinese dissidents violated the four principles, even before they were published, the government made an example of some of these people. At least three democracy movement leaders (Wei Jingsheng, Xu Wenli, and Fu Yuehau) were given fifteen years in prison, the same penalty as one member of the Gang of Four. Most recently, in the wake of student demonstrations in January of 1987, China's top party leader, Hu Yaobang, was relieved of his post as party secretary. Others, such as Liu Binyan and Fang Lizhi, were criticized or removed from positions of responsibility.

Some foreign observers, as well as Chinese democracy movement leaders, have argued that successful economic development requires increased levels of civil and political rights. Unfortunately, the case must be made as much on faith and principle as on evidence from case studies. The examples of the Soviet Union, Cuba, and China have shown that Western levels of civil and political rights are not necessary for economic growth in socialist societies. Even the World Bank has predicted continued growth for China at 4 to 6 percent, 3 to 4 percent capita, with no increases in civil and political liberties.[43] Recent research suggests that capitalist societies are also able to develop without permitting greatly increased civil and political rights (Korea, Taiwan, Singapore)[44] and that democracy itself does not necessarily lead to rapid growth, as in the case of India.

Nevertheless, the Chinese democracy movement has certainly pointed the way that China might move in its gradual democratization. There also are pressures that may increase civil and political rights, such as the dependence of advanced technologies on the free flow of computer-based data. Soviet Premier Gorbachev believes that *glasnost*, or openness in Soviet society is required for revitalizing the Soviet economy in the computer age. Another factor that will affect China is that at least 29,000 of China's best and brightest students have come to the West and particularly to the United States to study. Their Western experiences will surely influence their views on civil and political rights, just as many of the previous generation of Chinese who studied in the Soviet Union came home with a deep commitment to Stalinism.

Despite the hopes of the Chinese democratic movements that change will occur quickly, civil and political liberties will probably come to China only gradually and only so long as the Communist leadership feels civil and political liberties will not be used to undermine its rule. Two less likely scenarios that could increase demands for civil and political rights are a re-emergence of radical policies (followed by yet another widespread pro-democracy reaction) or the total failure of China's current market reforms, and therefore of its economy.

Conclusion

There does not have to be a trade-off between social and economic rights and civil and political rights, and the 1948 Universal Declaration of Human Rights holds all human rights to be of equal importance. In the case of the People's Republic of China, however, social and economic rights have come more easily than civil and political rights. From 1949 to 1978, China made impressive gains in social and economic rights regardless of political leadership. A brief comparison of China's PQLI with other poor countries' PQLIs shows that China also performed very well in comparison with equally poor and even much more economically advanced countries. Civil and political rights levels were much more modest, however, and even those modest levels were mostly lost during periods of radical leadership, such as 1957–1958 and 1966–1976.

China's major market reforms have so far not greatly harmed progress in social and economic rights and may hold the prospect for increased civil and political rights levels. Despite a modest regression in social indicators, China's social and economic rights performance has not significantly deteriorated as a result of the market reforms from 1979 on. Many groups, particularly in the urban and wealthy rural areas, are doing much better economically and should continue to do so. It will be important, however, to continue monitoring infant mortality and life expectancy figures, particularly for poor provinces or areas. Societal and technological pressures associated with the market reforms, as well as the tragic experiences of the Cultural Revolution, have led Chinese leaders to grant greater civil liberties. China's market reforms have also contributed to civil liberties by permitting some Chinese, particularly those in the countryside, to be free of the all-embracing *danwei*. So far, however, civil and political rights are being granted only up to the limits seen in other Leninist-socialist countries with a developed socialist legal system. Major future increases in civil and political rights will probably come only through the willingness of small number of dissidents to risk ruined careers and prison terms.

Notes

1. See World Bank, *China: Socialist Economic Development, the Main Report* (Washington, D.C.: World Bank Documents, 1981), p. 68. Dwight Perkins gives the figure 25 years for the rural population in 1949. Communist sources say that urban life expectancy near Beijing in 1949 was about 52. See *Statistical Yearbook 1981* (Hong Kong: Economic Information Agency, 1982), p. 104.

2. See World Bank, *China*, p. 47; and Arthur G. Ashbrook, Jr., "China: Shift of Economic Gears in Mid-1970's," in *The Chinese Economy Post-Mao*, (Washington, D.C.: U.S. Government Printing Office, 1978), p. 227.

3. World Bank, *China*, p. 47.

4. Ibid. According to the World Bank, India had achieved an average annual per capita growth rate of 1.4 percent from 1957 to 1979.

5. Ibid., p. 6.

6. Morris D. Morris, *Measuring the Condition of the World's Poor: The Physical Quality of Life Index* (New York: Permagon Press, 1979), pp. 128–131.

7. John S. Aird, "Responses to Ten Questions on Family Planning Policies in China by U.S. House of Representatives, Subcommittee on Human Rights and International Organizations, Subcommittee on Asian and Pacific Affairs," unpublished manuscript, Washington, D.C., October 10, 1985, p. 5.

8. Judith Banister,"Statement of the Representative of the Bureau of Census Before the Subcommittee on Human Rights and International Organizations and the Subcommittee on Asian and Pacific Affairs, U.S. House of Representatives," unpublished manuscript, Washington D.C., October 31, 1985).

9. John P. Lewis and Valeriana Kallab, eds., *U.S. Foreign Policy and the Third World: Agenda 1983* (New York: Praeger, 1983), pp. 210–211.

10. *People's Daily*, April 9, 1980, p. 1, cited in David Zweig, "Economic Development and Social Conflict: The Politics of Prosperity in Rural China," unpublished manuscript, p. 1.

11. Lewis and Kallab, *Agenda 1983*, pp. 210–211.

12. World Bank, *China*, p. iii.

13. Ibid., p. ii.

14. Ibid., p. iii.

15. Morris, *Quality of Life Index*.

16. Norman Hicks and Paul Streeten, "Indicators of Development: The Search for a Basic Needs Yardstick," *World Development* 7 (1979), pp. 567–580; David Larson and Walton Wilford, "The Physical Quality of Life Index: A Useful Social Indicator?" *World Development* 7 (1979), pp. 581–584; and Rati Ram, "Composite Indices of Physical Quality of Life, Basic Needs Fulfillment, and Income: A 'Principal Component' Representation," *Journal of Development Economics* 11 (1979), pp. 227–247.

17. John W. Sewell, Richard Feinberg, and Valeriana Kallab, eds., *U.S. Foreign Policy and the Third World: Agenda 1985–86*, New Brunswick: Transaction Books, 1985, pp. 219–221.

18. World Bank, *China*, p. 49.

19. Estimate reported by Ann F. Thurston, author of *Enemies of the People* (New York: Knopf, 1987) as having been given by high Chinese leaders in her unpublished interviews.

20. World Bank, *China*, p. 49.

21. Ibid., p. 98.

22. Cited in Lowell Dittmer, "Ideology and Organization in Post-Mao China," *Asian Survey* 24, no. 3 (March 1984), pp. 368–369; and *People's Daily*,

April 9, 1980, p. 1, cited in Zweig, "Economic Development and Social Conflict," p. 1.

23. "Economic Growth and Rural Development, *Beijing Review*, no. 10, March 10, 1986, p. 20.

24. Ibid, pp. 14–16.

25. Ibid.

26. William Hsiao, "Transformation of Health Care in China," *New England Journal of Medicine*, April 5, 1984.

27. Banister, "Statement." See also Table 8.2 in this chapter.

28. Harry Harding,"Political Development in Post-Mao China," in A. Doak Barnett and Ralph N. Clough, eds., *Modernizing China: Post-Mao Reform and Development* (Boulder, Colo.: Westview Press, 1986).

29. Jack Donnelly, "Human Rights and Development: Complementary or Competing Concerns?" *World Politics* 36, no. 2 (January 1984), pp. 255–283.

30. Nicholas Lardy, "Runaway Subsidies," *China Business Review* 10, no. 6 (November–December 1968), pp. 21–24.

31. Hsiao, "Transformation of Health Care."

32. Jeffrey Taylor, *Employment and Unemployment in China: Results from 10-Percent Sample Tabulation of 1982 Population Census*, Foreign Economic Report No. 23 (Washington, D.C.: U.S. Department of Commerce, September 1985), p. 26.

33. Ibid.

34. Ibid. p. 27.

35. Erika Platte, "China's Fertility Transition: The One-Child Campaign," *Pacific Affairs* 57, no. 4 (1984–1985), pp. 646–671.

36. Banister, "Statement.".

37. World Bank, *China*, p. 6.

38. Taylor, *Employment and Unemployment*, pp. 20 and 22.

39. "Prospect and Retrospect: China's Socialist Legal System," *Beijing Review* 4, no. 2 (1979), p. 27, cited in Hungdah Chiu, "Socialist Legalism: Reform and Continuity in Post-Mao People's Republic of China," Occasional Papers Reprint Series in Contemporary Asian Studies, no. 1, 1982, p. 2.

40. David Zagoria, "China's Quiet Revolution," *Foreign Affairs*, Spring 1981.

41. Dittmer, "Ideology and Organization," pp. 368–369.

42. Brantly Womack, "Modernization and Democratic Reform in China," *Journal of Asian Studies* 43, no. 3 (May 1984), pp. 417–436.

43. World Bank, *China*, p. xx.

44. See Donnelly, "Human Rights and Development," pp. 265–266.

9

A Chinese View on the Reform of the Economic Mechanism in Hungary: A Comment

Su Shaozhi

Different conditions in different countries give rise to different ideas guiding the reform of the existing economic mechanisms. Each country has to work out its reform program in the light of its specific socioeconomic reality. Consequently, no country can offer a universally applicable model to be copied mechanically by others. It is in this sense that Jozsef Szabo, president of the Political College under the Central Committee of the Hungarian Socialist Workers' Party (HSWP) said, "There does not exist any `Hungarian model.' What exists is but Hungarian practice."[1]

The economic reforms in the Soviet Union and the East European countries have had their respective characteristics, and all have led to varying degrees of positive results in different respects. But in the words of Wlodzimierz Brus, "Hungary has displayed a far greater degree of internal stability than perhaps any other East European country, including the USSR. . . . As for the economic reform, the prevailing (but not unanimous) view is that it [Hungary] made a substantial positive contribution to economic performance, particularly by increasing flexibility and making it possible to adjust the structure and quality of output to internal and external demand."[2] Facts have proved that even though the postreform Hungarian economic mechanism is unavoidably plagued by a number of problems, some of which are rather serious, it now possesses greater vitality and functions more smoothly than in the years before the 1968 reform.

In the past dozen years or more, there have been both favorable and unfavorable comments by the domestic and international press on Hungary's economic reform. During the last few years in particular, there have been differing views and some resultant arguments about certain difficulties besetting the Hungarian economy and about the measures taken to cope with them. Some people think that Hungary has been strengthening its centralized management system, which will thus lead to the collapse of its economic reform. Others say that Hungary's economic reform adds fuel to pure utilitarianism, and that this will cause the development of liberalization and of the capitalist factors.

Most people, however, subscribe to the view that the reform of the Hungarian economic mechanism has produced obvious results; that it is in keeping with the objective laws of development to make some readjustments along with the changes in actual conditions; and that because the reform itself is a protracted and constant process of development and the 1968 reform was but the beginning of this process, it is hard to say when the reform has been fully completed. Bela Csikos-Nagy wrote, "Looking on the 1968 abolition of regulation based on compulsory plan directives as the first stage of the reform, and the introduction of competitive pricing in 1980 as the second stage, then, in the eighties, a possible foreign exchange reform may well be the third stage."[3]

Basic Features of the Reform

Fundamentally, Hungary's 1968 economic reform was directed at the maladies of the highly centralized Stalin-type system of economic control and management. These maladies were seen in the serious political and economic problems that existed in the years when Rakosi was in power 1947–1956. Touching on the circumstances after the conclusion in 1950 of Hungary's first three-year plan, Matyas Timar wrote:

> Politically, these years were characterized by wilful methods, the peak of personal power and the beginning of its decline. Although there were remarkable results in industrialization and the formation of socialist agriculture, the economy was characterized by forced industrial development, by an insufficient consideration for domestic endowments in shaping the structure of industry, by certain autarkic tendencies, by a highly bureaucratic system of control, by deviations from the Leninist principles in agricultural policy, by expenditure on armaments beyond the capacity of the country, by stagnating and at times declining living standards. All that led to grave economic tensions and contributed to the intensification of those political problems which became obvious after Stalin's death.[4]

The problems Matyas Timar listed are, as a matter of fact, common to the highly centralized Stalin-type system of economic management in the East European countries.

Although some partial reforms were carried out in Hungary from 1956 onward, they did not touch on the old economic control and management system and so could not propel forward the development of the Hungarian economy. Reform of this very system therefore became imperative in the mid-1960s.

> In the last instance, the reform is economically necessary because earlier important sources and reserves of economic growth are being exhausted, and future rapid growth will only be possible through a more intensive

exploration of the economy's internal reserves and through the acceleration of technical development. The political significance of the reform lies, first of all, in that it is necessary to ensure a swift raising of the living standard of the masses in the future and to ensure that the living standard of every worker is determined, to a greater degree than now, by the social effectiveness of the work of an individual, by the production results that are attributed to an individual and by the achievements of collective labour. The political objective of the reform also lies in the elimination of the excessive restrictions that hinder individual creativeness and responsibility and in the checking of the tendency of bureaucratism.[5]

It is thus clear that Hungary's economic reform of the mid-1960s was aimed at purging the maladies enumerated by Matyas Timar and that it was launched in full consideration of its economic and political objectives.

As pointed out in the decision adopted in 1966 by the Central Committee of the Hungarian Socialist Workers' Party on the reform of the Hungarian economic mechanism, the basic feature of such reform is "the organic coupling of the planned central guidance of the national economy with the active role of the commodity relations and of the market on the basis of the socialist ownership of the means of production."[6] It is very important to understand this basic feature in studying Hungary's economic reform, for only in that way can a superficial and one-sided analysis of the reform be avoided. The quotation indicates the following:

- Hungary's economic reform has been made "on the basis of the socialist ownership of the means of production." This characteristic does not mean any considerable increase in the proportion of the private economy, but it means the readjustment of certain basic relations within the existing economic sectors. This demolishes the assertion that the economic reform entails the development of the capitalist factors.

- The economic reform does not mean abolition of the basic principles of national control because the various major targets and ratios in the plans for national economic development are still determined by the central authorities.[7] The method of planned central control, however, does not stress administrative but rather economic means. The state has at its disposal various means of economic regulation in order to ensure the more effective fulfillment of plans. Meanwhile, in the overall economic setup, "market mechanism is assured of a broad scope of operation, that is to say, the demand and supply prices are allowed to exert their influences directly."[8] Nonetheless, there should be no laissez-faire market of free competition: In the new economic mechanism, the market is an organized market subject to regulation by the state. In other words, there is a system similar to what Brus calls a "centrally planned economy with a regulated market mechanism." Bela Csikos-Nagy put it clearly: "Hungary has never really entertained the idea of abandoning planned economy of the socialist type in favour of a certain form of socialist market economy."[9] Instead of weakening central control and guidance, Hungary's economic reform aims at improving and strengthening them. Meanwhile, facts have refuted the view that all measures to reinforce central control and guidance simply mean renewed emphasis on centralization and will thus cause the failure of the economic reform.

A most concentrated expression of the 1968 reform of the Hungarian economic mechanism was the discontinuation of the practice of the central authorities imposing annual plan targets on the enterprises through the relevant ministries: The enterprises are allowed to draw up their own plans, which serve as their work programs and need not be approved by the government. At the same time, use is made of the positive role of commodity relations between buyer and seller and of the market mechanism. This relieves the central government of the impossible task of taking into consideration, while working out plans, the innumerable and constantly changing actual processes and their mutual relations.[10] In place of state plan targets assigned to the enterprises are the various regulation systems of the state. Direct and indirect means of economic regulation are used to influence the activities and decisionmaking of the enterprises, to readjust the interests of the state and the collectives and individuals, and to ensure the accomplishment of the national economic plans.

The Hungarian economic mechanism comprises the planning system, the regulation system, and the institutional system. Combining to form an integrated whole, these three systems have assumed the following characteristics as a result of the 1968 reform:

1. The planning system seeks adherence to planned economy while abolishing the method of the central government assigning plan targets to enterprises. The central authorities take charge of the chief macroeconomic policy decisions. National economic plans principally set the major targets and ratios of development and the means of control and management for ensuring the fulfillment of the plans. National economic plans are binding only on the government and economic administrative departments, and there are no plan instructions to the enterprises. Ordinary decisionmaking power is delegated to enterprise directors, whereas the state concerns itself mainly with the accomplishment of the plans by utilizing the regulators. The state issues administrative orders to enterprises only in some specific circumstances, such as in the case of the production of military hardware and certain consumer goods. In these cases, the state stipulates how much should be produced and exported and where the state can interfere when production deviates from the plans.

2. The regulation system is an integral part of the Hungarian economic mechanism. Through the regulation system, the state influences the activities and decisionmaking of enterprises so as to ensure the implementation of the state's economic policies and the fulfillment of the national economic plans and to coordinate the interests of the state and the collectives and individuals. There are systems for the regulation of prices, of the income of enterprises, of wages, of enterprise development, of the circulation of products, and of foreign trade. All these regulation systems may be readjusted from time to time in the light of changed domestic and international conditions.

Because market mechanism is brought into the orbit of planned economy, the system of price regulation plays a particular role. Bela Csikos-Nagy holds that "market price movement is a prerequisite for the rational solution of the economic problems."[11] Hungary has adopted the method of gradual transition to market prices with the aim of developing the role of market mechanism. With the 1968 reform, a system of double-channel prices was introduced, whereby the part of profit contained in the prices is proportionate partly to production funds and partly to wages. Prices themselves are determined by three factors: production costs, value judgments prevailing on the market, and state preferential treatment. In Hungary, prices are divided into the producer prices (i.e., prices of products sold by the producer enterprises) and the consumer prices (i.e., prices at which products are bought by the consumers). As the central factor of price, the price of production is meant to make price approach value, make the producer price increasingly approach the price of production, and make the consumer price increasingly approach the producer price. In Hungary, prices take the following forms: (a) fixed prices; (b) negotiated prices, which fluctuate but are subject to official restrictions and are further subdivided into state-set ceiling prices and prices fluctuating within state-set limits; and (c) free prices. With readjustments, the proportion of fixed prices will tend to decrease while that of free prices will tend to increase. In 1979, the proportion of fixed prices in the producer prices was about 30 percent; that of negotiated prices, another 30 percent; and that of free prices, 40 percent. The respective proportions in the consumer prices in the same year were 40 percent, 30 percent, and 30 percent.

3. In the institutional system, management of the macroeconomic processes is firmly in the hands of the relevant central departments, while management of the microeconomic processes rests with the operative departments. This division is seen in (a) the strengthened control by the government and the functional ministries; (b) the reduced role of the administrative ministries and their simplified organizational setup; and (c) the extended decisionmaking authority of enterprises. Owing to some specific circumstances, however, there have been no marked organizational changes in the postreform years, which means that some of the original reform ideas remain unfulfilled.

Theoretical Prerequisite of the Reform:
The Relationship Between Planning and Market

One major theoretical question confronting Hungary and some other countries in their economic reforms is the relationship between planning and the market. This is also a question that has evoked heated debates. As Bela Csikos-Nagy wrote:

> In recent years, a number of Marxist economists have wanted to give the impression that the discussions about the economic reform were an alternative between *socialist planned economy or socialist market economy* . . . whether socialist societies should continue to develop in the system based on planned economy or should become transformed into market economies. They, so to speak, set the plan against the market as well as social consciousness against economic spontaneity. On this basis, however, a fruitful discussion can scarcely be carried on. A true alternative only exists between commodity production and direct exchange of products (barter economy). . . . Practically, the main point always is the *synthesizing of plans and market*, for market economy without plan or planned economy without market are out of the question.[12]

On the question of the relationship between planning and the market, the following views have been so extensively prevalent among the Hungarian economists that they have become the starting point, both in theory and practice, for the country's economic reform:

1. Although the necessity of instituting a planned economy in a socialist society is determined by the public ownership of the means of production, one cannot equate planned economy with the system of plan instructions from the central authorities. In the words of Bela Csikos-Nagy, "the economic policy of 1968 meant abolition of the practice of equating planned operation with plan instructions from the central authorities, and consequently it meant a reassessment of the concept of planned development."[13] Without a specific level of development of the productive forces, it is difficult to realize a high degree of centralization and unified guidance in matters of planning, as envisaged by Marx. The planning departments can only set the main orientation, ratios, and tasks for the development of the national economy. Enterprises are given decisionmaking authority and the power of independent operation within the framework of microeconomy. On their part, the central authorities use regulatory means to influence the enterprises and make their activities conform to the requirements of the national economy and thus ensure the fulfillment of plans.

2. Economy of a socialist society is still organized on the basis of commodity production. Despite Marx's and Engel's assumption that commodity

production would wither away once society acquired possession of the means of production, practice shows that nationalization of the means of production and collectivization of agriculture in a socialist society do not mean the end of commodity production. Commodity relations exist not only among the state and the collectives and individuals and in foreign trade but also among the different units of the state itself. These relations continue because there exist in a socialist society interests of the entire nation and the collectives and also of enterprises and individuals. It will be impossible to satisfactorily coordinate the interests of all quarters in the absence of commodity relations. Commodity production will erode only when there is great abundance of material wealth—only when distribution according to need becomes a reality. Because of differences in social and economic systems, the function of socialist commodity production and of the associated categories is different from that of capitalist commodity production and of the associated categories. But there is a point of similarity between the two cases in the sense that commodity production and the associated categories can serve as regulatory means in the economic mechanism as a whole.

3. The function of market mechanism is an objective reality in socialist society. Nonetheless, market mechanism should be definitely brought into the orbit of planned economy. Because commodity production exists in socialist society, it is necessary to recognize the existence of market for commodity exchange and to recognize the function of the economic law of commodity production—the law of value. The law of value expresses itself through the market law of supply and demand, whereas market mechanism functions through prices. Consequently, "One of the pillars supporting the reform of the economic mechanism is to set up a price system suited to the character of the new overall system. . . . The price system in the new economic mechanism should be a flexible system. Therefore, officially-set prices should be limited to a narrow scope. Attention should be paid to the indirect method of price regulation by the state, namely, to the economic means used by the state to influence price formation."[14]

There always exists the spontaneous regulatory role of the market. When the state restricts the function of the market mechanism in one sphere, the mechanism will make itself felt in others. With the present level of development of the productive forces, planning, and management, it is an objective necessity to utilize market mechanism on a wide scale. Inasmuch as a market mechanism can supply varied economic information and help shape a favorable relationship between production and demand, higher economic efficiency can be achieved through such a mechanism than through regulation merely by instructions from the central authorities. There is, however, a major drawback in market mechanism because its regulation often comes after the event and is unstable and likely to precipitate losses. For this reason, it is necessary both to recognize the workings of market mechanism and to place it within the orbit of planned economy so that there may be an organic coupling of the central authorities' planned control of the economy with market mechanism. On the one hand, this means that the central authorities decide on the major issues concerning the development of the national economy, determine the main orientation, ratios, and targets of the economic growth, and muster the proper means to ensure the fulfillment of all these. On the other hand, it means that market mechanism should be assured of a broad scope of action in the whole economy—namely, that the supply and demand prices should be allowed to play their roles, that there should be genuine commodity relations between buyer and seller, and that enterprises should be given the power to make decisions on most of the related economic matters. The organic link between planning and the market also implies that there should be no laissez-faire market—no free competition—but a market subject to central control and state regulation. At the same time, the market can affect planning insofar as it helps in the formation of plans and in the supervision of their implementation, and it can cause partial revision of those plans. There is no need for the compulsory implementation of the original targets if such partial revision does not detract from the accomplishment of the major planned ratios or if it can bring greater benefit to the national economy.

Only with a proper understanding and recognition of the basic views listed above can there be a correct understanding of the reform of Hungary's system of economic control and management and of its development.

Progress of the Reform

The Preliminary Stages

Preparation for the economic reform was formally begun in December 1964. The planning evolved through roughly three stages:

The stage of criticism of the old system of economic control and management. At its plenary session in December 1964, the Central Committee of the HSWP decided on a comprehensive critical examination of the old economic mechanism. The party's Central Committee and the State Economic Commission took charge of this work which was to be completed early in 1966, whereupon a report was to be filed to the Central Committee. Then, with the direction of a theoretical economists' group under the Central Committee, a dozen working panels were formed. Drawing in practical and theoretical experts, these panels were to deliberate on matters of planning, prices, income sharing, wages, material interests, investment, foreign and home trade, agriculture, the local councils, finances, and some other questions. Following about a year's effort, the critical examination was finished and a consensus achieved. Subsequently, a comprehensive reform plan was drawn up, charting the general orientation.

The stage of working out specific plans. The Central Committee of the HSWP called a plenum in November 1965 to discuss the question of the reform of the country's system of economic control and management. It adopted the "Preliminary Guidelines for the Reform of the System of Economic Management," which analyzed the disadvantages of the old system, pointing out that "it stands in contradiction to Hungary's economic reform, and constitutes an obstacle to the latter." The document also put forth some tentative ideas on the economic reform, stressing that the reform "should not be rash, nor dilatory." The departments concerned were asked to set aside reserves of certain commodities and foreign exchange so as to cope with any urgent situation that might appear during the early days of the reform. Following its adoption by the HSWP Central Committee, the document was distributed among the party, government, academic organizations, and the various enterprises for comments.

In early 1966, the HSWP Central Committee set up political, economic, and legal committees to further deliberate the proposed economic reform; these three committees put forward a number of suggestions.

In May 1966, the HSWP Central Committee again held a plenum, which passed the "Guidelines for the Reform of the Economic Mechanism" and another document based on it, "Decisions on the Reform of the Economic Mechanism," giving specific stipulations and explanations on a series of matters of principle. Compared with the original ideas and proposals, there were some necessary compromises on a number of questions.[15]

Trial reforms and arrangements. The reform was first carried out on a trial basis in a number of enterprises between 1966 and 1967. Meanwhile, different courses were organized for the training of cadres. The working panels completed their tasks, and the vocational departments were asked to work out the various regulatory systems and the detailed rules for their application. In June 1967, the HSWP Central Committee passed another decision, calling on most enterprises to determine the new producer prices within one month (the deadline set for the machine-making and construction departments was September of the year) and on all enterprises to familiarize themselves with the new financial and legal stipulations before the end of November. The decision also stressed the further publicity of the new system of economic control and management, in addition to raising a number of questions meriting the attention of all.[16]

The Overall Reform

The year 1968 saw the countrywide introduction of Hungary's new economic mechanism. Then two significant measures were taken: The first was the establishment of schools for teaching managerial personnel modern management techniques and schools for commercial studies. The other was revision, beginning from 1971, of the penal code to specify punishments for economic offenses committed under the new economic mechanism and to provide new interpretation of such offenses as illegally raising commodity prices, jeopardizing the interests of the customers, selling manufactured goods of inferior quality, and giving bribes. All these combined to ensure the smooth working of the new economic mechanism.

Hungary's success in its economic reform has been inseparable from adequate preparations. The deep criticism of and debates about the old system helped to achieve a consensus of opinions and to chart the general orientation of the reform. After the general orientation was determined, detailed guidelines were formulated and relevant decisions made after discussions. With definite stipulations on a series of matters of principle, people have something to go by in their work. Instead of a piecemeal effort, the reform has been guided by a comprehensive plan, which means that the measures taken in various fields have been well coordinated and many loopholes thus avoided. Nationwide study and discussion of the reform program enabled the masses to gain an adequate understanding of the party decision, and there have been timely measures for the training of cadres and for legislation. Thus, the many-sided arrangements have ensured the satisfactory implementation of the economic reform.

An analysis of the economic conditions of Hungary between 1967 and 1974 fully testifies to the positive changes produced by the reformed system of economic control and management (see Table 9.1). In this period, national income showed an annual rate of growth of 5.5–7.0 percent, the average annual rate of growth being substantially better than the corresponding figure both in the previous and the subsequent years.

There were other positive changes. Labor productivity achieved a notable rise in this period. Between 1971 and 1975, the increased proportion in the total output value of industry that was attributable purely to higher labor productivity reached as much as 97 percent. The earlier chronic deficit in the balance of payments in relation to the capitalist market was overcome, and then growth proceeded in a balanced way so that foreign exchange reserves even showed an increase. All this was accomplished without restricting imports; in fact, the share of imports grew with respect to consumer goods needed by the ordinary people. There was an unprecedented improvement in the livelihood of the people, and commodity supplies became more abundant, with shortages limited to certain typical products. The smooth economic development in this period caused some scholars to call it a "golden age" for Hungary.

At the beginning of the 1970s, changed conditions on the world market made Hungarian economic development more and more difficult. First came the suspension of the convertibility of U.S. dollars to gold and the oil price hike. In the 1970s, the price of gold rose 20-fold and that of oil 10-fold while world market price levels—excluding oil—increased only 2.5-fold. As 55 percent of Hungary's energy needs (including 80 percent of its oil needs) were dependent on imports, changes in the world market prices caused its terms of trade to deteriorate by nearly 20 percent. In other words, the country lost 10 percent of its national income.[17]

Table 9.1   Average Annual Growth Rate of National Income

1950–1955 (under Rakosi's regime)	5.7
1957–1967 (decade before economic reform)	5.8
1967–1974 ("golden age")	6.3
1973–1979	5.3

Source: Statistical Pocket Book of Hungary, 1980, (Budapest: Statistical Publishing House, 1981).

In the face of the rather successful expansion of the Hungarian economy during the "golden age," the critics of the economic reform generally kept silent. In the years 1974–1978, however, debates on the economic mechanism were resumed because of the many difficulties besetting the national economy. People began to seek new principles and methods of adjustment in the light of the new situation. Some economic literature terms this period (1974–1978) the "period of gestation" for the Hungarian economic reform.

The first argument appearing in this "period of gestation" was that given the worsening world market conditions, the new economic mechanism introduced in 1968 should be discontinued. Favoring renewed centralization, advocates of this view held that planned economy itself sufficed to protect a socialist society against the unfavorable changes on the international market and that better planned economy and government control would be able to delay the inroad of the negative effects. Some believed that Hungary would have to return to a centrally determined economy and once again apply compulsory plan directives. Prevalence of these views made timely response to the impact of the world market crisis impossible, thereby aggravating domestic economic difficulties.

Experience has shown that for an economy like Hungary's, which is very sensitive to fluctuations in foreign trade, the only alternative for it when faced with difficulties is to adopt flexible regulatory measures to surmount them. It is ineffective to resort to an economic mechanism that institutionally abolishes reaction to world economic impulses instead of strengthening it. It finally became clear through the debates that steps must be taken to eliminate the negative consequences of the excessively restrictive measures and to apply more consistently and determinedly the basic principles of the new economic mechanism started in 1968.

The arguments in the "period of gestation" also centered around the question of whether equilibrium in international trade and payments could be restored through accelerating or decelerating economic growth. The fifth five-year plan (1976–1980) tried to do away with the balance-of-payments deficits through an ambitious development. It was argued that the export increment necessary for restoring the balance in international payments could be created relatively quickly through accelerated growth without affecting the improvement of the Hungarian people's living standard. This approach proved unrealistic: According to the 1978 data, economic growth of 1 percent demanded increased imports from the non-ruble areas at a rate of 1.3 percent; and the latter rose to 2 percent when the country's economic growth surpassed 3–4 percent. In other words, the rate of its economic growth could not keep pace with the increase in non-ruble imports, and this imbalance could not be offset by exports.[18] In order to maintain the balance of payments in equilibrium, more foreign loans had to be raised than planned.

The conclusion was reached in the course of debates that economic growth had to be slowed in the medium term, at least until a new course was found along which growth could proceed in a balanced manner. The sixth five-year plan (1981–1985), which was in harmony with this concept, centered on adjustment to the conditions of the international division of labor and on the restoration of international balance of payments. It set the average annual increase of national income at 2.8 percent and earmarked two-thirds of the increment for additional exports.[19] To maintain the living standard of the people in the face of slowed growth, the level of accumulation in the domestic utilization of the national income must be lowered. It amounted to 20 percent in 1980.

The preceding discussion shows that in this period, Hungary's economic policy did not aim at a high rate of growth but rather at balanced growth. At the same time, the people were to be assured of a better supply of consumer goods. These factors would facilitate a fairly stable economic and political development. Nevertheless, Hungary's economy failed to respond in good time to the world market crisis. To a certain degree, this failure had something to do with the inadequate flexibility of the country's system of economic management, which had yet to develop an automatic mechanism capable of making timely reaction. As pointed out by Béla Csikos-Nagy: "Price reform did not lead to an ideal system capable of ensuring a harmonious relationship between foreign trade prices and domestic prices through maintenance of relatively stable prices, even in conditions of inflation on the world market."[20] Thus, a further overall revision of Hungary's economic regulation system was put on the agenda.

In the second half of the 1970s, studies centered on the requirements that had to be met in the production structure in order for the country to become internationally competitive under more difficult conditions. A resolution was adopted in 1977 on the guidelines for a long-term external economic policy and the development of the production structure. A strategy for industrial growth in the 1980s was worked out in line with this major document. Development was to serve primarily the export potential, and the specific material and energy utilization in the national economy was to be reduced.

The price system has a substantial role to play in the formulation and implementation of Hungary's industrial strategy. Market mechanism was introduced following the 1968 economic reform, and greater autonomy was allotted to enterprises in purchase, production, and marketing—though effective central regulation was still considered necessary in developmental policy. Prices, however, still failed to reflect the value judgments prevailing on the market or to reflect work efficiency. Excessive price subsidies by the state served to distort the reform principles. It was felt that particularly in an economy sensitive to foreign trade, there was the need of a more flexible adjustment to the changing world market condition and that price should play a greater guiding role in the macrostructure as well as in the microstructure. These factors were the main reasons for the modification of the economic regulators in 1980. Introduction of competitive price formation became one of the most important elements of the revision of the Hungarian economic mechanism in that year.

The essence of "competitive pricing" lies in identifying economic efficiency on an international scale of competitiveness. Thus the relative prices of raw materials and semifinished and finished products, as well as the price ratio between products substituting for each other, are regulated by the world market or by foreign trade contract prices. Accordingly, the chief features of the Hungarian price system introduced in 1980 may be summarized as follows: (1) In the domestic evaluation of the natural resources (fuels and raw materials), adjustment to the ruling non-ruble import price is made universal; and (2) in competitive industries, adaptation to the non-ruble export price is necessary. To put it more precisely, the enterprise price level and the average enterprise rate of profit respectively are regulated by the export price level and the profitability of exports, whereas the relative price of goods sold at home is adjusted to supply and demand. Thus, the enterprises are compelled to economize on raw materials and energy, raise efficiency, and develop an even more effective production structure.

Béla Csikos-Nagy explains the situation,

> The government has at its disposal, for the influencing of the spontaneous market process, an appropriately varied economic policy tool chest. These tools can be summed up under the headings of production and distribution policy, prices and incomes policy, as well as monetary and budgetary policy. Within the range of the various manifestations of economic policy, monetary policy differs from all the others in being able to apply indirect measures, in addition to direct ones, thus offering great opportunities for economic incentives.
>
> The public ownership of the means of production, as well as the system of requirements of planned development, cannot be brought into harmony with a market-adjusted economic policy relying on the principle of the free market. The latter applies only indirect instruments. Nevertheless, flexible adjustment to the changing conditions of the international division of labour makes it desirable that indirect regulation should be the rule and direct regulation the exception. This, however, assumes the fuller effectiveness of the monetary function. This is why the monetarization of the economy should be taken as the main line of the socialist economic reform."[21]

In addition, Béla Csikos-Nagy maintains that the introduction of competitive pricing should be followed by foreign exchange reform: "In a foreign trade sensitive economy, the relaxation of internal restrictions must be accompanied by the mitigation of foreign exchange restrictions in order to make it possible for the rational function of price to flow more freely."[22]

In the foreign exchange reform, there was the demand that the dual (commercial and noncommercial) exchange rate be replaced by a uniform exchange rate. On October 1, 1981, the National Bank of Hungary announced that an official uniform exchange rate would be applied to convertible currencies. The use of a uniform exchange rate serves to raise the international prestige of the forint, help simplify the accounting procedure, and contribute to the making of economic policy decisions. In economic regulation, strengthening the monetary function raises the question of the convertibility of the currency, namely, the question of making the forint a freely convertible currency. In this respect, debates are still going on. Some people hold that convertibility is conducive not only to the coordination of the socialist planned economy but also to the expansion of international trade.

For political reasons, Hungary at first did little in reforming the institutional system. Since 1980, however, the country has adopted many major reform measures in this area. Some government departments were abolished or merged, and the central ministries reduced from 17 to 13. Eleven trusts restricting labor productivity were disbanded, and some big enterprises were encouraged to change over to decentralized management or break into medium-sized or small enterprises. More enterprises have been given greater autonomy in foreign trade. All these measures are aimed at further reducing state interference in the activities of the enterprises, extending their decisionmaking power, and encouraging them to develop emulation campaigns among themselves. To apply in industry the positive experiences gained in developing small-scale agricultural production, the Hungarian government decided to implement, as of January 1982, a new law concerning small-handicraft industry. It also put forth the principle of making an active use of the private enterprises, chiefly in the fields of consumption and services. The enterprise law contains the following provisions:

- Private enterprises each employing fewer than 30 workers and staff members shall be allowed to operate.
- In the fields of consumption and services, medium-sized and small enterprises shall be allowed to combine into cooperatives each with not more than 150 workers and staff members.
- All affected enterprises shall apply the system of independent accounting.
- Social insurance shall be extended to cover artisans and merchants operating on their own.

The purpose of these provisions is to set up an elastic supply system capable of coping with the changes in market demand.

Lessons from Hungary's Economic Reform

When setting out to reform its economic structure, a socialist country must keep in mind its own actual conditions and draw up a plan that reflects these realities. There is no universal pattern to follow, nor is it possible to copy the models of other countries. However, because the socialist countries before reform had all adopted a Soviet-type, highly centralized management system—the command economy—the reform efforts of those countries did have something in common: The goal was to effect a change from the command economy to a market-oriented economy of various forms. Therefore, their experiences in reform, positive or negative, are mutually applicable for reference.

Hungary since 1968 had made considerable achievements in its economic reform; however, from the second half of 1980, a rather severe economic situation began to grip the country. It was characterized by intensified inflation, economic stagflation, accumulated foreign debt ($17.7 billion hard currency debt by 1988) and deteriorated living standards—with no sign of improvement.[23] Thus the assessment of Hungary's reform has become a controversial subject. As Alec Nove maintains: "Hungary's experience shows clearly both the advantages and the difficulties which follow from an attempt to introduce what can be called 'market socialism.' On balance the positive features seem to predominate, and this despite some major inconsistencies in the application of the New Economic Mechanism."[24] Nove's book was published in 1983, but it would seem his conclusion is still valid today.

Hungary's success in its economic reform was attributable to a number of factors worthy of consideration.

1. Hungary's leaders had a clear and fairly correct objective for the economic reform. First, they made a scientific and critical analysis of the problems and mistakes that had existed in the old economic system. Then, after studying the realities of Hungary with reference to the basic principles of Marxism, they decided on the goal of the reform: to switch the command economy over to a regulated market economy by replacing orthodox centralization with market regulation, replacing extensive development with intensive development, and meeting the consumption requirements of the people. The central purpose of reform was to raise efficiency.

2. A relatively comprehensive program to reform the economy had been worked out. The reform was intended to be fundamental and principled and have long-term significance.

3. The implementation of the reform was carried out at a steady pace. Hungary's reform was introduced gradually after fairly substantial preparation, and the actual process of reform has been accompanied by timely legislation and education on the subject. These factors promoted satisfactory implementation.

However, there were setbacks in Hungary's economic reform later on. Apart from external reasons (e.g., the world economic situation and the oil crisis of 1974), the following factors deserve attention:

1. There were shortcomings in the program for restructuring the economy. As mentioned above, the goal for the reform—to establish a regulated market—was correct. But being overcautious about a market economy, the Hungarians made a compromise between planning and the market. This is shown by the fact that the state put undue emphasis on government intervention and the method of planned central control. As has been discussed earlier, Hungary had made it quite clear from the outset that the economic reform should by no means weaken the control and guidance of the central government but rather improve and strengthen them. As a result, government control had largely been preserved in state-owned enterprises. This situation was in fact very similar to the old command system; few features of a substantive market system could be found. The price system failed to be rationalized; a climate for competition was not created; little autonomy was granted to enterprises; the private sector of the economy did not develop to the full; the income of enterprises and individuals still did not hinge on their performance; enterprises that suffered losses could still get subsidies from the state; and egalitarianism in distribution had not been eradicated. Under such circumstances, the objective of raising efficiency through the workings of market mechanism and the pressure of competition, which had been anticipated by the reform, was far from being achieved.

2. Several important problems failed to be resolved, both in theory and in practice. These included certain critical questions:

- The regulated market advocated by Hungary, which is the same as China's planned commodity economy, meant in theory to bring about a synthesis of plan and market or to have a market mechanism definitely brought into the orbit of the planned economy. But how this is to be realized, especially in the context of public ownership, is a problem remaining to be solved even today. Such being the case, no effective measures could be offered in practice.

- The two contradictions raised by János Kornai were not able to be resolved. These were the contradiction between the socialist principles of efficiency and those of what he calls "socialist ethics"; and the contradiction between efficiency and the socialist principles of solidarity, security, and full employment.[25] In order to raise efficiency, there had to be a system of incentives. If the incentives had worked, the inevitable outcome would have been a widening difference in workers' incomes and greater income inequality. Enterprises of low efficiency would have been threatened by bankruptcy, and workers would have been laid off. Socialist security and solidarity would then have been at stake. There were no effective measures to deal with these problems either.

3. Shortcomings also existed during the process of implementing the program for reform. It is sometimes necessary to make changes in the course of carrying out a plan. But in the case of Hungary's reform, political pressure often precipitated compromises, twists and turns, and even a degree of backsliding. Several reasons account for this. First, there was a lack of consistent adherence to the original plan, and when new circumstances emerged in and outside of the country, the leaders failed to respond in a prompt, flexible, and effective way. Second, certain manifestations of formalism, such as formalism in the execution of the regulations of the Enterprise Committee, gave rise to bureaucratism and irresponsibility. Third, there was an excessive number of changes in rules and regulations in the process of the implementation.[26] Changes are necessary sometimes. But frequent changes often caused confusion among the managers who could not respond to the frequently changing rules of the game. And the masses, who were at a loss for what to do, lost their confidence in the reforms.

4. The political reform was not able to proceed at the same pace as the economic reform. The blurring of party and government responsibilities, an aged leadership, a cumbersome administrative structure, and a mysterious and fossilized work style all prevented the economic reform from developing smoothly. As the masses lost confidence in the reforms and even lost their interest in politics, they gave little support to the reforms, which inevitably created difficulties.

It was in the context of such a situation that the National Congress of the Socialist Workers' Party of Hungary was held in Budapest in May 1988. This congress, putting its emphasis on reform of the political structure and personnel changes, adopted a resolution on the party's tasks and improvement of the political structure. The most important aspect of the new political structure was the rejuvenation of the party, including the separation of the party and government, the streamlining of organizations, the substantial reshuffling of the Politburo and the Central Committee, and the formation of a new leading body made up of younger, vigorous people with creative new ideas. In the thirteen-member Politburo, eight members (including János Kádár) have been replaced by younger and more radical reformers. Hungary's reform has now entered upon a new stage, which gives encouragement to reformers of the other socialist countries in Eastern Europe as well as to China. This revitalization has an important bearing on the political and economic reforms of the socialist world.

Notes

1. See *Freedom of the People*, Hungary, January 9, 1982.

2. Wlodzimierz Brus, "Political System and Economic Efficiency: the East European Context," *Journal of Comparative Economics*, No. 4, 1980, pp. 48, 52.

3. Bela Csikos-Nagy, "The Competitiveness of the Hungarian Economy," *The New Hungarian Quarterly*, Autumn 1981, p. 34.

4. Matyas Timar, *Reflections on the Economic Development of Hungary, 1967–1973* (Budapest: Akadémiai Kiado, 1975), pp. 11–12.

5. "Guidelines Formulated by the Central Committee of the Hungarian Socialist Workers' Party for the Reform of the Economic Mechanism," May 1966, *Principles of Hungary's Economic Reform and Management System* (Beijing: Chinese Financial and Economic Publishing House, 1980), Chinese edition.

6. Ibid.

7. See "Resolution Concerning the Reform of the Economic Mechanism" adopted by the Central Committee of the HSWP, May 1966, *Principles of Hungary's Economic Reform and Management System* (Beijing: Chinese Financial and Economic Publishing House, 1980), Chinese edition.

8. Ibid.

9. Bela Csikos-Nagy, *The Economic Mechanism of Hungary—the Period 1976–80*, New China News Agency, *Cankao ziliao*, May 20, 1982.

10. See "Guidelines," May 1966.

11. Bela Csikos-Nagy, "The Price Policy of Hungary," *Economic Problems*, USSR, No. 7, 1982.

12. Bela Csikos-Nagy, *Socialist Price Theory and Price Policy* (Budapest: Akadémiai Kiado, 1975), English edition, pp. 79–80.

13. Csikos-Nagy, *Economic Mechanism*.

14. See "Guidelines," May 1966.

15. Timar, *Reflections*, p. 7.

16. See "Decision of the Central Committee of the HSWP on the Preparation for the reform of the Economic Mechanism," June 1967, *Principles of Hungary's Economic Reform and Management System* (Beijing: Chinese Financial and Economic Publishing House, 1980), Chinese edition.

17. See Bela Csikos-Nagy, "The Competitiveness of the Hungarian Economy," *The New Hungarian Quarterly*, English edition, Autumn, 1981, pp. 26–27.

18. Ibid., p. 28.

19. Ibid., p. 29.

20. Csikos-Nagy, "Price Policy."

21. Csikos-Nagy, "Competitiveness," p. 34.

22. Ibid.

23. *International Herald Tribune*, July 11, 1988, pp. 1 and 6.

24. Alec Nove, *The Economics of Feasible Socialism* (London: Allen & Unwin, 1983), p. 133.

25. See ibid., pp. 123–124.

26. Ibid., p. 124.

PART 3

SOCIALIST REFORMS AND THE WORLD MARKET ECONOMY

If for the purpose of our analysis we view the CMEA countries as a separate economic world-system,[1] then socialist countries in theory have three alternative choices in their international economic policies: (1) to become a part of the CMEA economic system (all of Eastern Europe except Albania and Yugoslavia are members, plus Mongolia, Cuba, and Vietnam); (2) to attempt autarchy or self-reliance (for which China became a model during 1960–1976); or (3) to integrate their economies into the capitalist world market system (as Yugoslavia did after the break with Moscow in 1948 and as China has done since 1978). Each of these alternatives is examined in this section on international economic policies.

Since Yugoslavia's break with Moscow in 1948, Soviet power (including troops stationed in Eastern Europe and the history of Warsaw Pact intervention to keep unorthodox states in line, like Czechoslovakia in 1968) has assured that for the CMEA countries of Eastern Europe, there has in fact been only one option—economic integration with the Soviet Union.[2] But even these relationships have changed substantially over the years, both within the bloc and between the bloc and the world market economy.

In Chapter 10, Valerie Bunce, a political scientist at Northwestern University, examines the relationship between the Soviet Union and the Eastern European member countries of CMEA, what she calls "the Soviet empire." Bunce analyzes the changes that have taken place since 1945 through the Stalin, Khrushchev, and Brezhnev eras, asking who has benefited and how? She later extends her analysis from an examination of Soviet–East European relations to an assessment of how the entire CMEA bloc has fitted into the capitalist world market system.

The second foreign economic policy option for socialist countries—self-reliance—is assessed in Chapter 11 by William Loehr and Peter Van Ness, formerly colleagues at the University of Denver. Taking China as a case study, they attempt to calculate statistically the cost to China in lost economic growth of Mao Zedong's insistence on a strategy of self-reliance in China's international economic policy during 1960–1976, a time when China's strategy of self-reliant development was influential in much of the Third World.

In Chapter 12, Guocang Huan, one of the first PRC students to receive doctorate degrees from U.S. universities in political science, analyzes the third option, integration in the capitalist world market economy, again using China as a case study. Huan assesses China's "open door policy," which encourages foreign investment, trade, and cultural and educational exchanges with the West. Begun in 1978, this effort to acquire capital and technology for China's development by building economic ties with the United States, Japan, and Western Europe has been a fundamental part of the PRC's domestic market reform strategy.

In fact, China is the best example of the third policy option because the PRC has moved further than any other socialist country to integrate its economy into the capitalist world market economy. As data in the Appendix show, only 7 percent of China's total foreign trade was with other socialist countries in 1983. By comparison, even Yugoslavia directed 42 percent of its trade toward the East, and for all of the other countries analyzed, the majority of their trade was carried out with other socialist countries.

Moreover, China has joined the World Bank and the International Monetary Fund and applied for status as a contracting party to the General Agreement on Tariffs and Trade (GATT). World Bank lending to China by 1987 was at about $1.5 billion a year, and is expected to double by the early 1990s. Mooen Qureshi, the World Bank's senior vice president for operations, is quoted as saying that "in no other country does the bank have such a varied and diverse role," which combines both advisory and financial functions. He sees the most important aspect of the bank's role to be facilitating China's integration into the World market economy.[3]

The final contribution to this section on international economic policy, Chapter 13, is an essay by James Caporaso, a political scientist at the University of Washington. Invited specifically to comment on the three other contributions to this section, Caporaso draws out several common themes in the three chapters and then points to other important issues not directly addressed by the authors (e.g., socialist countries as "late developing societies") that in his view are central to the relationships among "International Economic Strategies, the State, and Domestic Society."

Notes

1. See the discussion of Wallerstein, Chase-Dunn, and Szymanski in Chapter 1.

2. For a detailed description of Soviet and Warsaw Pact military forces and their deployment, see International Institute for Strategic Studies, *The Military Balance 1987–1988* (London, 1987), pp. 33–53.

3. Robert Delfs in *Far Eastern Economic Review*, October 1, 1987, p. 71.

10

The Political Economy
of the Soviet Bloc

Valerie Bunce

A socialist system "only works if state control over the surplus is accepted by society."[1]

From the economic standpoint, the late capitalist grouping can renounce its former 'rollback' policy, since our bloc is . . . being integrated into the unitary world market which they dominate.[2]

The highly asymmetric distribution of resources among and within states in the Soviet bloc suggests that this empire, in direct contrast to empires of the past, should work to the clear economic and political benefit of the imperial power.[3] Few colonial powers in history, for example, have been able like the Soviets to insulate their colonies from both foreign and domestic competition over economic resources and political authority. Moreover, few imperial powers in history have been so able to ensure colonial compliance with imperial demands. The Soviets can wield the stick of imperial monopoly over all the vital economic and political resources within the empire. They can also offer the carrot of a regional system that manages to forge a mutually beneficial relationship between powerful elites in the center and powerful but dependent elites in the periphery. Finally, ease of imperial control is combined in this case with unusually sizable advantages to be gained from control. Whereas most territories in history have been annexed to serve either economic or geopolitical interests, Eastern Europe has managed to serve both. It generates a sizable and easily transferred social surplus, and it enhances Soviet national security through partial socialist encirclement. Eastern Europe, therefore, would appear to be that rare example of an ideal colony, eminently worthy of and highly amenable to imperial exploitation.[4]

Appearances, however, are deceiving. In this chapter, I argue that Soviet gains from control over the "ideal" empire in Eastern Europe have in fact declined sharply over time. I explain this paradox of sizable Soviet resources yet declining returns as a function, ironically, of the longer-term consequences of setting up an ideal empire—in particular, the costs at the domestic, regional, and eventually the global levels of combining a regional hierarchical system and dependency relations within the bloc with derivative Stalinist political economies in the client states. This combination had the effect at the domestic level of placing the East European states in a bind by the mid-1950s. They needed to expand consumption in order to purchase short-term domestic support, yet in doing so, they mortgaged economic growth and thereby the prospects for longer-term stability. These domestic pressures on the client states were passed on to the Soviet Union by virtue of the Soviet monopoly over markets, primary products, regional borders, and political authority—that is, because of the Soviet roles within the bloc as regional hegemon, political core, and economic periphery. These domestic and regional factors converged in turn to push the bloc to reintegrate with the global capitalist system in the 1970s.[5] The decision to terminate regional autarchy, however, exacerbated the very problems the policy was meant to counter. Pressures for political liberalization and reform of the economy through expanded use of markets both increased and thereby challenged the interlocking monopoly enjoyed by the Soviet and East European Communist parties. And as the states of Eastern Europe became more dependent on the West for markets and capital during the 1970s, so they became even more dependent on the Soviet Union for the same—an outcome counter to Soviet and East European elite interests.

It can be concluded, therefore, that the empire in Eastern Europe "struck back" for two reasons. First, the Soviet Union was in effect "hoist by its own petard." In establishing an "ideal" empire, Soviet "power" was translated in practice into Soviet weakness. Second, the burdens of empire allowed the Soviets to be hoist by the petard of late capitalism—that is, by the pressures Western trade placed on command economies, by the need of Western banks to recycle petrodollars in the 1970s, and by the global recessions of 1973–1974 and 1979–1982. Indeed, in setting up an autonomous world system and an ideal empire, the Soviets had merely laid the groundwork for outcomes opposite to those originally envisioned. By the time Gorbachev became General Secretary in 1985, the empire in Eastern Europe had become a mixed blessing.

The Ideal Empire

In order to assess changes over time in how valuable Eastern Europe has been to the Soviet Union, a standard is needed for evaluation. The approach I take is to construct an ideal empire—one that has optimal outcomes insofar as Soviet interests are concerned—and then assess the extent to which Soviet gains meet these ideal outcomes.

What, then, are Soviet interests in Eastern Europe? At the most general level, the Soviet Union wants Eastern Europe for the same reasons all states want colonies. Acquisition of outside territory helps the state maximize national security, economic growth and stability, and domestic political stability. From this perspective, an ideal colony would be easy to control, cheap to administer, and highly valuable in economic and geopolitical terms. When translated into specific outcomes resonant with Soviet values and interests, the ideal empire should accomplish three sets of tasks. First, with regard to national security, Eastern Europe should behave as a reliable ally, should contribute to the Soviet and regional defense burden, and should enhance Soviet power in the international system. Second, with respect to economic interests, Eastern Europe should be relatively cheap to administer and yet at the same time provide the Soviet Union with greater economic stability through assured, stable, and malleable markets and through a growing and easily transferred surplus; needed primary and secondary products at low cost; and favorable terms of trade. Finally, with respect to domestic stability, the empire in Eastern Europe should be seen by the Soviet population and dominant interests within that system as an asset; it should provide an added barrier to any external influences that might in a hostile international system challenge domestic stability or undercut the domestic control exercised by the Soviet state; and it should help dampen conflict among powerful interests within the Soviet Union by achieving the goals noted above, thereby easing the Soviet state's task of allocating money, power, and privilege at home.

To what degree has Soviet dominance over Eastern Europe managed to accomplish these objectives? I approach this issue by assessing the extent to which these ideal outcomes were achieved in the Stalinist period (1945–1953), the Khrushchev period (1953–1964), and the Brezhnev era (1964–1982). As will be seen, Soviet returns from empire were remarkably close to the ideal during the Stalinist period. By the end of the Brezhnev era, however, it could be concluded that control over Eastern Europe was meeting only one of the three sets of objectives: the maximization of Soviet national security. And even in this sphere it could be argued that the outcome was less favorable than in the past, because security was purchased at a much higher cost.

The Stalinist Period

Most empires in history have featured a mix of assets and liabilities insofar as imperial interests were concerned. One major reason is that the various goals of empire often dictate policies that are inherently contradictory. For example, there are inherent tensions between exerting maximum political control over colonies (in order to ensure the generation and easy transfer of capital) and the burdensome administrative and military responsibilities such control generates. There is also a tension between acquiring colonies that are attractive in economic and geopolitical terms and, as a result of their worth, having to deal with competitors for political power and the social surplus. Finally, there is a logic in maintaining local power structures in the colonies as a way of minimizing disruptions and discontent; yet the very fact of indirect rule places coopted elites in a position of power that over the long run will lead to a diversion of capital into local coffers and, more generally, decreasing compliance with the demands of the center.

Imperial powers, therefore, usually have to make hard choices among goals. Indeed, it is difficult to imagine an empire that maximizes national security and access to a sizable surplus while simultaneously keeping administrative and military costs to a minimum.

The Soviet bloc during the Stalinist period seemed to accomplish all of these seemingly contradictory objectives. The bloc was unique in its domestic and regional structure, unique in its relationship to the international system, and unique, as a result, in its capacity to maximize the imperial power's domestic and foreign interests. More specifically, the empire in Eastern Europe had three characteristics: Stalinism in the domestic sphere; complete Soviet control over the borders of the system and over the primarily bilateral interactions between states within the region; and isolation of the region from the international system. As a result, client states within the bloc depended on the Soviet Union for political power, economic stability, and economic growth.

The re-creation of the Stalinist experience in Eastern Europe was a two-stage process, which took place from approximately 1945 to 1953. The first stage involved the destruction of the old system. Much had been accomplished by the bitter interwar experience and the war itself, especially in Yugoslavia, Hungary,and Poland. The destruction was completed by Soviet occupation, the assignment of Eastern Europe to the Soviet zone of influence, the use by Communist parties of popular appeals including calls for land reform and punishment of fascist collaborators, and the discrediting by wartime and interwar experience of alternative elites, governing parties, and governing formulas. The second stage involved the creation of a new political economy that adhered closely to the Stalinist model. On the economic side, the new system included the introduction of state ownership of the means of production, central planning, collectivization of agriculture, and rapid industrialization both through controlled consumption and through the funneling of considerable forced savings into heavy industry. On the political side, Stalinism involved the concentration of resources in the hands of an authoritarian party and the use of terror to destroy old allegiances and power structures, force allegiance to the new order, and further concentrate power in the upper reaches of the party—in particular in the hands of those trained in Moscow and obedient to Soviet wishes.

In practice, Stalinization meant—as in the Soviet experience—that the familiar boundaries separating the polity, the economy, and the society in most systems were nonexistent. Instead, political, economic, and social arenas, roles, and resources were interdependent and fused.[6] Control over these pooled (and therefore sizable) resources, moreover, was highly concentrated at the top of the party and state hierarchies. Those elites exercised monopolistic and monopsonistic control over a rapidly expanding economy, and they had considerable incentives to maximize that growth. Fusion forged an interdependence between political fortunes and economic performance and between control over political power and control over economic resources.

Stalinist political economies in the client states thus allowed the Soviet Union to avoid many of the common problems that have undercut the value of empires in the past. In particular, the Soviets avoided governance over internally weak colonial states. They sidestepped all those considerable costs attached to choosing either cooptation or replacement of indigenous elites. And they did not face the common dilemma of having access to either unwanted goods in the colonies or, given the diffusion of power and the need to placate interests when establishing external control, a social surplus constrained by far too many claimants. Instead, by establishing Stalinist systems in Eastern Europe, the Soviet Union guaranteed, at least initially, that its colonies would be stable, that their governing parties would be subject to few political or economic pressures from below, and that the economies in the client states would grow, and grow in an optimal way.

The impressive array of resources available to the party elite in Eastern Europe and the Stalinist expansion of those resources, however, did not lead to the seemingly logical outcome. Eastern European party elites did not grow more autonomous. Instead, in expanding the resource base of colonialized elites, the Soviet Union in fact expanded its control over resources throughout the bloc. The symmetry at the time between Eastern European elite and Soviet elite interests helps explain this historically peculiar outcome; so does the political and economic dependence of Eastern European elites on the Soviet Union.

That political dependence had four main components. The first was the minimal domestic mandate of many of these parties as a result of Soviet "liberation" (especially in the cases of Poland, Hungary, Romania, and the German Democratic Republic).[7] The second was the role of the Soviet Union in either creating these Communist parties (as in Romania and the GDR) or in effect re-creating them (as in Poland and Hungary). The third was the Soviet demonstration in 1948 that Moscow controlled leadership selection in Eastern Europe and in all cases preferred Moscow-trained Communists over indigenous elites. The fourth consideration was the role of the Soviet Union as hegemon within a closed regional system, which, given bipolarity in the international system and the structure of the bloc, was left outside the zone of Western intervention and, as the Czechoslovak crisis with respect to the Marshall Plan indicated, Western aid as well. The considerable power of Eastern European elites, made possible by Stalinism, was in reality—to use Wladyslaw Gomulka's apt phrase—"a reflected brilliance, a borrowed light."[8] The power of these elites was derivative and dependent.[9]

The states of Eastern Europe were also economically dependent on the Soviet Union. Wartime destruction had been particularly great in Poland, Hungary, and Yugoslavia. East European economies were generally small, had a limited industrial base (except in Czechoslovakia), and were weak in primary products; the Soviet economy, by comparison, was large and had a considerable resource base. Finally, the Soviet Union could exert control over the region because the Soviets controlled the primarily bilateral political and economic transactions within the region and the primary products necessary for industrialization.

The Soviets, therefore, had ample control over both the powerful elites and the expanding economies they had in effect created in the client states. Eastern European elites acted as willing and capable transmission belts, maximizing Soviet foreign and domestic interests. The Soviets gained all the benefits of partial socialist encirclement, including greater security from the West and greater control over the domestic population. In the immediate postwar period they also received capital from the client states of an amount roughly equal to what the United States transferred to Western Europe through the Marshall Plan.[10]

What made these arrangements particularly successful was that Soviet gains were in many respects Eastern European gains as well. The reproduction of the Soviet model, the decision by Stalin to maintain separate states and separate economies in the bloc, and the decision to continue the prewar Soviet practice of autarchic development all indicated that Soviet interests in the area were primarily related to national security. The elites in Eastern Europe had in fact a great deal of control over their own economies, especially after the Soviets completed postwar reconstruction. Eastern European elites had opportunities to retain much of the surplus and to use the economy as a major mechanism for expanding their political power at home.

Fusion, rapid industrialization, and incorporation into a regional system also provided some concrete payoffs, among them a sense of national security, the proliferation of groups and individuals who benefited from rapid growth and one-party control, and protection from Western business cycles for a region severely affected by those cycles before 1939. Stalinism also brought some relief from the negative effects, so acutely felt during the interwar period, of Eastern Europe's primary-product dependence, its small domestic markets, and the typical combination in peripheral societies of too many intellectuals with too little economic growth.[11] Indeed, as George Konrad and Ivan Szelenyi have persuasively argued, the rapid expansion of power and resources during the Stalinist period gave the intelligentsia in Eastern Europe the role they had always sought—teleological power brokers—and the system they had always wanted—rational redistribution.[12]

Finally, these arrangements provided a means for linking these fractious societies to a new and more coherent political order. For example, the Stalinist stage saw a tremendous expansion of powerful positions in the party and in the economy, as one might expect in a command economy controlled by an authoritarian party and bent on rapid industrialization. For the citizenry as a whole, moreover, the compression of the modernization experience brought enhanced opportunities for upward political and social mobility.[13] Attachments were forged through the exhilarating experience of participating in the creation of a new society characterized by an expanding social wage, job security, and rapid socioeconomic transformation. Finally, in an area long the typical periphery, whose countries had functioned as the pawns of global powers because of an unfortunately strategic geopolitical location, Stalinism allowed for the possibility of achieving "national mobility" as well.[14] Stalinism created, in short, many vested interests. Although Stalinism had its costs to the coopted elites in Eastern Europe, these costs were not so large when viewed from the perspective of the turbulent interwar period.

From the Soviet perspective, of course, the costs were even smaller and the gains even more significant. Eastern Europe was an important counterweight to the West, and Soviet borders were secure as never before. The bloc's compliance with Soviet concerns was high and at a low cost. And the colonies were essentially self-supporting, deficient only in areas of Soviet largesse: primary products and political power.

Eastern Europe at this time, then, was an ideal empire, easy to control and highly valuable in economic, political, and national security terms. It provided the Soviets with what appeared to be an autonomous world system that they dominated.[15]

Some Deviations from the Ideal: 1953–1964

The impact of Stalin's death in 1953 demonstrated that certain conditions had to be met if Eastern Europe was to continue functioning as an ideal empire. More specifically, the degree to which the bloc functioned as a Soviet asset depended upon four conditions: rapid economic growth in the client states such that domestic conflict could be moderated; continued Soviet control over world communism and, hence, continued unity and obedience within the bloc; continued ability of Eastern parties to maintain absolute control over their societies and their economies such that the parties functioned as both powerful political and economic monopolies at home and dependent and obedient allies abroad; and a continued congruence between the political interests of Soviet and East European elites. Over the course of Khrushchev's tenure, all four of these conditions were challenged to some degree. The empire, as a result, lost some of its gloss.

The first complication grew out of Khrushchev's relations with the communist world and his encouragement, by accident and some design, of different roads to socialism. His rapprochement with Tito, for example, had the effect of weakening all the elites in Eastern Europe because each had ridden to power on the back of the anti-Titoist purges in 1948–1949. This shift undercut to some degree the control these elites had over the working class. Their spirited attacks on Yugoslav self-management after 1948 contrasted sharply with the implication in improved Soviet-Yugoslav relations that some tolerance, albeit severely limited, of the Yugoslav model was permissible.

At the same time, the increasingly deviant behavior of Albania and China, along with Soviet tolerance of deviance in Poland in 1956, indicated to the Eastern European party elites that they had some bargaining power. Indeed, if the party maintained control (which was itself in the elites' interest), some deviance was possible, especially if linked to the continuation of domestic tranquillity. This recognition was particularly pronounced in those states that were close to the Soviet border yet had weak governing mandates and limited legitimacy. The Romanian and Polish parties, for example, needed to put a distinctive stamp on their roads to socialism and had the resources to do so.[16]

De-Stalinization, however, made control over domestic populations in the periphery more difficult. One can debate at length about whether de-Stalinization was an accidental by-product of the Soviet succession struggle in a regional system where dissent as well as power flow westward, a ploy by Khrushchev to gain control over the satellites by installing his own people in power, or a conscious decision reflecting Khrushchev's genuine aversion to Stalinist excesses and his commitment to stimulating a moribund system through semipopulist principles and a shift from power to authority.[17] What is not debatable is that what happened in Hungary from 1953 to 1956, in the German Democratic Republic and Czechoslovakia in 1953, and in Poland once Boleslaw Bierut, the head of the party, died placed elites in all of the client states in a vulnerable position. They had been installed by and were beholden to Stalin. They had forced (especially in Hungary) tremendous social sacrifices in a very short period of time in the name of Stalin. They headed historically fractious, rapidly changing, and very new societies, which were the creation not of domestic Communist parties so much as interwar turmoil, the war itself, and the Red Army. Moreover, in Hungary and to a lesser extent Poland, Czechoslovakia, and Romania, terror against the party had nearly equaled the Soviet experience of the 1930s, but it had happened in new societies of more recent but equally revolutionary vintage and through a process telescoped into a few short years. Indeed, in the Polish case the party had been purged three times—during the 1930s, during the Soviet occupation, and during the anti-Titoist purges. Finally, in the more developed economies in the north, party elites faced slower growth. Given fusion between the polity and the economy, this slowdown exacerbated intraparty conflict, especially when combined with an ongoing succession crisis as in Hungary, Poland, and Czechoslovakia. In the Hungarian case, in particular, Khrushchev's juggling of Rákosi and Nagy mobilized competitive groups within the party, replacing the consensual and authoritarian one-party control so necessary for domestic stability.

As a result, de-Stalinization in Eastern Europe was a dramatic and difficult break with a past that was neither as institutionalized nor as resonant with historical traditions as in the Soviet experience. It was also a break made easier by remnants of elites and ideologies from the past, remnants long gone from the Soviet scene by 1956. The impact of de-Stalinization was, not surprisingly, greatest in those systems that combined in extreme form all of the factors noted above—in particular, Hungary, Poland, and eventually Czechoslovakia. In these states de-Stalinization translated (with some ease, given fusion and intraparty conflict) into demands by intellectuals and, to a lesser degree, workers for a new leadership (especially in Poland) and substantial political and economic reforms (especially in Hungary). All three countries demanded immediate economic recompense, so long promised, for the sacrifices made during the brief Stalinist industrialization drive. Elites in Bulgaria, Romania, Albania, and Czechoslovakia managed to put off reforms until the invasion of Hungary sealed the fate of many of these measures. But the impact of reforms elsewhere was dramatic: For a brief period, domestic politics reappeared in the periphery.

Domestic demands strained both elites and empire. Within the periphery, they by definition implied a dispersion of the party's monopoly over political and economic resources, a monopoly essential to the continued stability of these systems and to their role as transmission belts for Soviet interests. Indeed, Eastern European elites were caught between their longer-term interests (and the interests of the Soviet Union) and the immediate concerns of their various publics. Domestic demands—direct in some cases, feared in others—implied dispersion of political and economic power through an opening up of the party, decentralization of the economy, the establishment of "national communism," and increased emphasis on domestic consumption over capital investment.[18]

The elites' dilemma, in brief, was that their long-term needs for rapid growth and party control were inconsistent with short-term political pressures from below. The resolution they chose was to shore up inroads into Eastern European (and thereby Soviet) elite control over economic and political resources in Eastern Europe, while ameliorating mass discontent in ways that would not threaten the highly skewed distribution of political and economic power at home and within the bloc.[19] Serious reform in the aftermath of Poland and Hungary in 1956, therefore, was rejected in favor of retracting the worst abuses of Stalinism, particularly insofar as terror against the party was concerned. Symbols of reform were provided, either through the inauguration of new leaders who had suffered under Stalin (Gomulka in Poland, Kádár in Hungary) or through decollectivization (in the Polish case). In the short term, public consumption was primed. To have responded in any other way would have led to the dismantling of the whole system, because the forfeiture by the party of either economic or political power would have been the forfeiture of both. It would also have meant the forfeiture of Soviet dominance over the region.

The fiscal burden of these decisions seems to have fallen primarily on Soviet shoulders. It did so, ironically, because of Soviet power and Eastern European weakness. Soviet strength involved Soviet monopoly over all the fiscal, political, and military resources necessary for purchasing short-term stability in the bloc. The Soviets were the political patrons of domestically weak party elites in the client states; they had the liquidity—in economic as well as political terms—to get through a crisis; they were autarchic whereas Eastern Europe needed Soviet primary products in order to maintain growth; and, finally, because of bilateralism and the redundancy of Eastern European economic strengths and weaknesses, the Soviet Union was the central participant in what were at that time limited trade relations within the bloc.

At the same time, the Soviets had what might be called a political as well as an economic monopoly; they had unusually strong incentives to bail out Eastern European elites. The region was critical for defense, especially in the context of U.S. economic and military superiority. Unrest "in one country" was not safe in a regional system where contiguous states were similar in their origins and political-economic arrangements. De-Stalinization and the costs of the Hungarian invasion had already limited the domestic tools available for "encouraging" public restraint.

Eastern Europe's party elites had a very strong set of arguments in support of economic aid. Dissent could cross Soviet borders by passing through the Baltic republics and the Ukraine. Moreover, the elites could argue, decisions in such circumstances should be based on the "worst-case scenario." It was safer to assume that unrest was contagious—to assume otherwise and be wrong would have necessarily dangerous consequences for bloc stability. Finally, there was an ideological consideration. Both purchasing stability and introducing some reforms were consistent with Khrushchev's concerns with creating a more positive basis for regime-society relations in the post-Stalinist period.

The weakness of Eastern European elites, who had few resources to deal with the consequences, real and feared, of de-Stalinization, thus enhanced their ability to bargain with Moscow. As a result, the Soviet Union functioned in the short term as the fiscal guarantor of political stability throughout the region. In practice, the Soviets helped pay for increases in public consumption throughout Eastern Europe during the second half of the 1950s. They provided relatively cheap primary products to all of Eastern Europe, allowed some deterioration between 1956 and 1964 in Soviet terms of trade within the bloc, and extended emergency and nonrepayable aid to regimes in trouble—the German Democratic Republic and Czechoslovakia in1953, Hungary and Poland in 1956.[20]

Once implemented, however, Soviet aid in the form of implicit trade subsidies became standard operating procedure, and for three reasons. First, there was by the early 1960s an economic slowdown in much of Eastern Europe.[21] The result was that Eastern European elites lost the capacity to respond to domestic economic demands while continuing to fear that failure to respond would spark unrest, particularly in countries that had avoided de-Stalinization, such as Czechoslovakia. Indeed, every state in the bloc had some bargaining resources in regard to its demonstrated or potential vulnerability. Second, small economic subsidies were far less costly for the Soviet Union than was the risk of unrest and its threats to national security and domestic political stability. The size of the Soviet economy, its autarchic structure, and the fact that Eastern Europe's economic needs were in areas of Soviet excess—that is, primary products—all reduced potential cost. Finally, given the importance of growth for moderating the heated competition for economic and political resources, the economic downturn in Eastern Europe and rising mass expectations produced substantial political conflict within these systems, as one would expect.

The Eastern Europeans, then, had a powerful set of arguments for the continuation of favorable terms of trade. As a result, by the end of Khrushchev's tenure, the empire in Eastern Europe had become less profitable for the Soviets.[22] The rising costs associated with trade and periodic unrest in the periphery were, however, minimal when compared with all the assets involved. Eastern Europe provided a Soviet bridgehead in Europe, helped shoulder a defense burden that was growing rapidly in response to East-West competition, provided the Soviet economy with some needed items, and enhanced Soviet control over their domestic population through partial socialist encirclement. This was still a lot to receive for a few rubles, especially because they seemed to produce desired ends. The bloc was, after all, stable from the late 1950s to the end of Khrushchev's tenure, despite an economic slowdown.

The Empire Strikes Back: 1964–1982

The Brezhnev regime tried to return intrabloc relations to their previous footing. Brezhnev wanted the bloc to continue to further Soviet foreign policy interests; he wanted at the same time to improve upon his predecessor's record in maximizing economic growth and political stability. He failed. By the end of Brezhnev's tenure, a pattern common both to empires of the past and to military alliances had evolved. National security was purchased at higher and higher cost, both because there were tensions inherent in Soviet interests insofar as Eastern Europe was concerned and because fears of sacrificing growth and stability on the altar of national security led to decisions that, ironically, undermined all three Soviet goals.

The concern with national security led the Soviets, in the aftermath of Czechoslovakia in 1968,[23] to tighten their control over the Warsaw Pact and over leadership selection in Eastern Europe. Demanding Eastern European help in their arms build-up, the Soviets stipulated through the Brezhnev doctrine the limits of deviance for client states in domestic and especially foreign policy behavior.[24] They were relatively successful. However, these achievements in national security were offset by some loss, albeit impossible to measure, of influence in the Third World as a result of the Sino-Soviet rift; the crisis in Czechoslovakia and the Polish crises of 1970–1971, 1975–1976, and 1980–present; the Romanian deviation in foreign policy and the Albanian alliance with China; the continued thorn of Yugoslavia; a decline over time in bloc cohesion;[25] and the ability of most members of the bloc during the 1970s either to reduce their defense burden (expressed as a percentage of GNP) or, as with Bulgaria and the GDR, to hold contributions to the regional defense burden relatively constant.[26] These costs were important, but, the foreign policy benefits the Soviets reaped from empire were still sizable. Eastern Europe still carried about 10 percent of the bloc-wide defense burden, for example.

The same could not be concluded for Soviet gains from intrabloc economic relations. From 1961 to 1965 the average annual rate of growth in the Soviet GNP had slowed to 5 percent, a postwar low.[27] In part this slowdown reflected the natural limits to rapid growth, once an economy matures, and the particular limits to growth, once command economies deplete new sources of labor and capital and confront more directly the costs of distorted prices, inferior technology, imbalanced growth, and, more generally, inefficient utilization of the factors of production. In part, however, the slowdown also reflected the costs of empire: for example, the unfavorable terms of trade within the Soviet bloc, the costs of having extended aid to regimes in trouble, and the structural inability of Eastern Europe to provide the Soviet Union with needed—let alone high-quality—products.

The Brezhnev regime approached these problems by instituting (or, more accurately, trying to institute)[28] economic reform at home and changing economic relations abroad. The Brezhnev regime charged more for Soviet primary products because it used five-year moving averages based on world market prices. It pressured the bloc to coordinate economic plans to a greater extent and to increase the level of capital investment. It also pressured Eastern Europe to specialize; the northern tier would focus on the production of consumer goods and machine tools, the southern tier on agriculture and the processing of raw materials. The Soviets went along with economic reforms in Hungary and the GDR, in the hope that such measures would bolster growth and improve the quality of products. Moreover, they encouraged Eastern Europe to use detente to open up trade relations with the West.[29] Western trade would take some pressure off the Soviet economy and encourage, through the imposition of Western standards, an improvement in the quality and diversity of goods produced in the bloc.

These measures were not successful, and the economic burdens of empire increased rather than declined. Bloc specialization and plan coordination proceeded in a stop-and-start manner because of the autarchic legacies and the vested economic and political interests generated by Stalinism. Eastern Europe also feared that a regional division of labor would make it more dependent on the Soviet Union. In practical terms, moreover, shortages of capital, weaknesses in technological innovation, the commitment to full employment, and the significant growth of the second half of the 1960s in most of Eastern Europe limited incentives for such a strategy.[30] Indeed, there were few good political or economic reasons for Eastern Europe to go along with Soviet demands for major structural changes in their economies.

The biggest failure, however, was in intrabloc trade and Soviet transfers of explicit subsidies. Although the Soviet terms of trade within the bloc did in fact improve over the course of the Brezhnev era, particularly during the 1970s, the rate of improvement paled against dramatic improvements in the Soviet terms of trade with the West.[31] Soviet exports to the West and to the bloc were essentially the same products and increasingly attractive in the world market. As a result, the opportunity costs attached to Soviet trade within, as opposed to outside, the bloc were substantial. Indeed, one estimate (and, it must be emphasized, an estimate) of these opportunity costs by Jan Vanous and Michael Marrese places the loss to the Soviet Union from intrabloc trade at $21.7 billion (current U.S. dollars) from 1974 through 1980.[32] As Table 10.1 indicates, moreover, the Soviet Union's implicit and, it must be noted, nonrepayable trade subsidies to Eastern Europe rose sharply over the 1970s. The rise reflected the fact that intrabloc prices for Soviet raw materials and energy had not kept pace with world market prices and the extent to which Eastern European states had neither the economic incentives nor the structural capacity to cut back on Soviet imports. In other words, the economic burden of the bloc, so far as trade was concerned, had become much heavier over the course of the Brezhnev era.

These estimates of implicit trade subsidies may be on the high side.[33] Also, the recent downturn in world market prices for many primary products (in particular, energy products) and the impact of moving averages based on earlier, higher prices would necessarily reduce Soviet burden since 1980.

Nevertheless, there are other ways in which the costs to the Soviet Union of trade within the bloc may be underestimated in Table 10.1. First, the table omits the substantial trade subsidies extended to Poland after the crisis of 1980. In 1981, for example, Poland received raw material and energy supplies from the Soviet Union that were valued at about $6.7 billion but that cost the Poles approximately half that amount. Indeed, in that year the Soviets charged the Poles one-half of the OPEC rate for Soviet oil, the charge to the rest of the bloc was 70 to 80 percent of OPEC prices.[34] Second, these figures on losses from intrabloc trade do not include the costs of reduced Soviet access to Western markets as a result of Eastern European trade dependence or the costs to the Soviets of the combination of Soviet economic power and Eastern European weakness. With regard to the first point, primary products, aside from gold, are the means through which the Soviet Union can gain access to Western trade. And Western trade is critical, because the Soviets rejected a policy of producing valued technological and consumer items during the 1970s in favor of importing such items from the West.[35] Continuing high demand in Eastern Europe for Soviet primary products, therefore, reduces Soviet access to Western markets.

Sizeable Soviet exports of necessary items to the bloc mean sizeable Soviet imports from the bloc but minimal Soviet control over the quality of these imports. If autarchy has meant in practice redundancy, production for domestic consumption, and weaknesses in consumer goods, then high demand for exports means that the Soviet Union functions, in effect, as a captive monopsony receiving redundant and unwanted items. The social surplus, in short, may be

Table 10.1. Estimated Implicit Soviet Trade Subsidies to Eastern Europe
(in million current dollars)[a]

	Bulgaria	Czecho-slovakia	GDR	Hungary	Poland	Romania	Total
1974	1,081	1,174	2,023	877	1,067	43	6,265
1975	919	1,097	1,665	598	1,027	19	5,325
1976	877	1,195	1,786	671	1,021	45	5,595
1977	1,015	1,226	1,896	645	1,106	50	5,938
1978	1,087	1,086	1,914	661	897	109	5,754
1979[b]	2,000	2,000	3,400	1,200	1,700	100	10,400[c]
1980[b]	4,100	4,100	7,200	2,600	3,500	200	21,700[c]

[a]These figures represent the estimated opportunity costs of Soviet trade to Eastern Europe,
or the gap between what the Soviets charge the Eastern Europeans for goods imported from
the Soviet Union and the higher prices the Soviets would receive if these goods were
exported to the West. Although these estimates are subject to debate, given the difficulties
involved in establishing exchange rates, spot market prices for oil, and the like, they would
seem to be reliable estimates because (1) a great majority of the goods in question are
primary products and therefore relatively insulated from problems associated with estimating
quality or elasticity of demand and (2) the arguments supporting the exchange rates used are
convincing. For arguments that question whether these estimates may be too high, see
Paul Marer, "The Political Economy of Soviet Relations with Eastern Europe" in Sarah
Meiklejohn Terry, ed., *Soviet Foreign Policy in Eastern Europe* (New York: Council on
Foreign Relations, 1984), pp. 155–188.

[b]These are preliminary estimates.

[c]The huge jump in 1979 and 1980 reflects (1) the degree to which the Soviets were not able
to take advantage of sharp increases in world market prices for energy supplies in intrabloc
trade and (2) the extent of Eastern European energy and trade dependence on the Soviet Union.
For example, excluding Romania, a range of 75 percent to 93 percent of all energy imports
in Eastern Europe comes from the Soviet Union, and 1/2 to 1/3 of all trade in these countries
is with the Soviet Union. See Morris Bornstein, "Soviet-East European Economic Relations,"
in Morris Bornstein, Zvi Gitelman, and William Zimmerman, eds., *East-West Relations and
the Future of Eastern Europe* (London: Allen & Unwin, 1981), pp. 105, 111.

Sources: Jan Vanous and Michael Marrese, "Soviet Subsidies to Eastern Europe," *The Wall
Street Journal*, January 15, 1982.

easy to transfer within the Soviet bloc, but its form, from the Soviet
perspective, has become less and less controllable and attractive.

The growth of implicit trade subsidies and other losses from intrabloc trade
are not the only economic costs of empire. The Soviet Union also transfers
explicit subsidies to its clients in Mongolia, Vietnam, and Cuba, as well as in
Eastern Europe (see Table 10.2). As the estimates in this table indicate, the
Soviets have extended substantial hard currency loans—approximately $6.2
billion in 1981, for example—at what appears to be very low interest and with
very flexible, perhaps nonexistent, repayment schedules. At the same time, the
Soviets appear to have given extensive ruble credits—approximately $5

Table 10.2 Estimated Soviet Economic Subsidies to Client States

	Estimated Hard Currency Subsidies 1981 (in $U.S. millions)	Present Value of Ruble Credits 1971–1980 (in 1980 $U.S. billions)	Present Value of Trade Subsidies 1971–1980 (in 1980 U.S. Billions)[a]	Total Debt and Nonrepayable Soviet Aid, 1971–1980 (in 1980 $U.S. billions)	Soviet Share of Total Eastern European Debt, 1971–1980 (in percentages)[b]
Bulgaria	127	.8	13.5	16.3	88
Czechoslovakia	344	.4	15.3	18.5	85
GDR	292	1.4	26.6	38.4	73
Hungary	167	.4	9.7	16.5	61
Poland	1,900[c]	.5[d]	13.6	36.4	43
Romania	460	-.5	.8	7.7	4
Total	3,290	3.0	79.5	133.8[e]	63
Cuba	1,860	na	na	na	na
Mongolia	86	na	na	na	na
Vietnam	1,040[f]	na	na	na	na
Total	2,986	na	na	na	na
Grand Total	6,276	na	na	na	na

[a]This column is the opportunity cost for the Soviets of trading within the bloc as opposed to trading at world market prices. This figure is critical because it is a nonrepayable cost of empire, and, as this table indicates, it is growing at a rapid rate. Note the impact of geopolitical considerations; that is, the favored treatment of Poland and East Germany, which on a per capita basis have received $1,700 and $2,274, respectively.

[b]This column is the proportion of total debt to the Soviets, including credit and trade subsidies to overall debts, including Western hard currency debt. In other words, the percentages indicate how much of overall Eastern European external debt (defined to include Soviet subsidies of all kinds) is to the Soviet Union as opposed to the West.

[c]This figure is most likely on the low side. Other estimates range from 2.0 to 2.5 billion. See Frank Lipsius, "Poland's Cost to the East," *New York Times*, February 7, 1983; John Burns, "Poland an Increasing Economic Burden for Soviets," *New York Times*, December 23, 1981; and "Soviets May Seek New Loans," *New York Times*, January 8, 1982.

[d]In 1981, this figure jumped to $3.8 billion for coverage of Polish trade deficits with the Soviet Union. See "Soviets May Seek New Loans," *New York Times*, January 8, 1982.

[e]This figure is for Eastern Europe only.

[f]This figure may also be on the low side. Estimates in 1981 indicated that out of a $3 billion debt, Vietnam owed $1.6 billion to the Soviet Union. See "Vietnam in Economic Straits Seeks U.S. Contact," *New York Times*, December, 28, 1981.

Sources: Michael Marrese and Jan Vanous, *Implicit Subsidies and Non-Market Benefits in Soviet Trade with Eastern Europe* (Berkeley, Calif.: Institute for International Studies, 1983), pp. 125–130, 143–147, 198–204, 213–226, and 228–234; Michael Marrese and Jan Vanous, "Soviet and Western Financial Support of Eastern Europe," unpublished paper summarizing their monograph (1983): "Now Russia Asks for Time to Pay," *The Economist*, February 6, 1982, p. 79; "Vietnam in Economic Straits Seeks U.S. Contacts," *New York Times*, December 28, 1981; John Burns, "Poland and Increasing Economic Burden for Soviets," *New York Times*, December, 23, 1981.

billion(see Table 10.2 and note c)—to Eastern Europe, reflecting in part the growth across the 1970s of Eastern Europe's trade deficits with the Soviet Union. When these estimates are combined with the estimated implicit trade subsidies noted above, Soviet aid in all forms to Eastern Europe amounted to (very) approximately $133.8 billion between 1971 and 1980. Indeed, as column 5 in Table 10.2 indicates, this figure easily outdistanced Eastern European debt to the West.

While a serious drain on the Soviet economy, these implicit and explicit subsidies presented in Tables 10.1 and 10.2 do not tell the whole story. For example, ruble credits (and trade subsidies) extended to allies outside Eastern Europe are not included in these two tables, yet they are known to be sizeable. Although Cuba may be worth $3 billion to $5 billion a year to the Soviet Union and Vietnam worth $2 billion a year, the fact remains that these colonies are significant economic drains. In addition, Table 10.2 does not include credits (approximately $3.8 billion in 1981 alone) extended to the Poles to cover Soviet-Polish trade imbalances; such aid has very probably continued. Finally, indirect evidence suggests that the figures for hard currency loans to Poland in Table 10.2 are too low. Poland did eventually pay the interest due in 1981 to Western banks and was able to reschedule the principle due in the same year, despite a GNP that declined for the third straight year, falling exports to the West, and a sharp decrease in industrial output between 1980 and 1982. Austerity measures in Poland, moreover, did not seem to be as austere as the size of the debt would make one expect.[36]

Did the Soviets provide more to the Poles than Table 10.2 indicates? Soviet behavior during 1981 indicates a substantial drain on Soviet hard currency reserves. Examples include the large but difficult-to-explain increase in Soviet debt to the West (from $17.5 billion to $19.0 billion); a large increase in Soviet gold sales, despite depressed market conditions; and the failure of the Soviets to use up Western trade credits. Despite depressed economic and unstable political times, the Soviets pressured Eastern Europe to pay more for fewer Soviet goods and to ride out the disruptions in intrabloc trade brought on by the sagging Polish economy and, indeed, sagging Hungarian, Czechoslovak, and East German economies.[37] The final evidence concerns the performance of the Soviet economy during this period. Industrial growth, for instance, was supposed to be 4.7 percent in the first half of 1982 but reached only 2.7 percent. Unprecedented in history, moreover, the economic plan for 1982 called for *no* increase in the Soviet standard of living.[38] The burden of the Polish crisis, therefore, would seem to have fallen even more heavily on the Soviet economy than Tables 10.1 and 10.2 suggest.

The nature of Soviet trade in the bloc and the size of Soviet loans and credit to client states together demonstrate that Brezhnev's hopes for a reversal of the trends of the 1960s in intrabloc trade and in Soviet emergency aid did not materialize. The measures taken to limit the economic costs of empire had precisely the opposite effect, as the relationship between Soviet price increases within the bloc, on the one hand, and expansions of implicit and explicit subsidies, on the other, seems to indicate. Originally, the size and resource base of the Soviet economy, Soviet dominance in intrabloc trade, and the Soviet role as a political and economic monopoly had formed the basis of Soviet strength in intrabloc bargaining. Now, all of these characteristics seemed to increase Soviet weakness within the bloc. All economic roads led to Moscow, especially in hard times.[39]

It is hardly surprising that the growth of the Soviet GNP has slowed in recent years, averaging in one estimate only 2.7 percent per year from 1976 to 1980 and actually declining by 1.4 percent in 1980.[40] The reasons for this slowdown are many, of course, and they include a variety of domestic and international factors. Nevertheless, one reason must be the mounting costs of what may be termed Soviet national security: that is, the costs of "empire maintenance" (or the substantial nonrepayable subsidies noted above—emergency aid, ruble and hard currency loans) and the burden of heavy defense outlays (approximately 11 to 12 percent of the Soviet GNP or about 90 percent of all bloc defense expenditures through the 1970s).[41]

The burden of maintaining control over Eastern Europe has important political costs as well. Imperial conquest is based on the assumption that control over colonies will not only maximize various economic and national security interests but also enhance domestic political stability. The ledger here resists summary with figures, but we can nonetheless make some inferences.

The diversion of scarce economic resources to the client states has contributed to Soviet policies of stringency at home and greater pressure on workers in particular, as well as on the party, to produce more with less.[42] These policies, needless to say, breed resentment, especially in a time of worker unrest in Eastern Europe and when more Soviet citizens have seen firsthand how well off Poles, East Germans, and others are in comparison with their own position in a consumer-deficit society.[43] The figures in Table 10.3 are suggestive (in a rough sense only) of the contrast over time between Soviet and Eastern European economic priorities and between the quality of life in Warsaw or Prague and Moscow. When this contrast is combined with the belief in many quarters in the Soviet Union that Eastern Europe siphons off Soviet goods and with the mirror-image belief within the client states, the result is a great deal of domestic discontent, in the Soviet Union as well as in the satellites.

This discontent, moreover, will only increase in the future. As the costs of domestic austerity become clear and as the Eastern European regimes, with the plausible exception of Hungary, fall prey to their past habit of failing (and indeed fearing) to prepare a discontented populace for hard times, Eastern European states will undoubtedly turn to the Soviets to lessen the burdens that hard times impose.[44] The result will undoubtedly be greater pressure on the party to reform and on the regional hegemon to subsidize reforms. The Polish crisis and unrest in Romania in 1977 in response to economic pressures on workers are, of course, cases in point.[45] And they are especially telling examples

Table 10.3 Comparisons of Average Annual Rates of Growth in the
Economy, Productive and Unproductive Investment, and Wages: The
Soviet Bloc, 1971–1980 (in percentage growth)

	Soviet Union	Bulgaria	Czecho-slovakia	GDR	Hungary	Poland	Romania
1971–1975							
Economy (GNP-constant prices)	3.7[a]	3.9	2.7	3.8	3.0	5.2	5.7
Productive investment	8.1	8.5	8.4	3.7	6.0	20.1	11.6
Unproductive investment	3.9	9.0	7.2	6.0	9.4	12.6	10.8
Difference between productive and unproductive investment[b]	4.2	-0.5	+1.2	-2.3	-3.40	7.5	.8
Wages	2.7	2.6	2.5	n.a.	4.22	6.7	3.7
Difference between wage growth and economic growth	+1.0	+1.3	+0.1	n.a.	-1.2	-1.4	+2.0
1976–1980							
Economy (GNP-constant prices)[c]	2.7	1.8	1.3	2.8	2.1	1.3	5.7
Productive investment	3.6	3.6	3.0	n.a.	2.4	-3.5	9.4
Unproductive investment	2.8	5.3	2.2	n.a.	2.4	2.6	4.6
Difference between productive and unproductive investments	+.8	-1.7	+.8	n.a.	0.0	-6.1	+4.8
Wages	2.2	4.6	2.0	n.a.	5.0	5.7	4.7
Difference between wage growth and economic growth	+0.5	-2.8	-0.7	n.a.	-2.9	-3.4	+1.0

[a] The Soviet figures for GNP are not directly comparable to the East European figures because they were derived from different estimation procedures. The Soviet figures are taken from Joint Economic Committee, U.S. Congress, *USSR: Measures of Growth and Development, 1950–1980* (Washington, D.C.: U.S. Government Printing Office, December 1982), pp. 15–16. The East European figures are estimates made by Thad Alton and are reported in Paul Marer, "Economic Performance and Prospects in Eastern Europe: Analytical Summary and Interpretation of Findings," in Joint Economic Committee, U.S. Congress, *East European Economic Assessment: Part II* (Washington, D.C.: U.S. Government Printing Office, 1981) p. 26. The GNP figures for Eastern Europe are for 1976–1979, not 1976–1980.

[b] The point here is that Eastern Europe in general shows more commitment to unproductive investment, as revealed in the negative figures.

[c] The point here is that wage increases have outstripped economic growth in many cases, as signified by the negative numbers.

Sources: The sources for GNP are in note a. The sources for the rest of the table are *Statisticheskii ezhegodnik stran; chlenov soveta vzaimopomoshchi (Statistical Yearbook of the Countries in the Council of Mutual Economic Assistance)* (Moscow: Central Statistical Office, 1978), pp. 404–406, 138; and SEV (Moscow: Central Statistical Office, 1981), pp. 415–418, 144. It must be noted that these figures must be treated with caution, because the figures on GNP are Western estimates and the figures on wages and investment are from official sources. If official sources were used for economic growth, the contrast between wages and economic growth would be smaller, though the trend would be in the same direction.

when one considers the unique position of Janos Kádár and the more typical and vulnerable position of other leaders in a bloc prone to spillover effects. If partial socialist encirclement seems to enhance the domestic and foreign security of the hegemonic power, it does so only if the proximate periphery is quiescent, economically productive, deficient in the quality of life by comparison with the hegemon's culture. When these conditions are not met, as the Soviets discovered in the Czechoslovak case in 1968, partial socialist encirclement can in fact threaten domestic security and stability.[46]

What began as an ideal empire has evolved in just thirty-five years into an empire that although still valuable, features fewer assets and many more liabilities. Soviet and Eastern European elites still share interests, and the Soviets still hold a monopoly over political and economic resources within the bloc. But if the value of empire is based on the degree to which the colonies help the colonial state achieve its central objectives of economic growth, national security, and domestic political support and political stability, then the value of this empire has declined sharply over a relatively brief span of time.

Why the Empire Struck Back

Why has Soviet control over Eastern Europe generated fewer and fewer returns? A full explanation must take into account the impact of domestic, regional, and global pressures on intrabloc relations. More specifically, the analysis thus far points to four issues that must be addressed in any full explanation of declining Soviet returns from Eastern Europe. First, why did Eastern European publics demand so much of the state, how were they so cohesive in their actions, and why did they focus their concerns on the issue of immediate improvements in the standard of living? Second, why were these obviously authoritarian states so vulnerable to demands from below and so responsive to them, despite their considerable capacities to behave otherwise? Third, whereas Soviet emergency aid is easy to explain, other economic transactions within the bloc are not. More specifically, how did all the Eastern European states manage to bargain so consistently well with the Soviets in terms of implicit and explicit subsidies, the defense burden, and domestic investment priorities? In other words, why were the Soviets so accommodating, even during periods of tranquillity within the bloc? Finally, why did the Soviets and the Eastern Europeans decide to terminate regional autarchy and rejoin the global capitalist system? That decision, after all, went deeply against the historical and ideological grain, threatened Soviet monopoly over the region, and eventually undercut the domestic and the foreign interests of both the Soviet Union and the client states.

Some of the answers to these questions can be found in extant assessments of trade-offs that evolve over time in empires in general and, more specifically, of changes over time in the costs and benefits to member states in this particular empire. Analysts who have focused on relations within the bloc and who treat the nation-state as the unit of analysis emphasize how susceptible bargaining within the sytem is to free-rider dynamics. Susceptibility increases when bargaining is bilateral, when the system is regional-hierarchical in structure, and when the smaller states within the regional system manage to gain access to resources outside the bloc.[47] Other analysts have treated the region as the unit of analysis and focus on the place of the Soviet bloc within the global capitalist system.[48] They argue that the Soviets had to pay a price for attempting to isolate the region from the global capitalist system and had to pay an even higher price for allowing the bloc to evolve into a semiperiphery of the global capitalist system.[49] A final approach, which has been applied in only a limited way to the Soviet bloc, has argued that declining Soviet returns reflected both the natural limits to expropriation of the surplus in empires and the mounting costs associated with imperial control. The growing costs of Eastern Europe can be explained from this perspective as a function of the inherently contradictory objectives of empire and of the long-term costs of expansion. These two factors seem to have led to the development of Janus-faced elites in the colonies.[50] They also led to the expansion of foreign and domestic competition for political authority and economic goods and to the necessary translation of these pressures into what Robert Gilpin has characterized for empires in general as "the growing conflict among guns, butter or productivity."[51]

Each of these arguments provides some pieces to a puzzle that might be summarized as obvious Soviet power but apparent Soviet weakness. Each, however, fails to provide complete answers to the four questions specified above and fails to examine the full range of imperial costs and benefits. The first approach, with its focus on state-level bargaining within the bloc, provides good explanations of why the Soviet Union has been so accommodating to Eastern European demands. It recognizes the susceptibility of the bloc to free-rider effects and the predictably high costs to Soviet security of a failure to respond quickly to Eastern European demands. But because of its focus on the state, it says little about the *origins* of demands in the client states or about variation in ability to bargain successfully with the Soviet Union over defense contributions, trade, and aid. Moreover, it makes little sense to treat (as such analyses do) what were in reality severe costs of growing Eastern European dependence on the West and eventually on the East during the 1970s for all concerned as increases in the "resources" available to Eastern European states when bargaining with the Soviets. It is also difficult to explain why the Soviets cut into their own resources and allowed Eastern Europe to gain leverage in intra-bloc bargaining by encouraging the termination of regional economic autarchy. In sum, it is difficult to explain the events of the 1970s—or to explain the conflicts between regimes and their societies in Eastern Europe—by relying on arguments that focus on bargaining among states within the bloc. International and domestic forces, in short, are too influential to be treated as givens.

It is precisely these two issues—domestic tensions and global pressures—that are of central interest to those who examine the Soviet bloc in the context of center-periphery dynamics in the global system. This approach is helpful in explaining why peripheralization of the bloc led to growing tensions within Eastern Europe and led as well to a decline in the resources available to all the states in the bloc. However, this line of argument is less helpful in other regards. First, an analysis that fails to distinguish among bloc states, and at times between the dominant and the small states within the bloc, does not address the variations by state and time in costs over the postwar period. Second, the analysis is not clear about how isolation of the region from the global capitalist system in the 1950s and 1960s translated into growing burdens on the Soviet Union in general, a deterioration throughout the bloc in the terms of trade, and a decline as well in Eastern European contributions to the defense burden. Finally, it is not clear why Soviets willingly opened the bloc to Western penetration. Such a policy, after all, created essentially "double-dependency" relations, only heightening tensions between Eastern European regions and their publics and between these states and the Soviet Union.

The third approach, the "decay of empires" thesis, explains why interests shared between Soviet and Eastern European elites in growth and party control generated over the longer term regime-society tensions in the colonies, increased Eastern European pressures on the Soviets to purchase growth and stability in the empire with Soviet rubles, and forced the Soviets to respond to those pressures. But this approach also leaves important questions unanswered. The central issue—why this empire, which was usually well organized to avoid such costs, had such familiar results—cannot be resolved through a focus on imperial decline. Second, why did the Soviet Union ask for trouble by "inviting in" foreign competition over resources and authority during the 1970s? Such behaviour is, needless to say, contrary to normal imperial policy.

A full explanation of why the Eastern Europeans became so demanding and the Soviets so accommodating demands a combination of these three explanations and hence a sensitivity to the interaction among domestic, regional, and global factors. I first examine the unusual structure of Eastern European states, assessing how the combination of Stalinist political economies at home with political and economic dependence abroad had the effect of poising these states against their publics and focusing public dissatisfaction on the state. I then move from the domestic to the regional level, assessing how the combination of domestic pressures in client states with an asymmetric distribution of political and economic resources among states in a regional hierarchical system had the effect of making the Soviet Union not just a monopoly, but, perhaps of greater importance, a political and economic monopsony as well. Control over bloc resources meant that Soviet power within the bloc was not just the "power to persuade" but also, and increasingly, the power to "process" all demands in the bloc and the power to "prevent" their proliferation. Finally, at the global level I argue that the costs to all bloc members generated by growing Eastern European dependence on the Soviet Union led the bloc to increase interaction with the global capitalist system.

Indeed, the decision was ideal, in that it met in varying degrees the concerns of all the parties involved. It would reduce the burden of Eastern Europe on the Soviet Union while in turn reducing Eastern European burdens at home.

In practice, however, the decision had the opposite effect. Eastern European dependence on the Soviet Union increased domestic pressures within the client states. The Soviet Union was forced into the unenviable position of using Soviet resources to prevent economic and political bankruptcy in the bloc. By the 1980s the empire had become more, not less, of a burden for the Soviet Union, and at a time when such burdens could not easily be assumed. Eastern Europe's purported growth in "bargaining power" with the Soviets merely reflected in fact how weak these states had become as a result of their growing economic dependence on Western markets. Soviet losses from empire were not Eastern Europe's gains; growing Eastern European dependence on the Soviet Union could not be construed as Soviet gains. Instead, the resources of *all* the states in the bloc declined, and that decline was accompanied by a decline in Eastern Europe's value to the Soviet Union.

The Consequences of Stalinism for Domestic Pressures in the Periphery

A Stalinist political economy has the effect, noted earlier, of creating a very strong party-state, one that fuses and concentrates the political, social, and economic resources of society. In such a system the party-state functions as a political and economic monopoly and monopsony. In the initial Stalinist years in Eastern Europe, such a description said a lot about the power of the parties in Eastern Europe, the power of the Soviet Union, and, as a result, the weakness of society throughout the bloc. In later years, however, it said more about the vulnerability of the Eastern European parties and the Soviet Union to the economic demands of society in the client states.

The combination of Stalinism at home and dependence on the Soviet Union abroad made Eastern European states highly vulnerable to public pressures, and it did so because of five factors. First, states in Eastern Europe were derivative systems, highly dependent on the Soviet Union for primary products and political authority. This dependence reduced the political and economic means that elites in these systems could use to win popular compliance. Nationalist appeals, for example, were difficult to make, and actions opposed to Soviet wishes were difficult to take. At the same time, dependence left the Soviet Union with control over all those resources that might be used to prevent or deal with popular unrest in the bloc. The Soviets, therefore, had a monopoly over political, military, and economic resources. They functioned as a captive market for, as well as a captive supplier of, economic goods and political authority.

Second, a Stalinist system generates very high levels of conflicts among elites and among functional interests. Fusion between political and economic arenas, roles, and resources expands and concentrates the stakes associated with losing or winning in the political, economic, or social arenas. Fusion also implies an absence of all those safety valves that in more pluralist societies work to diffuse or to rechannel societal conflict. A Stalinist system, as a result, has clear winners and losers. It is unable, in contrast to its pluralist counterparts, to blur the distinction between the two through, for example, a focus on the system's ability to deliver either money, power, or status; through an emphasis on the justice of the allocative processes rather than on unjust outcomes; or through tolerance for political, economic, or social nonconformity. High stakes and the absence of alternative arenas in which to mediate conflict and distribute desired goods work to concentrate and heighten political conflicts over the allocation of power, money, and status.

Third, responsbility for allocating all three is concentrated in the hands of the party. Conflict in such systems, therefore, is not only very focused but focused on the party. The party has all the resources, the party is the arena for interest intermediation, and the party serves as the expediter in a highly bureaucratic system. Moreover, the party claims sole responsibility when things go well; it must therefore bear responsibility when things go badly. The party functions as a political monopsony as well as a political monopoly. Such states, in short, must be understood not simply as powerful but also as besieged.

Fourth, just as conflict in Stalinist political economies is intense, "bundled," and concentrated on the party, so also are the structure and interests of the party clear—and clearly antagonistic to the interests of society. The party wants to maintain control over the economy and the polity, and the party wants to promote rapid economic growth. Indeed, these goals are interdependent. Political careers in a Stalinist system depend on economic performance, political power is expressed through control over economic resources, and power in the economy carries with it power in the polity and society. Moreover, strong economic performance is unusually important to the functioning of such a system because a sizable surplus helps regulate and dampen the considerable conflict among dominant and always economically based interests built into such systems. Finally, economic success is one of the few available means for legitimating and supporting the prevailing, highly asymmetric distribution of power and economic resources. The maintenance of party control thus requires low consumption, high investment, and acceptance of these priorities by all those "weak" interests that, if strong would undercut economic growth. Party power, therefore, depends on peasant and worker weakness.

The weakness of society in Stalinist systems, however, is more apparant than real, especially in states that are derivative and externally dependent. The final factor that made many Eastern European states vulnerable to pressures from below was the growing ability of workers to define their interests in opposition to those of the party and to translate those antagonistic interests into tangible and influential demands. More specifically, workers face a system that prevents popular access to political and social channels, bases its legitimacy in the last analysis on favourable economic comparisons with the presocialist past and on governance for the benefit of workers, and pressures workers with norms. Workers eventually begin to focus on the system's performance as the measure of its legitimacy. At the same time, they tend to evaluate that performance from a perspective that is short-term, economic in focus, and concerned with outcomes at odds with the short-term goals of the party. Workers want reduced pressure at the workplace, more consumption, and expanded opportunities for maneuver in the economy and society—and because of fusion, eventually in the polity as well.

Just as workers in these systems have interests antagonistic to the party, so too do they have considerable resources to transform anomic anger into cohesive concerns and cohesive actions. Workers' protest in a workers' state is embarrassing to these regimes. More important, it threatens the underlying dynamics of the system, as no economic grievance in a Stalinist political economy is without political or social impact. And the very structure of these systems tends to encourage the development of working-class cohesion. One can point, for example, to the great postwar expansion of the working class in these rapidly developing societies, their concentration into large factories, and the similarities in worker experiences—similarities that result from regime policies and policy shifts that because of fusion and centralization, affect all workers in the same way at the same time. Blame for bad conditions can easily be assigned to the party, and strength comes from guaranteed employment, labor shortages in many cases, and the sizable social wage that exists in state-socialist systems.[52] Workers have additional power, albeit potential, as a result of growing deficiencies in capital and the precedent of periodic worker unrest in the bloc. Finally, the party's ability to win working-class compliance grows more limited as opportunities for social mobility and income redistribution narrow with lower growth and completion of the initial industrial breakthrough.

This list has several additions: the short-term horizons of workers, a result of their emphasis on policy outcomes rather than public inputs into the policy process; the failure of such systems to provide the public with information on political or economic issues; and the inherent difficulties elites in state-socialist systems have in blaming workers for decreased growth. All in all, it is easy to see why workers often become demanding and why elites in such systems are vulnerable to worker demands. It is also easy to see why communist parties in Eastern Europe respond to popular unrest in the way they do. It is eminently sensible for them to buy working-class compliance in the short-term through expanded consumption and thereby protect the privileged position of the party by maintaining the basis of party power: centralization and fusion of the polity and the economy. They give up a little to protect what they have.

The responsiveness of Eastern European elites to economic demands from below has forced elites in the periphery to mortgage economic growth over time by responding to short-term economic demands and short-term political needs.

These issues were introduced by de-Stalinization in the 1950s, and the ways in which these issues were then resolved in Eastern Europe have become standard operating procedures (see Table 10.3). Indeed, given the considerable and mounting costs to both Soviet and Eastern European elites of extrication from this political consumption cycle, concern with public consumption in the satellites became a necessary procedure. A social compact evolved in Eastern Europe as a result. These states exchanged tangible economic benefits, greater equalization in the distribution of income, low norms for worker productivity, and some loosening of cultural barriers and social norms for the continuation of party dominance over the polity and economy, worker compliance with social, economic, and political norms, and public tolerance for Soviet influence and protection abroad.[53]

A compromise was forged at the intersection between public and party interests, constraints, and bargaining capacities. That compromise translated domestic pressures in the periphery into an ongoing economic courtship of the population.[54] It was particularly noticeable in those countries with a history of worker unrest, a sizable working class, access to the West, and limited domestic support for the revolution and the party—Hungary, Poland, Czechoslovakia, and the GDR. The most extreme case, as recent events and the data in Tables 10.1–10.3 indicate, has been Poland. Here, ethnic and religious homogeneity, the precedents set by regime receptiveness (and Soviet acquiescence) to mass discontent in 1956, 1970, 1975–1976, and 1980, historical tensions between Poland and the Soviet Union, a party that continually postponed its economic and political day of reckoning for short-term political reasons, and an economy that in the 1970s provided a textbook case of unrest as a function of rising expectations—all led, when combined with factors noted above, to what might be termed the first historical case of a genuine (if not periodically repressed) proletarian revolution.[55]

The uneasy truce between party and society in Eastern Europe maximized the short-term interests of both: It kept the party in control and society in some economic comfort. But the truce worked against two long-term interests that these parties and their publics necessarily shared—reduction of economic and political dependence on the Soviet Union and maintenance of a rapidly growing economic surplus that would help contain intraelite and party-society conflict over the distribution of vital resources. By the late 1960s it was clear that Eastern Europe depended more and more on the Soviet economy. It was also clear that the rate of growth in these economies (in particular in Poland, Hungary, and Czechoslovakia) was not equal to meeting the social contract, continuing high levels of economic investment (particularly vital, given declining returns on capital), satisfying defense obligations, and meeting the concerns of all those interests that were accustomed to privilege. Something had to give. That something was the Soviet Union.

The Costs of Power and Weakness:
The Impact of a Regional Hierarchical System

The dependence of Eastern European regimes on economic growth and rising consumption at home and on the Soviet economy, the Soviet military, and Soviet party patronage abroad proved to be a source of some strength, not weakness, in bargaining with the Soviet Union. The Soviet Union was at the same time the largest market, the dominant trade partner, and the central supplier of primary products in the bloc. As regional hegemon, moreover, the Soviets supplied crucial political resources to their derivative client states, dominated all political transactions within the bloc, and defined the boundaries of the system. Soviet "strength" was considerable. This strength opened the Soviets up to the free-rider problem. Moreover, the derivative and dependent nature of these states and Soviet concerns with domestic security made the Soviets highly vulnerable to fears of unrest in the colonies and highly responsive to the argument that domestic Communist control in Eastern Europe—the linchpin of Soviet control over the bloc—had to be maintained at all costs. Finally, economic subsidies were far less costly than political and economic reforms. The latter course of action would have jeopardized the necessary linkage in the bloc between sizable domestic and sizable international inequalities in power and control over economic resources.

The empire, therefore, was worth a lot to the Soviet Union, and it was (in practice or by way of contagion) vulnerable to domestic unrest. At the same time, only the Soviets had the capacity to do something about such effects, and only opting for substantial economic subsidies would keep the system intact and strengthen the bonds between powerful elites in the center and the "reflective" power of the elites in the periphery.

As noted above, the Soviets initially saw the logic of subsidies as a small price to pay for bloc stability. By the late 1960s, however, it was clear that subsidies were not a viable long-term solution. The Soviet Union, with its declining domestic reserves, could do only so much. Moreover, capital was scarce throughout the bloc; and because of labor shortages and structural limits to worker output, higher productivity depended more and more on technology unavailable inside the bloc. Finally, a policy of enhancing the purchasing power of the public in Eastern Europe could not quell discontent if there was little for the public to purchase with the money and if the goods they wanted were not easily produced and distributed by centrally planned economies.

Together, these problems of Soviet "strength" and Eastern European "weakness" eventually pointed the bloc toward Western trade. In the context of global recession, they also pointed it toward an accumulation of large Western debts and a deterioration in the Eastern European terms of trade.[56] With the termination of regional autarchy, dependency relations within the bloc merely deepened in consequence of the semiperipheralization of the bloc within the global capital system. In turn, all the contradictions noted above deepened as well, enhancing the already sizable burdens generated by the social contract and the pressures that the contract exerted on the bloc.

Joining the Periphery of the Global Capitalist System

The termination of regional economic autarchy involved two related policy shifts: a lessening of political tensions between East and West, or *razriadka*, and Soviet encouragement of economic transactions between the bloc and developed capitalist systems. From the perspective of both Soviet and Eastern European elites, such dramatic shifts in policy seemed at the time to resolve pressing problems at home and abroad. For the Soviets, in particular, the successful pursuit of *razriadka* held open the possibility of expanding domestic economic flexibility by easing the pressure of high military outlays over time. The defense burden was especially great in the Soviet case because of lower growth, because the Soviet economy was a little more than one-half the size of its U.S. competitor, because of economic inefficiency (which meant higher costs attached to producing hardware similar to that in the West), and because the Soviets were also defending against the Chinese and the East European "threat." Some easing of the fiscal burden on the state carried other appealing outcomes, among them the release of all the human as well as the material capital that a sizable defense sector had been absorbing. In addition, detente promised as much, if not more, flexibility in Soviet dealings with the rest of the world. There would be greater predictability in Western actions if East-West relations and spheres of influence were clearly defined. One source of tension in Soviet bloc relations—the growing pressures on Eastern Europe to shoulder more of the defense burden— would be removed. Finally, and perhaps more realistically, East-West political cooperation could act as a wedge to expand economic and scientific exchanges with the West. In this sense, Brezhnev, Nixon, and Kissinger saw eye to eye on the benefits of detente.[57]

Razriadka went hand in hand with the decision to terminate regional economic autarchy. Trade with the West offered the Soviets and the Eastern Europeans a way out of the dilemmas posed by too little growth and too many claimants on the surplus, by growing pressures for political and economic reforms that would necessarily undercut "planner" and, with that, party sovereignty, and by the necessity of moving toward capital-intensive growth and the provision of more consumer goods.[58] Trade with the West and Western credits were ways of getting out of bottlenecks—political as well as economic.

Certain external benefits were foreseen as well from greater economic contact with the West. Eastern European political and economic dependence on the Soviet Union might lessen. Domestic pressures were to be ameliorated by growth and an infusion of Western goods. The smaller countries could maximize their advantages by plugging into the international division of labor (which was critical, given the parallel deficiencies dictated by derivative economic systems). Moreover, the proportion of trade with the West could reduce the enormous economic pressures on the Soviet Union within CMEA, the regional trade organization.[59] Some Soviet and Eastern European economists also felt that producing for the world market rather than for captive consumers would force an improvement in the quality of goods produced within the bloc. All the benefits of Western market mechanisms could be imported, then, while avoiding all the problems that a wholesale adoption of such mechanisms at home would generate—for example, widening income differentials by class as external prices took over, increasing unemployment, and reduction in the economic and political control exercised by the party.[60]

On the Western side, similarly positive calculations were made. Detente, before it was misconstrued as a result of short-term political pressures (particularly in the United States), was seen as advantageous to Western interests.[61] It offered savings and reduction in global tensions and promised greater flexibility in foreign policy. It also held out the attractive prospect of access to a huge, untapped market capable of absorbing both the dregs and the growth exports of the Western economies—for example, lower-quality consumer goods, German steel, U.S. grain, manufactured goods in general, and high (and not so high) technology. Access in the process to the Soviet bloc's raw materials and energy supplies was only enhanced by the congruence of these markets with bankers' ideals: the presence of captive consumers, steady demands, strong governments, and the Soviet fiscal and political umbrella. Western bankers thought "centrally planned economies [in contrast to the Third World] could always be kept solvent."[62] Indeed, as David Rockefeller has summarized, "In terms of straight credit risk, the presumption is that there is greater continuity of government in certain socialist states than non-socialist systems."[63]

As Western politicians sought a strong economy, Western bankers sought reliable clients and, after 1974, outlets for petrodollars. For both groups, the opening up of the Soviet bloc was a very positive prospect. Convergent interests between East and West led to a rapid expansion of East-West trade over the course of the 1970s—an eightfold increase from 1970 to 1981 of Western exports to the bloc and an eightfold increase in the same period of Western imports from the Soviet bloc (see Table 10.4).

The impact of this expansion on the East and West, however, was asymmetrical. Western involvement was somewhat greater than is implied by the small percentage of Soviet bloc trade in overall Western trade (rarely reaching 5 percent of overall trade, except in West Germany and Austria).[64] Nevertheless, the fact remains that the opening up of the East to the global economy had far more dramatic effects on the East than on the West. In the Soviet bloc the expansion of trade with the West moved Eastern Europe toward somewhat greater trade dependence in general (see Table 10.5). Trade expansion led to a deterioration for Eastern Europe in the terms of trade with the West and also with the Soviet Union because the Soviets increased the price they charged for primary products and because the market for Eastern European manufactured

Table 10.4 Structure of Soviet Bloc Trade with the West

	1971	1973	1977	1978	1979	1980	1981[a]
Exports ($U.S. billions)	6.7	12.9	27.5	32.5	41.1	47.1	51.4
Imports ($U.S. billions)	7.6	16.4	–33.8	–38.3	–45.1	–51.6	–56.9
Trade deficits	–.9	–3.5	–6.3	–5.8	–4.0	–4.5	–5.5
Current account	n.a.	n.a.	–8.5	–5.5	–3.2	–4.6	–6.2

[a]Recent trends indicate an improvement on the current account, with Eastern European imports from the West down 16 percent in 1982. See "Curtain Call," *The Economist*, December 3, 1983, p. 92.

Sources: Roger Kanet, "East-West Trade and the Limits of Western Influence," in Charles Gati, ed., *The Internatinal Politics of Eastern Europe* (New York: Praeger, 1976), p. 205; *World Economic Outlook* (Washington, D.C.: The International Monetary Fund, June, 1981), p. 154. The figures for 1981 are estimated. Broken down, the data indicate that (1) growth in trade with the West was particularly large for Poland, Hungary, the Soviet Union, and East Germany and declining for Bulgaria and Romania; (2) the Soviet Union remained easily the dominant trade partner for the Eastern European states (with the exception of Romania); (3) the primary decline in trade over time was inter-Eastern European trade; and (4) the trade deficits were produced by Eastern Europe, not for the most part by the Soviet Union.

Table 10.5 Overall Trade as Percentage of Gross Material Product[a]

	1966–1970	1971–1975	1976–1979
Bulgaria	20.0	25.0	26.0
Czechoslovakia	15.0	16.0	17.5
GDR	16.0	19.0	20.3
Hungary	20.0	23.0	24.8
Poland	10.0	12.0	13.7
Romania	11.0	13.0	14.8
Soviet Union	3.9	4.7	5.1

[a]When broken down by region, the data indicate that Eastern European trade in general focused on the West and the Soviet Union and that Poland, Hungary, and the Soviet Union show the largest increaes in trade with the West over the mid- to late 1970s. See Arpad Abonyi, "International Development of Labour and Industrial Readjustment in Hungary: Dependent Industrialization and the Limits of State Strategy—The consequences for the Automobile and Machine Tools," paper delivered at the International Studies Association convention in Cincinnati, Ohio, March 24–29, 1982.

Sources: Eleftherios Botsas, "Pattern of Trade," in Stephen Fisher Galati, ed., *Eastern Europe in the 1980s* (Boulder, Colo.: Westview, 1981), pp. 80, 94; United Nations, *Economic Bulletin for Europe*, vol. 33 (New York: United Nations, 1981), p. 1.8.

goods was weak. It also led to mounting trade deficits with the West (registered in Table 10.4) and rising surpluses in Soviet trade with Eastern Europe.[65]

Of greater importance to the East, and increasingly to the West as well, was mounting Soviet bloc debt to Western banks and Western governments, especially in the wake of the energy crisis of 1973–1974, the global recession in 1979–1981, and the surfeit of petrodollars in Western banks (see Table 10.6). As the figures indicate, gross debt to the West (only an average of 63 percent of Eastern European total debt, broadly conceived, to the Soviet Union) grew rapidly, from $6.5 billion in 1970 to approximately $88.1 billion by 1981.[66] The seriousness of this economic burden for Eastern Europe is revealed in the dramatic increases in the debt-service ratio since 1977 and the ratio of total debt to annual hard currency export earnings (see Table 10.7).[67] Indeed, by 1980 the average ratio of total medium- and long-term hard currency debt to hard currency export earnings averaged 145 for the bloc as a whole.

By the late 1970s, then, the global recession and the substantial difficulties that autarchic economies of the state-socialist type face in expanding hard currency trade had together turned what seemed to be a rational decision into one carrying grave economic consequences. Indeed, Eastern Europe had taken on many of the characteristics of a semiperiphery within the global capitalist system. There was growing indebtedness to the capitalist core, growing trade dependence in general and on the West in particular, a deterioration in the terms of trade, and negative trade balances (see Tables 10.4, 10.5, and 10.8).[68] There were also the familiar externalities associated with high levels of debt in small, rather specialized economies unable to adjust to changing market conditions. Examples were many: structural difficulties arising from planning and the bloc division of labor in expanding the range of export items and pursuing import-substitution policies; the importation of Western business cycles with their clear effects in 1973–1974 and 1979–1981 on deficits, debts, and development; some indications of growing income inequalities;[69] reduced fiscal flexibility of the state; "creeping" market-oriented reforms; in some cases growing imports of food;[70] and the imposition, first in Bulgaria and then in Romania, Poland, Hungary, and the GDR, of domestic austerity measures.[71]

For the Soviet economy, the economic dislocations in Eastern Europe led to a number of contradictions. By the end of the 1970s the Soviet Union had in a sense the worst of all worlds. The Soviets functioned as a periphery economy but enjoyed few of the benefits associated with that role. They were, for example, unable to "capitalize" on primary-product strength during a period of high demand for such products. The Soviets also functioned as a core economy within the region but again enjoyed few of the associated benefits. Because of Eastern European economic problems, for instance, they were unable to convert economic dominance into international political and economic leverage.[72]

Eastern European demands increased and Western bankers became more powerful because these economies opened up to the West on the eve of a global recession. Eastern Europe had to be helped because severe disruptions in

Table 10.6 Estimated Eastern Bloc Hard Currency Gross Debt to the West ($U.S. billions)

	1970	1974	1975	1976	1977	1978	1979	1980	1981[a]	1971–1980
Bulgaria	0.7	1.2	1.8	2.3	2.7	4.3	4.5	4.5	4.8	16.3
Czechoslovakia	0.3	1.1	1.5	2.1	2.7	3.2	4.0	4.5	4.8	18.5
GDR	1.0	2.8	3.8	6.0	5.9	8.9	10.1	11.5	12.5	38.4
Hungary	0.6	1.5	2.1	2.8	3.4	7.5	7.8	8.9	8.0	16.5
Poland	0.8	3.9	6.9	10.2	13.0	17.8	20.5	23.0	27.0	36.4
Romania	1.2	2.6	3.0	3.3	4.0	5.2	6.9	9.5	12.0	7.7
Total	4.6	13.1	19.1	25.7	31.7	46.9	53.8	61.9	69.1	133.8
Soviet Union	1.9	5.0	10.0	14.0	16.0	16.5	17.2	17.5	19.0	n.a.
Total for bloc[b]	6.5	18.1	29.1	39.7	47.7	63.4	71.0	79.4	88.1	n.a.

[a]Recent estimates indicate that bloc debt to the West fell to about $62 billion in 1982. See "Curtain Call," *The Economist*, December 3, 1983, p. 192.

[b]This figure does not include debts incurred by CMEA banks, which range from $0.1 to $2.8 billion, 1970–1981.

Sources: Morris Bornstein, "Issues in East-West Economic Relations," in Morris Bornstein, Svi Gitelman, and William Zimmerman, eds., *East-West Relations and the Future of Eastern Europe* (London: Allen & Unwin, 1981), p. 37; Michael Marrese and Jan Vanous *Implicit Subsidies and Non-Market Benefits in Soviet Trade with Eastern Europe* (Berkeley, Calif: Center for International Studies, 1983), pp. 38–43; Allen Lenz and Robert Teal, "Projected CMEA Hard Currency Debt Levels Under Selected Growth Assumptions," p. 745, and Paul Marer, "Economic Performance and Prospects in Eastern Europe: Summary and Interpretations of Findings," p. 57, both in Join Economic Committee, U.S. Congress, *The Eastern European Economies* Vol. 2 (Washington, D.C.: U.S. Government Printing Office, 1981).

Table 10.7 The Burden of Debt in the Soviet Bloc and Some Comparisons

	Total Western Debt by Year-end 1980 as Percentage of Hard Currency Export Earnings	Western Debt-Service Ratios[a] (percent)		
	1980	1970	1977	1980
Bulgaria	347	35	85	35
Czechoslovakia	143	8	34	22
GDR	290	20	40	40
Hungary	307	20	44	45
Poland	390	20	60	105
Romania	264	36	42	28
Soviet Union	71	18	28	6
Average	145	22	47	40
All non-oil developing nations		25.8	23.7	26.6
Brazil	52[b]	n.a.	n.a.	58
Mexico	33[b]	n.a.	n.a.	45

[a]The ratio of payments (interest and principal due) to exports of goods and services earnings in Western interactions only.

[b]This figure is on long-term debt only, so it is not directly comparable to the overall debt.

Sources: International Monetary Fund, *World Economic Outlook* (Washington, D.C.: The International Monetary Fund, June, 1981), pp. 135–137; "Sanctions After Poland," *The Economist*, January 30, 1982, p. 30.

Table 10.8 Terms of All Trade for the Soviet Bloc (Indexed with 1975 = 100)

	1975	1977	1978	1979	1980	1981 (first half)
Soviet bloc	100	104	106	109	110	113
Eastern Europe[a]	100	98	99	97	95	93
Soviet Union	100	113	115	126	131	143

[a]When these figures are broken down by country, it is clear that although Poland's terms of trade improved somewhat over the 1970s (with 1976 being the high point), the rest of the bloc states showed a clear deterioration (with Hungary being the most extreme case). See Paul Marer, "Economic Performance and Prospects on Eastern Europe: Analytical Summary and Interpretation of Findings," in *Joint Economic Committee, U.S. Congress, East European Economic Assessment: Part II* (Washington, D.C.: U.S. Government Printing Office, 1981), Chart 9, p. 51.

Source: United Nations, *Economic Survey of Europe*, vol. 33 (New York: United Nations, 1981), p. 1.6.

intrabloc trade would hurt the Soviets. The tie between growth and stability in the client states meant that domestic stringency might lead to political instability in the satellites—and perhaps in the Soviet Union as well. Moreover, bankruptcy in any country of the bloc would close Western markets to the entire bloc, including the much stronger Soviet economy.

That final point gave Western bankers leverage. The Soviet Union needed Western trade and capital. But one default would in effect return the whole bloc to autarchy,[73] which would create, because of bloc integration, a serious recession throughout the region. Recession in turn would lead to more pressures on the Soviet Union, either to rescue its clients or else risk the political disintegration of the empire. As a result, the economic and the political—and the domestic and the foreign—interests of the Soviet Union would be severely undermined. The regional hierarchical system replaced the normal "debt regime" that governed transactions between Western bankers and governments on the one hand and Turkey, Jamaica, Zaire, and the like on the other.[74] This "debt regime" was unusually effective precisely because of Soviet strength and because one default would lead to a bloc-wide freeze-out—an outcome against the interests of the entire bloc.[75]

Hence the Soviets had little choice but to aid their allies, through continued trade subsidies and explicit subsidies as well and through pressure on more solvent states to help shoulder the burdens. As a result, Eastern European dependence on the Soviet Union for markets and basic commodities increased. Indeed, this trend extended to Romania and Yugoslavia, both of which came back to the fold at least insofar as trade was concerned. Soviet aid in the form of trade subsidies and positive trade balance increased, the bloc was forced to endure severe disruptions in trade, and the hard currency earnings capacity of the Soviet Union began to fall.

There was a high and understandable correlation between Eastern European debt to the West and debt to the East, but the Soviets forfeited the gains that usually come from deepening dependency relations. Core-periphery dynamics within a regional hierarchical system—combined with some of the core-periphery dynamics within the global economy at a time of crisis—led, for the Soviet Union, to the worst of all possible outcomes: "double dependency" for Eastern Europe, the semiperipheralization of the entire bloc, and a sizable reduction for the Soviets in the gains from empire.

In the early 1970s it seemed rather reasonable to argue that capitalist and socialist economies needed each other, especially as they both faced lower growth (though for different reasons), and that global trade would expand in the 1970s as it had in the 1960s. The experience of the 1970s was quite different— protected markets in the West, an energy crisis, an expansion of attractive and highly competitive markets and suppliers in the Third World, and Eastern Europe's failure to use economic reforms or trade with the West to improve on the efficiency of capital usage or the quality of items produced. As a result, all those decisions made in the early 1970s produced precisely the opposite of what had been expected. Opening up to the West resulted in more, not less, pressure for economic reforms and more, not less, political and economic dependence of Eastern Europe on the Soviet Union. It also led to greater strains in intrabloc relations because of domestic austerity measures and the escalating burden of Poland. It led to less, not more, economic flexibility because of the tug-of-war between external and internal demands over the diminishing surplus. It led to lower, not higher, Soviet and Eastern European economic growth. Finally, it led to serious challenges both to party control over the polity as well as the economy in Eastern Europe and to Soviet control, or at least the benefits of that control, over the region. Dealing with capitalism in crisis, rather than "plugging up" holes, served "to stretch the system at its most sensitive points."[76]

The Polish crisis is, of course, an extreme but illuminating case in point. Although precise figures are hard to come by, it appears that by 1981 Poland owed Western governments and banks about $27 billion (see Table 10.6). This burden was enormous: $27 billion translates into a debt of about $770 per capita, a debt-service ratio for 1981 of about 105, and a ratio of total debt to export earnings of more than 400 percent (assuming export earnings in 1981 at about $6 billion). By mid-1982 it was clear that the Poles could not pay the interest, let alone the principal, due in 1982, and a substantial rescheduling was arranged among the five hundred banks and numerous Western governments involved. The Polish economy was and is in a shambles. It is burdened by severe debts and in a structural sense cannot do much about it. Not only are few items available for export to the West, but the country depends on imports for food, raw material, and energy, its planned economy is unusually inflexible, and there is a political stalemate between the party and the Solidarity trade union.

The impact of debt on the domestic political economy of Poland and the whole region has been enormous. Shortages throughout the bloc have increased because of distortions in trade within CMEA and with the West. The cost of living throughout the bloc has increased as well because of the effects of domestic austerity measures. Moreover, the trend toward greater income inequality throughout the bloc is likely to continue, for two reasons. First, state pressures on the countryside and the factories to hold down labor costs will continue to increase. Second, the class-differentiated impact of budgetary and investment cutbacks funnels money into the most "productive" economic sectors and reduces, as far as is politically feasible, state subsidies for such basic goods as foodstuffs and housing.

The alliance of the early 1970s between "Western bankers and Polish housewives" necessarily led by the late 1970s to the dropping of one member of that coalition—Polish housewives. The pursuit of regime interests in combination with "lax Western credit was the creator of Solidarity," but such credit was also "its (Solidarity's) executioner."[77] Bankers wanted a reassertion of state control over consumption and over payment of the external debt in Poland. Their interests intersected with Soviet interests in Poland and the interests of the Polish elite in reinstating central control over the distribution of power and the rapidly diminishing economic surplus. There were "common interests between East and West in a rescue plan for the Polish economy."[78]

The debt crisis had created what were from the perspective of global politics strange bedfellows, but from the perspective of global economics was a familiar alliance. It was an alliance between the capitalist core and the periphery's core—that is, a form of comprador collusion. But in this case none of the parties gained much from what was (from an economic and therefore political perspective) a necessary but not a terribly productive alliance. Western bankers gained little hope of recouping their money, the Soviet Union added to its financial and political burdens, the Polish party lost its limited domestic support and became more dependent on the Soviet Union, and Polish workers lost political and purchasing power. The bloc as a whole—because of fusion, their derivative structures, and integrated trade—faced the possibility of economic and perhaps political bankruptcy.

Conclusions

The evolution of the Eastern bloc during the postwar period suggests that even those empires that are ideally structured to maximize imperial interests are subject to the law of declining returns over time. Indeed, the history of the Soviet bloc contains a number of ironic developments. One is that Soviet power translated in practice into Soviet weakness. As the regional hegemon, the political core, and the economic periphery in the bloc, the Soviets functioned increasingly as a political and economic monopoly and monopsony. As such, the Soviets faced an intractable dilemma by the early 1980s. If they withdrew support from Eastern Europe, they would merely enhance the prospects for instability in the bloc—an outcome damaging to Soviet domestic stability and national security. If they continued aid, they would drain their already weakened domestic economy, would reinforce the inefficiency of Eastern European economies, and would enhance the dependence of Eastern European elites on both the Soviet Union and domestic groups pressing for higher consumption. If they encouraged reforms, they could only look forward to the dispersion of political and economic resources so vital to Eastern European control over their societies and Soviet control over the bloc. The Soviets, in short, were long on resources and short on viable options.

A second irony is that the combination of authoritarian politics and central planning, when added to external dependence, opened up Eastern Europe to two problems that have traditionally been understood as problems peculiar to capitalist polyarchies—short-term horizons and the political business cycle.[79] This vulnerability occurred because such systems have clear lines of conflict between state and society, concentrate conflict on issues of current economic gains and losses, and thereby pressure the party to purchase political support through economic means. The costs of the Soviet role as a monopoly and monopsony within the bloc, therefore, was repeated in a sense within the client states as well. Elite power in both cases implied elite vulnerability to the demands from below.

A final irony was that the very characteristics that allowed the bloc to form an alternative world system were the same characteristics that over time pressured it to rejoin the global capitalist system. As noted above, the Soviet bloc could function as an alternative world system because it was autarchic, and because autarchy was combined with Soviet monopoly over vital political and economic resources (including the control over regional borders), Stalinism at home, and East European dependence abroad. These features, however, led to the ironic developments noted earlier and to the seemingly optimal decision to end regional isolation. That decision was made simply because it maximized the interests of all the players—in particular, the desire of both the Soviets and the East Europeans to lessen dependence, expand capital and access to consumer goods and high technology, and therefore maximize growth, stability, and national autonomy. Other solutions to deficits in capital, technology, and political authority (such as continued Soviet subsidies, domestic reforms, or a loosening of bloc integration) of course were less attractive—difficult to achieve and with clear short-term costs. In "going West" to resolve internal contradictions and to buttress the power of the party-state, however, the bloc managed to deepen domestic and regional contradictions. Rather than safeguarding socialism, the bloc ended up "playing a functional role in the reproduction of capitalism."[80] The end of economic autarchy, therefore, opened up the possibility that political autarchy might end as well, in both the domestic and the regional realms.

As a result, the Soviet Union ended up mediating between the core-periphery dynamics within the bloc and those dynamics within the global capitalist system. As broker, however, the Soviets managed to bear all of the costs and enjoy few of the benefits. They lost money, access to Western markets, and economic as well as political control over the empire. The combination of political and economic dependence of Eastern Europe, bloc integration through bilateral trade skewed toward the Soviet Union, sizable Soviet economic resources, and the Soviet Union's external position as regional hegemon and global power proved to be an unfortunate combination of strengths.

The dynamics of a regional hierarchical system and the dynamics of the world capitalist system in economic recession led to the semiperipheralization of the Soviet bloc in the global economy. Because of the structure of Stalinism in the client states, these dynamics led as well to the development—most notably in Poland—of Janus-faced elites unable to please domestic or foreign clienteles and subject to the constraints of "double" dependency. Finally, for the Soviet Union, all these forces led to growing contradictions among the goals of empire. If the Soviets were to try to maximize their economic benefits from control over Eastern Europe, they would jeopardize Soviet national security and Eastern

European, and therefore Soviet, domestic stability. If they were to opt for policies promoting greater national security and bloc-wide stability, they would necessarily mortgage Soviet domestic economic growth. And such economic burdens would, of course, over time make it more and more difficult for the Soviets (or the Eastern Europeans) to purchase political stability at home. A declining surplus would eventually terminate the policy of priming public consumption in order to woo the population.

These were the contradictions which Mikhail Gorbachev inherited when he became General Secretary in 1985. His approach to these problems, which I have addressed in detail elsewhere,[81] has been to place a great deal of emphasis on improving regional economic performance. This will reduce, he hopes, Eastern European burdens on the Soviet economy. Toward this end, Gorbachev has prodded Eastern Europe to mimic his domestic political and (especially) economic reform package, to integrate their economies more fully with the Soviet Union, and to join expanding economic contracts with the West with greater intra-bloc coordination of research, development, and production. At the same time, Gorbachev has been willing to make some compromises with Eastern Europe and has, as a consequence, lowered Soviet expectations about what the Soviet Union can and should gain from empire. More specifically, Gorbachev has been willing to recognize diverse interests in the bloc, tolerate a fair amount of political and economic diversity in the region, and, thus, allow the bloc to become more of an alliance—at least in political terms—than a bloc. His strategy, therefore, recognizes that compromises must be made, and that the least unpleasant solution for all concerned is one that deals first and foremost with economic problems throughout the bloc. If these economies continue to stagnate, after all, then none of the goals of empire will be served. Weak economies cannot buy public support indefinitely.

Gorbachev's strategy, therefore, is one that makes the best of a bad situation. But will it work? It will not, of course, return the empire to its once ideal status. The contradictions analyzed in this chapter are too embedded for that to happen, and Gorbachev's minimalist reform strategy is premised on this very fact of life. Will his reforms at least increase the benefits of empire? This is not entirely clear for two reasons. First, there is a decided possibility that the reforms will not work, even if we assume that they will be implemented. Planning will be at war with markets, East-West trade will be at war with intra-bloc trade, domestic autarchy will clash with regional integration, and the transition costs may be so great that few benefits will materialize. Second, it is not at all clear that Gorbachev's reforms will be implemented. His reforms are under attack at home and abroad and have already produced, even in their infancy, considerable costs. Planners are threatened, ministries are in disarray, parties are dividing and publics are angry—about higher prices, more strict work norms, and the prospects of unemployment, more steeply-graded pay scales, and a declining social wage. These constraints are joined, moreover, by four other factors that only increase the costs of and the resistance to reform in Eastern

Europe. These four factors are: (1) ongoing succession struggles in most of these regimes; (2) the implementation at present of domestic austerity measures in Hungary, Romania and Poland; (3) the continuing crisis in Poland. and; (4) growing ethnic strife within, and in the cases of Hungary and Romania, between states in the bloc.

The road to reform is paved with potholes. The reform process, itself, might very well lead in the short-term to greater instability, lower economic performance, and less national security. And the short-term is, as this chapter has demonstrated, what politics and economics in the Soviet bloc are all about.

Notes

This chapter is a revised version of "The Empire Strikes Back: The Evolution of the Eastern Bloc from a Soviet Liability," *International Organization* 39 (Winter 1985):, pp. 1–46..

1. Samir Amin, *Unequal Development* (New York: Monthly Review Press, 1976), p. 372.

2. Rudolf Bahro, *The Alternative in Eastern Europe* (London: NLB, 1978), p. 237.

3. The term *empire* is used here, because the nature of Soviet dominance over Eastern Europe—that is, the primary motives behind Soviet control, the structure of the bloc, and the distribution of resources within the bloc—is in many (but hardly all) respects similar to the nature of empires. See, for example, Robert Gilpin, *War and Change in World Politics* (New York: Cambridge University Press, 1981), pp. 110–115, 139–140, and Daniel Chirot and Thomas Hall, "World-System Theory," *Annual Review of Sociology* 8 (1982), pp. 81–106.

4. For further evidence on this point, see Gilpin, *War and Change* pp. 144–168.

5. The Romanian case is an exception. Pressures from below were minimal (until the late 1970s), and the decision to expand economic relations with the West was part of a larger concern with enhancing Romanian autonomy, Ceausescu's domestic control, and Stalinist economic priorities. See William Crowther,"Romanian Politics and the International Economy," *Orbis* 28 (Fall 1984), pp. 553–574.

6. I use the term *fusion* to emphasize how uniquely merged, concentrated, and interdependent resources are in a Stalinist political economy. The significance of fusion for the role of the state and the structure of conflict in Eastern Europe will be assessed later in the chapter. For assessments of how the structure of the Stalinist political economy evolved and how fusion affects the distribution of power in these systems, see George Konrad and Ivan Szelenyi, *The Intellectuals on the Road to Class Power* (New York: Harcourt Brace Jovanovich, 1979), especially pp. 147–148; Hans-Hermann Hohmann, "The State and the Economy in Eastern Europe," in J.E.S. Hayward and R. N. Berki, eds., *State and Society in Contemporary Europe* (New York: St. Martin's, 1978), pp. 141–157; Mihaly Vajda, *The State and Socialism* (New York: St. Martin's, 1981), p. 135; and Alec Nove, "Socialism, Centralized Planning and the One-Party State," in T. H. Rigby, Archie Brown, and Peter Reddaway, eds., *Authority, Power and Policy in the USSR* (New York: St. Martin's, 1980), pp. 77–97. Fusion should not be confused with corporatism; the latter implies, particularly in its liberal variant, some separation

of arenas and a state that has some autonomy. For further discussion of both terms and their application to the contemporary Soviet case, see Valerie Bunce, "The Political Economy of the Brezhnev Era: The Rise and Fall of Corporatism," *British Journal of Political Science* 13 (January 1983), pp. 129–158.

7. The Hungarian case suggests that public consensus on the need for revolutionary change was sizable. What was at considerable issue, however, was Soviet domination. See Charles Gati, *Hungary and the Soviet Bloc* (Durham, N.C.: Duke University, 1986), Chs. 3–4.

8. Quoted in Christopher Jones, *Soviet Influence in Eastern Europe: Political Autonomy and the Warsaw Pact* (New York: Praeger, 1981), p. 7; see also pp. 2–23. For analyses that assert, in contrast to Jones, that the domestic structure of Eastern Europe and the structure of the bloc had less to do with pressures imposed by Soviet expansionism than with necessary actions arising from Soviet concerns with limiting the influence of capitalism and thereby preserving the Soviet state, see Christopher Chase-Dunn, "Introduction," in Chase-Dunn, ed., *Socialist States in the World System* (Beverly Hills, Calif.: Sage, 1982), pp. 9–18; David Ost, "Socialist World Market as Strategy for Ascent?" in Edward Friedman, ed., *Ascent and Decline in the World System* (Beverly Hills, Calif.: Sage, 1982), pp. 229–254.

9. The one exception, of course, was Yugoslavia. In the rest of this paper, the Yugoslav case will be discussed only tangentially because it left the bloc in 1948 and by the early 1950s created a unique political economy.

10. See Paul Marer, "Has Eastern Europe Become a Liability to the Soviet Union: (II) The Economic Aspect," in Charles Gati, ed., *The International Politics of Eastern Europe* (New York: Praeger, 1976), pp. 59–81. Also see Marer, "The Political Economy of Soviet Relations with Eastern Europe," in Steven J. Rosen and James R. Kurth, eds., *Testing Theories of Economic Imperialism* (Lexington, Mass.: Heath, 1974), pp. 231–260.

11. See Wlodzimierz Brus, "Stalinism and the 'Peoples' Democracies," in Robert Tucker, ed., *Stalinism* (New York: Norton, 1977), pp. 239–256; Paul Johnson, "Changing Social Structure and the Political Role of Manual Workers," in Jan Triska and Charles Gati, eds., *Blue Collar Workers in Eastern Europe* (London: Allen & Unwin, 1981), pp. 29–42, especially pp. 34–36; Andrew C. Janos, "The One-Party State and Social Mobilization: East Europe Between the Wars," in Samuel Huntington and Clement Moore, eds., *Authoritarian Politics in Modern Society* (New York: Basic Books, 1970), pp. 204–236; and Bahro, *The Alternative in Eastern Europe*, pp. 117–119.

12. Konrad and Szelenyi, *Intellectuals on the Road*. They note, among other things, the tremendous expansion, given centralized planning and authoritarian one-party rule, of managerial positions during Stalinism.

13. Walter Connor, "Socialism, Work and Equality," in Irving Louis Horowitz, ed., *Equity, Income and Policy* (New York: Praeger, 1977).

14. Christopher Chase-Dunn, "Socialist States in the Capitalist World Economy," *Social Problems* 27 (June 1980), p. 515.

15. See Albert Szymanski, "The Socialist World System," in Christopher Chase-Dunn, ed., *Socialist States in the World System* (Beverly Hills, Calif.: Sage, 1982), pp. 57–84. As I will argue below, however, the autonomy of the Soviet bloc was more apparent than real. While the bloc does not conform to the concept of a periphery within the world system, it is also not autonomous. Its initial structure grew out of the peripheral role of these states prior to the revolutions and Soviet competition with the West, and its changing structure from the 1960s onward testified to the continuing impact of the capitalist world system.

16. See William Zimmerman, "Hierarchical Regional Systems and the Politics of System Boundaries," *International Organization* 26 (Winter 1972), pp. 18–36; Kenneth Jowitt, *The Leninist Response to National Dependency* (Berkeley: University of California Institute of International Studies, 1978); Kenneth Jowitt, "The Romanian Communist Party and the World Socialist System: A Redefinition of Unity," *World Politics* 23 (October 1970), pp. 38–60; Chris Jones, "Soviet Hegemony in Eastern Europe: The Dynamics of Political Autonomy and Military Intervention," *World Politics* 29 (January 1977), pp. 217–241; Cal Clark, "The Evolving Nature of Hierarchy in the Soviet–East European International System," paper presented at the annual meeting of the American Political Science Association, Chicago, September 2–4, 1983; and Cal Clark and Donna Bahry, "Dependent Development: A Socialist Variant," *International Studies Quarterly* 27 (September 1983), pp. 271–294.

17. Compare, for example, Jones, *Soviet Influence*, p. 8, with Jeremy Azrael, "Varieties of De-Stalinization," in Chalmers Johnson, ed., *Change in Communist Systems* (Stanford, Calif.: Stanford University Press, 1970), pp. 135–152; and George Breslauer, *Khrushchev and Brezhnev as Leaders: Building Authority in Soviet Politics* (London: Allen & Unwin, 1982), pp. 23–60.

18. See Jan Triska, "Workers' Assertiveness and Soviet Policy Choices," in Triska and Gati, *Blue Collar Workers*, pp. 268–269; Konrad and Szelenyi, *Intellectuals on the Road*, pp. 155–157.

19. See Valerie Bunce, "Neither Equality nor Efficiency: International and Domestic Inequalities in the Soviet Bloc," in Daniel Nelson, ed., *Communism and the Politics of Inequalities* (Lexington, Mass.: Heath, 1983), pp. 5–34; Zvi Gitelman, "The Politics of Socialist Restoration in Hungary and Czechoslovakia," *Comparative Politics* 13 (January 1981), pp. 187–210.

20. For evidence on the linkages between the crises of 1956 and increases in public consumption in the bloc, see Frederik Pryor, *Public Expenditures in Communist and Capitalist Nations* (Homewood, Ill.: Dorsey, 1968). For Soviet responsibilities to foot the tab, see Marer, "Political Economy"; Triska, "Workers'Assertiveness."

21. Jan Vanous, "East European Economic Slowdown," *Problems of Communism* 31 (July–August 1982), pp. 1–19.

22. See Marer, "Political Economy"; Marer, "Has Eastern Europe." For an assessment of Soviet costs and benefits at this time and the difficulties involved in making such assessments, see also Paul Marer, "Prospects for Economic Assistance," in Jan Triska and Paul Cocks, eds., *Political Development in Eastern Europe* (New York: Praeger, 1977), pp. 256–274.

23. For an analysis of Soviet interventions, see Jiri Valenta, "Revolutionary Change, Soviet Intervention and Normalization in East-Central Europe," *Comparative Politics* 16 (January 1984), pp. 127–152.

24. Jones, *Soviet Influence*; and William Zimmerman, "Soviet–East European Relations in the 1980's and the Changing International System," in Morris Bornstein, Zvi Gitelman, and Zimmerman, eds., *East-West Relations and the Future of Eastern Europe* (London: Allen & Unwin, 1981), pp. 87–104.

25. Richard Flashkamp and Daniel Nelson, "Detente and the Warsaw Pact: East European Military Expenditures in an Era of Decreased East-West Conflict," paper delivered at the Western Social Science Association meeting, Denver, Colorado, November 12, 1981; Zimmerman, "Soviet–East European Relations."

26. See the data reported in William M. Reisinger, "East European Military Expenditures in the 1970s: Collective Good or Bargaining Offer?" *International Organization* 37 (Winter 1983), pp. 147–155. For assessments of trends over time in the bloc's military outlays, see International Institute for Strategic

Studies, *The Military Balance, 1982–1983* (London, 1982), pp. 124–146; and Stockholm International Peace Research Institute, *World Armaments and Disarmament: SIPRI Yearbook*, 1983 (New York: Taylor & Frances, 1983), p. 162.

27. This is the CIA estimate. See U.S. Congress, Joint Economic Committee (JEC), *USSR: Measures of Economic Growth and Development, 1950–1980* (Washington, D.C., December 8, 1982), pp. 15–16. Although Western estimates of Soviet GNP vary, the trends over time are similar from one study to the next.

28. See Fyodor Kushnirsky, "The Limits of Soviet Economic Reform," *Problems of Communism* 33 (July–August 1984), pp. 24–32. Nor is this likely to change under Gorbachev. See, for example,V. Zagladin, "Strategiia Razvitiia, blagosostoianiia mira," (Strategy for Development and Social Well-being of the World) *Novoe Vremia* 22 (March 22, 1985), pp. 5–7.

29. The debt crisis, however, has made the Soviets more skeptical. Indeed, they have begun to resist Hungarian proposals for further decentralization of the economy and increased economic transactions with the West. See Alfred Reisch, "CPSU Fails Formally to Endorse Hungary's Economic Reform," *Radio Free Europe*, April 27, 1985, pp. 19–24. For an insightful assessment of the costs and benefits of integration by socialist states into the global economy, see Josip Zupanov, "Otvaranje prema ekonomiji—hoce li ovaj put uspjeti?" (Is Opening up the Economy the Way to Success?) *Socioloski Pregled* 18 (January–February 1984), pp. 3–18.

30. Vanous, "East European Economic Slowdown." Also see JEC, *USSR: Measures of Economic Growth*, pp. 15–16. It is important to note that the Soviets were also ambivalent about specialization within the bloc, because such a policy would allow some states to gain added leverage through monopoly over vital products—in particular, machine tools.

31. For evidence on this point, see Eleftherios Botsas,"Trade Patterns," in Stephen Fischer-Galati, ed., *Eastern Europe in the 1980s* (Boulder: Westview, 1981), p. 98; United Nations, *Economic Bulletin for Europe*, vol. 33 (New York, 1981), pp. 1.6, 1.14–1.18.

32. Jan Vanous and Michael Marrese, "Soviet Subsidies to Eastern Economies," *Wall Street Journal*, January 15, 1982; see also their *Soviet Subsidization of Trade with Eastern Europe: A Soviet Perspective* (Berkeley: University of California Institute of International Studies, 1983).

33. See Paul Marer, "The Council for Mutual Economic Assistance: Integration or Domination?" in Sarah M. Terry, ed., *Soviet Foreign Policy in Eastern Europe* (New Haven: Yale University Press, 1984). The central problems addressed by Marer have to do with the degree to which the calculation of subsidies is inflated by assuming seller markets outside the bloc; by postulating too liberal an exchange rate; and by the skewed availability of data on what the Eastern Europeans send to the Soviet Union versus what the Soviets send to Eastern Europe.

34. See Frank Lipsius, "Poland's Cost to the East," *New York Times*, February 7, 1982; "Now Russia Asks for Time to Pay," *Economist*, February 6, 1982; John Burns, "Poland an Increasing Economic Burden for Soviets," *New York Times*, December 23, 1981; Paul Lewis, "As Poland's Economy Slides, Comecon Feels the Backlash," *New York Times*, January 10, 1982; and Richard Portes, *The Polish Crisis: Western Economic Options* (London: Royal Institute of International Affairs, 1981). For a recent summary of the Polish crisis, see "Poland's Economy," *Economist*, February 12, 1983, pp. 71–73. For an analysis of Polish deficits from intrabloc trade, see Paul Lewis, "Poland's Slump: Endangering Economies of the Soviet Bloc," *New York Times*, January 8, 1982.

35. For an excellent analysis of these decisions and their relationship to detente, see Peter M. E. Volten, *Brezhnev's Peace Program: A Study of Soviet Domestic Political Process and Power* (Boulder, Colo.: Westview, 1982).

36. It is interesting to note, for example, that the impact of Yugoslavia's austerity policies seemed to have been greater, if only because the Yugoslavs lacked the Soviet umbrella. For estimates of the costs of austerity in Yugoslavia, see OECD, ed., *Yugoslavia* (Paris: OECD, 1985); Desimir Tochitch, "Titoism Without Tito," *Survey* 28 (Autumn 1984), pp. 1–24; and Cyril Zebot,"Yugoslavia's Self-Management on Trial," *Problems of Communism* 31 (March–April 1982), pp. 42–49.

37. See Steven Rattner, "Impact of Soviet Gold Sales," *New York Times*, January 5, 1982; Ellen L. James, "Is Moscow Reducing Assistance to Cuba?" *New York Times*, April 7, 1982; "Soviet Fails to Use Gas Pipeline Credit," *New York Times*, April 1, 1982; "East Germany Tries to Cope," *New York Times*, July 19, 1985; Vanous,"East European Economic Slowdown."

38. See *Pravda*, July 21, 1982, and the Yugoslav analysis of Soviet economic problems at the end of the Brezhnev era in "Odlazak velike lichnosti" (Departure of an Important Person) *NIN* (Belgrade), November 14, 1982, pp. 8–11. More recent diagnoses of Soviet economic problems since Gorbachev's accession to power, moreover, are surprisingly blunt in their pessimism. See "Na vstrechi XXVII S'ezdy KPSS," *Pravda*, April 25, 1985.

39. In the face of hard currency problems, two of the more "uppity" states in the region—Romania and Yugoslavia—turned more of their trade toward the Soviet Union. See *Statisticki godisnjak Jugoslavije, 1981* (Belgrade: Central Statistical Office, 1981), p. 747, Jeanne Kirk Laux, "The Limits of Autonomy: Romania in the 1980s," in U.S. Congress, Joint Economic Committee, *Eastern European Economic Assessment, Part II* (Washington, D.C., 1981), pp. 107–127; Crowther, "Romanian Politics"; O. Djurdjevic, "Ekonomska saradnja Jugoslavije; clanica SEV" (Economic Cooperation between Yugoslavia and CMEA) *Nase Teme* 28 (December 1984), pp. 2799–2818.

40. JEC, *USSR: Measures of Economic Growth*, p. 58.

41. For the figures on defense, see SIPRI, *World Armaments*, p. 162; JEC, *USSR: Measures of Economic Growth*; Charles Wolfe, Jr., "Costs of the Soviet Empire," *Wall Street Journal*, January 30, 1984; Seweryn Bialer, "The Politics of Stringency," *Problems of Communism* 29 (May–June 1980), pp. 19–33. It must be noted that defense outlays, while they cannot be termed "losses" to the same degree that nonrepayable subsidies can, are nonetheless a very inefficient form of economic investment.

42. See the exhortations directed to the party and the workers to tighten discipline, produce more with less, and to link pay with output in the November 1982 and the June 1983 Central Committee Plena and in Twenty-Seventh Party Congress. See "Peredovaya: na vazhneishikh uchastkakh nashei raboty" (Editorial: On the Important Contributions of our Labor) *Kommunist* 50 (July 1983), pp. 3–13, "Luchshe rabotat'—luchshe zhit'" (Better Work—a Better LIfe) *Kommunist* 49 (April 1982), pp. 3–12, and "Na vstrechi XXVII." Recent figures on the growth of labor productivity, investment in productive versus unproductive investment, consumption as a percentage of GNP, and economic growth all show the effects of austerity. See A. Bagdasarov and S. Pervushin,"Proizvoditel'nost truda: teorizya, praktika, rezervy rosta" (Productivity of Labor: Theory, Practice, Reserves of Growth) *Kommunist* 50 (January 1983), pp. 14–23; and JEC, *USSR: Measures of Economic Growth*.

43. Consider the implications, for example, of the sharp growth in Soviet tourists visiting Eastern Europe, as noted by John Bushnell, "The New Soviet

Man Turns Pessimist," in Stephen Cohen et al., eds., *The Soviet Union Since Stalin* (Bloomington: Indiana University Press, 1980), pp. 177–199. Consider as well the implications of higher levels of consumption among party members in consumer-deficit societies, as discussed by Mervyn Matthews, *Privilege in the Soviet Union* (London: Allen & Unwin, 1978), and the implications of polls citing resentment over inequalities in privilege cited in David Paul and Maurice Simon,"Poland Today and Czechoslovakia 1968," *Problems of Communism* 30 (September–October 1981), pp. 25–39 and James P. McGregor,"Polish Public Opinion in a Time of Crisis," *Comparative Politics* 17 (October 1984), pp 17–36.

44. See the arguments by Zvi Gitelman, "The World Economy and Elite Political Strategies in Czechoslovakia, Hungary, and Poland," in Bornstein et al., *East-West Relations*, pp. 127–61; and Walter Connor, "Workers and Power," in Triska and Gati, *Blue Collar Workers*. It should be noted that the austerity measures imposed by Eastern European regimes of late are not as austere—insofar as one can gauge such things—as similar measures in nonsocialist Third World countries. The social wage, for example, has not been reduced much and is still substantial. This moderation reflects, among other things, Eastern European fears of austerity-measure "riots" similar to those occurring in Third World countries and seeming Soviet willingness to lessen the domestic costs of the debt crisis in the satellites.

45. See Laux, "Limits of Autonomy," Arpad Abonyi, "Eastern Europe's Reintegration," in Chase-Dunn, *Socialist States in the World System*, pp. 181–202; and Crowther, "Romanian Politics."

46. Grey Hodnett and Peter Potichnyj, for example, have argued that a key factor influencing Soviet intervention in Czechoslovakia in 1968 was the feared effects of Slovak irredentism on the Ukrainians. See their *The Ukraine and the Czechoslovak Crisis* (Canberra: Australian National University, 1972).

47. For relevant arguments focusing on the distribution of resources available to states for bargaining within the bloc, see Zimmerman, "Regional Hierarchical Systems"; Zimmerman,"Soviet–East European Relations"; Reisinger, "East European Military Expenditures"; Jowitt, "Romanian Communist Party"; Clark, "Evolving Nature"; and Vanous and Marrese, *Soviet Subsidization*, chap. 8.

48. See Chase-Dunn, "Introduction"; Chase-Dunn, "Socialist States;" David Ost, "Socialist World Market as Strategy for Ascent," in Friedman, *Ascent and Decline*, pp. 229–254; Jowitt, *Leninist Response*; Gitelman, "World Economy"; Abonyi, "Eastern Europe's Reintegration"; William Zimmerman, "Dependency Theory and the Soviet–East European Hierarchical Regional System: Initial Tests," *Slavic Review* 37 (December 1978), pp. 604–623; Clark and Bahry, "Dependent Development."

49. It is important, however, to note that there are differences of opinion about whether the Soviet bloc is part of or separate from the global capitalist system. Compare, for example, Chase-Dunn, "Socialist States" with Szymanski, "The Socialist World System." As I will argue below, the particular costs associated with setting up a separate system, particularly given East-West military conflict, led to pressures to rejoin the global capitalist system. The result was that the bloc increasingly took on the characteristics of the semiperiphery—a position reminiscent of presocialist historical experience.

50. See Theda Skocpol, *States and Social Revolutions* (New York: Cambridge University Press, 1981).

51. Gilpin, *War and Change*, p. 167. See also Chirot and Thomas, "World System Theory"; Gilpin, *War and Change*, pp. 10–16, 146–185; and Triska, "Workers' Assertiveness," especially p. 275.

52. This contrasts, of course, with the Yugoslavs, who through self-management and market socialism have structured a system that blurs the clear lines of confict between workers and the state by atomizing the working class. For an analysis that addresses why the Yugoslavs have avoided the Polish experience despite austerity, see Josip Zupanov, "Trziste rade; samoupravni socijalizam" (The Labor Market and Self-Managing Socialism) *Nase Teme* 27 (1983), pp. 266–271; and Valerie Bunce and Alexander Hicks, "Capitalisms, Socialisms and Democracy," forthcoming in Maurice Zeitlin, ed., *Political Power and Social Theory*, vol. 6 (Beverly Hills, Calif.: Sage, 1987), pp. 90–132

53. See in particular Zvi Gitelman, "Power and Authority in Eastern Europe," in Johnson, ed., *Change in Communist Systems*, pp. 235–264; Zygmunt Baumann, "Twenty Years After: The Crisis in Soviet Type Systems," *Problems of Communism* 20 (November–December 1971), pp. 45–53; Gitelman, "World Economy"; Alex Pravda, "East-West Interdependence and the Social Compact in Eastern Europe," in Bornstein et al., *East-West Relations*; Triska,"Workers' Assertiveness"; Bahro, *Alternative*, p. 207; Konrad and Szelenyi, *Intellectuals on the Road;* Brian Silver, "Political Beliefs of the Soviet Citizen: Sources of Support for Regime Norms," unpublished manuscript, December 1985; and Wayne D. Franceisco and Zvi Gitelman, "Soviet Political Culture and 'Covert' Participation in Policy Making," *American Political Science Review* 78 (September 1984), pp. 603–621.

54. Bogdan Mieczkowski, "The Relationship Between Changes in Consumption and Politics in Poland," *Soviet Studies* 30 (1978),pp. 263–269; Triska and Gati, *Blue Collar Workers*; and Longin Pastusiak, "Origins and Nature of the Polish Crisis, 1980–1981,"unpublished paper, Ohio State University, Mershon Center, February 9, 1984.

55. The limits of worker power are analyzed by Connor,"Workers and Power"; Adam Przeworski, "The 'Man of Iron' and Men of Power in Poland," *PS* 15 (Winter 1982), pp. 18–31; and David Mason, "Policy Dilemmas and Political Unrest in Poland," *Journal of Politics* 45 (1983), pp. 397–421. Mason's analysis suggests that in the Polish case at least, worker power is central and worker pressure on the regime's priorities is evident even *prior* to succession.

56. It was hoped, according to the arguments supporting the new stage of "developed socialism," that greater equalization in income distribution by class during the 1960s would enhance productivity. See Bunce, "Political Economy"; Walter Connor, *Socialism, Work, and Equality* (New York: Columbia University Press, 1979); and Bogdan Mieczkowski, *Personal and Social Consumption in Eastern Europe* (New York: Praeger, 1977), pp. 149, 196–198, 225, 273, and 311. As Jozef Prajestka put it (quoted in Mieczkowski, p. 189), "A better satisfaction of human needs favors faster economic growth."

57. For Soviet views of *razriadka*, see G. L. Rozanov, *Politika sotrudnichyestva-veleniye vremeni SSSR i kapitalisticheskiye strany, 70-ye gody (The Policy of Cooperative Relations Between the USSR and the Capitalist Countries During the 1970s)* (Moscow: Mezhdunarodnye otnosheniya, 1977); E. S. Shersnev, *SSSR-SShA: ekonomicheskiye otnosheniya i problemyi vozmozhnosti* (Moscow: Nauka, 1976,). Compare how similar these arguments are with those of Richard Nixon, *RN: The Memoirs of Richard Nixon.* vol. 2 (New York: Warner, 1978), pp. 89–105. For an exhaustive analysis of detente, see William Garthoff, *Detente and Confrontation, American-Soviet Relations From Nixon to Reagan* (Washington, D.C.: Brookings Institution, 1985).

58. The relationship between detente and economic reform is analyzed perceptively by Volten, *Brezhnev's Peace Program.*

59. See in particular Kalman Pesci, *The Future of Socialist Economic Integration* (Armonk, N.Y.: Sharpe, 1981); Fredrich Levcik and Jan Stankovsky, *Industrial Cooperation Between East and West* (White Plains, N.Y.: Sharpe, 1979), pp. 41–54; Bornstein, "East-West Economic Relations"; and Franklyn D. Holzman and Robert Levgold, "The Economics and Politics of East-West Relations," in Erik Hoffman and Frederic Fleron, eds., *The Conduct of Soviet Foreign Policy*, 2d ed. (New York: Aldine, 1980), pp. 428–478.

60. Pesci, *Future*, p. 162; Friedrich Levcik, "The Prospects for East-West Trade in the 1980s," in Bornstein et al., *East-West Relations*, pp. 62–86; Zupanov, "Otvaranje prema ekonomiji." Such calculations, of course, were fanciful, as Zupanov and others have noted.

61. On the U.S. misconstrual, see in particular Lawrence Radway, "The Curse of Free Elections," *Foreign Policy* 40 (Fall 1980), pp. 61–73; Coral Bell, "Soviet-American Strategic Balance, the Western Alliance, and East-West Relations," in Bornstein et al., *East-West Relations*, pp. 11–30; and Volten, *Brezhnev's Peace Program*. For a Soviet analysis of how U.S. electoral politics defeated detente, see A. A. Kokoshin,"Vnutrennie prichiny peremen vo vneshnei politike" (Domestic Sources of Change in Foreign Policy). *S SH A* 11 (July 1980), pp 3–13.

62. Paul Marer, quoted in Paul Lewis, "Role of Western Banks in Poland's Debt Crisis," *New York Times*, February 3, 1982. For a Soviet view of these issues, see L. Bauman and B. Grebnikov, "The Socialist Community: Economic Integration," *International Affairs* (Moscow) 22 (1981), pp. 73–81.

63. Quoted in Anthony Sampson, "So, Give Credit Where Credit is Due (Poland)," *New York Times*, January 10, 1982. See also Gabriel Eichler, "Country Risk Analysis and Bank Lending to Eastern Europe," in JEC, *Eastern European Economic Assessment, Part II*, pp. 759–775; "The Country Risk League Table," *Euromoney*, February 1982, p. 46; and Franklyn Holzman, "Credit Worthiness and Balance-of-Payments Adjustment Mechanisms of Centrally Planned Economies," in Steven Rosefielde, ed., *Economic Welfare and the Economics of Soviet Socialism* (Cambridge: Cambridge University Press, 1981), pp. 163–184.

64. For example, it has been estimated that such trade furnishes 1 percent of the West German GNP, provides 92,000 jobs to West Germany (particularly in steel), and with the pipeline deal, will provide some 20,000 more jobs to the seven European nations involved. Finally, there is energy dependence. In the early 1980s, 17 percent of West German domestic gas consumption was provided by the Soviets, a figure expected to rise to 30 percent by the 1990s and to 20 percent for other West European countries. See Angela Stent, "The USSR and Germany," *Problems of Communism* 30 (September–October 1981), pp. 1–23; John Tagliabue, "Bonn Needs the Business Even More Than the Gas," *New York Times*, August 14, 1981.

65. See Joan Parpart Zoeter, "Eastern Europe: The Hard Currency Debt," in JEC, *Eastern Europe Economic Assessment*, vol. 1 (1981), pp. 716–731.

66. The debt burden has declined, however, in the bloc since 1981. The total regional hard currency debt stood at about $55 billion in 1983, almost half of which was Polish ($25.2 billion). This reflects austerity, Soviet help, and an upturn in Western economies. See Seth Mydans, "East Bloc Lending Climate Improves," *New York Times*, March 5, 1984.

67. By 1976–1977, for example, Poland was borrowing for current consumption needs. See Karin Lissakers, "The Polish Debt," *New York Times*, January 8, 1982. For a discussion of the mechanics of the "debt regime," see Charles Lipson, "The International Organization of Third World Debt," *International Organization* 34 (Autumn 1981), pp. 603–631; Ortmeyer, "Poland's

Foreign Debt"; Portes, "The Polish Crisis"; Zoeter, "Eastern Europe"; and Lawrence Brainard, "Eastern Europe's Uncertain Future: The Outlook for East-West Trade and Finance," in JEC, *Eastern European Economic Assessment*, vol. 1, pp. 751–758.

68. In 1979 Eastern Europe's current account balance was negative $5 billion. In 1980 the figure was –4.8, and in 1981 –5.5. The Soviet Union, by contrast, ran considerable trade surpluses in the bloc and in the world. See United Nations, *Economic Bulletin for Europe*, vol. 33 (New York, 1981), p. 116.

69. The linkage between external dependence and patterns of income inequality in Eastern Europe is examined in Bunce,"Neither Equality Nor Efficiency." For interesting insights into this linkage from an Eastern European perspective, see Zsuzsa Ferge, *A Society in the Making: Hungarian Social and Societal Policy, 1945–1975* (White Plains, N.Y.: Sharpe, 1979), pp. 159–191.

70. For example, Poland traditionally has been a net food exporter, but by the late 1970s was a net food importer. This change reflected sharp declines in livestock beginning in 1977 and sharp declines in crop production beginning in 1978. See Paul Lewis, "Economic Revival Called Polish Aim," *New York Times*, December 15, 1981. Hungary, by contrast, has become a net food exporter, in part because the Hungarians have instituted significant organizational reforms in the countryside and have capitalized on Western technology and cooperative agreements to maximize output. See Sheila Thefft, "Hungary Harvesting the Fruit of U.S. Farming Know-How," *Chicago Tribune*, June 24, 1982; Paul Lewis, "What Poland Lacks, Hungary Has Aplenty," *New York Times*, December 16, 1981. Indeed, by 1979 only Czechoslovakia, Hungary, and Romania were net agricultural exporters. But see Crowther, "The Romanian Economy."

71. See "Curtain Call," *Economist*, December 3, 1983, p. 92; Binder, "Czechs Are New Economic Casualties"; Egon Neuberger, Richard Portes, and Laura D'Andrea Tyson, "The Impact of International Economic Disturbances on the Soviet Union and Eastern Europe: A Survey," in JEC, *Eastern Europe*, vol. 2 (1981), pp. 128–147; Paul Hare, "The Beginnings of Institutional Reform in Hungary," *Soviet Studies* 35 (July 1983), pp. 310–330. For a general description of austerity measures as an economic tool, see Andrew Crockett, "Stabilization Policies in Developing Countries," *IMF Staff Papers* 28 (March 1981), pp. 54–79. It must be noted that austerity measures in these countries differ from those imposed by the IMF on the Third World. First, these measures involve primarily a stabilization, not in most cases a decline in per capita income in the Eastern bloc. Second, the social wage is left intact while pressures increase to work more for the same remuneration. In other words, austerity policy in these countries is not as austere as it has been elsewhere. This approach is because of Soviet aid, because of the ways in which fusion makes a tie between economic austerity and political protest highly likely, and, finally, because these countries, unlike the Third World periphery, are considerably less trade-dependent and much closer to an autarchic economic structure. Finally, on the East German case in particular, West German aid cannot be discounted—see B. V. Flow, "The GDR: Strange Hard Currency Cushion," *Radio Free Europe—Radio Liberty Background Report*, December 28, 1984. All these factors explain as well why Eastern Europe could prune so much of the region's external debt—a reduction of $8 billion in 1982 and $6.6 billion in 1983—and could slash imports from the West by 16 percent in 1982. See "Curtain Call."

72. For example, almost 90 percent of Soviet imports from West Germany—their largest trade partner in the West—are manufactured goods and high-technology items, most of which are unavailable in the East or of poorer quality. See Flora Lewis, "Split Among Allies Runs Deeper Than Sanctions," *New*

York Times, January 3, 1982; and Steven Rosefielde, "Comparative Advantage and the Evolving Pattern of Soviet International Commodity Specialization, 1950–1973," in Rosefielde, *Economic Welfare*, pp. 185–222.

73. Indeed, the Soviets were in early 1982 denied a loan by the West Germans that would normally have been routine. At the same time, of course, the Soviets had several sources of strength in bargaining as well, albeit weak ones. One is the necessity of the banks admitting overexposure, another is the dearth of assets available in the West for seizure if bankruptcy were to occur.

74. See Lipson, "International Organization."

75. The one constraint on Western banks was the difficulty, in lieu of any formal role for the IMF (except in the Romanian case), of forging cooperation. In the Polish case, the banks involved—over 500, and many of them small—had difficulty organizing and admitting their exposure. See Ortmeyer, "Poland's Foreign Debt."

76. Alex Pravda, "East-West Interdependence and the Social Compact in Eastern Europe," in Bornstein et al., *East-West Relations*, p. 184.

77. "Now Russia Asks for Time to Pay," *Economist*, February 6, 1982, p. 81.

78. See Clyde Farnsworth, "Poles Ask Admittance to IMF," *New York Times*, December 21, 1981. For an analysis of the domestic and international origins of the Polish crisis, see Valerie Bunce, "The Polish Crisis of 1980–1981 and Theories of Revolution" in Terry Boswell, ed., *Revolution and the World System* (New York: Praeger, forthcoming).

79. See Charles Lindblom, *Politics and Markets* (New York: Basic Books, 1977); and Edward Tufte, *Political Control of the Economy* (Princeton: Princeton University Press, 1979). For an elaboration of these arguments, see Bunce and Hicks,"Capitalisms, Socialisms."

80. Chase-Dunn, "Socialist States," p. 513. The conflict in the literature about whether the Soviet bloc is separate from (Szymanski, "The Socialist World System") or part of the global capitalist system (Chase-Dunn, "Socialist States") is resolved through the argument that the costs of separation and of reform together pressured the bloc to reintegrate with the global capitalist system.

81. Valerie Bunce, "The Soviet Union as a Declining Hegemon: The Gorbachev Reforms and Eastern Europe." Paper presented at the annual meeting of the American Political Science Association in Chicago, September 2, 1987.

11

The Cost of Self-Reliance: The Case of China

William Loehr and Peter Van Ness

During the last fifteen years of Mao Zedong's rule, China was a model for the Third World of self-reliant development. Many developing countries at different times have pursued policies that could be called policies of "self-reliance." In many cases, these policies appeared in the form of import-substitution economic strategies, aimed at replacing imported goods with domestic production. Import substitution is normally carried out within the context of functioning markets, with government intervention in the form of subsidies, taxes, and exchange rate manipulation. In other cases, countries have simply chosen to shut themselves to the outside (e.g., Albania and Burma), sharply restricting imported goods along with other forms of foreign influence. In these cases, self-reliance policies are often based on fear that importing creates a dependence upon foreigners that is not conducive to national development. Socialist Third World countries have been particularly anxious that integrating their economies with the world market would distort their domestic development and result in dependency relations with the capitalist West.[1]

But self-reliance may come at a cost. Importing is the source of capital goods, technology, and productive inputs that may not be available locally. Some countries pursuing self-reliance policies assume that this is only a temporary necessity and that after an adjustment period they will be able to supply their own capital goods, technology appropriate to their needs, and other productive inputs.

It is the purpose of this chapter to assess the net economic cost of the attempt at self-reliance made by the Maoist leadership in China during the period 1960–1976 by comparing economic performance in that period with the record of China's economic performance since the establishment of the People's Republic in 1949. Our assessment is empirical. We will first lay out the logic of the empirical test that we will perform. Then, we briefly discuss the history of the Chinese case. Next, we discuss the statistical procedures that we use and the data to which they are applied. Finally, we present the results of the analysis, indicating that indeed there was a cost to China associated with attempts to seek self-reliance.

Our empirical test rests upon the observation that policies of self-reliance are normally designed to reduce or even to do away with imports. Part of the fear of imports—perhaps the major fear—is that all else being equal, increased imports imply a tendency toward a deficit in the balance of trade and therefore a surplus in the capital account of the balance of trade. The latter normally implies borrowing from foreigners and the accumulation of debt, along with the constraints imposed by creditors upon the economic development policies that may be put in place.

Not surprisingly, the balance of payments must balance. There are two main accounts in the balance of payments—the current account and the capital account. A deficit in one by definition implies a surplus in the other. The current account records all transactions associated with trade in goods, services, and unilateral transfers. The capital account records all transactions associated with changes in the holdings of net assets, such as the transactions that stem from making investments or loans or from the accumulation of foreign exchange. A negative balance in the current account—for example, because of importing more than is exported—must be "balanced" by a positive figure in the capital account. Such a positive figure in the capital account can come about voluntarily by investors who make a direct investment in the country or by a foreign financial institution that lends the cash required to import. In some cases, the positive figure can come about involuntarily. For example a country imports but simply does not have the means to pay. The exporting country is therefore forced to make a "loan" to the importing country, and this exchange is simply recorded as a short-term capital transaction in the capital accounts of both countries. It appears as a positive figure in the capital account of the importer, just as if the "loan" were a voluntary one.

China's Economic Policies

For Mao Zedong, self-reliance meant controlling one's own future to the greatest extent possible and preventing powerful outside forces from establishing structural control over the productive life of one's country. Specifically, the international economic strategy of self-reliance prohibited private foreign investment in China, refused Chinese participation in the major financial institutions of the capitalist world economy (like the World Bank and the International Monetary Fund), and even saw the acceptance of long-term foreign loans as compromising. China argued that the foreign aid programs of both the United States and the Soviet Union were essentially efforts to control Third World countries, and Beijing designed its economic assistance to Asia and Africa during these years as an alternative model based on principles of purportedly true equality and mutual benefit.[2]

China has attempted three different approaches in its international economic policy over the four decades since the Communists came to power in 1949. During the 1950s, China leaned toward the Soviet Union and cooperated closely both in security and economic matters with the Soviet bloc. In the 1960s, China broke with Moscow, initiating its own particular road to socialist development, which included an international economic policy of self-reliance that continued until Mao's death in 1976. Finally, Deng Xiaoping and the post-Mao leadership in the present period have launched a third alternative policy, the "open door" to the West, which calls for integrating China's economy with the world market.

During the self-reliance period in China, 1960–1976, many of the practices subsequently undertaken by the post-Mao party leadership were at that time denounced as contrary to the principles of self-reliance and independent development: for example, establishing joint ventures in China with foreign multinational corporations; building a foreign tourist industry in China; contracting with foreign companies and governments to send PRC workers and engineers abroad to work in order to earn foreign exchange; importing foreign consumer goods to satisfy consumer demand in China; and sending thousands of Chinese students and scholars abroad for academic training in capitalist countries.

However, as Doak Barnett has observed, Beijing "never advocated complete autarchy" or relying solely on one's own economic resources.[3] Mao's concern was to avoid economic ties with "strings attached"—relationships with powerful states that gave them leverage over the other country's domestic affairs—not to avoid international exchange. For example, during the 1960–1976 self-reliance period, China's total foreign trade first declined somewhat and then expanded. By 1976 the total value of China's imports and exports combined (trade turnover) had more more than doubled.[4] Hence, self-reliance under Mao Zedong was not incompatible with expanding foreign trade, just as long as a balance was maintained and China did not incur long-term foreign indebtedness.

The Chinese Communist Party (CCP) government's decision to undertake a strategy of self-reliance was prompted in part by the Soviet Union's decision to cut off aid to China after a decade of close Sino-Soviet economic and technical cooperation during the first years of the People's Republic. The Soviets provided an estimated $2.2 billion in credits during the PRC's first ten years[5] and had committed themselves to providing aid through China's initial three five-year plans for a total of fifteen years.[6] When they unilaterally broke that commitment in 1960, the Soviets were apparently attempting to discipline a rebellious China (from their point of view), trying—unsuccessfully as it turned out—to force China back into the socialist camp by withdrawing their aid.

Soviet loans to China had been accompanied by vitally important technical assistance, including the sending of foreign experts from the Soviet Union and Eastern Europe to China, the training of Chinese students and scientists both in China and abroad, and the purchase of entire factories complete with technology as part of the Soviet aid package. Credits from the USSR to China during the first years of the People's Republic, 1950–1957, constituted an average of more than 13 percent of Beijing's capital construction budget per year.[7]

When the Soviet advisers in China were ordered home by Moscow in the summer of 1960, taking their blueprints with them, they left the Chinese in the lurch. Many aid projects were only partially completed and had to be abandoned. Other new plants already constructed could not be operated for lack of trained Chinese personnel. Industrial production dropped in one year—1960 to 1961— by 42 percent,[8] in large part because of the withdrawal of Soviet aid.[9]

One might speculate in hindsight that China at this point might have turned to the West as an alternative source of capital and technology, as Yugoslavia had done in 1948 when it broke with Moscow. But China's political position at the time seemed to have precluded such an accommodation with the West. China's foreign policy since 1958 had been focused on building relations with the Third World, attempting to construct a broad anti-imperialist united front comprised of both newly independent Asian and African goverments as well as revolutionary "national liberation" movements. The United States and the "Pax Americana" post–World War II establishment were the main targets for this radical attack on the global status quo.

Self-reliance in a strictly economic sense can be interpreted as a condition in which imports relative to exports are as small as possible and the volume of trade is small. A country that avoids running a balance-of-trade deficit depends less upon foreigners for credit than do countries with large trade deficits. By contrast, reliance on the outside world appears when countries are importing to obtain technology and inputs that they do not produce internally. For them, trade balances are more likely to be negative (or at least less positive), and the accumulation of debts to foreigners a normal occurrence. Another dimension of this kind of "reliance" can be related to the sheer magnitude of trade, even if trade is in balance. Resources a country does not have can be obtained by exchanging for them resources it does have. When trade is in balance, a large volume of trade implies that even though the total amount of resources remains unchanged overall, there is a qualitative change in the resources available from those that are available locally to those that are not. Thus, two important dimensions of self-reliance include the trade deficit and trade volume. Large values on either dimension indicate less self-reliance than do small values.

To determine whether policies of self-reliance of the types described above are conducive to economic growth requires examining the relationship between the trade balance and changes in some measure of national income (such as gross domestic product, national income, etc.). If "reliance" is conducive to growth, there would be a negative relationship between trade balances and growth. That is, when trade balances are increasingly negative, growth tends to be increasingly high, as the country takes advantage of the technology, capital, and inputs that are "lent" by foreigners. Similarly, the converse would be the case. Furthermore, as the volume of trade increases, growth also would be expected to increase. This positive relationship occurs as domestically available resources are traded for resources available only from abroad.

Here we want to test the hypothesis that in the Chinese case, importing is good for growth. If we can reject that hypothesis, we can infer that policies of self-reliance come without cost to growth or that they may even be compatible with improved growth prospects. As discussed above, importing and depending upon foreigners would be indicated by low or even negative trade balances, as well as by a large volume of trade. Thus, in a formal sense we are interested in testing two null hypotheses:

H1: There is a negative correlation between trade balances and economic growth.

Conversely, rejection of this null hypothesis implies the alternative:

Ha1: There is either no relationship or a positive relationship between trade balance and growth.

H2: There is a positive relationship between the relative volume of trade and growth.

Rejection of H2 then implies the alternative:

Ha2: There is either a negative relationship or no relationship at all between growth and the volume of trade.

In the cases where either or both of these hypotheses are rejected, the alternatives imply that policies of self-reliance could be either costless or even beneficial to growth, as their proponents claim.

Data and Analysis

To test these hypotheses in the case of China, we have used the data shown in Table 11.1. Ashbrook has provided calculations of real gross national product (GNP) for China for the years 1950 to 1980, with all data expressed in billions of dollars of 1980. As an alternative measure of economic activity, an index of China's net material product (NMP) as reported by Dernberger has also been considered. Because there are two major ways in which economic activity is often measured for China (GNP and NMP) and the use of these alternatives is not without controversy, we have chosen to perform our statistical work using both measures to check for the robustness of our conclusions. The choice of economic activity index affects our results very little. Davie and Carver have calculated trade balances for the period. Their data are in millions of current dollars, and so we have put them in "real" terms by deflating them by the U.S. Wholesale Price Index. Trade volume and its relationship to Chinese gross domestic product (GDP) have been put forward by Gregory C. Chow. Chow's measure of trade volume is represented by the total amount of trade (exports plus imports) as a proportion of GDP for each year.

We use statistical regression techniques to test the hypotheses using the data from Table 11.1. Generally, our regression equation is of the form

Table 11.1   China's Economic Performance: Basic Data

	Gross National Product (billions of 1980 $)	Net Material Product (1952=100)	U.S. Wholesal Price Index	Trade Balance (millions of U.S. $)	Trade (as percentage of national income)	Exports minus Imports (millions of U.S. $)
1949	71	58.90				
1950	86	70.10	0.30	98.59		30
1951	100	81.10	0.31	−1096.77		−340
1952	118	100.00	0.32	−444.44	11	−140
1953	123	114.00	0.32	−671.88	12	−215
1954	127	120.60	0.33	−707.69	12	−230
1955	140	128.30	0.35	−807.37	15	−285
1956	150	146.40	0.34	444.44	13	150
1957	159	153.00	0.35	504.32	12	175
1958	180	186.70	0.35	326.80	12	115
1959	170	202.10	0.35	482.13	12	170
1960	156	199.20	0.35	−198.30	11	−70
1961	125	140.00	0.35	99.46	9	35
1962	140	130.90	0.35	1049.35	9	370
1963	158	144.90	0.35	1066.86	9	375
1964	182	168.80	0.35	794.78	8	280
1965	203	197.50	0.36	528.81	9	190
1966	232	231.00	0.37	471.44	8	175
1967	226	214.30	0.37	13.44	7	5
1968	228	200.40	0.38	354.05	8	135
1969	252	239.10	0.40	568.04	7	225
1970	282	294.70	0.41	267.97	6	110
1971	301	315.30	0.42	919.38	6	390
1972	312	324.50	0.44	1433.73	7	635
1973	351	351.40	0.50	937.94	9	470
1974	364	355.20	0.60	−125.97	12	−75
1975	388	384.70	0.65	468.94	12	305
1976	395	374.40	0.68	2504.77	11	1705
1977	429	403.60	0.72	2076.41	10	1500
1978	479	453.20	0.78	−301.82	12	−235
1979	520	489.90	0.88	−644.83	13	−565
1980	552	514.50	1.00	−305.00	15	−305

Sources: R.F. Dernberger, "Economic Policy and Performance," in Joint Economic Committee, Congress of the U.S., *China's Economy Looks Toward the Year 2000*, vol. 1, 1986; A. G. Ashbrook, Jr., "China: Economic Modernization and Long-Term Economic Performance," and J. L. Davie and D. W. Carver, "China's International Trade and Finance," in Joint Economic Committee, Congress of the U.S., *China Under the Four Modernizations*, 1982; and G. C. Chow, *The Chinese Economy*, Harper & Row, 1985.

$$GNP = f \text{ (trade balance, trade volume, other variables).}$$

It is necessary to recognize that trade balances are not the only factors affecting economic growth. China has gone through several episodes during which domestic economic strategy has shifted greatly. Both the Great Leap Forward and the Cultural Revolution were major efforts to change economic strategy, and both of these had a great effect on economic performance. These attempts at strategic shift were efforts to make China more self-reliant in the sense that has been discussed above. If these two periods were not accounted for by our statistical procedure, we would be mixing the influence of other important factors with the influence of trade balances. Also, our period of analysis extends from 1950 to 1980, a period over which, with some interruption, there has been an upward trend in most indicators of Chinese economic performance, such as measures of GNP. Thus, we should include a time trend to account for the general upward drift in the dependent variable caused by factors that we are not now considering.

The self-reliance period is generally recognized as covering the time from the Soviet aid cut off in 1960 until Mao's death in 1976. During that period, 1960–1976, both the Cultural Revolution and economic depression caused by the the Great Leap occurred. To recognize the influence of the Great Leap downturn and the Cultural Revolution, as well as the trend in GNP, we have included in our analysis several variables in addition to the trade variables. The trend is easiest to incorporate by including simply the year of observation, a fairly standard way to account for "all influences otherwise omitted." The influences of the Great Leap and the Cultural Revolution, within the context of the self-reliance period, are considered by the use of "dummy variables."

The addendum at the end of this chapter discusses dummy variables in more detail, and they are extensively explained in statistics and econometrics texts. In brief, dummy variables are designed to recognize shifts that occur either in the dependent variable or in the relationship between the dependent variable and some independent variable whenever dichotomous conditions exist. For example, either we are dealing with one of the years associated with the Great Leap or we are not; years are associated with the Cultural Revolution or they are not. These are dichotomous conditions that can be recognized by dummy variables. Procedurally, a dummy variable takes on the value of one when the condition exists and a value of zero when it does not. This dummy variable (a series of zeros and ones) is then treated like any other variable. The interpretation of the use of dummy variables should become clear as we discuss our results. In the statistical work that we have done, we have subdivided the self-reliance period (1960–1976) into two parts. One part covers the years that fell within the Great Leap depression and recovery (1960–1965), the other the years generally associated with the Cultural Revolution (1966–1976). Separate dummy variables distinguish between these two subperiods. Together they account for the self reliance years.

In the regression equations that follow, the following definitions and acronyms apply. (See Table 11.1 for sources.)

Dependent variables:

GNP = real GNP as reported by Ashbrook

NMP = an index of net material product (NMP) as reported by Dernberger. The base year for the index is 1952.

Independent variables:

year = the years from 1950 to 1980

tradbal = trade balance as reported by Davie and Carver and deflated by the U.S. Wholesale Price Index (1980 = 1.0)

trade% = total trade (i.e., exports plus imports) divided by GDP

Leap = a dummy variable equal to one for 1960 through 1965, zero otherwise

Cultrev = a dummy variable equal to one for 1966 to 1976, zero otherwise

bal-lp = *tradebal* x *Leap*

bal-cr = *tradbal* x *Cultrev*

trad-lp = *trade%* x *Leap*

trad-cr = *trade%* x *Cultrev*

The last four variables use dummy variables to check for the influence of the two major shifts in Chinese economic strategy. *Leap* and *Cultrev* are used to check for shifts in the average level of economic activity during the periods when they apply. The variables *bal-lp* and *bal-cr* are designed to check for a change in the relationship between economic activity and the trade balance during the Great Leap and the Cultural Revolution respectively. Similarly, *trad-lp* and *trad-cr* are designed to check for a change in the relationship between economic activity and trade as a proportion of GDP. The interpretation of these variables will be explained along with the results.

Table 11.2 shows the estimate of a regression equation relating GNP to the five variables, *year, trade%, tradebal, Leap,* and *Cultrev.* The coefficients are the numbers of interest to our hypothesis, and we have highlighted them in the table. (In this discussion we will round off the numbers for brevity.) Most coefficients shown in the table are of very high statistical significance (better than the 95 percent level), and the fit to the data is very tight ($R^2 = .99$). The coefficient attached to the variable *Year,* 15.18, indicates that over the entire period, there has been a tendency for real GNP to increase by $15.18 billion (1980 dollars) on average each year for the period 1950–1980. The negative coefficients on *Leap* and *Cultrev* indicate that each of these changes in strategy had a tendency to reduce GNP. The coefficients tell us that, on average, the Great Leap reduced GNP by $66.71 billion per year, and the Cultural Revolution reduced it by about $48.98 billion per year. Because the trade balance and trade volume are included as separate independent variables, these statements about the Great Leap and Cultural Revolution are net of the effect

Table 11.2

	Righthand Variable	OLS—Dependent Variable: gnp Estimated Coefficient	T-Statistic
1	Year	15.18	T = 36.0
2	Trade%	609.81	T = 3.3
3	Tradbal	−0.0073	T = −1.7
4	Leap	−66.71	T = −6.9
5	Cultrev	−48.98	T = −4.7
6	Constant	−29604.78	T = −36.1

R-squared	=	0.99
F-statistic (5, 23)	=	387.66
Durbin-Watson statistic	=	1.64

that these two periods may have had on GNP through their influence on the trade variables.

The important relationships to our hypotheses are the ones between GNP and the trade variables, after "controlling for" the other variables. The relationship between trade volume and GNP is positive (609.81) and highly significant (better than the 99 percent level), and we therefore cannot reject Hypothesis 2 (H2). Also as expected, the relationship between trade balance and GDP is negative, the coefficient being -0.0073. H1 as well appears difficult to reject.

We should not move too quickly to make statements about rejecting hypotheses based simply upon the results shown in Table 11.2. The effect that the trade balance appears to have had on real GNP is the average for the entire period (1950–1980). That average includes the influence that the Great Leap and the Cultural Revolution may have had on making China's real GNP less (or more) sensitive to changes in the trade balance. For example, assume for the moment that the Cultural Revolution did have one of its intended effects— namely, that it made China's real GNP less sensitive to the trade balance. How would this appear statistically? Using the same statistical procedure used to produce the coefficients appearing in Table 11.2, we would find that during the Cultural Revolution period, there was a positive coefficient attached to a dummy variable representing the *combined effect* of the Cultural Revolution and the trade balance. That is, the Cultural Revolution would have the effect of making the coefficient on the trade balance less negative.

Table 11.3 tests whether the Great Leap and the Cultural Revolution were successful in decreasing China's dependence upon trade. Four new variables are included in addition to those used in the equations of Table 11.2. Two of these are labeled *trad-lp* and *trad-cr*. They are constructed, as shown above, by multiplying the *trade%* by the dummy variable for each period. The coefficients attached to these two "slope" variables should be added to the coefficient on the *trade%* to get the effect of the volume of trade on GDP during the periods of the Great Leap and the Cultural Revolution respectively. The coefficient on *trade%* alone (i.e., as it appears in Table 11.3) should be interpreted as the relationship

Table 11.3

	Righthand Varible	OLS—Dependent Variable: gnp Estimated Coefficient	T-Statistic
1	Year	15.45	T = 38.23
2	Trade%	179.19	T = 0.49
3	Tradbal	–0.020	T = –3.03
4	Leap	–200.80	T = –1.48
5	Cultrev	–105.20	T = –2.19
6	Trad-lp	1324.26	T = 0.97
7	Bal-lp	0.014	T = 0.67
8	Trad-cr	339.29	T = 0.85
9	Bal-cr	0.02	T = 2.85
10	Constant	–30086.48	T = –38.79

R-squared   =   0.99
F-statistic (9, 19)   = 265.00
Durbin-Watson statistic =   1.58

between the volume of trade and GDP after the influence of self-reliance during the Great Leap and the Cultural Revolution have been removed. Similarly, there are two other variables labeled *bal-lp* and *bal-cr*. As in the case above, these are formed by multiplying the dummy variables by *tradbal*. This will allow us to see the independent relationship between the trade balance and growth in GDP while controlling for the effect of the Great Leap and the Cultural Revolution. To see the relationship between growth in GDP and the trade balance *during* the Great Leap depression and recovery or the Cultural Revolution periods, we would add the coefficients on *bal-lp* or *bal-cr* to the coefficient on the trade balance (*tradbal*).

In Table 11.3 we can see that of the four new variables, only one appears to have any statistical significance. The coefficient attached to *bal-cr* is .025, has a "t" value of 2.85, indicating a level of significance better than the .05 level. This coefficient would be expected if indeed China became more self reliant during the period of the Cultural Revolution. That is, during the Cultural Revolution, China's growth in GDP appears to have become less influenced by the trade balance. The overall coefficient on the trade balance (*tradbal*) is negative, but the coefficient on *bal-cr* is positive. The influence of the trade balance on GDP during the Cultural Revolution is the sum of these two coefficients, and that sum is less negative than the coefficient attached to *tradbal* alone. Overall, the results of Table 11.3 indicate that during the Great Leap downturn (1960–1965), there is no statistical evidence that China became less reliant on trade. During the period corresponding to the Cultural Revolution (1966–1976), there was some movement toward self-reliance acting through the trade balance, though the importance of the volume of trade remained unaffected. During both subperiods, GDP was greatly lowered because of forces acting through variables other than the trade volume or trade balance.

When the addition of the *trad-lp, bal-lp* and *trad-cr* variables did nothing of statistical significance to add to the analysis, they were dropped from further consideration. Table 11.4 shows the statistical relationships without them. The estimates made in Table 11.4 allow us to make some rough estimates of the effects of the two major efforts to gain self-reliance. Take the Great Leap downturn and recovery period first. We have seen that it had no discernible effect upon China's sensitivity to changes in the trade balance or the overall volume of trade. However, the average effect of the Great Leap was to reduce real GDP below what it would otherwise have been for reasons other than the ones being considered here (thus the negative coefficient on the *Leap* variable). The coefficient on the variable *Leap*, -65.91, indicates that during the period 1960–1965, GNP was $65.91 billion less than it would have been, all else being equal. Using average values for the independent variables for the 1960–1965 period (from Table 11.1), we find the equation in Table 11.4 predicts that real GNP would have averaged about $219 billion during 1960–1965 in the absence of the Great Leap rather than averaging $153 billion with it. This change represents a reduction averaging about 30 percent, but it ignores the observations that during the Great Leap, trade balances turned sharply more positive as China repaid its debt to the Soviet Union and the volume of trade declined substantially compared with the 1955–1959 period. Both of these forces would depress GNP below what it would have been had levels of prior periods been maintained.

The Cultural Revolution appears to have achieved one objective—to make the country's GDP less sensitive to changes in the trade balance. The net effect of the trade balance during the Cultural Revolution years is the average effect (-0.017) plus the coefficient attached to the variable *bal-cr* (+0.022). The net effect of the trade balance is therefore determined by applying the coefficient +0.005, (-0.017 + 0.022) to the trade balance. Instead of the normal negative relationship between the trade balance and GDP, the Cultural Revolution apparently was able to reverse that relationship slightly. The trade balance averaged $710 million during the 1966–1976 period. Thus, instead of producing balanced trade, the effect was to increase real GDP by about $3.5 billion rather than decrease it by $12 billion.

The main effect of the Cultural Revolution, however, was to reduce real GDP by an average of about $64 billion because of factors other than trade balance. Using the equation from Table 11.4 as we did for the Great Leap, we must compare the average trade balance for the period 1966–1976, $710 billion, with some counterfactual situation because part of the effect of the Cultural Revolution was to make the economy less sensitive to the trade balance. Compared with the situation of balanced trade, the net effect of the Cultural Revolution was to reduce GNP by an average of $49 billion annually. The net loss because of the Cultural Revolution, therefore, was about 14 percent of real GNP for the period. The equation from Table 11.4 predicts that GNP would have averaged $335 billion without the Cultural Revolution and $286 billion with it. The reduction in GNP is the combined effect of the $64 billion

Table 11.4

	Righthand Variable	OLS—Dependent Variable: gnp Estimated Coefficient	T-Statistic
1	Year	15.31	T = 41.47
2	Trade%	472.92	T = 2.83
3	Tradbal	−0.017	T = −3.35
4	Leap	−65.91	T = −7.83
5	Cultrev	−64.29	T = −6.12
6	Bal-cr	0.022	T = 2.91
7	Constant	−29859.71	T = −41.58

R-squared	=	0.99
F-statistic (6, 22)	=	429.67
Durbin-Watson statistic	=	1.81

reduction in GNP on average that is associated with factors other than trade and a $15.5 billion increase due to the favorable impact the Cultural Revolution seems to have had on the relationship between trade balances and growth. In the absence of the Cultural Revolution, the $710 million positive trade balance would have implied a reduction of GNP of about $12 billion. However, the Cultural Revolution was apparently able to turn that relationship around, causing the actual trade balance to boost GNP by about $3.5 billion due to improved self-reliance. In short, the Cultural Revolution did achieve one of its objectives: It reduced China's dependence upon imports relative to exports. However, the benefits of achieving that particular objective were far outweighed by the losses in GDP occurring for other reasons.

We performed statistical analyses similar to those described above, but using an index of net material product (NMP) as the dependent variable instead of real GNP. The results, shown in Table 11.5, are generally the same as they are for real GNP, though there is one major difference. Unlike the analysis dealing with GNP, the relationships with NMP indicate that the Great Leap period did have some influence on the importance of the volume of trade. The variable *trad-lp* comes into the analysis with a very strong relationship with NMP during the 1960–1965 period. However, the relationship is positive, indicating that during that period the growth of NMP was more strongly affected by trade than in other periods and that that effect is the opposite of what one would call "self-reliance." Indeed, it appears that China became more reliant upon trade during the period, and the fact that trade volume fell sharply during that period hurt growth in NMP greatly.

The preceding analysis of the impact of selected variables during the two subperiods on GNP could also have been conducted with a focus on NMP. The results would have appeared about the same. Using the equation of Table 11.5, we would be able to predict that the NMP index would have averaged 229 during the 1960–1965 period in the absence of the Great Leap, but the effect of the Great Leap was to reduce the index to only 166, a 27.5 percent reduction. During the 1966–1976 period, instead of averaging 334 (as predicted

Table 11.5

	Righthand Variable	OLS—Dependent Variable: netmatpr Estimated Coefficient	T-Statistic
1	Year	14.3	T = 26.46
2	Trade%	336.74	T = 1.36
3	Tradbal	−0.01	T = −1.63
4	Leap	−361.60	T = −3.32
5	Culture	−56.81	T = −3.67
6	Trad-lp	3362.54	T = 2.84
7	Bal-cr	0.02	T = 1.77
8	Constant	−28039.47	T = −26.52

R-squared   =   0.98
F-statistic (7, 21)   = 150.32
Durbin-Watson statistic =   1.09

without the Cultural Revolution), the NMP index averages only 291, a 13 percent drop.

The discussion of the quantitative impact of the policies pursued in China during the self-reliance period—and particularly during the two major subperiods of the Great Leap and the Cultural Revolution—could have been carried out using a number of counterfactual situations. The numbers would have changed a bit, but the overall points would remain. During the 1960–1965 period, there is no indication that China became more self-reliant and some indication self-reliance was less. The Cultural Revolution does seem to have achieved some self-reliance in that China's growth became less associated with maintaining a negative trade balance. However, in both subperiods, any effects on trade-related factors was vastly overpowerd by the strong and negative impacts of factors other than trade. Both periods implied large losses in economic activity, whether measured by GNP or NMP, and little if anything was gained in self-reliance. In general, we cannot reject the hypotheses that growth in China is positively associated with trade volume and negatively associated with trade balances. This result remains despite the country's efforts at achieving self-reliance during the 1960–1976 period.

Conclusion

"Development is dependent development," concludes Edward Friedman. "The developing nation remains vulnerable to mighty forces beyond its control." He continues his assessment of developing countries, focusing particularly on socialist countries: "There is no such thing as autonomous, autarkic, self-reliant development. That goal is not only a mirage, it is poisoned; it is not an oasis. It confuses sovereignty with development. It substitutes nationalism of an extreme type for economics. It is a consequence of what may be called utopian Leninism."[10]

Our empirical study of China's attempt to achieve self-reliance shows that Friedman's conclusion, at least in the case of the PRC, is much too strong. During the self-reliance period, the Chinese economy continued to grow at a substantial rate. Moreover, Stephen Thomas's chapter (Chapter 8), in this volume also shows that China made significant achievements in social and economic human rights during the first three decades of the People's Republic, before the post-Mao decision in 1978 to integrate China's economy with the world market.

But China paid a price for its self-reliance policy. The statistical analysis presented here is an attempt to estimate the cost in lost economic growth during the self-reliance years 1960–1976. Also, losses in economic growth were only part of the cost to China. Compare, for example, the Heymann analysis of China's technology acquisition and diffusion during the self-reliance period with accounts of China's vastly improved access to foreign capital and technology under the current "open door" policy.[11]

Nonetheless, our empirical study shows that the Maoist economic policies during the Cultural Revolution helped to reduce the adverse effects on annual economic growth rates in the period 1966–1976. Hence, self-reliance, at least in the 1960s and 1970s, was possible for a large, resource-rich country like China—if the leadership was prepared to pay the price.

Notes

1. For a general survey of radical assessments of these and related issues, see Keith Griffin and John Gurley, "Radical Analyses of Imperialism, the Third World, and the Transition to Socialism: A Survey Article," *Journal of Economic Literature* 23 (1985), pp. 1089–1143.

2. John Copper, *China's Economic Aid* (Palo Alto: Hoover *Institution*, 1976).

3. A. Doak Barnett, *China's Economy in Global Perspective* (Washington, D.C.: Brookings Institution, 1981), p. 157.

4. State Statistical Bureau, People's Republic of China, *Statistical Yearbook of China 1983* (Hong Kong: Economic Information & Agency, 1983), p. 420.

5. Feng-hwa Mah, *The Foreign Trade of Mainland China* (Chicago: Aldine Atherton, 1971), pp. 248–249.

6. "In the 1950s—the era of close Sino-Soviet cooperation—China eagerly accepted what was undoubtedly the most comprehensive technology transfer in modern history. During that decade the Chinese obtained from the Soviet Union the foundation of a modern industrial system. In the process, however, the Chinese became heavily dependent on Soviet tutelage and were induced to adopt a Soviet model of forced industrialization inappropriate to China's resource endowment." Hans Heymann, Jr., "Acquisition and Diffusion of Technology in China," in Joint Economic Committee, Congress of the U.S., *China: A Reassessment of the Economy* (Washington, D.C.: U.S. Government Printing Office, 1975), p. 678.

7. Calculated from data in Mah, *Foreign Trade*, p. 152; and *Statistical Yearbook*, p. 448.

8. Arthur G. Ashbrook, Jr., "China: Economic Modernization and Long-Term Performance," in Joint Economic Committee, Congress of the US, *China under the Four Modernizations* (Washington, D.C.: US Government Printing Office, 1982), Part 1, p. 104.

9. The general economic downturn in China that began in 1959 was also the result of bad weather and the failure of the economic strategy of the Great Leap Forward. There have been many assessments of the cost of the failure of the Great Leap (1958–1960). For example, see Alexander Eckstein, *Communist China's Economic Growth and Foreign Trade* (New York: McGraw-Hill, 1966), pp. 84–86; and Mark Selden, "Cooperation and Conflict: Cooperative and Collective Formation in China's Countryside," in Mark Selden and Victor Lippitt (eds.), *The Transition to Socialism in China* (Armonk, N.Y.: M.E. Sharpe, 1982), pp. 86–87. Ashton and associates estimate on the basis of their independent analysis of Chinese census data that the famine caused by the Great Leap resulted in the loss of 30 million lives in China. B. Ashton, K. Hill, A. Piazza, and R. Zeitz, "Famine in China, 1958–1961," *Population and Development Review* 10 (1984), No. 4, pp. 613–645.

10. Edward Friedman, "Introduction," in Edward Friedman (ed.), *Ascent and Decline in the World System* (Beverly Hills: Sage, 1982), pp. 9–23.

11. Compare Heymann, "Acquisition and Diffusion," for example, with Denis Fred Simon, "The Evolving Role of Technology Transfer in China's Modernization," in Joint Economic Committee, Congress of the US, *China's Economy Looks Toward the Year 2000* (Washington, D.C.: US Government Printing Office, 1986), volume 2, pp. 254–286. See also Frederich W. Wu, "Socialist Development of Self-Reliance within the Capitalist World Economy: The Chinese View in the Post-Mao Era,": in Harish Kapur (ed.), *The End of Isolation: China after Mao* (Dordrecht, the Netherlands: Martinus Nijhoff, 1985); and Bruce Cumings, "The Political Economy of China's Turn Outward," in Samuel S. Kim (ed.), *China and the World: Chinese Foreign Policy in the Post-Mao Era* (Boulder: Westview, 1984).

Addendum: Introduction to Dummy Variables

The purpose of this addendum is to give a brief introduction to dummy variables as they are used in regression analysis and as they are used in this chapter. More technical detail can be found in almost any introductory econometrics text; for example, see R. J. Wonnacott and T. H. Wonnacott, *Econometrics* (New York: John Wiley and Sons, 1970); and P. Rao and R. L. Miller *Applied Econometrics* (Belmont, Calif.: Wadsworth Publishing Co., 1971).

In general, dummy variables are used to recognize dichotomous variables. They are often used to distinguish separate relationships that are due to gender, race, different time periods, and so on.

Normal linear regression analysis estimates the linear relationship between a dependent variable (Y) and any number of independent variables (X). Computational procedures calculate parameter estimates (coefficients) such that equations of the following form can be specified:

$$Y = a + bX + e,$$

where e is a random error term and a and b are the coefficients. The coefficient of primary interest is (usually) the b, which tells us the relationship between Y and X. The coefficient a, often called the "intercept term," tells us what the average level of the dependent variable is other than that determined by the independent variable(s).

For example, suppose we are interested in the relationship between consumption (dependent variable) and income. If we obtain data for some country over a period of years, we might estimate a regression equation like

$$C = 15 + .80I + e,$$

where C and I are obviously consumption and income respectively and where $a = 15$ and $b = .80$. The error term (e) is random and has an expected value of zero, so discussion can proceed without further consideration of it. The equation tells us that on average, there is some amount of consumption that is not associated with income ($15); in addition, for every $1 of income, $.80 is spent on consumption.

Let us assume that during the time period we are using to estimate the example equation, the selected country fought a war. We suspect that the consumption/income relationship was different during the war period and that inclusion of that period distorts the average for other years. Dummy variables are used to test the hypothesis that the war years were different.

Define a new variable, D, such that $D = 1$ for war years and $D = 0$ otherwise. This is the dummy variable. Include the new variable as an additional variable in the regression equation and re-estimate. The resulting equation might be

$$C = 20 + .80I - 10D.$$

Since $D = 1$ during the war years and $D = 0$ otherwise, when we "plug in" values for the independent variables, we get two different situations. During war years we get

$$C = 20 + .80I - 10,$$

or

$$C = 10 + .80I.$$

Thus we confirm our hypothesis that during war years, consumption was lower, on average, for reasons other than income. When we consider nonwar years and $D = 0$, the coefficient attached to the dummy variable drops out because we multiply by zero. Thus, during nonwar years, the relationship is

$$C = 20 + .80I.$$

Overall, we see that the inclusion of the war years lowers the average amount of consumption not accounted for by income. We see that when we take out the influence of the war, the consumption attributable to factors other than income is \$20. In our first equation, when the effect of the war was not taken into account, the average consumption attributable to factors other than income appeared to be \$15. This finding is important because \$15 represents *neither* the war period nor the nonwar period.

Figure 11.1A illustrates this example. Consumption is represented on the vertical axis and income on the horizontal one. Our original equation is labeled #1. The second equation is labeled #2-war and #2-nonwar. Graphically what the dummy variable does is to shift the relationship. The slope of the line remains unchanged (in this example), but the line is shifted by the influence of the dummy variable on the intercept term. We have also drawn in the location of hypothetical observations of consumption/income combinations on the figure. These are labeled n and w, for nonwar and war observations. Note that the line #1, which does not recognize relationship differences arising from war, gives us an average of all observations. It tends to "split the difference" between two different clusters of points.

Suppose we also suspect that during the war, the relationship between income and consumption was also changed. This shift might result from special taxes or rationing imposed during the war. We would like to check to see if the

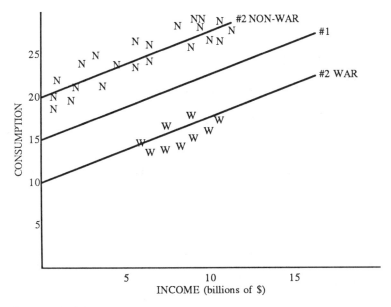

Figure 11.1A

slope of the relationship between consumption and income was different during the war compared with the nonwar years.

Create another variable by simply multiplying the original dummy times income;

$$D \times I.$$

Then include this variable as another independent variable. The results may look something like

$$C = 20 + .85I - 10D - .25(D \times I).$$

Note that during the nonwar years, when $D = 0$, the two righthand terms are also zero and the equation is

$$C = 20 + .85I.$$

For the war years, when $D = 1$, the equation becomes

$$C = 20 + .85I - 10 - .25I,$$

or

$$C = 10 + .60I.$$

Thus, we have found that during nonwar years, consumption increases by $.85 for every additional dollar of income. During the war years, that relationship was sharply reduced. Consumption then increased by only $.65 for every dollar of increased income.

The findings are illustrated with Figure 11.2A. The axes are the same as before, as is the original regression line labeled #1. Again we label the war and nonwar situations as #2-war and #2-nonwar. The diagrams now show that there is a sharp distinction between the two periods. Consumption was generally lower during the war years for reasons other than income, and income had a much reduced influence on consumption. From a policy point of view, we would be greatly misled by not accounting for the war influence. During nonwar periods, consumption is higher than an equation not recognizing the wartime influence would indicate. Failure to recognize the wartime's reduced consumption gives a misleading impression of the average relationship between consumption and income.

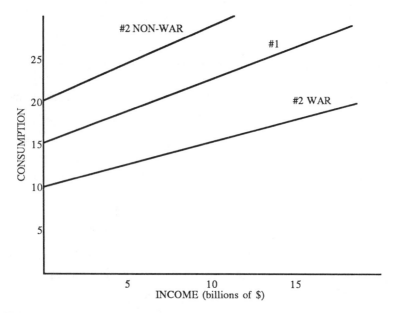

Figure   11.2A

12

China's Open Door Policy, 1978-1988

Guocang Huan

In 1978 the Chinese government adopted a new policy that Westerners have referred to as the "open door policy." This policy has altered China's developmental strategy from one based on self-sufficiency to one of active participation in the world market. Under this policy, China's foreign trade has rapidly increased and now amounts to about 8 percent of its gross national product (GNP).[1] China has become more active in international economic organizations such as the World Bank and International Monetary Fund (IMF). In the past ten years, the Chinese government has set up four Special Economic Zones (SEZs) and has allowed the district of Hainan Island to enjoy the same special rights of attracting foreign investment; the government has opened up another fourteen coastal cities. In Spring 1988, the Chinese government proposed a new strategy to develop processing industries on the entire Chinese coastal area. Meanwhile, several thousand foreign companies and banks are now operating in China. During the past seven years, the Chinese government has sent more than fifty thousand scholars and students to Western countries and Japan for study and training. In turn, thousands of foreign scholars have been invited to China to give lectures and seminars on various academic subjects. Furthermore, the government of China has loosened its control over the flow of information from abroad. China has rapidly expanded its tourist industry and received over twenty million visitors during the first six months of 1988. The Chinese government has made it easier for Chinese citizens to leave the country. Over the past few years, China has also expanded its export of labor to the international market.

Two basic, interrelated questions deserve to be raised here. First, what are the necessary and sufficient domestic and international conditions for China to adopt the open door policy effectively? Second, what is the relationship between China's open door policy on the one hand and its domestic, political, and economic development on the other? In order to answer these two questions, this chapter will discuss the political and economic background of the open door

281

policy, review the process of how China adopted it, and finally examine the policy's success and key problems.

Roots and Reasons

The open door policy is deeply rooted in the following important factors. First, it represents a continuation of China's efforts to modernize itself by "learning from the West." These efforts, begun when China suffered internal crises and invasion by Western powers, Japan, and Russia in the middle of the nineteenth century, were aimed at narrowing the gaps between China and foreign powers in the areas of economic development, technology, and military power. The basic strategy both the government of the mid-nineteenth-century Qing dynasty and later the Nationalist government chose was to import technology and science from the west while maintaining China's traditional cultural values and political and economic system. This strategy was referred to as "zhong xue wei ti, xi xue wei yong." That is, Chinese traditional culture would remain at the center while Western technology would be imported as the method for developing China's economic and military power. In pursuing this strategy, China sent a large number of students to industrialized states, imported Western technology for building up China's national industries (largely owned by the state), and introduced Western science into Chinese educational institutions. The introduction of Western humanist thought into China, however, faced strong resistance from the supporters of official ideology and traditional popular culture. Moreover, this strategy did not include a policy of actively expanding China's foreign trade and attracting foreign investment into China. Under strong political and military pressure by foreign powers, though, China was forced to open up its markets.

The process of adopting this strategy was difficult and painful, owing largely to China's long history of internal political and economic crises, its strong nationalism and cultural tradition, and its unfavorable international environment. The lack of a strong government capable of pursuing fundamental political and economic reform and changing traditional Chinese culture was one of the major reasons why this strategy was not fully successful in modernizing the country.

Despite many difficulties and disruptions during the 100 years between the middle of the nineteenth century and the end of the 1940s, when the Communist Party took power and directed China first to lean on the Soviet Union and then to minimize its contacts with the outside world—especially the West—this strategy was never fully banned. Rather, it gradually changed China's political, economic, and social structure, mixed traditional Chinese culture with Western culture, and promoted the process of the country's modernization.

Second, the Cultural Revolution (1966–1976) created a domestic political atmosphere that made it possible for the post–Cultural Revolution government to adopt the open door policy. The Cultural Revolution disrupted the process of China's political and economic development. It greatly damaged the shape and authority of the country's political institutions. It brought about a long-term economic depression and reduced the living standard of the majority of the population. It also intensified political tensions and conflicts between society and the state, and undermined official ideology and legitimacy. As a result, the post–Cultural Revolution leadership in China was under strong popular pressure to raise living standards and expand individual freedoms.

The failure of the Cultural Revolution also created a solid base for the new leadership. This leadership, largely composed of those who survived the Cultural Revolution, is less orthodox and more pragmatic than the leadership it succeeded. Led by Deng Xiaoping, it has been impressed by the rapid, worldwide progress in economic development and the evolution of technology—especially in the industrial market economies and Asia's newly industrialized countries, and during the ten years when the Cultural Revolution reversed China's economic development. In its view, to reform the economic system, to gain foreign technology and capital investment, and to increase China's participation in the world market form China's alternative development strategy.[2]

Third, political development in China after the second half of 1978, especially following the Twelfth National Congress of the Chinese Communist Party (CCP) in the fall of 1982, created a favorable environment for the adoption of the open door policy. The reform group, led by Deng Xiaoping and Zhao Ziyang, has rapidly strengthened its position within the party, government, and army. It has decentralized the decisionmaking system, promoted a process of professionalizing government bureaucrats and even has partly reformed official ideology. In addition, a large number of conservative cadres have been replaced by better-educated, younger, and more open-minded people.

In the national economic arena, the government has begun to further its reform of the urban industrial and commerical sectors, following China's successful agricultural reform. The government has decentralized the planning system, introduced a reform of the pricing system, and strongly promoted the development of private sectors in both urban and rural areas. During the past few years, the government has leased out thousands of state-owned enterprises, which are not profitable, to individuals.

At the microeconomic level, the Chinese government has reformed the management system and granted enterprises greater autonomy in deciding what, how, and how much to produce in response to the market situation. The government has played down the role of party organization and political cadres in enterprises. Instead, a large number of technicians and well-educated managers have been promoted to key positions. Thus the ongoing economic reform has narrowed and will further reduce the institutional gap between the Chinese economy and market economies, and has created a better environment for the adoption of the open door policy.

Fourth, the dynamics of China's international environment have favored the adoption of the open door policy. Since 1971, when Henry Kissinger made his first trip to Beijing, the political structure of the Asia-Pacific region has undergone gradual and fundamental changes. The United States and China no longer regard each other as the principal threats to their basic security interests in the region but rather as potential strategic partners against the Soviet Union and its allies in Asia. The rapid Soviet military buildup in the Far East has gradually intensified Soviet-U.S. competition in the region. This trend has become even stronger since the middle of the 1970s, when the United States withdrew from Vietnam, and political order was reestablished in China with the turn away from radical Maoist policies. Washington has repeatedly announced that "a stable, strong and independent China can best serve its long-term interests and contribute to the region's peace and stability."[3] As such, China will not only help Washington counter Moscow's pressure, but also cooperate with U.S. allies in the region on various subregional security issues. This political atmosphere has favored China's efforts to open its door to develop cooperation with the West, especially the United States, and Japan.

In economic terms, the Asia-Pacific region has been the most dynamic region in the world. It has had the highest growth rates and enjoyed the most rapid growth of trade. Given the fact that China does 80 percent of its foreign trade with this region, the prosperity of the area provides the necessary external conditions for China, a country rich in natural and human resources, to gain technology and capital investment and rapidly expand its trade.

Fifth and finally, the post-Mao leadership—especially since 1978 when Deng Xiaoping consolidated his power—has taken a more rational and realistic approach toward both Hong Kong and Taiwan. In September 1984, the Chinese government signed an agreement with the British government to allow Hong Kong to maintain its existing capitalist system after 1997, when Hong Kong will be returned to China and become a "Special Administrative Zone" of China. In addition, Beijing has changed its policy from the "liberation of Taiwan" to "reunification with Taiwan," and made great efforts to reduce tensions and increase contacts with Taipei. The success or effectiveness of this new approach depends largely upon two related key factors: whether China is able to maintain its political stability and continue its liberal reform program; and whether China can continue to expand its cooperation with market economies, increase direct and indirect business ties between the Chinese mainland on the one hand and Hong Kong and Taiwan on the other, and adopt a flexible foreign economic policy that will narrow the institutional gaps, reduce tensions, and increase common interests among the Chinese mainland, Hong Kong, and Taiwan. Adopting the open door policy can help the government enhance its political credibility. For these five basic reasons, the Chinese government had strong incentives to adopt, and has strong incentives to continue, the open door policy.

For A New Policy, New Strategy

The first important change that the open door policy has brought about during the past ten years is the Chinese government's new foreign trade strategy. This strategy is based on the assumptions that the contemporary world economy is an interdependent one, and that each state should stress its own comparative advantages when participating in the international division of labor. No longer should China pursue the Maoist strategy of self-sufficiency and isolation; it should exploit its rich natural and human resources, develop labor- and natural resource–intensive industries, expand its foreign trade, and integrate the Chinese economy into the world economy. To improve knowledge and experience of, and connections in the international manufactured goods market, the government should encourage local authorities and enterprises to develop export-oriented industrial processing.[4]

Based on these assumptions, the Chinese government has decentralized its foreign trade institutions. Under the new rules, local authorities, especially at the provincial level, have been granted greater power to do business directly with foreign corporations without requiring approval from the central government. Most provincial governments now have trade representatives in Hong Kong, Japan, the United States, and Europe. These representatives are directly responsible to the provincial authorities, not to the Ministry of Foreign Trade and Foreign Economic Relations in Beijing. Generally, provincial authorities are required to keep their foreign exchange in balance, but the percentage of foreign exchange that they have made and are allowed to keep has been raised. Enterprises, too, have been encouraged to expand their exports. They now can directly negotiate business and sign trade agreements with foreign partners. They are allowed to keep a certain percentage of the foreign exchange they have made. With the exception of a few key industries—some heavy industries and energy and mine industries where the central government maintains full control—this policy has been widely implemented.

There has been a foreign exchange market for enterprises, on which exchange rates are determined by supply and demand. In order to solve the problem of the price gap between China's domestic market and international market and to give an incentive to exporting companies, the Chinese government has created a system of double exchange rates. Under this system, the exchange rates between renminbi (the Chinese currency) and foreign currency used for domestic accounting purposes is determined by supply and demand for foreign exchange on the market. Newly established private enterprises in China are also allowed to deal directly with foreign companies. As a U.S. observer has noted, many private consulting firms in China are now playing an active role as middlemen to promote business with foreign companies.[5]

The second component of the open door policy is the new strategy of technology transfer. Chinese leaders have repeatedly emphasized the importance of gaining advanced technology from industrial market economies. In particular, they are interested in importing technology in computer, energy, and other dual-use high-technology areas. The Chinese leaders have frequently attended foreign exhibitions of high technology in China, and openly urged foreign governments, especially the U.S. and Japanese governments, to make further efforts to promote technology transfer to China.[6] The Chinese government substantially reduces import duties on items that are considered technically "advanced." The tax rate on those Chinese-foreign joint venture projects that bring in "advanced" technology are much lower than those on other projects.[7] The Chinese government is also willing to open its domestic market to these joint venture projects, and a balance of foreign exchange is not necessarily required.[8] In addition, thousands of foreign scientists and engineers have been invited to give lectures in China; hundreds of research institutions have been formed to gather and analyze information about the most recent technology developments abroad; and thousands of engineers, scholars, and students have been sent overseas, especially to the United States, Japan, and Western Europe, for study and training. The Chinese have become more active than ever in various international conferences on technology and science. The Chinese government has passed laws to protect the interests of those foreign companies that have transferred technology to China.[9] In 1984 and 1985, China signed agreements with the Soviet Union and a few Eastern European states to acquire technical assistance to replace the 156 large industrial projects that China imported from the Soviet bloc during the 1950s.[10]

The third aspect of the open door policy is the strategy of attracting foreign direct investment into China. This strategy began with the efforts to establish four SEZs—Shenzhen, Zhuhai, Xiamen and Shantou—in 1979, when the government's ten year plan (1976–1986), based simply upon taking out foreign loans and importing equipment and technology, failed, and fundamental economic reform began to be implemented. The government has granted special rights to the SEZs and, later, to many "open areas" on the Chinese coast. For instance, the SEZs enjoy great autonomy in making the majority of their decisions. They can sign joint venture contracts with foreign companies. The corporation tax rate is only 15 percent in the SEZs; it is 33.3 percent outside them. Within the SEZs, many industrial, scientific, and construction projects enjoy a tax holiday of two to five years.[11] There is little political control by the Communist Party; instead, technocrats and foreign investors play the key role in the decisionmaking process.

Politics is no longer the most important factor in determining hiring, wages, bonuses, and promotion. Rather, these are largely determined by the education and skills of the employees. Managers in the SEZs have full responsibility in making decisions about production and marketing, and they do not have to follow the government plan. Prices are determined by supply and demand and are directly related to the international market. In enterprises that are 100-percent owned by foreign investors, foreign investors enjoy full control of management. In joint venture enterprises, the Chinese and foreign investors usually share the responsibility of management and profits.

Theoretically, there is no fixed sales quota for enterprises in the SEZs. Nevertheless, most enterprises there are expected to sell their products mainly in the international market. During the past few years, however, about 70 percent of the SEZs' total products have been sold in the Chinese market.[12] The Chinese government guarantees foreign investors the right to transfer their profits into foreign exchange. It does not charge import duties on production goods needed by the SEZs.

Most of these policies have been implemented in the district of Hainan Island as well. The Chinese government, however, has encouraged local authorities around the country to make efforts to attract foreign direct investment. Except for market-sharing allocation (distributing the products of joint ventures in China's domestic and international markets—the key policy guaranteeing China's balance of payments and still tightly controlled by the central authorities), each provincial government is allowed to give foreign investors favorable financial and fiscal treatment in order to encourage them to bring capital and technology into China.

As noted, in 1984 the Chinese government announced the decision to open fourteen coastal cities, which hold roughly 40 percent of China's total industrial capacity, to foreign investors. In 1987, the government further opened the entire Chinese coast to foreign investors. The two largest industrial cities, Shanghai and Tianjin, enjoy the right to approve contracts with foreign investors for up to U.S. $30 million without permission from the central authority, while the limits for Guangdong and Fujian provinces and the city of Dalian are U.S. $10 million. Other provinces can approve contracts with foreign corporations for up to U.S. $5 million.[13] They can also reduce the corporation tax rate on joint venture enterprises to 15 percent. In joint venture enterprises in the fourteen coastal cities, as well as in locations outside the SEZs, foreign investors enjoy the same rights and benefits that they enjoy in the SEZs. Two major restrictions apply to the opening in coastal cities: They have to make their foreign exchange payments roughly on balance, and the joint venture enterprises should sell most of their products in the international market.

In order to strengthen foreign investors' confidence in the Chinese market, Chinese leaders have repeatedly announced that the open door policy will not be abandoned and that attracting foreign direct investment is the long-term policy of the Chinese government. In addition, since 1980 the government has passed over 200 laws and regulations pertaining to trade and foreign investment in China. The Chinese government has signed investment protection agreements with over twenty Western countries.[14] These efforts have reduced the legal gap between China and foreign countries and have increased business confidence in the Chinese market. The Chinese government has allowed many major foreign banks to open business offices in China.

The fourth aspect of the open door policy is the Chinese government's new attitude toward international economic and financial organizations. China joined the World Bank and IMF in 1980, and it has become increasingly active in other institutions such as the United Nations Industrial Development Organization (UNIDO). Since 1980, the relationship between China and the World Bank and IMF has developed rapidly. During the past five years, the World Bank and IMF have sent many work teams to China to do field research on the Chinese economy. These work teams have developed a very good working relationship with various government institutions and gathered detailed data about the country's economy, which had never before been made public in China. The World Bank has supported a number of industrial, construction, agricultural, and educational projects in China and given China long-term and low-interest loans. Because China is one of the few developing countries with large foreign exchange reserves, the IMF's financial resources, used mainly to help countries with serious balance-of-payments problems, are not yet available to China. The Chinese government has paid a good deal of attention to the World Bank and IMF analyses of and suggestions for the Chinese economy, taking them into consideration in its policymaking.[15] In 1986, the World Bank opened an office in Beijing. Both the World Bank and the IMF have frequently sent their staff members to China to conduct seminars. They have also contracted leading Western consulting companies to help China to reorganize its financial and industrial institutions, redefine its business strategies, and improve efficiency. The Economic Development Institute of the World Bank has established a training program for high-level Chinese officials who are in charge of economic affairs. In the long run, these efforts will help China create a new generation of economic policymakers.

The fifth aspect of the open door policy is the large number of scholars and students going abroad, especially to industrial market economies, to study and receive training and then to introduce foreign culture and academics into China. Begun in 1978, this policy has been increasingly rational and flexible. Except for those who have political or legal problems, most Chinese citizens are now allowed to go abroad to study.[16] The government also allows the families of those who study abroad to leave the country. Chinese embassies and consulates abroad now send Chinese publications to Chinese students and organize Chinese students' associations on school campuses. More important, the government has remarkably increased the proportion of students majoring in the social sciences, business, and law. Recently, Chinese corporations and banks based in Hong Kong and overseas have begun to recruit Chinese students who have completed their studies abroad but been reluctant to return to China.

During the past ten years, thousands of scholars from different countries have been invited to China to give lectures and seminars on various subjects. Chinese leaders have frequently received leading Western economists and discussed openly with them problems occurring in the country's economic reform and adoption of the open door policy. Many Chinese universities have established direct exchange programs with universities abroad. Chinese universities and colleges have received large numbers of students from abroad, and many foreign scholars have been allowed to go to China to do field research.

Also significant has been the government's efforts to introduce foreign culture and new developments and trends in foreign academics. Hundreds of public and internally circulated materials are now published in China to introduce Western literature, music, art, philosophy, economics, management science, and other subjects. More and more books in different languages are translated into Chinese and published in China. The government has invited hundreds of art and music delegations to visit China. The government has loosened its control over the channels of information: Listening to the Voice of America, for instance, is no longer regarded as bad behavior. In sum, Chinese society enjoys much greater access to information from and about the outside world than at any period since 1949.

Sixth, to implement the open door policy, the Chinese government has rapidly expanded its tourist industry and made efforts to export its labor services to the international market. During the past ten years, through cooperation with foreign investors, the government has built a large number of hotels and restaurants. It has eased the customs and the visa application process for foreign visitors. The Chinese government has opened many areas that were inaccessible to foreign tourists before.[17] During the past ten years, the government has encouraged local authorities and construction companies to undertake projects in different countries. Unlike the 1960s, when China sent its construction teams to Third World countries (especially in Africa) simply as part of its foreign aid program, under the open door policy Chinese construction companies are sent mainly to Middle East oil-exporting states to earn hard currency. In addition, the Chinese shipbuilding industry has begun to enter the international market.

Judging the Successes

Generally, the adoption of the open door policy has been successful, although it also has encountered serious difficulties. The government has partially reached its goals: The open door policy has promoted China's economic reform and development; it has deepened the country's political development; and it has significantly changed China's relations with the outside world.

China's foreign trade has increased from U.S. $21.11 billion in 1978 to over U.S. $82.7 billion in 1987.[18] This increase is likely to continue in the years ahead. China's position in the world market has been strengthened and the proportion of manufactured goods in its total exports has increased significantly.[19] China's foreign trade decisionmaking and implementing mechanisms have been decentralized and are therefore more rational, flexible, and effective. The country has created a new generation of 'businessmen' who better understand international business practice and enjoy more confidence and greater decisionmaking power. Local authorities and enterprises now have greater incentives to expand their exports. In 1987, China had a foreign exchange reserve over U.S. $15.5 billion.[20]

China has received more advanced technology from industrialized countries—particularly important to its energy, transportation, and computer industries.[21] More important, many technology-transfer projects have been undertaken in the form of either joint venture or compensation trade. Usually, the Chinese side does not have to pay immediately in cash for the technology. These projects also have helped the Chinese improve their knowledge of and capabilities for industrial and scientific management.

During the past ten years, China has utilized various foreign loans totaling U.S. $20.1 billion. Between 1980 and 1987, about U.S. $17.9 billion of foreign direct investment has been pledged in China. During the first three quarters of 1988, China utilized over U.S. $5.7 billion foreign investment.[22] According to one set of official data, by the end of 1987, Chinese and foreign investors had signed 4,516 agreements of equity joint venture; 5,080 contracts of cooperative ventures; and 183 agreements of wholly foreign-owned ventures.[23] In comparison, six years ago, when the majority of overseas direct investment came from Hong Kong, it went mainly into small-scale projects paying short-term returns. Since the second half of 1983, the proportion of direct capital investment from industrial market economies in the total investment that China receives has increased. More large-scale and long-term projects with advanced technology have been undertaken. Over 60 percent of the total projects are industrial.[24] Since the second half of 1984, more and more foreign investment has been made in China's coastal industrial cities, such as Shanghai, Tianjin, Qingdao, and Guangzhou, where developed infrastructure and skilled labor are available, and market potential is greater.

China's working relationship with both the World Bank and the IMF has been strengthened. In 1986, the World Bank issued its second country report about China's economic development. After detailed analysis of the trends and dynamics of the Chinese economy, the World Bank proposed its policy recommendations and suggestions to the Chinese government.[25] As noted above, these policy recommendations and suggestions have been well received. In addition, the training programs and seminars that both the World Bank and the IMF have sponsored for middle- and high-ranking Chinese officials in charge of economic affairs have improved their knowledge of Western economics, and their ability to analyze economic problems and formulate relevant policies.

The open door policy has also promoted the process of legal reform in China. As mentioned above, in order to attract foreign investors and narrow the legal gap between China and market economies, the government has passed over 200 laws and regulations, which account for 40 percent of the total number of laws that the government passed during this period. China has sent hundreds of students and scholars to Western countries to study law, opened many law schools in China, and encouraged the establishment of thousands of law firms. These efforts have strongly affected the ongoing legal reforms in China. Many principles in these 200 laws and regulations can be and already have been applied to domestic legal institutions. Major western law firms have begun to practice in China. The new generation of Chinese lawyers has begun to introduce Western legal principles into both the reformed Chinese legal institutions and Chinese legal practice.

Although China has reduced its own economic aid to other countries, it has received economic aid from other countries. In addition to the low-interest and long-term returns on loans that it has borrowed from the World Bank, China has received loans from foreign governments and private financial institutions. During the past few years, under contracts with both foreign governments and foreign companies, China has sent over 70,000 workers and technicians to work on construction projects abroad. Because of its relatively low wage levels and its qualified workers, China has become increasingly competitive in the international labor market. In 1987, according to the Chinese government, Chinese workers abroad earned over U.S. $1 billion in hard currency.[26] China has also become more active in investing overseas. By the first half of 1988, China had invested over U.S. $500 million in a few hundred joint venture projects around the world.[27]

China has become more attractive to foreign tourists. Over 30 million tourists visited China during the first half of 1987. About 85 percent of them were from Hong Kong and Macao. The rest were mainly from Japan, the United States, and Europe. Tourists now visit most parts of China without special permission from the government.

More than 50,000 Chinese scholars and students have been studying abroad. Many of them are working on their doctorate degrees. The number of students who study law, economics, political science, business, and subjects in the humanities continues to increase and now amounts to about 15 percent of the total. Some scholars and students already have completed their studies and returned to China. A new generation of Western-trained scholars, managers, and policymakers is gradually growing up and playing an increasingly important role in various governmental, business, and academic institutions. In the long run, this development will strongly influence the future direction in which China will move.

The open door policy has changed the Chinese leadership establishment. Today's Chinese leaders and high-level officials visit industrialized countries more frequently than did their predecessors. They are much better informed about economic, political, and scientific developments in the West, and about various international issues. Their behavior has become more acceptable in the international community. More important, they have paid more attention to the reactions of the international community to their policies. Because of the stronger interdependent relationship between the Chinese economy and the world market, China's economic interests increasingly have been considered as an important factor in the formulation of domestic and foreign policies. One important reason why the Chinese government stopped the "anti-bourgeois liberalization" campaign (meant to reverse the reform progress, alter the open door policy, and strengthen bureaucratic control over the society) in the beginning of 1987 was the consideration that such a conservative and repressive campaign would hurt (and actually already had hurt) business confidence in the Chinese market. Increased information about the outside world and travel to industrialized countries have given Chinese leaders a broader perspective with which to analyze their own policy issues.

The open door policy has rapidly changed China's traditional culture and values, especially among the youth and intellectual establishment. A consumer revolution, which is based largely upon a sampling of Western culture and lifestyle, has taken place. The old official ideology has been increasingly undermined, while Western values and humanist thoughts have become increasingly popular. In short, the new information that the open door policy has brought into China has challenged both Chinese traditional culture and old ideological orthodoxy.

The open door policy has promoted economic reforms in China. The SEZs, for instance, have been regarded as the place where the government tests its new economic policies. In the SEZs the government has established new systems of wage, bonus, management, pricing, and enterprise autonomy. The government also encourages the development of private sectors and the consumer revolution in the SEZs. To a large extent, these policies have become the models for government promotion of urban industrial reform outside the SEZs. Furthermore, in the SEZs the workers gain higher wages and bonuses; managers enjoy greater power and higher salaries; enterprises have more autonomy; and the residents' living standard is higher than in the rest of China. These developments have become strong incentives for the reformers to implement similar policies outside SEZs.

Finally, the open door policy has changed the structure of the Chinese economy and its relationship with the world market as a whole. The total amount of China's foreign trade now is about 8 percent of the country's GNP. China has become increasingly dependent upon advanced technology and equipment imported from industrial market economies. International economic organizations' and Western scholars' views of the Chinese economy have had an increased influence on policymakers in China. Foreign corporations and banks have also deepened their involvement in China's many important development projects. In sum, the degree of interdependence between the Chinese economy and the world economy as a whole has increased.

Noting the Problems

There are four serious difficulties regarding China's open door policy. The first problem concerns the shortcomings of Chinese political, economic, and legal institutions and some unfavorable effects of China's domestic, political, and economic developments on the adoption of the open door policy. The plausible course of action to solve issues in these areas is further reform of the political, economic, and legal systems and rationalization of the policymaking process.

As mentioned above, political developments in China favored Deng Xiaoping's reform program and the open door policy. The reform group has successfully expanded its influence and power. But several obstacles remain.

In the first place, the reform group does not fully control party ideology, nor has it developed a new ideology to justify its policies. The conservatives still wield great influence on economic policymaking. They are particularly strong in the middle and low levels of party and government institutions where the open door policy has been implemented. Furthermore, the future pattern of political succession contains some uncertainties. The final results of the succession will depend largely on two interrelated factors: the dynamics of the power structure and the success of the ongoing reform program and open door policy.

These political problems and uncertainties have hurt foreign investors' confidence in China's market. Such business confidence is essential when a foreign investor considers the wide gaps between political, economic, and legal systems in China and those in industrial market economies. Many Chinese students have had bad personal experiences in the Cultural Revolution. The political stability and continuation of the reform program and the open door policy are two important factors in deciding whether to return to China after their studies abroad.

In the fall of 1983, when the campaign against "spiritual pollution" took place, foreign investment in China immediately declined. There was strong reaction to this campaign from Chinese students abroad. Many of them suspected that conservatives in China were launching another "anti-rightist" campaign (such as the mass terror against intellectuals in 1957). In the spring of 1985, when the SEZs and the district of Hainan Island appeared to have problems in balancing their payments and competing in China's domestic market, the conservatives once again exploited this opportunity to attack the open door policy. In January 1987, Hu Yaobang, a prominent reform leader and general secretary of CCP, was ousted. The reform group was undercut and the conservatives launched the "anti–bourgeois liberalization" campaign. The conservatives also seem worried about the increasingly stronger Western cultural influence on Chinese youth and made consistent efforts to eliminate such influence. During the summer of 1988, the conservatives again challenged directly the new trends and ideas in Shukou Industrial Zone, which are largely associated with Western culture.

The bureaucratic system is another obstacle to the implementation of the open door policy. Many foreign businesspeople have complained about the inefficiency of the Chinese bureaucracy, the slow process of business decisionmaking, and the complicity of relations between different governmental institutions. During the past several years, the decisionmaking process has been decentralized, and local authorities and enterprises now enjoy greater autonomy. This development, however, has not been fully legitimized by legal institutions, but rather only by the government's "policies." The central government maintains and frequently exercises its power to intervene in local businesses' dealings with foreign companies, especially in the areas of foreign exchange control, marketing distribution, and tax rates. Chinese students who have returned from abroad have complained that they have been misplaced and unable to find a favorable environment to use the knowledge they gained abroad.

Many foreign investors consider Chinese legal institutions and those recent laws specific to foreign economic relations to be too "vague," "general," "ambiguous," and "simplistic." Furthermore, there is no clear legal mechanism in China for resolving disputes. No law, for instance, spells out what should be done to resolve, or which regulations governing contract principles, commercial law, or international business practice are the basis for resolving, potential disputes between Chinese authorities and foreign companies. Some foreign companies also question whether China has lawyers qualified to provide legal representation or to work in the appropriate courts. There is no law to protect private ownership. In addition, the Chinese government has not allowed foreign companies to enter the Chinese insurance market. This policy has already discouraged many foreign investors from making deep commitments to a highly risky market such as China.

The government has advanced its urban economic reform, especially to decentralize planning, reform the pricing system to reflect market supply and demand, and encourage the development of the private sector. The reform process, however, still faces some challenges. These challenges have also affected the open door policy. The reform of the pricing system was undertaken rapidly during the last quarter of 1984 and the first quarter of 1985—when the Chinese economy was overhauled, and its growth rate was over 20 percent. The sudden and wide relaxation of government control of price-making together with a loose monetary policy then led to an immediate jump in the inflation rate. In Spring 1988, a similar situation occurred, and the inflation rate jumped to over 30 percent. Unlike Western economies, the four basic features of the Chinese economy—capital, labor, commodity, and capital goods markets—have been structured separately. The price reform affected only the commodity market, not the other three; its effectiveness, therefore, is constrained. In the same way, the ability of enterprises to respond to changes in market supply and demand is equally constrained by the old system of decisionmaking mechanisms as well as by the allocation of capital and the labor force and the production of goods. The price reform has thus caused a long-term "structural" inflation.

The development of the private sector is a serious challenge as well. Politically, it is in sharp conflict with party ideology. Economically, the authorities have been increasingly uneasy about the mechanism for coordinating the private and public sectors, as the government does not plan to reform fundamentally the system of the allocation of capital, human resources, and natural resources. As the competition between the private and public sectors has intensified, state-owned enterprises have become more and more dependent on the government's protection and subsidies.

The lack of coordination between the decentralization of the decisionmaking process and the reform of banking and pricing systems has also made it difficult for the central government to control national investment and the speed of economic growth. In 1984 (mainly during the last quarter), the government issued 28 billion more yuan than it did in 1983. The economic growth rate jumped over 20 percent. During the second half of 1987 and the first half of 1988, the central government again increased money supply while loosening its control over commodity prices. As a result, the inflation rate jumped up, but the growth rate declined sharply. A similar situation can be seen in the issue of balance of payments. Policies of decentralization and promoting exports (discussed above) give local authorities and enterprises strong incentive to increase their exports. They are also allowed to keep a high proportion (about 30 percent, on average) of the hard currency they have earned. As a result, when the government decided to encourage the country's imports of both production and consumer goods in the last quarter of 1984 and the first quarter of 1985, China's foreign reserves suddenly declined from U.S. $17 billion to U.S. $12.5 billion. Thus the government has had to implement a policy tightly to control imports.

All these political, legal, and economic problems have weakened the reform group's position vis-à-vis the conservatives, decelerated the process of urban economic reform, and slowed the adoption of the open door policy. It has made foreign investors wary of investing in China and has diminished the confidence of supporters of the China open door policy.

The second basic problem of the open door policy is functional and technical: China lacks the knowledge and experience to manage it. This deficiency can be overcome through the process of learning and education.

During the past ten years, China has remarkably improved its knowledge of the international market. Several serious problems, however, remain. In the first place, the government appears to lack the knowledge to formulate its open door policy. In particular, there are not enough qualified policy research centers to develop feasibility studies of the open door policy. Nor do policymakers seem fully to understand the relationship between the open door policy and the ongoing urban economic reform. As a result, the government frequently must adjust the open door policy. There is no coordinating mechanism between the open door policy and other policies of economic reform. One example is the recent proposal made by Zhao Ziyang in Spring 1988 regarding the development strategy of Chinese coastal areas. After the government announced that it would develop industrial processing projects on the Chinese coast as the major strategy to enter the international market, it discovered a few months later that the proposal lacked basic support from both business community and provincial authorities. Economists have debated the proposal and found that the strategy did not include detailed policy surveys. The Chinese coast lacks sufficient infrastructure to implement this strategy. With limited knowledge of and connections in the international manufactured goods market, the existing institutional weaknesses make it very difficult for Chinese enterprises to compete with their counterparts abroad. The government itself is unable to finance the building of infrastructures. In addition, it will be increasingly difficult for the government to manage its balance of payments. Consequently, in the summer of 1988, the government decided to cease the discussion about this strategy. Such a policy shift, however, has created a psychological crisis both domestically and internationally.

The development of SEZs is a good example. The Chinese side has made huge investments to build up the infrastructure in SEZs, especially in Shenzhen, needed to attract foreign investors, but no one has seriously considered how the Chinese can get back returns on their investment. Moreover, the Chinese authorities have not selected foreign investment projects in the SEZs carefully, nor have they strictly established the proportion of products that SEZ enterprises must sell to the domestic market. As a result, over 40 percent of foreign investment projects in the SEZs are not manufacturing but rather tourist or commercial projects. Many manufacturing projects, especially those financed by Hong Kong businesspeople, do not apply advanced technology, nor are they competitive in the world market. Rather, they greatly depend upon China's domestic market. As a result, only 30 percent of the SEZs' total products are for export. Some Chinese economists have complained that through the SEZs, foreign companies have gradually monopolized the Chinese market.[28] The government finds it increasingly difficult to balance the SEZs' payments.

The expansion of Chinese corporations' operations in Hong Kong and other parts of the world is another example. As mentioned above, thousands of Chinese corporations are now operating in Hong Kong, and some of them have already begun operations in North America, Europe, and Japan. These corporations have played an increasingly important role between China and the foreign business community. By taking advantage of their foreign connections and the right of keeping all hard currency that they made, these corporations have become a powerful force to manipulate the Chinese domestic market. There has been no mechanism to guide the competition between these corporations and their Chinese counterparts. In October 1988, the central government suddenly decided to "clean up" these corporations by closing some of them and restricting others' activities both abroad and in China.[29]

Furthermore, many Chinese managers who negotiate with foreigners know little about technology and international business. Some overseas corporations have defrauded the Chinese, delivering commodities of poor quality or depriving them of the loans and commissions to which they were entitled. A Chinese economist complains that in one SEZ in Guangdong, only 65 percent of the contracts signed with foreign investors are viable; 25 percent of them are difficult to implement or entail disputes between Chinese and foreigners; a further 10 percent present a serious problem.

The third basic problem of the open door policy concerns the dynamics of China's international environment and its advantages and disadvantages with competing markets abroad. Although the international environment is generally favorable for China to adopt its open door policy, there are still some problems. First, the protectionism has become rampant. The United States has been restricting and probably will continue to restrict China's exports, especially textile goods. China, as well as other nations, finds it increasingly difficult to enter the Japanese market. In 1985, China's trade deficit with Japan was over U.S. $6 billion. The figures for 1986 and 1987 are U.S. $4.2 billion and U.S. $0.9 billion, respectively.[30]

Furthermore, there are many restrictions, particularly in the United States, on technology transfer to China. It takes ninety days for U.S. companies to apply for permission from the U.S. Department of Commerce to transfer certain items of technology to China. To export some technology items to China, it is necessary to get approval from the Department of State. There are also other items that are not allowed to be exported to China. Although in many cases China can buy equivalent technology from either Western European countries or Japan, this restriction reduces China's possible choices and thereby weakens China's bargaining position in the international market. Like other countries, China finds it difficult to import technology from Japan.

It is important for foreign investors to compare China's advantages and disadvantages to those of other Asian countries. Such a comparison should be based upon several criteria, including the economic development, political stability, market potential, infrastructure, and resources of the countries under consideration. It should also include an analysis of investment opportunities and the possibilities for developing potential markets in specific countries.

Compared with the wages paid in Hong Kong and the Export Processing Zones (EPZs, established to attract foreign investment and technology and promote exports) in Indonesia, Malaysia, Taiwan, and South Korea, the Chinese SEZs' average wage is between 30 and 70 percent lower. It is close to that in the Philippines' EPZs and about 50 percent higher than the average in EPZs in Thailand, India, Sri Lanka, and Pakistan. It is unclear, however, how much of a gap in productivity exists between China's SEZs and other Asian EPZs. Some businesspeople in Hong Kong believe that, on average, the productivity in the SEZs is 50 percent lower than it is in Hong Kong. Lower wages in SEZs, therefore, do not compensate sufficiently to attract foreign investors. In addition, because the average wage in SEZs is about 50 percent higher than it is outside the SEZs, more and more foreign companies tend to invest outside the SEZs.

In China, no enterprise is allowed to buy land; land can only be rented, and the duration of leases ranges from twenty to forty years. In Hong Kong, Macao and South Korea, foreign corporations may buy land. In Taiwan, Singapore, and the Philippines, there is no limitation on the period of land use. In Thailand, Singapore, Sri Lanka, and Malaysia, land can be leased for thirty-three to ninety-nine years.

In South Korea, Singapore, and Taiwan, foreign investors can get low-interest and long-term loans from the local governments to buy or build industrial buildings. Except for the Philippines and Macao, rental costs in most Asian EPZs are similar to those in China's SEZs. The highest rents in Asia are in Japan and Hong Kong. But rent in Hong Kong has declined recently because of a loss of confidence in the colony's future. Inside China's SEZs, moreover, rent is much higher, which is another important reason that foreign companies tend to invest in other parts of China.

Except for two free-trade posts (Hong Kong and Macao) and the Ryukyu Islands, where there are no customs duties on imports and exports, Asian EPZs have for the most part adopted customs policies similar to China's policy toward SEZs. They offer tax waivers to enterprises that import production goods and raw materials and export to international markets. Such policies have not been fully implemented in all of the enterprises in other parts of China that have received foreign investment and technology.

Similarly, China's corporate income tax rate in the SEZs, Hainan Island, and other open areas—15 percent—is lower than the rates in most Asian EPZs, where the range is between 20 and 40 percent. Only Malaysia and Macao have the same tax rate as China. Hong Kong's corporate income tax rate is 18.5 percent. Outside the SEZs, however, the Chinese government raised the tax rate to 33.3 percent, though it may be reduced if foreign corporations bring "advanced" technology into China.

China's great market potential is one of the key factors in its ability to attract foreign investment. The Chinese government has made efforts to encourage a "consumer revolution" in China, which has strengthened the popular demand for high-quality consumer goods imported from abroad. The recent difficulty of balancing payments has nevertheless led the government to lessen its flexibility in further opening China's internal market. In most cases of joint ventures, compensation trade, or 100-percent foreign-owned projects, the Chinese side now demands that foreign corporations balance foreign exchange. This policy has dampened enthusiasm for China's market, especially if investors are unable to make their production costs in China lower than elsewhere.

Finally, the open door policy has also created certain new problems for the government. These difficulties are largely inevitable, but correct policies can reduce their negative effects. Politically, the employees in either SEZs or other foreign-involved enterprises receive payments that are usually 70 percent higher than employees elsewhere. This serious income gap has already caused popular grievance. The efficiency gap and different management styles of foreign and Chinese managers have also presented a political challenge to official ideology as well as to the party's authority outside the SEZs. Furthermore, the surfeit of information from abroad and the strong Western cultural influence have weakened the dominance of official ideology and created tensions between different generations. In the long run, the government also will face the problem of lessening the tension now existing between those who have benefited from education and training in the West and Japan and those who have not had the opportunities of going abroad. In addition, the expanded ties with foreign countries have also increased corruption, smuggling, and pornography, thereby provoking strong nationalism in society and giving conservatives within the party excuses to attack the open door policy.

Economically, the government has had difficulty in controlling its balance of payments as the foreign trade system has been decentralized, and foreign corporations can enter China's domestic market through either the SEZs or other joint venture projects outside SEZs, Hainan Island, and other open areas. Moreover, it will be increasingly difficult for the government to deal with the price gap between the Chinese internal market and the international market as the increased intake of foreign commodities by China's market has a strong effect on China's domestic pricing structure. In the long run, therefore, the Chinese economy is likely to be more affected by the high inflation rate in the international market. The open door policy has increased and will continue to increase the degree of interdependency between the Chinese economy and the world economy. This interdependency is likely to increase the vulnerability of the Chinese economy. Under certain political conditions, such as difficulties in the forthcoming succession of Deng Xiaoping and the lack of cadres' experience in managing the urban economic reform program, this development may encourage the conservatives within the government to pressure the reform group to alter the open door policy.

Conclusions

China is still at a historical turning point. Its ongoing political and economic reform has made fundamental domestic changes and will continue to do so. Its open door policy has strengthened China's position in the international market, introduced foreign technology, capital investment, and management skills into China, and gradually created a new generation of policymakers who have broad international perspective as well as knowledge about modern societies. The open door policy has also changed Chinese culture and created the possibility of developing a pluralistic cultural structure in China.

On the other hand, the open door policy has been facing serious challenges, both domestically and internationally. These challenges may slow the process of adopting the open door policy as well as the country's political and economic development. Yet the fundamental social and political changes taking place during the past decade have already become deeply rooted in Chinese society. Time and well-researched policies should allow even further progress toward modernization.

Notes

1. *China Business Review*, May–June 1987, pp. 56–57.

2. *People's Daily* (overseas edition), 1985, 7, 24, p. 1; 1985, 9, 36, p. 3; 1988, 10, 1, p. 1; and 1988, 10, 6, p. 1.

3. R. Reagan, "A Historical Opportunity for the US and China," *Realism, Strength, Negotiation, Key Foreign Policy Statement of the Reagan Administration*, U.S. Department of State, p. 70.

4. *Outlook Weekly* (Beijing, China), 1985, no. 2, pp. 32–34; and *Nineties* (Hong Kong) 1988, no. 3, pp. 41–44.

5. *People's Daily*, 1985, 9, 26, p. 3; and 1988, 10, 13, p.3; and M. Ross, "Changing the Foreign Trade System," *China Business Review*, May–June 1985, pp. 34–37.

6. C. Bogert, "Consulting Groups Proliferate," *China Business Review*, July–August 1985, pp. 11–12.

7. *Outlook Weekly*, 1985, no. 2, pp. 9–11; *People's Daily*, 1985, 7, 27, p. 1; 1985, 9, 11, p. 1; and 1988, 10, 19, p. 1.

8. *People's Daily*, 1985, 8, 25, p. 2.

9. *China Reconstructs* (North American edition), Vol. 34, No. 6, June 1985, pp. 20–21.

10. *Peoples' Daily*, 1985, 7, 2, p. 1.

11. *Beijing Review*, vol. 27, no. 51, November 17, 1984, p. 3.

12. *People's Daily*, 1985, 8, 25, p. 2.

13. *Beijing Review*, vol. 27, no. 48, November 26, 1985, p. 48; and *Nineties*, 1988, no. 7, pp. 64–67.

14. *Outlook Weekly*, 1985, no. 32, pp. 21–23.

15. *Outlook Weekly*, 1984, no. 41, pp. 24–25; and *China Business Review*, September–October 1988, pp. 46–48.

16. *People's Daily*, 1985, 9, 21, p. 1; and K. Green and S. Ruwart; "Joining the World Economy," *China Business Review*, May–June 1988, pp. 32–33.

17. *People's Daily*, 1985, 8, 27, p. 1; and 1988, 10, 8, p. 1.

18. *People's Daily*, 1985, 9, 26, p. 1.

19. *China Business Review*, May–June 1988, pp. 56–57.

20. *Outlook Weekly*, 1985, no. 5, p. 18; and *People's Daily*, 1988, 10, 13, p. 3.

21. *Far East Economic Review*, May 26, 1988, p. 99; and *China Business Review*, May–June, pp. 56–57.

22. *People's Daily*, 1988, 10, 21, p. 1.

23. *China Business Review*, May–June 1988, p. 57; *World Economy Herald* (Shanghai, China), July 19, 1985, pp. 2–3; and *People's Daily*, 1988, 10, 21, p. 1.

24. *People's Daily*, 1988, 10, 21, p. 1.

25. World Bank, *China: Long-Term Issues and Options* (office use only), May 22, 1985, Washington, D.C.

26. *People's Daily*, 1988, 7, 23, p. 3.

27. S. Poole, "China Builds Overseas Business," *China Business Review*, September–October, 1988, pp. 20–23.

28. *Outlook Weekly*, 1984, no. 52, pp. 11–13; and 1988, 10, 21, p. 3.

29. *People's Daily*, 1988, 6, 24, p. 3; and 1988, 10, 18, p. 3.

30. *China Business Review*, May–June 1988, p. 57; and *People's Daily*, 1988, 10, 22, p. 1.

13

International Economic Strategies, the State, and Domestic Society: A Comment

James Caporaso

Perhaps the most important practical political economy issue facing leaders of countries today concerns the predominant ways of orienting toward the international political economy. The international debates have been dominated by calls for a New International Economic Order (NIEO), collective bargaining among members of the South, outward-oriented versus autocentric development, and global market integration versus self-reliance. Domestic political controversy has not been immune from choices that involve the international dimension. Indeed, it is impossible to understand the full meaning underlying the debates on industrial policy, corporatism, protectionism, and economic restructuring without also understanding the international implications of these options.

The chapters in this section all, in somewhat varying degrees, deal with the domestic and international aspects of various international economic strategies. First, there is the chapter by Valerie Bunce, "The Political Economy of the Soviet Bloc." It is a complex discussion that tries to weave together several themes (political, economic, military) across several levels (domestic, regional bloc, capitalist world economy), none of which is in principle reducible to the others. To the individual countries, the global economy presents itself as a giant payoff matrix—a structure of rewards, penalties, opportunities, and constraints. The regional bloc (CMEA, Council of Mutual Economic Assistance) is the historical *cordon sanitaire*, a belt of countries between the Soviet Union and Western Europe. This regional component takes on its most important meaning in raw political and military terms. Finally, domestic society is obviously important, for it is here that real decisional capability and the capacity to mobilize resources lie. All three levels are extremely important in understanding the politics of the Soviet Union and Eastern Europe, and Bunce tries to juxtapose and integrate them without reducing any to reflections (or effects) of others.

The chapter by William Loehr and Peter Van Ness examines the economic costs of self-reliance for the People's Republic of China. China, convinced of the dangers of too deep an enmeshment in the capitalist world economy, and persuaded further that re-entering the world economy would yield benefits only if the domestic infrastructure were first in place, embarked on a policy of self-reliance. The key question addressed is what impact this inward strategy had on Chinese economic performance.

The chapter by Guocang Huan, "China's Open Door Policy: 1978–1988," is a very useful complement to the Van Ness–Loehr chapter. First, they are historically complementary—China's self-reliant period dated from 1960 to 1976 while the open door policy dates from 1978. Second, Huan examines in detail the PRC's progressive involvement in the international system, detailing the changes made in foreign trade policy, investment policy, the creation of Special Economic Zones, and the exchange of students, bankers, and business managers.

Themes

These chapters return to a number of important themes, three of which I single out here.

The first theme is—not surprisingly—the form and content of the international economic strategies themselves. The first three, inseparable questions are whether to integrate in the international economy, whether to integrate in the socialist or capitalist world system, and on what terms should this integration take place. These questions raise monumental issues that involve structural and historical givens. To decide whether to be socialist or capitalist is not simply a question of technique, like raising or lowering tariffs. It raises questions regarding organization of the macro society. Huan explores the potential (as well as the brief historical record) of capitalist integration. Van Ness and Loehr assess the economic costs. Bunce analyzes the politics and economics of world capitalist integration pursued simultaneously with the regional political economy of CMEA. Whether to join, on what terms, with what supporting domestic coalition, and with what combination of state power and market forces—these are some of the critical questions faced.

A second theme concerns everyone's lack of insulation from the international economy—like it or not, whatever the strategy pursued. The international economy proves to be inescapable, if only (and rarely was it only) in its shadowy opportunity-cost form. In a separate volume Michael Marrese points out that the implicit subsidy of the Soviet Union to Eastern Europe ran into billions of dollars.[1] The question can always be asked: How would things have been different if greater international involvement had occurred? Van Ness and Loehr most explicitly ask this question, but it lies behind the calculations of the others too. Beyond this opportunity-cost notion, the international economy affected China and the Soviet bloc in a number of ways. The first

OPEC shock increased the availability of international capital. Contrary to almost all advanced capitalist countries, which instituted deflationary responses, Eastern Europe was attracted by the opportunities presented by cheap foreign capital. Thus, borrowing and debt increased during the 1970s in Eastern Europe.

A third theme is the powerful and alluring role of the market both in China and Eastern Europe. This is a tacit first premise for Huan, whose paper is mostly concerned with how the Chinese could more effectively capitalize on the opportunities presented by the open door policy. The market, large and anonymous, directed only by aggregate movements of relative preferences and relative prices, has been and continues to be a truly revolutionary force. The epochal significance of the rise and spread of markets, the "Great Transformation" in Karl Polanyi's phrase,[2] continues to play itself out in the modern era and in arguably the strangest of all places—socialist societies.

Neglected Themes

Perhaps it is unfair to identify themes not dealt with, or dealt with in a minor way, in the chapters. Yet a number of ideas are important enough that their absence makes for a particular silence.

The first omission concerns the problem of "late development." All countries except England were late developers in different ways. The 1986 volume of *International Organization*[3] on international economic strategies of socialist states adopts a late-development perspective on socialist states and, as a result, provides itself with a historical link to earlier development efforts and a comparative link with the newly industrializing countries of today. The important variations are many, but the key problem faced by late-developing societies—socialist or capitalist—is that other more developed states already populate the international system. Thus Smithian arguments about the advantages of scale and the division of labor, as well as Ricardian demonstrations of the welfare effects flowing from exploitation of comparative advantages, do not tell the entire story. As John Ruggie points out, after Great Britain, nearly every European country had a spokesperson for a delayed development, semiprotectionist strategy.[4] These individuals, the most famous of whom was Friedrich List, took into account the superior strength (economic and political) of established industrialized countries and devised strategies to capitalize on this "environment of superior strength."

The second neglected theme is really a series of themes that have to do with the probable trade-offs in going down the "capitalist road." These points concern the relationship between capitalist market reforms and what might be termed the socialist project.

A market is a large, impersonal institution for allocating resources that operates by transmitting signals about relative prices and preferences. Nearly all recognize the market as an efficient allocative instrument. What is not always recognized is that it is also a method for transferring wealth. Insofar as markets are accompanied by capitalist relations of production (private ownership of wealth-producing capital, free wage labor), markets embody rules for creation and distribution of the surplus. But even if a pure market socialism were possible, differentials in wealth would occur because of uneven sectoral growth, uneven ties to the global economy, the clustering of external economies in distinct areas, and so forth.

Another component of the second theme concerns the absence of treatment of the market as a linked phenomenon—that is, as a component of a larger social constitution. Huan's paper seems to argue for market reforms without full appreciation of the effects of the market on other aspects of life, among them kinship, religion, locality, the relation between locality and work life, and stability of social relations. "Expanding the market" is not a technical procedure, and it is not something that occurs in an isolated manner from the rest of society. The economy, as Polyani argues,[5] is not a natural given. It is and still continues to be an instituted process—a process that is continually establishing itself as part of the rest of society. Today, we talk easily about land, labor and capital as factors of production, as if these phenomena were always separate and alienable objects of exchange. It was not always so. Will market reforms be capable of being limited to carefully circumscribed spheres of economic life? Can the incentives, private capturability of profits, price mechanisms, and allocative efficiency of the market be successfully incorporated without serious implications for family structure, distribution of wealth, stability of social relations, material aspirations, the centralization of bureaucracy, desire for participation, and social ownership of capital?

The social ownership of capital is certainly the centerpiece of the socialist project. The key question here is whether there is any inherent link between the market as a decentralized—almost private—mechanism of allocation and the form of ownership of wealth-producing capital. That form of ownership and mode of allocation are at least analytically separate leads to hybrids such as "market socialism" and "state capitalism." The question is not whether these historical-social combinations exist at the moment but whether, over a much longer evolutionary path, they are stable or unstable types. Christopher Chase-Dunn has argued persuasively that as long as commodity exchange dominates relations among economic units, the units themselves will be influenced.[6] In other words, one cannot have "capitalism à la carte," taking some of its market logic but leaving its dominant form of production relations behind. This key issue is one that leaders of developing and developed countries must face. It is sometimes lost in debates about isolation versus interdependence.

Notes

1. Michael Marrese, "CMEA: Effective But Cumbersome Political Economy," in Ellen Comisso and Laura D'Andrea Tyson, eds., "Power, Purpose, and

Collective Choice: Economic Strategy in Socialist States," *International Organization* 40, no. 2 (1986), (special issue).

2. Karl Polyani, *The Great Transformation: The Political and Economic Origins of Our Time* (Boston, Mass.: Beacon Press, 1944).

3. Comisso and Tyson, "Power, Purpose."

4. John Gerard Ruggie, "Introduction: International Interdependence and National Welfare," in Ruggie, ed., *The Antinomies of Interdependence* (New York: Columbia University Press, 1983).

5. Polyani, *Great Transformation.*

6. Christopher K. Chase-Dunn, "Socialist States in the Capitalist World Economy," in Chase-Dunn, ed., *Socialist States in the World System* (Beverly Hills, Calif.: Sage, 1982), pp. 29–30.

14

Conclusion

Joel Edelstein

It is no surprise that the movement for market-oriented reform has grown in the state-socialist countries. In all economies in which centralized economic planning is utilized, there is extensive waste and inefficiency in the allocation of resources. There are production stoppages caused by bottlenecks in materials supply. Goods spoil or go unused because of poor quality or overproduction. Management often maintains idle and unneeded workers. Workers commonly do not apply themselves to their tasks. Fields are often poorly kept and equipment poorly maintained. Bureaucracy results in a substantial absorption of time, energy, and creativity, including the waste of those who work in it and those who must overcome its obstacles. Consumers buy whatever becomes available regardless of quality, buying to trade if not to use, and there is a daily experience of waiting lines. These problems are some of the costs of interfering with the market and its powerful incentive structure and of locating decisionmaking authority at a distance from the enterprise.

In the 1960s, some of the socialist economies began to react to the deficiencies of centralized economic planning and the problems caused by inadequate work incentives. In the late 1980s, movements for greater use of the market, more individual incentives, and, in some instances, enlargement of the private sector have made headway in nearly all of the state-socialist countries. But the meaning of the policy changes introduced and considered is unclear. Do they suggest that centralized economic planning is unworkable and should never be used? To what extent do they represent basic change beyond technical adjustments in economic management? Has the problem been one of too much equality? And what of the future of socialism?

Is Centralized Economic Planning Ever Useful?

The enthusiasm of many Eastern European and Chinese economists for reform might make one wonder what could have lured reasonable people into these departures from the wisdom of Adam Smith and the virtues of the market. However, it should be recalled that state ownership and economic planning were introduced in the socialist countries at points in their respective histories when the benefits of the market were generally of tertiary significance. Immediate economic goals were the mobilization of underemployed resources and economic surplus for economic development and industrialization and, to a lesser degree, the improvement of social welfare. In China, social revolution in the country-side was a major goal, as well as a route to power. In general, expropriation of privately held property was a means to the consolidation of political power. Though the economies became plagued with waste and inefficiency, the primary objectives were accomplished with the use of state ownership and centralized economic planning.

Everywhere, in capitalist as well as in socialist countries, the project of industrialization has been accompanied by misery for those whose product was appropriated as economic surplus to be invested. In the socialist economies, greater efforts have generally been made to avoid the worst deprivations, and real hunger has been far less frequent. Nonetheless, the planned pace of development often has been overly ambitious. In an effort to maximize the rate of accumulation, the share of the economic product allocated for current consumption has been too low and the portion for savings too high. Although much of the economic surplus has been successfully directed to investment, the resultant sacrifices were substantially offset by losses caused by a lack of work incentives as well as by deficiencies in organization and management.

The countries of northern Europe that pioneered the path of industrial capitalism did so by virtue of propitious internal conditions and a favorable international environment. In the United States, Germany, and Japan, governing class alignments ultimately gave support to policies that overcame potential obstacles. Countries in which industrialization was not substantially under way at the beginning of the twentieth century have faced external forces that have precluded the rise to power of internal political forces that would lead a capitalist project of nationally oriented general industrialization. For these countries, industrialization has only occurred in a partial fashion within the model of dependent development.

In the countries in which revolutions led by socialists have come to power, it is unlikely that industrialization could have been achieved without consider-able centralization. Use of the market was problematic because the market tends to reward and reinforce strength and punish weakness—of enterprises, sectors, regions, and nations. It reflects the current situation and, therefore, normally is not a source of leadership for economic transformation. Moreover, societies exhibit a tendency toward internal consistency among their respective economic, political, and sociocultural spheres, the economic tending to be predominant: The locus of political power and the style of political organization tend to follow the locus of control over production. It is likely that if authority had been decentralized to the level of the enterprise, there would not have been sufficient central direction to pursue change.

Conditions for centralized planning were lacking. To date, though a number of revolutions have come to power led by people who advocate the ideas of Marx, there has been no revolution of the sort to which the *Communist Manifesto* refers. No revolution has taken place as a result of the contradictions of advanced capitalism. The immediate conditions for revolution have come about in the course of wars among imperialist powers and from the contradictions of uneven development. The new regimes have lacked the degree of economic concentration necessary for efficient planning as well as the personnel with the requisite education and skills. The principal virtues of state ownership and centralized planning were their superior capacity to mobilize resources and the absence of alternative methods of organization for economic development.

Now, the gains that have been made under centralized economic planning will permit the market to be used as it could not have been before. Generally, there is a sufficient industrial base to generate profit that can be reinvested by decentralized management for further expansion. Production of agricultural inputs and consumer goods can now induce farmers to produce and exchange agricultural surpluses. Mobilization is no longer an issue. It is appropriate that efficiency in the use of resources should grow in importance. With primitive accumulation completed, the flexibility to participate in creating more advanced technologies is possible. Failing to do so would have serious consequences.

How Far-Reaching Are the Changes?
Contending Views of Tasks and Policies for the Present Period

There are a number of ways of viewing the stage of societal development characterized by bureaucratic state socialism. Each has a distinctive perspective regarding the historical tasks attributed to the stage, attendant problems, and appropriate policy responses. Between social democracy on one hand and two variants of Marxian thought on the other lies the question of whether socialism is exclusively a political economic system to meet the needs of a society as it is presently constituted. Or is it a transitional form that serves most importantly as the medium for the qualitative transformation of society?

For social democracy, as for liberal capitalism, egoistic individualism and individual material incentives are the only sound basis for the organization of complex human societies. Social democracy does not entertain the Marxian vision of a communist future toward which present society should be directed. Individuals will always deal with the human condition as individuals. Some degree of economic planning, along with some forms of social ownership, is useful to reduce fluctuations in the rate of accumulation while ameliorating social problems and enhancing social welfare. However, the social democratic understanding identifies socialism as a means to meet the present needs of a society. Reform should proceed pragmatically to achieve the greatest degree of social security consistent with the maintenance of work incentives, efficiency of management, and for some, entrepreneurial freedom.

Marxism, on the other hand, looks to a potential future society qualitatively different from societies that have existed until now. In the context of the evaluations of socialist experience so far, it is with the risk of appearing passé that I recall the Marxian vision. Marxism understands human beings to have a broad repertoire of behaviors but at the core to be creative animals whose fulfillment requires expression through work. Accordingly, life in societies in which most must labor under conditions of exploitation and other alienating circumstances simply to survive is frustrating and oppressive. In the Marxian understanding, human liberation arises in the elimination of alienating conditions so that work can be an expression of individuality and of the social nature of humanity. These conditions require social ownership of the major means of production, thus ending private ownership, which generates antagonistic social class divisions. According to the Marxian vision, the elimination of social classes obviates the need for coercive state power to maintain a system that benefits a dominant class at the expense of a subordinate class. A major step in reaching for this future occurs when private ownership and the bourgeois power that defends it are overthrown. The revolution that ends capitalism initiates a stage of society in which the conditions for communism are developed. In this Marxian understanding, socialism is most importantly a period of transition.

Conservative Marxism

Marxian thought is generally regarded as politically radical because it identifies within capitalism the seeds of socialist revolution. The end product of capitalist accumulation is the creation of a numerically preponderant working class aware that its interests lie in socialism. In creating ever greater productive potential, capitalism also produces increasing crises and increasing misery, bringing about the mobilization and organization of the proletariat toward revolution. Revolution occurs when the fullest potential of this mode of production has been achieved. Capitalist social relations have become fetters on further development of the forces of production. With the downfall of capitalism, accumulation can continue, based upon the productive potential created by capitalist accumulation.

Capitalist development creates a broad range of conditions necessary for socialist development. For example, both the concentration of capital and the extension of capitalism into the countryside force members of the *petite bourgeoisie* and the peasantry into the working class. This enlargement of the proletariat at the expense of other classes reduces class conflict after the seizure of power. Development of the productive forces under capitalist accumulation obviates the need for substantial centralization of the economic surplus under socialism. And economic concentration facilitates the introduction of socialized ownership and control through economic planning.

To the extent that Marxian thought finds capitalist development a necessary prerequisite for socialism, it does not identify present bureaucratic state-socialist countries as socialist. Rather, they are postcapitalist societies. The mere fact that the leaders of a regime identify with Marxism does not establish the conditions for socialism. These societies are transitional regimes in which accumulation must create the conditions for socialism. As we have seen, this stage is characterized by serious economic and political contradictions. This conservative Marxian perspective tends to concur in the Maoist analysis of the contradictions of socialist development, though not with Mao's voluntaristic response. Conservative Marxism is more deterministic in perceiving the limitations of what can be accomplished in this stage. Furthering accumulation is the fundamental task on which advancement depends. Nothing more than that can be achieved. Seeking to overcome the limitations of the market results in the problems of overcentralization. The teleological strain in this conservative Marxism also asserts that whatever distortions occur in the social relations of production will eventually be overcome when sufficient accumulation has occurred. Conservative Marxism, unlike social democratic thought, places importance on the transitional character of bureaucratic state socialism, but it gives even less significance than does social democracy to values other than accumulation (e.g., equality).

Voluntaristic Marxism

In the voluntaristic Marxian perspective, the transition is not only a characteristic of the stage but an active project that guides policy. Advanced socialism is a prediction and a program as well. The future is not determined but depends in a rather immediate sense on the management of present contradictions. This perspective is perhaps best exemplified by the efforts of Chairman Mao to struggle against the tendencies toward the rise of "capitalist-roaders"—tendencies that he identified as inherent within the process of socialist development. In Cuba, Che Guevara called for a program of centralized budgeting and collective incentives, arguing that an advanced stage of imperialism had given rise to an advanced level of revolutionary consciousness. This consciousness, he contended, could serve as an advanced level of productive forces to support the production relations he advocated. Adopting Guevara's position, Fidel Castro urged "moral incentives" to avoid the Soviet Union's "selfishness amidst abundance."

With the urgency of its premise that the present organization of the social relations of production shapes the future, voluntaristic Marxism sometimes transforms analytical statements into prescriptions. In this vein, the Marxian understanding that what artists create is a social product becomes a policy that artists *will* reflect what society *should* be articulating: the struggle to transform itself. Although Marx postulated that the creations of artists are a social product emanating from consciousness shaped by the artists' material existence or "social being," revolutionary leaders with state power have often engendered contradictions by *directing* artists to reflect the new society still in the process of being born.

Voluntaristic Marxian thought recognizes the importance of accumulation, but tends to reject use of the market and other practices considered to be backsliding into capitalism. Reform promoting individual private ownership is also inconsistent with this perspective. Reform oriented toward increased worker ownership and management relative to bureaucratic state planning could be consistent with voluntaristic Marxism despite increased use of the market.

Reform Agendas

Public statements by advocates of reform do not provide conclusive evidence of their perspectives or their ultimate agendas. Except for self-described revolutionaries, advocates of change tend to justify their proposals in terms that do not depart substantially from the present officially accepted framework. As we have seen, market reform is consistent with a broad range of ideological perspectives and agendas. Conservative Marxists could be among the advocates, having concluded that only the market can build the forces of production to eventually support socialist relations of production. Pragmatic social democrats seeking to maintain accumulation with equity could join, as could capitalist-roaders who might even seek the primitive quality of U.S. capitalism. Nonetheless, it is clear that decentralizing decisionmaking authority to the level of the enterprise must at least reinforce the interests and perspectives of managers and technocrats. Implementation of market reforms represents both an ascendancy already achieved by these strata vis à vis party cadres and further establishment of their position. When the intentions of those individuals with new influence or the ultimate results of the reforms they advocate are unknown, market reform constitutes significant political change.

What of the Future of Socialism?

Paradoxically, the movement toward greater use of the market occurs as the conditions for planning improve in the socialist countries. Economic modernization tends to bring about larger enterprises and, in some sectors, a smaller number of them. The capacity for data collection and processing grows with more sophisticated communications system and higher educational levels.

This potential may suggest that the complexity that complicates both planning and the need for flexibility grows faster than the capacity to deal with complexity. Alternatively, this situation could be an intermediate stage with respect to either the development of more subtle and flexible planning systems or in the achievement of higher levels of productivity. In the future, the ability to deal with complexity may increase more rapidly than the difficulty of the planning process. A more efficient, though still less than optimal, central planning system could become more acceptable, especially if substantial advances were made in productivity. In other words, in the future, societies might better be able to afford trade-offs of efficiency for other values.

For the immediate future, it will become clear that market-oriented reforms are not the panacea suggested by the works of Milton Friedman. Among the problems that will emerge rather quickly will be uneven development, inflation, stagnation, the tendency of enterprises to externalize costs through environmental contamination, the lack of correspondence of the product mix with social goals, and the tendency to undermine the remaining public sector by transfers of resources from it to the private sector.

The capacity to ameliorate most of these tendencies will be available to some extent through the planning mechanism and welfarist policies. However, there is a real question of political will. The managerial and technical strata found the problems of centralized planning intolerable. With a more economistic perspective, these defects of the market may be an acceptable trade-off for new efficiencies. It remains to be seen how workers and peasants, who greet reforms with a sense of relief, will react to the results of change.

Appendix

The data in the table provide a basis for comparing China and Hungary with other selected communist-party states regarding their size, standard of living, growth performance, and international economic policies.

To take China as an example, the data show that the PRC is vastly larger in population than the others (in fact, two and one-half times larger than all of the other countries taken together). China's standard of living, with respect to all four measures, is by far the lowest among the nine countries, but significantly, regarding life expectancy at birth, the PRC (at 67 years) scores only three years below the average for the other eight countries (70 years). According to estimates by the World Bank, which sees this statistic as one of the best indicators of citizen well-being, China's life expectancy at birth is thirteen years higher than India's, for example. Regarding growth performance, China's record in recent years is by far the best of the nine countries, including the important consumer-goods indicator, food production per capita. Since 1978, China has experienced significant inflation (and probably the number here underestimates the actual situation substantially), but it has not suffered the debilitating problems of inflation that countries like Yugoslavia and Poland have. Finally, China's foreign economic policy is least typical of the nine countries in that all of the others, including Yugoslavia, are substantially tied to trading relations with the socialist world, which China is not, and the PRC has the lowest debt problem of the nine, except for the Soviet Union.

Hungary can be compared with the other eight countries in a similar fashion. Its performance has not been so impressive as China's to date, in part because of the oil shocks of the 1970s (a problem that China and the Soviet Union avoided—and in fact benefited from because they are petroleum-exporting countries). However, Hungary's problems of inflation, indebtedness, and declining growth have thus far not been so serious as similar problems that have plagued Poland and Yugoslavia. It is important to keep in mind that the success

Table A. China and Hungary Compared with Selected Socialist Countries: Social and Economic Indicators

	Standard of Living					Patterns of Growth				International Economic Policy	
	Population, 1986 (millions)	GNP Per Capita, (US $) 1986	Population Per Physician, 1981	Daily Calorie Supply, 1985	Life Expectancy at Birth 1986	Average Annual Rate of Growth in Real GNP, 1976–1981 (%)	Average Annual Growth of National Income 1981–1985 (%)	Index of Food Production Per Capita, 1983–1985 (1979–1981=100)	Price Index of Consumer Goods, 1984 (1980=100)	Direction of Foreign Trade: % to Socialist countries 1983	Net Foreign Debt as % of Exports to OECD, 1984
Bulgaria	9.0	6800	400	3663	71	1.5	3.7	101	103.0	78	120
China	1059.4	260	1730	2602	67	5.8	9.8	125	108.9	7	57[a]
Czechoslovakia	15.5	9280	350	3465	71	1.7	1.7	118	107.9	77	85
German Democratic Republic	16.6	11300	490	3791	72	2.4	4.6	105	100.3	65	147
Hungary	10.6	7920	300	3482	70	1.8	1.6	111	129.9	53	263
Poland	37.5	6930	550	3280	71	-0.7	-0.8	106	341.8	71	634
Romania	22.8	6030	700	3385	70	3.5	4.3	110	NA	53	175
USSR	281.5	8370	270	3440	70	2.5	3.5	110	104	56	35
Yugoslavia	23.3	6220	700	3602	68	5.2	0.5	102	403.7	42	400

[a] 1983.

Sources: World Bank, *World Development Report 1987* (Oxford: Oxford University Press, 1987); State Statistical Bureau, PRC, *Statistical Yearbook of China 1986* (Oxford University Press, 1986); *Handbook of Economic Statistics, 1982* (Washington, D.C.: Central Intelligence Agency, 1982); *Handbook of Economic Statistics, 1987* (Washington, D.C.: Central Intelligence Agency, 1987);[1] John L. Davie, "China's International Trade and Finance," in Joint Economic Committee, U.S. Congress *China's Economy Looks Toward the Year 2000*, vol. 2 (Washington, D.C.: U.S. Government Printing Office, 1986); William V. Wallace and Roger A. Clarke, *Comecon Trade and the West* (London: Frances Pinter, 1986), pp. 113–114; and *EIU Regional Review: Eastern Europe and the USSR 1986* (London: The Economist, 1986).

and failure of market reforms is only partially reflected in quantitative comparisons. Alec Nove in his assessment of Hungary's reforms provides detailed illustrations of qualitative changes that do not appear in the quantitative data.[2]

Notes

1. It should be noted that there is debate about the reliability of the CIA data. See William Safire in *New York Times*, March 28, 1988, p. 21; Anders Aslund in *International Herald Tribune*, May 21–22, 1988, p. 6; and Richard E. Ericson, "Soviet Numbers Game Threatens Perestroika," *Bulletin of the Atomic Scientists*, December 1988, pp. 20–25.

2. Alec Nove, *The Economics of Feasible Socialism* (London: Allen & Unwin, 1983), pp. 123–133. Also, on other measures of performance, such as educational achievement, Hungary scores very high when compared with other industrialized countries, East and West. See John Walsh in *Science*, March 11, 1988, p. 1237.

Index

About the Book

The economic problems that both Hungary and China have experienced are in many ways representative of a common set of serious difficulties faced by the entire communist world. Thus, the market reforms that have been designed to solve those problems may provide answers that are widely applicable to socialist command economies in general. In this book, eminent Chinese and Hungarian scholars evaluate the present status of market reforms in their countries and assess their own and each other's problems and achievements. Commentaries by U.S. specialists are also included. Although the authors primarily reflect the reform position—some are reform leaders, others are academic proponents of reform—alternative positions are represented as well.

Peter Van Ness is associate professor in the Graduate School of International Studies at the University of Denver. He is author of *Revolution and Chinese Foreign Policy*, as well as numerous articles and book chapters on China, and is on the editorial board of the *Bulletin of Concerned Asian Scholars*.